American Slavery and After

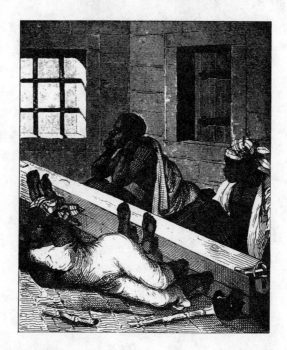

GEORGE OLSHAUSEN

Olema Press
San Francisco, California

Table of Contents

ABOUT THE AUTHOR

Great times produce men to match their tasks. Such was the case in America through the thirties and fifties. That was an era when the world saw more immediate political challenges on levels unmatched in the present era. Europe saw the rise of Fascism. Russia, the ascendancy of Stalin. America, the New Deal. The Great Depression and the rise of the labor movement were once again the order of the day in the U.S.

To understand George Olshausen is to understand an era and a place. The era, that of the thirties and their tumult, the forties, and their struggles for the rights of minorities attacked by the prejudices of war and racism, and the fifties, and the age of repression against all democratic rights and principles that were established in the two decades preceding. And the place is San Francisco and the West Coast.

San Francisco was not only the home of Bohemia and free thinking in the West, but the birth place of the International Longshoremen's and Warehousemen's Union, which rose out of the general strike of 1934, and the surrounding growth of militant unionism in California.

George was born in Ithaca, New York, in 1903. He attended the University of California Law School, Boalt Hall, in the mid-20's, and was editor of the California Law Review, preceding Roger Traynor. In the 30's and 40's he continued to contribute to that journal as well as to the State Bar Journal of California. But his political attitudes were shaped by the events of the era. First, with the New Deal, and the responses it drew from the conservative bar; then with the need for a progressive organization of lawyers. This soon crystallized in the National Lawyers Guild, of which George was a founding member.

In 1948, led by that paragon of jingo journalism, Walter Winchell, the United States picked out an innocent woman of Japanese-American ancestry who had been stranded in Japan by the war, and labeled her as "Tokyo Rose". She was indicted by a federal grand jury in San Francisco in 1948, and tried for treason in 1949. Of the seven overt acts of treason with which she was charged, the jury returned a verdict of guilty on only one count. George was one of the three attorneys who volunteered to represent her.

It was not a popular cause for the era. Of over one hundred specifications of error, the Court of Appeal found none warranting reversal even in their cumulative effect.

iii

But the Tokyo Rose trial was only the opening salvo in a new phenomenon, the charade of questioned loyalty. It was nothing but a dress rehearsal for the cold war and the wave of repressive court cases that came after. Afterwards came the renewed wave of Smith Act cases against political dissidents. Then the wave of "loyalty oath" cases against teachers and others. In all of them, George was an active participant for the defense.

An indication of the period was the inability of any opponent of the repression to make his way into print. Virtually all organs of opinion were closed to them. Only the small journals of the left and bohemian community could be used to make left positions known.

The city of San Francisco would not be recognized now by anyone who lived there at that time. There were relatively few lawyers, but the caliber of the bar was well-respected, even on a national level. George became one of the most widely known appellate lawyers in the state, if not the best. His greatest success, in terms of traditional civil law, was the victory in McGuire v. Hibernia Bank, where he reversed the trial court's position that depositors in the bank could not recover against the bank after Bank Holiday. But his greatest contribution in his own thinking, and in the thoughts of those who knew and worked with him, was to cases that challenged the internment and treatment of Japanese-Americans during World War II.

Not one "respectable" magazine in America could be found to raise its voice in defense of Iva D'Aquino, unjustly convicted of treason as "Tokyo Rose". Throughout the fifties, only three articles appeared in print in her defense. Two of them were by George. Both were in small journals published in San Francisco.

When she was released from Federal Prison in 1956, the United States Immigration and Naturalization Service moved to deport her as an alien. Realizing the urgent need for an independent public voice in her behalf, George quickly organized a committee in her defense, independent of her legal representation in the deportation proceedings, led by Wayne M. Collins, Sr., her chief attorney. The committee gathered almost no adherents. Operating from his apartment on Clay Street in San Francisco, it published pamphlets and leaflets in her defense, and George spoke to the few community groups that would listen to him, whenever possible.

This was how George Olshausen lived. By day, he was known as one of the best appellate attorneys in San Francisco. At night he was a denizen of a North Beach Bohemia that pre-dated, by many years, the Beat era of a later generation.

iv

No mistake would be more profound however, than to view George as a product of "local color". His articles throughout this period were printed in virtually every left-wing journal of non-sectarian circulation; Law and Society, the American Socialist, Monthly Review and Science and Society.

But through all those years, from the 30's through the 50' and 60's, George had another vocation. He was working on a history of American slavery to try and place it in its proper historical perspective, namely, as a stage of American capitalist development. And at the same time, as a development antithetical to capitalism. Friction between these two conflicting strands ultimately led to the Civil War.

George as a lawyer, looked to the jurisprudential history of slavery as a way to approach this thesis. For thirty years, he researched every case the U.S. courts had considered in terms of slavery, of relations of slaves to slaves, to their masters, to the land and to the developing states of the north. Every journal, every writer of the pre-Colonial, Colonial, pre-Civil War and Civil-War period was researched for information on the question.

With the scholarship he showed as a civil appellate attorney, which earned him the pre-eminent position in that field, George supported each paragraph of his text with footnotes and copious quotations.

In the late sixties, George left the U.S. for Yugoslavia. There, he finished his manuscript, but never edited it. All save the sixth chapter have been recovered, along with the footnotes for all the chapters. The footnotes are more voluminous than the text itself, and are not reproduced here because of prohibitive costs. George passed away in Yugoslavia in 1978. He left the bulk of his estate for the publication of this book.

The footnotes have been retyped and lodged with the Miklejohn Institute in Berkeley, California. Access to them, and references thereto may be obtained from the institute located at 1715 Francisco Street, Berkeley, California, 94703.

It should be noted that for the recent graduate of a progressive law school, or graduate of any law school who has progressive beliefs, to regard anyone of George's persuasion as exceptional must seem peculiar. But that was anything but the rule in the years that George practiced and fought. Again, that may seem unusual. But to have swum against the stream in the years of McCarthy, and worse yet, during the years of reactionary liberalism during the World War II, is a phenomenon that the Congressional hearings on internment have only recently begun to reveal to scholars.

All too often in the struggle for human progress, the men and women who led the struggle and made the greatest contributions, are soon forgotten and their work is overlooked by later generations. It is our hope that this will not be so with George.

Wayne M. Collins
San Francisco, California
April, 1983

THE FOOTNOTES

The numbers in the text refer to the voluminous footnotes Mr. Olshausen provided to document his text. The footnotes are copious and thorough. Unfortunately, they are more voluminous than the entire mansucript and could not be reproduced in this volume.

Scholars, or persons interested in seeking out these citations should contact the Miklejohn Civil Liberties Institute, Box 673, Berkeley, California, 94701.

An Empty Continent

The discovery of America was a <u>Volkerwanderung</u> in modern times. Where the latter-day immigrants from Europe met old civilizations in Mexico and Peru, they overwhelmed them as the Aegean migration had flooded across Egypt in the 12th century B.C., or as the Teutons had swept away the Roman Empire in the 5th century A.D.

But for the most part the European immigrants found an empty continent peopled by no more than one and a half million Indians—an empty land, yet[4] a fertile one.   To be developed, the country had to be filled by migration, voluntary or involuntary. Voluntary immigration could take place anywhere; it would take its own time. Forced migration could only follow the voluntary; its tempo was determined by the voluntary migrants. Where forced migration occurred, it had the necessary effect of complementing and accelerating the pace of settlement. Thus the slave trade, forcibly bringing Negroes from Africa to America, was a hothouse grown migration. Little good has been written of it since its abolition, but there is at least this in its favor. The slave trade helped to populate North America.

The first cargo of slaves were brought to Virginia in 1619. In 1654 the Dutch West India Company was authorized to import slaves into New Netherlands (New York) on the grounds that it would tend to increase the population and advance the colony.[6]

When the thirteen colonies were organized in 1775, all—with one exception—permitted slavery.   The exception was Georgia, the southernmost of the colonies, but also the newest to be established. Yet the prohibition against slavery in Gen. James Oglethorpe's charter of 1733 did not last. Only seventeen years later, in 1750, the Georgia planters secured "the one thing needful" in a legalization of slavery.[7-8]

So at the outbreak of the American revolution, all thirteen colonies had slaves. But the numbers were quite unequal. Differences in the staple crops made slavery profitable in the southern colonies but not in the north. The crops north of what would late of be the Mason-Dixon line were wheat and other cereals: the staples south of that line were tobacco in Maryland, Virginia and parts of North Carolina, and rice and indigo in South Carolina and in Georgia.[9]

1

Wheat or corn required only one laborer for each twenty acres, but tobacco crops needed one laborer for every two or three acres.[10] Slave cultivation of the northern crops would have required as many supervisors as slaves, making the cost of supervision prohibitive. Besides, periods of enforced idleness from cold weather were much shorter in the South.[10a] Consequently, slaves flowed into the more southern colonies. Virginia, the largest tobacco producer had, at the time of the revolution, as many slaves as the other colonies combined.[11]

The total population, state by state, was therefore greater in the southern colonies than in the northern colonies, though the white population in the south was considerably less than in the north. Chas. Cotesworth Pinckney's figures at the South Carolina Convention[12] in 1788 show a total population of 1,454,000 in the seven northern colonies, or an average of 207,000 people living in each one. The same figures show a total of 1,286,000 people for the six southern colonies, or an average of 214,000 in each. The white population of the six southern colonies was 766,000, meaning there were 520,000 slaves in the region.

The slave's dual character as both a human being and a chattel made the slave states the richest section of the Union. Not only did the slaves themselves constitute wealth,[13] but slave plantations were the only large-scale enterprises of the time.[13a] As long as land labor was cheap, slavery was the only way to keep a laborer on the job. As soon as a free worker had saved a little money he went off and bought his own tract of land; hence it was impossible to carry on operations with a large number of wage laborers.

Benjamin Franklin described this problem in 1751, saying:

> So vast is the territory of North America that it will require many ages to settle it fully, and till it is fully settled labor will never be cheap here, where no man continues being a laborer for others, but gets a plantation of his own; no man continues long a journeyman to a trade, but goes among those new settlers and sets up for himself, etc. Hence, labor is no cheaper now in Pennsylvania than it was thirty years ago, though so many thousand laboring people have been imported. The labor of slaves can never be so cheap here as the labor of workingmen is in Britain. Why then, will Americans purchase slaves? Because slaves may be kept so long as a man pleases, or has occasion for their labor, while hired men are continually leaving their masters (often in the midst of his business) and setting up for themselves.[14]

Thirty-one years later Franklin saw that cheap land still prevented the growth of large manufacturing establishments.[15]

The counterpart was the experience of the Georgia planters when they demanded permission to import slaves. In 1740, for example:

> . . . the Jew Delym, 'on whom were founded all our expectations for cultivation of vines and making wines, moved out,' giving as his reason, the want of Negroes, which cost but 6 pence a week to keep, whereas his white servants cost him more than he was able to afford.[16-17]

At the same time the slave plantations included large establishments which could benefit from large-scale operations. In Virginia the number of slaves belonging to one owner was as high as 400; in South Carolina, 172; in Louisiana, 130; in North Carolina, 80; in Georgia, 52; and in Maryland, seven.

The result was what might be expected: At the time of the revolution the southern states were both richer and more highly developed than those of the north. Excepting Gouverneur Morris of Pennsylvania, both northern and southern delegates to the Constitutional Convention agreed that the north was then the poorer region.

In the debate on slave representation, Rufus King of Massachusetts and Chas. Cotesworth Pinckney of South Carolina made almost identical appraisals:

> Mr. King had always expected that, as the Southern States are the richest, they would not league themselves with the Northern unless some respect were paid to their superior wealth.[20]

> Gen. Pinckney dwelt on the superior wealth of the Southern States, and insisted on its having its due weight in the government.[21]

The manner of living in the two sections faithfully reflected economic differences. Pinckney expressed his amazement at the rude and primitive life of the northern colonies:

> The southern citizen beholds, with a kind of surprise, the simple manners of the east, and is too often induced to entertain undeserved opinions of the apparent purity of the Quaker; while they, in their turn, seem concerned at what they term the extravagance and dissipation of their southern friends. . . .[22]

John Adams thought that the condition of the poor in New England was no better than that of the Southern slaves:

> The condition of the laboring poor in most countries—that of the fisherman particularly of the northern states—is as abject as that of the slaves.[22a]

Among the southern states, Virginia was by far largest. Logically, although the American Revolution originated in Massachusetts, it probably should have been run from Virginia. The small merchants and fishermen of New England may have instigated American independence, but the father of the country was a Virginia tobacco planter and slaveholder.

Coming events cast their shadows at the Constitutional Convention, but in a curiously transposed way. The future could be read if the present were viewed through a prism or an inverting lens. Eli Whitney's cotton gin still lay five years in the future; but it is an oversimplification to say that slavery was moribund and that in 1793, invention of the cotton gin reversed the course of events. The cotton gin did not do that. It merely retarded an overriding but still uneven trend, but it did render the first solution more difficult and painful.

It is an oversimplification too, to view the slave and non-slave states as monolithic blocks. Crops or industries, as well as relative age and development, not only created fissures between the free and slave states, but produced groupings quite different from the solid sections which were to confront each other in 1861. In 1787, some slave and free states combined against other coalitions of free and slave states. On the surface, the problem of slave labor versus "free" labor gave no inkling of its denouement. But there were a few critics and doubters at the conventions. Parodixically, it was they who gave a forecast of the future.

On an empty continent, colonies which found slave labor profitable had forged ahead of those whose unsuitability to the slave system limited them to small independent enterprises. But each social system as it develops, tends to build its own ceiling, as a mollusk builds its shell. It can grow until that ceiling is reached, but when it is reached, development goes no further. The society must then either stagnate or be replaced by another with higher potential.

Though the plantation colonies were predominant in the 1780's, a few individuals detected signs that things might not always be so. They thought that the slave colonies had about reached the limit of their development and could soon be surpassed by the wage system of the North. Their prescience was due either to wishful thinking, which happened to coincide with reality, or to longer experience. The delegates' point of view acquire significance when related to the position of the respective colonies from which they were uttered. Among the northern states, New England was engaged in the carrying trade and in fishing.[23] Pennsylvania was the state of the Quakers, who had been agitating against slavery since 1693.[24] New England, carrying goods for the slave states, was more favorable to their contentions than were the crusading Quakers.

In the South, Virginia stood at the opposite pole from South Carolina and Georgia. Importing slaves since 1619, Virginia's tobacco planters had begun to experience overproduction as early as 1671. In that year Sir William Petty, in his <u>Political Arithmetic</u>, noted the "overplanting of sugar, tobacco, and pepper" which had made these staples "unreasonably cheap."[26] In 1710 came a wail about "the great decay of the trade of tobacco".[26a] In 1730 the Governor of Virginia complained that the tobacco trade had "fallen into miserable condition."[26b] Tobacco growing was again in the doldrums in 1757, near the beginning of the Seven Years' War.[26c] Virginians felt that they had more slaves than they could use. Jefferson's original draft of the Declaration of Independence inveighed against the English king for refusing to allow the colonies to prohibit slave trade.[27]

Though further importation of slaves was forbidden by the Virginia constitution of 1778,[28] the Virginia convention spokesmen still felt in 1788 that the state was surfeited with slaves. At the Virginia convention on ratification of the United States Constitution, Governor Edmund Randolph expressed the state's sentiment when he said:

> Are we not weakened by the population of those whom we hold in slavery? One day may come when they may make impression upon us. Gentlemen who have been long accustomed to the contemplation of the subject think there is some cause of alarm in this case: the number of these people, compared to that of the whites, is an immense proportion; their number amounts to 236,000— that of the whites, only to 393,000.[29]

On the other hand, South Carolina and Georgia were relatively new and unpopulated. Their rice and indigo crops seemed to have been prospering, so they had a continuous demand for more slaves. Georgia, in fact, was as yet virtually unsettled. Her importing of slaves only dated back to 1750,[30] and her entire population at the time of the Constitutional Convention was only 78,000 whites and 20,000 slaves.[31]

Heavy importation of slaves into South Carolina began about 1708, when the smaller sugar planters of Barbados emigrated to the mainland.[32]   By 1787 the state still had so much undrained and unimproved swamp land that the demand for more slaves seemed insatiable. "I am of the same opinion now as I was two years ago," Chas. Cotesworth Pinckney declared at the South Carolina ratification convention.

> That while there remained one acre of swamp land uncleared of South Carolina, I would raise my voice against restricting the importation of Negroes. I am thoroughly convinced . . . that the nature of our climate, and the flat, swampy situation of our country, obliges us to cultivate our land with Negroes, and that without them South Carolina would soon be a desert waste.[33]

Madison thus summarized the "southern" position before the Virginia convention:

> The gentlemen from South Carolina and Georgia argued in this manner: We have now liberty to import this species of property, and much of the property now possessed has been purchased, or otherwise acquired, in contemplation of improving it by the assistance of imported slaves. . . . [34]

Besides developing late, South Carolina had lost many of her slaves during the Revolutionary War.[35] All these factors together put South Carolina and Georgia "in want of hands to cultivate their lands," a shortage which the slave trade was expected to alleviate.[36] Continuation of the slave trade was the price of their joining the Union.[37] Moreover, the Carolinas and Georgia thought of themselves as the fastest growing states.

> It was not supposed that North Carolina, South Carolina and Georgia would have more people than all the other States, but many more relatively to the other states than they have now. The people and strength of America are evidently leaning southwardly, and south-westwardly.[38]

Georgia's population was in fact increasing. The slogan of the hour was "Go south, young man."

These circumstances combined to put Virginia and the two southernmost states into an even sharper antagonism than the two northern subdivisions were toward one another; in fact, into hostility more acute than any between the north and the south as a whole. Two issues focused the cleavages which existed on the subject of slavery:

(a)   prohibition of the slave trade;   (b) counting slaves for purposes of representation.

The proposal to prohibit further importation of slaves was like a flash of lightning which suddenly illuminated the respective interests of the colonies. Georgia and South Carolina insisted on keeping the slave trade open at least for awhile. The decision to permit the trade until 1808 was one of the many compromises of the 1787 Constitutional Convention. In one paragraph, Chas. Cotesworth Pinckney summarized the attitudes of the different states at the Federal Convention:

> 'Show some period,' said the members from the Eastern States, 'when it may be in our power to put a stop, if we please, to the importation of this weakness, and we will endeavor, for your convenience, to restrain the religious and political prejudices of our people on this subject.' The middle states and Virginia made us no such proposition; they were for an immediate and total prohibition.[40]

So bitter was the feeling that General Pinckney even accused Virginia of wanting to stop slave importations in order to raise the price of her own slaves.

> South Carolina and Georgia cannot do without slaves. As to Virginia, she will gain by stopping the importations. Her slaves will rise in value, and she has more than she wants.[40a]

A motion to allow the importation until 1808 instead of 1800 carried at the federal convention by a vote of 7-4.[41-3]   The seven ayes came from the three New England states, the three southern states, plus the State of Maryland. The four noes were cast by Virginia, Pennsylvania, New Jersey and Deleware. What do these votes mean?

At the time of the Constitutional Convention, Maryland's Luther Martin complained that in 1787 the country had lost its revolutionary fervor against slavery.

> At this time we do not generally hold this commerce in such abhorrence as we have done. When our liberties were at stake, we warmly felt for the common rights of man.[43b]

Although the "eastern states" had an aversion to slavery, they were,

> . . . willing to indulge the Southern states at least with a temporary liberty to prosecute the slave trade, provided

the Southern States would in their turn gratify them by laying no restrictions on navigation acts.[43c-d]

Contrariwise, Virginia, overstocked with slaves, joined hands with the Quakers of Pennsylvania, who had been agitating for abolition of slavery (not merely the slave trade) since 1693.[43e] In 1787 Pennsylvania could afford to oppose slavery, having more indentured white servants than any other colony. New Jersey and Deleware apparently followed the lead of Pennsylvania. None of their delegates uttered a word about slavery throughout the convention.

The portents of Virginia's coming decline were seen by those who desired to see them, or by those who were particularly prescient. Gouverneur Morris of Pennsylvania had perceived the tendency of the slave states to stagnate. While other delegates north and south were seeking a formula of representation duly crediting the south's superior wealth, Morris questioned the premise:

> The probable revenue to be expected from the southern states has been greatly overrated. Compare the free regions of the middle states, where a rich and noble cultivation marks the prosperity and happiness of the people, with the misery and poverty which overspread the barren wastes of Virginia, Maryland, and other states having slaves. Travel through the whole continent, and you behold the prospect continually varying with the appearance and disappearance of slavery.

> The moment you leave the southern states, and enter New York, the effects of the institution become visible. Passing through the Jerseys, and entering Pennsylvania, every criterion of improvement witnesses the change. Proceed southwardly, and every step you take, through the great regions of slaves, presents a desert impression, with the increasing proportion of those wretched beings.[44]

George Mason of Virginia understood the weakness of the slave system which was destined to be decisive. Slavery kept out new immigrants.

> Slavery discourages arts and manufactures. They prevent the emigration of whites, who really enrich and strengthen a country.[45]

Here was the rub. On an empty continent, the slave areas developed first, but at the same time the slave regions did not develop either in commerce or manufacturing. Above all, subsequent immigrants from Europe avoided those areas worked by slaves. Soon the stage would be set for an "overstepping" of the south by the north.

The counterpart of Virginia's anticipation of no more immigrants, was Connecticut's certainty that immigration would make slaves unnecessary:

> As population increases, said Oliver Cromwell of Connecticut, poor laborers will be so plenty as to render slaves useless. Slavery in time will not be a speck in our country. Provision is already made in Connecticutt for abolishing it. And the abolition has already taken place in Massachusetts.[46-47]

Madison (from Virginia) even foresaw a wage proletariat:

> In future times, a great majority of the people will not only be without land, but any other sort of property.[48]

The passage of time would show the regions in a hare-and-tortoise relation, with the slow, steady advance of the north overtaking the quick but uneven development of the south.

The other bone of contention was the weight to be given slaves in determining the number of a state's representatives in Congress, and in the electoral college. Here there was a nearly sectional division. But the position of the sections was inverted. Each was at the opposite pole from the position it would take fifty years later.

The convention, under Hamilton's influence, wanted to make representation a function of both persons and property. The colonized property was slavery and land. Since no method of calculation was proferred, it was agreed that slave property alone should carry extra votes, since slaves could be more easily evaluated than land.[49]

In the debate which resulted in making five slaves equal to three free men, it was the Northern states (and Virginia) which contended that since slaves were chattels they should carry no more votes than cows or horses. Or in any event they maintained, a slave was less efficient than a free laborer. It was the southern delegates who argued forcefully that a slave was not only a person, but produced as much as any freeman. Luther Martin of Maryland, in the shadow of her two neighbors, Pennsylvania and Virginia, expressed the view of all who wanted to exclude the slave population from being counted toward representation in the House:

> It was urged that slaves could not be taken into account

as _men_, or citizens, because they were not admitted to the rights of citizens, in the states which adopted or continued slavery. If they were taken into account as property, it was asked what peculiar circumstances should render this property entitled to the high privilege of conferring consequence and power in the government to its possessors, rather than any other property, and why slaves should, as property, be taken into account rather than horses, cattle, mules, or any other species; and it was observed, by an honorable member from Massachusetts, that he considered it as dishonorable and humiliating to enter into compact with the slaves of the southern states as it would with the _horses_ and _mules_ of the eastern. (Author's italics)[50]

This referred specifically to Massachusetts' Elbridge Gerry's remark that:

The idea of property ought not to be the rule of representation. Blacks are property, and are used, to the southward, as horses and cattle to the northward; and why should their representation be increased to the southward, on account of the number of slaves, than horses or oxen to the north?[51]

Against this, Pierce Butler of South Carolina,

. . . insisted that the labor of a slave in South Carolina was as productive as that of a freeman in Massachusetts: that as wealth was the great means of defense and utility to the nation, they were equally valuable to it with freeman, and that, consequently, an equal representation ought to be allowed for them in a government which was instituted mainly for the protection of property, and was itself to be supported by property.[52]

North Carolina and Virginia supported the three-fifths rule.[53] In North Carolina slavery was weak.[54] Virginia recognized that counting slaves equal to freemen would be to her advantage, but rejected it as "unjust", an instance of the schizophrenia which dogged her throughout the convention. North Carolina, Virginia and Massachusetts considered three-fifths the golden mean.[55] Gerry of Massachusetts thought three-fifths the highest ratio which could be allowed.[56]

It did not escape the delegates that even during the debates, the sections had reversed themselves to suit their requirements of the moment.

> If the southern states contended for the inferiority of the blacks when taxation was in view, the eastern states, on the same occasion, contended for their equality. [57]

Likewise, the southern states were fully aware that their position was the necessary consequence of originally speeding immigration through the slave trade. Their total population was ample to hold political equality with the North. Should they treat the slaves as persons, and count them toward their political strength, or treat them as chattels, and thereby lose them for political purposes? For the southern delegates, the three-fifths rule represented not only a compromise with the North, but a resolution of their own dilemma.

The deepest problem of slavery, however, was revealed through the split personality presented by the Virginia delegation. They were inconsistent, opposing the slave trade, but favoring slavery and they chided one another for this inconsistency. In the last analysis, their dilemma was not one of slavery as such, but of an established institution which had reached the limits of its growth. Slavery had built Virginia, and had made her the most important state in the Union, but the institution could not be pushed further, at least not in the tobacco country. So the Virginians were both afraid to lose their slaves and afraid to augment them. They felt, as Jefferson later expressed it, that "We have the wolf by the ears, and can neither hold him nor safely let him go." [58a]

These fears came to the surface with speculation which ran rife through the convention. First, would abolition of the slave trade lead to abolition of slavery? Secondly, would the three-fifths rule encourage the slave trade? Virginia delegates, especially George Mason and Patrick Henry, complained that the new constitution permitted the slave trade too long a respite, and that it contained no guarantee against the abolition of slavery. [59-64]

Mason, in almost one breath, objected to the admission of South Carolina and Georgia if they wanted any continuation of the slave trade, and demanded assurance that slaveowners would not be deprived of the slaves they already possessed. Edmund Randolph, and George Nichols did not miss the opportunity to charge their colleagues with inconsistency, which, in Randolph's eyes, "proved in some degree the futility of their arguments."

Just one facet of the debate foreshadowed the future exactly as it would be, without refraction or inversion. Pennsylvania, one of the most vociferous opponents of slavery, objected to the three-fifths rule on the grounds that:

> the people of Pennsylvania would revolt at the idea of being put on a footing with slaves. They would reject any plan that was to have such an effect.

Thus, from 1787 to the Emancipation of 1865, the most fervent champions of Negro rights were also people who wanted nothing to do with Negroes personally.[65]

One other aspect of slavery caused little debate either at the Convention, or at the ensuing state conventions; the Fugitive Slave Law. This matter had been disposed of by the Continental Congress in framing the Ordinance for the Northwest Territory and establishing a fugitive slave law, on July 13, 1787, almost in the middle of the convention (May-September, 1787). The Convention had no need to re-argue it.

The census of 1790 gave the slave states a majority of the total population and a majority in the House of Representatives. Until this time the South was still cultivating its old crops; tobacco, rice, and indigo. In 1792 Kentucky was split from Virginia, and established as a separate slave state.[66]

The following year, 1793, Eli Whitney patented his cotton-gin. His invention revolutionized southern agriculture without changing its economic subdivisions. South Carolina, Georgia and to a lesser extent, North Carolina, switched to cotton. In short, the cotton-gin gave a push to the expanding slave states, but it had an effect on Virginia's incipient stagnation.

Cotton growing sprang up almost overnight.

> Cotton exportation from the United States increased from 487,000 pounds in 1793 to 1,600,000 pounds in 1794, the year in which Whitney's gin was first put into operation. In 1796, a year after he improved his machine, production rose to 10,000,000 pounds.[67]

As might be foreseen, the census of 1800 again gave the slave states a majority, even in the House of Representatives, where slaves were counted only as three-fifths. This occurred despite the fact that Georgia prohibited further importation of slaves in 1793, as South Carolina had done in 1792 and North Carolina did in 1794.[68]

In 1803 however, South Carolina reopened the slave trade.[69] And in the same year, Jefferson purchased Louisiana from France. Louisiana meant additional slave states. New England anticipated that the southern majority would now increase, and become too strong to oppose successfully. Rather than be indefinitely at the mercy of a different and antagonistic section, many New Englanders preferred to secede from the Union. Their reasons were nearly identical to the reasons slaveowners later gave when they felt themselves in a hopeless and permanent minority.

Rufus King and Timothy Pickering were the leaders of New England secessionism. Their letters to each other give a clear picture of their thinking. Interestingly enough, King first suggested a milder remedy— excluding slaves entirely in computing Congressional representation. On November 4, 1804, he wrote to his friend Pickering, "ought not an effort be made to limit the Representation to the free inhabitants only?"[70-71] In 1803 the sections were still divided along the same lines as in 1787. The opponents of slavery still wished to treat slaves solely as chattels.

Pickering first broached secession on March 4, 1804. In the spring of 1804 King had a conversation with O. Walcott, the notes of which have been preserved. The lines were now much sharper. The two sections, North and South, were in opposition, or, at least, had a "dissimilitude of interests." Admission of Louisiana into the Union had permanently altered and:

> . . .permanently settled the balance between the North and South in favor of the southern states. The only remedy is separation. Will (Vice President Aaron) Burr agree and pledge himself to this object?[72-73]

Those who opposed secession did so because they thought the remedy was too drastic. Everyone seems to have shared the foreboding of a permanent preponderance in the slave states. John Quincy Adams, reviewing the reaction to the Louisiana Purchase more than twenty-five years later agreed that:

> It was the acquisition of Lousiana which had been the immediate incentive of the plan. We agreed and lamented that the one lamentable consequence of the annexation of Louisiana to the Union would be to diminish the relative weight and influence of the northern section; that it would aggravate the evil of the slave representation, and endanger the Union itself by the expansion of its bulk and enfeebling extension of its line of defense against foreign invasions.[74]

New England in 1803 was unmistakeably continuing Gouverneur Morris's train of thought that:

> . . . the consequence of such a transfer of power, from the maritime to the interior and landed interest will be an oppression of commerce.[75]

But New England's secession movement was destined to sputter out like a firecracker which fails to explode. Not Gouverneur Morris, but Col. Mason of Virginia, had correctly gauged the trend of events. It was Mason who complained that slavery tended to keep out new immigrants. Less than two decades after the Louisiana Purchase in 1803, immigrants moving into the northern states were once and for all to end the worries of New England about a "permanent" southern majority.

Meanwhile, Virginians once more gave proof of their superb political insight. In 1803, the Indiana Territory made the first of several petitions to be relieved from the anti-slavery provision of the Northwest Territory Ordinance. The House Committee rejected the request. In a report written by John Randolph of Roanoke, Virginia, it said:

> The rapid population of the State of Ohio sufficiently evinces, that the labor of the slave is not necessary to promote the growth and settlement of colonies in that region. That this labor, demonstrably the dearest of any, can only be employed to advantage in the cultivation of products more valuable than any known to that quarter of the United States: and the committee deem it highly dangerous and inexpedient to impair a provision wisely calculated to promote the happiness and prosperity of the northwestern country, and to give strength and security to that extensive frontier. In the salutary operation of this sagacious and benevolent restraint, it is believed that the inhabitants of Indiana will, at no very distant day, find ample remuneration for a temporary privation of labor and emigration.[76]

Wise old Virginia, talking like a reformed roue: "Don't use it. It may speed your growth at first, but it will stunt your growth later." Here, the settlement of the Northwest Territory was correctly assessed in terms of peopling an empty continent.[77] The same forces were at work in the territory as had influenced the colonization of the continent as a whole. Introducing slaves would foster an early hothouse-grown migration but, Randolph felt, would keep away later immigrants.

Five years later, in 1808, the provision agreed to at the Constitutional Convention forbidding Congress from outlawing the slave trade ran out. A law to take effect on January 1, 1808, was enacted before that date, and a President from Virginia, Thomas Jefferson, signed it.[78] As in the Convention, the states which were overstocked with slaves combined with those who had no use for slavery, to end the slave trade.[79]

However the new law had no immediate effects. The sufficiency of the slave states in the House,[80] and the pressure for secession in New England, both persisted through the census of 1810. In 1809 there was correspondence by New England secessionist Rufus King and others, with Governor Craig of Canada, with a view to splitting the New England states from the Union and annexing them to Canada.[81] But the census of 1810 was the last one to reflect the old distribution of power.

For the North, the ensuing decade was the darkest. After the outbreak of the War of 1812, Cyrus King wrote to Rufus King:

> But the people in this part of the United States almost despair, by the ordinary means of our election, of a remedy for our distresses and for the disasters of our country, if the anti-commercial restrictive Virginia system is to predominate in our national councils four years longer.[82]

Two years later New England resentment against "the anti-commercial restrictive Virginia system" crystallized into the Hartford Conference, which made New England secession the subject of debate.

The spark which touched it off was a dispute as to whether the individual states or the federal government should pay for the militia needed to defend the New England coast against attacks by the British.[83] The New England states were determined to get their place in the sun, and contributed the slogan, "Peaceably if we can. Forcibly if we must." [84] Secession was approved in case of "extreme necessity" brought on by the unfriendly acts of the federal government. But the time was not ripe. The conference wound up with a number of innocuous resolutions, such as abolition of the three-fifths rule, assigning representatives based only on the number of free persons in a state, and a constitutional amendment providing that the President could not be elected from the same state more than twice in secession.[85] As these resolutions were filed with Congress on January 15, 1815,[86] the War of 1812 came to an end.

It is of no significance that New England's proposed secession was initially rejected. A divorce does not follow the first quarrel. Later in the century southern secession was to be broached many times before it was actually carried out. The time for New England secession was not yet, and no longer. Within five years, when the census of 1820 arrived, southern preponderance was a thing the past. Non-slaveholding states had a majority in the House of Representatives.[87] The tortoise had overtaken the hare. In spite of the cotton gin's fillip to slavery, steady immigration from Europe had enabled the northern states to pass their southern competitors. Eli Whitney's invention could slow the process, but did not reverse it.

So the movement for New England secession died as its causes fell away:

> Winds lose their force when they do empty fly
> Unmet of woods or buildings. Great fires die
> That want their matter to withstand them. . . . [88]

The shift in the balance of power came like an earthquake. Admission of Missouri to statehood was the main temblor, but it was preceded by a minor one over the acquisition of Florida and the ceding of Texas. When Spain transferred Florida to the United States in 1819, the United States, in exchange, ceded to Spain the Texas sector of the Louisiana purchase.[89] This cession was engineered by the New England interests who wanted to get rid of territory from which new slave states might be organized.[90] The significant thing is that at this juncture the North was no longer in the minority, even without the Texas maneuver.

In the same year, 1819, came the first debates over the admission of Missouri. Positions taken by the contending sections were a true key to the new equation of power, which the next year's census would confirm. Northern Congressmen wanted Missouri admitted only with a clause excluding slavery.[91] What basis was there for taking such a position? Historically and legally, Missouri was no different from Louisiana, which in 1811, had been admitted as a slave state without contest. Missouri was a part of the Lousiana purchase. Both Missouri and Louisiana had been French before annexation by the United States,[92] and both had slavery under French law.[93] The agitation over whether Missouri should be admitted as a free or slave state stemmed from one thing only: that the Westward migration of slaveholders and non-slaveholders had at length collided. And this event coincided with the moment when the free states had outstripped the slave states in population.

When the smoke of the Missouri Compromise fight cleared away, the North had lost a battle, but won a campaign. The act for the admission of Missouri provided that while Missouri might become a state without restriction, slavery should be prohibited in all other states carved out of the Louisiana purchase and lying north of 36° 30'.[94] The terms of the compromise left no doubt as to the new center of power. To the north of the Missouri line, slavery was prohibited. To the south of the line the question was left open. Slavery might still be prohibited. And all this came about less than ten years after New Englanders had been concerned over the "permanent" domination of the slaveholding states!

Other portents, less violent, but no less momentous, signalled the shift in sectional power. Monroe's individual popularity returned him to office to 1820, but with this lag of only one term, the shift of population coincided with the end of the "Virginia dynasty". The presidential election of 1824, a second turning so to speak, was the only election since the XIIth Amendment, which went into the House of Representatives. Theodor Mommsen has said that "every political alliance is inwardly broken up when the relative strength of the parties is materially altered."[95]

So after 1820, national politics suddenly changed from smooth to turbulent. In the nine presidential terms which preceded 1824, all but one president had been reelected; in the nine terms which lay ahead, only one more would be re-elected before the outbreak of the Civil War.

The 77-year old Jefferson grasped the meaning of the Missouri agitation, while echoing the general surprise which was due to the fact that the quake happened to precede the census returns. Jefferson's famous "fire bell in the night" letter was written to John Holmes on April 22, 1820:

> I had for a long time ceased to read newspapers, or pay any attention to public affairs, confident that they were in good hands, and content to be a passenger in our bark, to the shore from which I am not distant. But this momentous question, like a firebell in the night, awakened me and filled me with terror. I considered it at once the knell of the Union. But this is a reprieve only, not a final sentence. A geographical line, coinciding with a marked principle, moral and political, once conceived and held up to the angry passions of men, will never be obliterated; and every new irritation will mark it deeper and deeper.[96]

Presidential aspirant John Quincy Adams foresaw, not only the struggle, but also its outcome. He seemed pleased with the prospect:

> If the dissolution of the Union should result from the slave question, it is as obvious as anything that can be foreseen of futurity, that it must shortly afterwards be followed by the universal emancipation of slaves. . . . A

dissolution at least temporary, of the Union, as now constituted, would be certainly necessary. . . . The Union might then be organized on the fundamental principles of emancipation. This object is vast in compass, awful in its prospect, sublime and beautiful in its issue. [97]

From the Settlement to the Cotton Gin (1607-1793)

> The life of the law has not been logic, it has been experience. The felt necessities of the time, the prevalent moral and political theories, intuition of public policy, avowed or unconscious, even the prejudice which judges share with their fellow-men, have a good deal more to do than the syllogram in determining the rules by which men should be governed. The law embodies the story of a nation's development through many centuries, and it cannot be dealt with as if it contained only the axioms and corollaries of a book of mathematica—the substance of the law at any given time pretty nearly corresponds, so far as it goes, with what is then understood to be convenient. —Oliver Wendell Holmes: The Common Law - Lecture I

Franklin put his finger on the reason why the slave colonies flowered sooner than the free colonies when he said that no employee stayed on the job long. In the free colonies, having saved ever so little, a man could strike out for himself on his own land. On a fertile and empty continent, large-scale operations were impossible unless employees were legally chained to the job. A slave system supplied this need, as well as the demand for rapid introduction of laborers. Even slavery's opponents would later admit that "the great and almost the sole excellence of slave labour is . . . its capacity for organization."[1] Slave plantations were, therefore, the first large-scale enterprises on the North American continent. And slave-worked agriculture was the first undertaking of any kind to have the advantages of large-scale production.

A master's right to hold a slave to his employment could not exist in vacuo.[1a] The moment it was accorded, it entailed a whole system of rights and duties. Their rights and duties fell into four main categories: (1) between slaveowner and slave; (2) between slaveowner and slaveowner; (3) between slaveowner and the community at large; and (4) between "free" Negroes and whites.

The legal system governing the relations of masters and slaves in the colonies was one of the first products of the forcible settlement of the continent. We shall examine this system in detail. The features of the slave system constitute a key to the country's ensuing history. They help to answer the question: If the capacity for organization enabled slave labor to outstrip free labor on an empty continent, what enabled free (wage) labor to surpass and destroy slave labor on a populated continent?

The basic features of slavery sprang up quite uniformly throughout the English colonies, although the details soon varied with the different regions.

The first feature of the colonial slave law was wholly negative. Under European serfdom, the laborer was tied to the land.[1c] This was not the case with the slaves of the Western Hemisphere.[2] Fastening laborers to the land was practical only where the land was known and the master stationary. Settlement of an unpeopled continent was experimental and entailed moving around in search of the best land. Slaves brought over to aid this settlement had to be as mobile as their masters.[3]

But if the slave was not tied to the land, he was tied to his master. Otherwise, it would not have been possible to keep slaves any longer than "free" employees.

The first essential to the slave system was, therefore, the master's legal right to bring back the slave who had left his service. This included slaves who had gone among the slaves of another plantation, slaves en route, and "outlying slaves" (i.e., those who had made homes for themselves in the wilderness beyond the limits of white settlements). The last are the counterpart of the white settlers who left their employment to work their own farms.[4] All the colonies enacted fugitive slave laws soon after they were organized. The colonists initially seem to have assumed that they would hold their slaves to their employment. When it was found that slaves sometimes strayed from their masters' fields, laws were passed.

Virginia was settled in 1607. Slaves were imported in 1619. Legal records commence in 1622.[5] Although the first statute referring to slaves seems to have been enacted in 1661,[6] the Virginia colonists exercised the power to bring back fugitive slaves as early as 1640.[7] In that year six servants and a Negro slave of one Reynolds "plotted to run away into the Dutch plantation from their said masters". They "sailed down to Elizabeth River where they were taken and brought back again".

Once the colonial legislature began to deal with slaves, it lost little time in enacting a general fugitive slave law. A full-fledged system for retrieving fugitives went into effect in 1663.[8] From then on, fugitive slave laws were part of the slave system in Virginia.[9g]

Maryland's institution of slavery took shape along similar lines. As in Virginia, judicial decisions in particular cases preceded general legislation. The earliest case involving a runaway in Maryland also presented one of the other great problems of a slave society: the community's interest in the master's treatment of the slave. In ATTORNEY-GENERAL v. OVERZEE (1658),[10] the colony prosecuted Overzee for mistreating a Negro slave by having Indian slaves hold him and then pouring hot lard on him to make him move. The defense was that the slave had run away and lurked in the bush. The jury acquitted the master of mistreatment.

This case shows the paramount importance assigned to holding slaves to the master's service.[11] But it also shows how problems never arose singly and how the colonists had to create an entire jurisprudence of slavery almost at once.[12] Six years later, in 1664, Maryland's slave law was made statutory.[13] Successive acts were passed in 1676,[14] 1681,[15] 1692[16] and 1695.[17]

When Maryland adopted a runaway statute in 1699, it was extremely strict.[18-19] Not only were servants or slaves subject to be taken as runaways if found without a pass more than ten miles from their master's homes, but any person was made liable to be taken as a runaway if found without a pass outside the county of his residence and unable to give a good account of himself.[19]

This Act also provided for rewards to those apprehending runaways and set up legal machinery for dealing with the latter. Anyone taking a supposed runaway had to bring him "before the next magistrate" who held him until the next court, unless the prisoner could post bail.[21] Thenceforth, runaway laws were a permanent feature of the colony's social structure.[22]

None of the remaining southern colonies were organized as early as Virginia or Maryland. For other slave laws of the same period, one must look to those colonies which were later known as "free" states. The Dutch colony in New York (New Netherlands) records at least two lawsuits over fugitive slaves.[23] When the British took over the colony, they lost no time in passing an act to deal with runaways. The transfer of sovereignty took place on June 13, 1665.[24] In the same year there was issued the Easthampton Book of Laws, which established laws both for bond slavery in general [25] and for fugitives in particular.[26] Three judicial cases involving fugitive slaves are reported under the English government of New York before the Seventeenth century came to a close.[27] New York retained its fugitive slave laws for the remainder of the period ending in 1793.[28]

In its early history, New Jersey developed the same way, although the obsolescence of slavery was soon noticeable. The earliest New Jersey statutes were enacted in 1664.[29] A fugitive slave law made its appearance in 1682,[30] and was reenacted in 1713.[31] After that, slavery in New Jersey began to die on the vine. The statute of 1713 remained unchanged, and the only new legislation which even squinted at the subject of fugitives was that which in 1752 forbade slaves from hunting or going away armed from their master's house after 9 p.m.[32]

Puritans in Massachusetts, imbued with ideals of human freedom, hesitated to say that indentured servants or slaves could be returned to their masters. So the recapture of fugitives was practiced but not mentioned except indirectly. Massachusetts' "Body of Liberties", enacted in 1641,[33] provided in Section 85 that a servant should be protected if fleeing from the cruelty of his master. An even more pointed example of the Puritans' attitude toward slavery is found in Section 91, which provided that there shall be no slavery "unless it be lawful captives taken in just warrent and such strangers as willingly selle themselves or are sold to us".

Massachusetts went to the extreme of forbidding its slaves from associating with Quakers—a measure enacted in no other colony except Barbados. The Friends were preaching Negro emancipation. In RE SOUTHWICKE (1659)[33b] persons were fined for refusing to work and joining the Quakers; those who could not pay fines were ordered sold in Virginia or Barbados.

But slavery did not flourish in Massachusetts,[34] and the problems of runaways was met by further discouraging the importation of Negro slaves. In 1709, Governor Dudley and the Massachusetts Lords of Trade exchanged letters in which the Lords objected to the Governor's stand that "Negroes are not desired in New England because it being on the Continent the Negroes have thereby an opportunity of running away".

The Governor's view prevailed. That same year, 1709, the council passed an act to encourage the importation of white servants,[36] and in 1718 made its point even more explicit with a resolution "That the Importation of White Servants be encouraged, and that the Importation of Black Servants be discouraged".[37] The subject came to a close when Massachusetts abolished slavery by judicial fiat in 1781.

Connecticut drew up its first constitution in 1638[38] and its first code in 1650 without reference to fugitive slaves.[39] But by 1750 the colony had duly enacted a law authorizing the siezure of any Negro, Mulatto or Indian servant travelling without a pass.[40] This was the extent of the legislation however. In 1784 gradual abolition was enacted by providing that all Negroes born after March 1, 1784 should be free.[41]

Rhode Island recognized slavery by statute in 1652,[41] and at the same time tried to soften it by providing expressly that Negroes should be held only for a term of years, the same as white servants.[42] But no fugitive slave law was passed until 1714.[43] Most of the other colonies had by then already rounded out their jurisprudence of slavery. Thus, while Rhode Island started its slave laws early, the institution evidently did not flourish, and the development of a legal code lagged.

In 1757, a penalty was specially imposed on privateers and other vessels carrying slaves out of the state without the owner's consent.[44] Part of the problem of holding slaves to one employer was to prevent slave dealers from conducting raids in Rhode Island. During the revolutionary war, the policy of enlisting slaves in the army and manumitting them[45] sometimes proved attractive to runaways from other states who were discharged as soon as their status was discovered.[46] But by that time slavery in Rhode Island was near the end of its road. After a momentary hesitation during which slave enlistments were halted, the state, in 1784, adopted the gradual abolition of slavery by decreeing that all Negroes, Mulattoes, etc. born after March 1, 1784, should be free.[48]

New Hampshire, the most northerly of the original colonies, shows most clearly how slavery failed to take hold in these areas. While there were slave laws from 1686 on,[49] there was no special fugitive slave law. The nearest approach to such a law prohibited slaves from going out after 9 p.m. except on errands; but this was designed to prevent disorders rather than runaways.[50] Furthermore, that law was repealed in 1792,[51] and slavery "died a natural death in New Hampshire" without formal abolition.[52]

Incidentally, the earliest references to slavery in New Hampshire were instructions from the English King to pass legislation which probably had little relation to conditions in the colony.[53] This pattern suggests that a limited body of slave law, which had taken shape in the older colonies, was applied ready-made to the later ones.

Even Pennsylvania, the Quaker state,[54] organized its society with all the usual slave legislation. The Duke of York's book of laws running from 1676-1682 contains provisions relating to slavery in general but not specifically to runaways.[55] This lack was supplied in 1685.[56] Forty years later the right to recapture fugitive slaves was elaborated by providing that the errant Negro should be whipped and his "take up" receive a reward of five shillings. [57]

After 1685, there was only one further bit of legislation on this subject. Furthermore, as early as 1712, Pennsylvania sought to curb the importation of slaves by levying duty upon them.[58] This policy was maintained until gradual abolition was launched in 1780. [59] Although even the abolition act retained machinery for bringing back runaway slaves, it honored them by placing them on equal footing with white bond servants.[60] That runaway slaves were never really a major issue in Pennsylvania is suggested by the fact that only one case concerning fugitive slaves seems to have arisen in Pennsylvania during this entire period. [61]

In the Seventeenth century, the position of Jamaica was not essentially different from that of the colonies on the mainland. Having taken it from Spain in 1658, the English proceeded to govern Jamaica in the same way as their other American colonies.[62] In 1684, an elaborate slave law was enacted. Its very first section forbade masters of vessels from carrying off slaves without a pass from their owners. [63] Later sections set up machinery for handling runaways within the island.[64] Similarly, Barbados provided legal sanctions for the return of fugitive slaves at least as early as 1704.[65] This colony went to the unusual length of forbidding its slaves from associating with the Quakers[66]— foreshadowing southern reactions to the Abolitionists a century and a half later. But of course, while the Quakers of 1700 caused scarcely a noticeable ripple, the Abolitionists of 1850 would stir up a tempest. For by then slavery would have outlived its economic usefulness. And similar moral propaganda against slavery in a different economic setting would have totally different effects.

In discussing the slave laws of New Hampshire, we noted that they appeared to be modelled on the laws already developed in the older colonies. So by the time the later colonies—the Carolinas and Georgia— were settled, it was no longer necessary to improvise. A well-recognized body of slave law had already been formed. The emergent jurisprudence of North and South Carolina followed what had become the orthodox pattern.

The earliest statutes of North Carolina were carried over from Virginia. The first compilation of North Carolina slavery legislation made its appearance in 1715,[67] although there were already judicial decisions dating from 1703 and one in 1713 referred to "an act concerning servants and slaves."[68] No fugitive slave law appeared on the books until 1741.[69] The late enactment of slavery's legal

cornerstone reflects the looseness of the entire slave system in North
Carolina. From the time of the first settlement to the outbreak of the
Civil War, North Carolina slaveowners never seemed to be sure whether
they wanted their slaves to be slaves, or small independent peddlers and
artisans.[70]   Still, North Carolina's statutory scheme, having been
borrowed ready-made from other colonies, was retained with only
subordinate modifications until 1793.[71] Up to that time, no legal cases
involving fugitive slaves arose in North Carolina.[72]

South Carolina's original charter was granted in 1663. It made no
mention of slavery.[73] Legal decisions about slavery date from 1673,[74]
and, as in the other colonies, precede the enactment of statutes. The
first South Carolina statutes date from 1682.[75] And the earliest slave
law was passed in 1686. Although entitled "An act inhibiting the trading
with servants or slaves",[76] it also contained a section about the recapture and return of fugitives.[77] This law, cautiously made to run for only
two years,[78] was, in effect, permanent. It was substantially re-enacted
in 1690,[79] 1701,[80] 1712,[81] and remained as a part of the South Carolina
legal system until the invention of the cotton gin.[82]

Delaware was originally organized under the same government as
Maryland[82a] and did not have separate laws until 1700.[82b] A fugitive
slave law for Delaware itself was not enacted until 1740.[82c] In that
year the colony passed "An act for the better regulations of servants and
slaves within this government."[82c] The preamble recited that it was:

> For the due encouragement of servants in the discharge
> of their duty, and preventing of their desertion from their
> masters' and owners' service, and for the discouraging of
> those who corrupt, entertain, traffick or deal with any
> servant or slave.

Fines were imposed on those who dealt with servants or slaves;[82d]
free Negroes were to be whipped besides,[82c] and had to make satisfaction by servitude if unable to pay the fine.[82g] A penalty of 40 shillings was imposed for each 24 hours for harboring or concealing servants
or slaves.[82f] And a reward of five shillings and reasonable costs was
offered to anyone taking up a slave more than ten miles from his
master's home.[82h]

The lumping of servants and slaves in one statute, and the relatively
light penalties show that slavery was not much of a problem in
Delaware; it was not well developed. Although slave stealing was
punished by death under the Act of 1742,[82i] this punishment was found
too difficult to enforce and in 1779 was reduced to 39 lashes, pillory,
with cropping of the ears and double restitution. There is no record of

judicial decisions on slavery. The preceding short account, which covers the entire legal history of slavery in Delaware to 1793, indicates the limited importance of the institution there.

Georgia was at once the southernmost and the last of the English colonies to be formed on the continent. These two features were mutually contradictory, and tended to work against each other. While climate and soil made slavery profitable in Georgia, the colony's year of organization, 1733, was on the threshhold of the Industrial Revolution that would eventually destroy the institution. Georgia's history is unique. It is the only colony that first prohibited slavery but later allowed it.

General James Oglethorpe, to whom was granted the original charter in 1733, disapproved of slavery[83] to such an extent that he tried to put his ideas into practice. So the original Georgia charter provided that there should be no slaves in the colony. There were too few white indentured servants for large scale cultivation, and the small farm units in Georgia were so unable to compete with South Carolina that they found it less expensive to import from that territory than to grow their own products. During the years 1737-1741, the population of the colony dropped from 5000 to 500.[86]

In 1740 the Georgia colonists began renting slaves from South Carolina.[87] At length, in 1750, over the protests of Gen. Oglethorpe himself and some German settlers, the prohibition against slavery was repealed.[88] The ratio of Negro to white servants was fixed at four males to one, with a fine for violation.[89] Furthermore, laws for the government of slaves were promulgated in 1755.[89a] The earliest Code of laws appeared ten years later in 1765.[90] This included the Act of 1757, as amended in 1760, forming slave patrols and empowering them to pick up any slaves found outside the master's enclosure without a pass.[91]

In 1770 the owner was not only permitted to retrieve his slaves, but could forbid them wander without a pass.[92] Male slaves over seven years of age could not travel without a white supervisor.[93] Plantations always had to have six white supervisors, inasmuch as "plantations settled with slaves, without any white man thereon, may be harbours for runaway and fugitive slaves". These laws continued throughout the period ending in 1793.[94]

The judicial records of the period show only one case involving fugitive slaves. This is the grand jury report of 1772, entitled RE FUGITIVE SLAVES,[95] which recites that:

> The Presentments of the Grand Jury . . . was read and it
> appearing thereby that a number of fugitive slaves have

assembled . . . on or near the borders of the River Savannah, and are frequently committing depredations with Impunity.

Louisiana developed its codes from French and Spanish law. New Orleans was founded in 1717 and the Code Noir of Louisiana introduced from the Island Colonies in 1724.[98] The Code Noir of 1685, brought into Louisiana from the French West Indies,[98a] punishes fugitive slaves[98b] and free Negroes who harbor them,[98c] and so assumes the master's right to retrieve them. The judicial decisions of the period likewise show that the right to retrieve a runaway slave was as well established in Louisiana as in the English colonies. The earliest case, entitled, RE NEGRO,[99] dealt with "a certain negro boy who had deserted but was recovered at Mobile." Two years later, in RE INDIAN GODIN,[100] the "Attorney General . . . reports that an Indian slave who ran away two years ago has been caught and is now in prison." Repeating fugitives were flogged, as in the case of the INDIANS GUILLORY, et al.[101] The law governing fugitives remained unchanged from the first settlement until 1793.[102]

The United States Constitution provided for interstate rendition of fugitive slaves, and in 1793 Congress passed the first federal Fugitive Slave Law.[102b] These laws show that the right to recapture fugitive slaves was enforced wherever slavery existed. It was the key to the early difference in development between the southern and northern colonies. Where slavery was profitable, the right to hold slaves physically to their job made large scale enterprise possible. The north, on the other hand, could neither use slaves nor develop other large scale enterprises as long as her wage laborers were free to leave their employment and farm for themselves as soon as they had saved some money. Recapture of fugitive slaves was the linchpin of the system. Just as this right inaugurated the plantation economy in the Seventeenth century, so in the 1850's, the Fugitive Slave Law was the first focus of the attack which ended in abolition.

The conditions which called forth the slave system in North America also shaped the methods by which masters enforced discipline. The counterpart to the demand for fugitive slave laws was the impossibility of disciplining employees by discharging them. "Firing" a worker is a threat and a sanction only where it is easier for the employer to find another employee than it is for the employee to find another job (or to set up in business for himself). But, as shown in our discussion of the fugitive slave laws, the early colonial economy presented just the opposite picture. It was the employer, not the employee, who went out of his way to keep the employee on the job. Consequently any discipline which the employer enforced on his employees had to be enforced without separating the employees from their work.

The answer was corporal punishment.[102c] This was readily adopted since it was general in Europe in the 17th century,[103] and was also the simplest means for maintaining large bodies of subordinate workers under the conditions obtaining in the English colonies at the beginning of the settlement.

Corporal discipline soon went beyond corporal punishment. The methods used for keeping slaves under control divided into two types; physical punishment after the fact, and a system of patrols which operated like military police among the slaves, taking measure against potential slave insurrections.

In Virginia, corporal punishment always took two forms: less severe penalties could be inflicted by the master or his overseer, but more severe ones had to be administered by the public authorities. In the former category, runaways and women servants who became pregnant out of turn were whipped under the sheriff's authority.[104c] The Act of 1748 Governing Servants and Slaves, recognizes the master's right to physical chastisement by forbidding immoderate correction.[105] The act provided that white servants could be whipped naked only on the orders of a Justice of the Peace,[105] thus marking the distinction that less severe punishment could be inflicted by the master himself—more severe ones, only by public officials.

This act continued the practice of whipping runaways.[106] A slave wandering over to another plantation without his owner's leave was subject to ten lashes by the owner.[107] However, a slave wandering off and carrying firearms or gunpowder was punished with up to thirty-nine lashes by order of a Justice of the Peace.[108] For lifting a hand against a white person, up to thirty lashes were likewise imposed by a Justice of the Peace.[109] While forbidding "excessive" correction, this statute also goes out of its way to provide an enormous field of immunity to the slaveowners—probably more than was permitted in later years:

> And that where any slave shall happen to die, by Reason of any Stroke, or Blow given, during his or her correction, by his or her owner, or by reason of any accidental Blow whatsoever, given by such owner, no Person concerned in such correction, or accidental homocide shall be liable to any prosecution or punishment for the same, unless upon Examination before the County Court, it shall be proved by the Oath of at least one lawful and credible witness,

that such Slave was killed wilfully, maliciously or design-
edly; and no person, indicted for the murder of a slave,
and upon trial found guilty of manslaughter only, shall
occur any forfeiture of punishment for such offense, or
misfortune.[110]

These provisions were continued in the Acts of 1753,[111] 1769,[112]
1782,[113] 1792.[114-115]   The judicial decisions in Virginia up to 1793
present only a few odd situations growing out of the corporal punishment
of slaves.   Up to 1793 there were actually no Virginia cases directly
discussing the right of a master to chastise his own slave. HOOMES v.
KUHN,[115-116] decided in 1792, arose out of the whipping which Kuhn
administered to Hoomes' slave, whom he had suspected of theft. Civil
damages were awarded against Kuhn in favor of the slave's owner.

The only other cases even remotely touching the subject, are
THOMAS SCORRELL'S CASE[117] in which the hirer of a slave was
charged with his murder and found guilty of manslaughter, and
DANDRIDGE v. LYON[118] in which the court assures the parties that
there is a danger of cruelties to slave children from the mother's owners:

> If Negro children do perish, by cruelty of those with
> whom their mothers live, as is supposed, it is believed to
> be in cases where they are hired out, or are under the
> direction of overseers at places far distant from the
> inhabitants of their owners.

While arising only from bizarre situations these few cases do bear
out the master's right of physical chastisement. The right exists almost
as a matter of course, but it must not be abuse. More later about this
proviso.

Maryland likewise recognized the master's right to inflict corporal
punishment on a slave by regulating its abuse. And in Virginia, the
master could punish within limits; beyond that, punishment had to be
imposed by public authority. The Act of Justice of 1715, penalized the
master for giving more than ten lashes for any one offense.[119]   A
magistrate could order up to thirty-nine lashes. So constables could
inflict 39 lashes to slaves of a plantation who failed to aid the constable
in dispersing a gathering or even a plantation owner could administer 39
lashes to the trespassing slave of another owner.[122]   The case of
ATTORNEY GENERAL v. OVERZEE,[123] decided in 1658, has already
been noticed from the viewpoint of fugitive slaves. It illustrates the
extreme to which direct punishment by the master was allowed to go.

Though the master was prosecuted for having his slave held while he (the master) poured hot lard down his throat, yet the master was acquitted in 1703, when a slave broke into an Indian cabin, damages were performed and the owner was ordered to punish his slave by whipping.[124]

These few cases are the only ones recorded in Maryland up until 1793, involving the master's right corporally to punish his slaves.

In New York the Dutch permitted masters to chastise their slaves after obtaining official permission.[125a] After New York became English, the law of October 24, 1684[126] authorized corporal punishment at the discretion of a Justice of the Peace for slave trading independently. As in other colonies the statute recognized the master's right of physical chastisement by curbing its abuse. In 1702 doubts were removed by granting the rights expressly—a master was empowered to impose punishment "at discretion not extending to life or member."[128] Under this same act unlawful assemblies of slaves were punished by not more than forty lashes, which, however, were given by public authority. Cities were empowered to appoint a common whipper whose salary was paid by assessments levied on slaveholders. So a slave striking a freeman suffered corporal punishment at the discretion of the Justice of the Peace.

Corporal punishment was the mode of discipline which minimized the time during which a slave was withdrawn from his master's service; while Negroes from Africa were brought over in larger numbers than white settlers, there were not enough to satisfy the demands for labor.

> Slaves are the property of Christians and cannot without great loss or detriment to their masters or mistresses be subjected in all cases criminal to the strict rules of the Laws of England.[128a]

Where corporal punishment was authorized,

> . . . the slave shall receive corporal punishment, at Discretion of a Justice of the Peace, and immediately thereafter be permitted to attend his or her Master or Masters service, without further punishment.[128b]

These provisions were renewed in 1712,[129] 1726,[130] and 1730.[131] Under some statutes, such as that of March 9, 1774,[132] the master's right to punish the slave directly must be read between the lines. This statute fined violators 3 pounds for each offense if they were freemen, but provides that slaves shall be held in jail and given 39 lashes unless the 3 pound fine be paid within six days. In most cases the master probably found it cheaper to pay the fine and then deal with the slave himself, than to lose the slave's services during a period of imprisonment and disability resulting from 39 lashes.

By 1788, when New York's slave laws were redrafted into a single statute, the institution was dying out. There is no longer any provision for corporal punishment of the slave by the master.[133] Nor do such provisions reappear.[134] As in many other colonies judicial decision preceded enactment of statutes. Robert Seary and "Mingoe" were sentenced to ten lashes and branded for being runaways, as early as 1682.[134a] No further judicial decisions are reported from New York until 1800.

New Jersey established corporal punishment by private persons (other than the owner) in its very first slave law.[135] In an effort to stamp out independent trading by slaves, the colonial government authorized the prospective vendee to whip any slave attempting to sell him something—and required the slave's owner to pay the whipper half a crown reward. Stripes by official authority were the punishment for stealing swine, fowl, etc. in 1695.[136] New Jersey likewise followed the pattern of the other colonies in recognizing the master's right to whip his slaves by forbidding the abuse of corporal punishment.[137] As elsewhere, runaway Negroes taken up without a pass more than five miles from their master's plantation could be whipped.[138]

There seems to be no further legislation along those lines during the period through 1793—but laws passed soon after that show that corporal punishment continued as the customary mode of discipline.[139] No legal cases on slavery were recorded in New Jersey before 1789;[140] and none in the remaining four years through 1793 involved punishment of slaves.

The Pilgrim Fathers came to Massachusetts seeking religious liberty. The austere religion which they practiced contained elements of both sadism and masochism. In the nature of things they did not hesitate to beat and whip their slaves. They recognized the master's right of corporal punishment in the same way as the other colonies—by curbing its abuse. Under the Body of Liberties of 1641, indentured servants were accorded interim support if they left the master's service because of cruel treatment; and were released unconditionally if the master had knocked out an eye, a tooth, or had otherwise maimed the servant.[141] But whipping was also sanctioned directly.

In 1698 both parties were punished by whipping if a white person bought stolen goods from a Negro.[142] A law of 1705 decreed that in the case of fornication between a Negro man and a "Christian" woman, both parties should be whipped.[143] Under this same law, if a "Christian" man fornicated with a Negro woman, the man alone was whipped,[144] and "severe" whipping was the punishment for a Negro or Mulatto striking a

white man. While the decline of slavery in Massachusetts is reflected in
the paucity of laws dealing with master-slave relation (as distinguished
from the slave trade), an act of 1746 imposes 10-20 stripes on any slave
for swearing, if the usual fine was not paid forthwith.[145] In 1752
whipping, not more than ten stripes, was meted out to Negroes caught in
street riots,[146] or damaging street lamps.[147]

In fact, corporal chastisement was retained even after
Massachusetts abolished slavery in 1781.[148] Negroes who entered
Massachusetts from other states, and failed to depart when ordered,
received ten stipes under a 1787 law.[149] Judicial cases in which slaves
were whipped begin in 1638.[150] In Massachusetts, as elsewhere,
individual sentences precede general statutes. From that date on,
sentences of whipping or branding for slaves and free Negroes occur
fairly often until 1685.[151]

Between 1690 and 1737 there are no recorded judicial decisions in
the Massachusetts Colony. When the records reappear, the first case
involving corporal punishment comes after the revolution and after the
Massachusetts constitution which was later held to have abolished
slavery. The long blank indicates how far the institution had faded out.

In 1781 a Negro was granted 50 pounds damage for an assault by a
white man who, it was charged, "seized the said Quork and threw him
down and struck him . . . with the handle of the whip, and did . . .
imprison him."[152] The issue was raised as to whether Quork Walker was
a free man or the slave of the defendant, and this issue was decided in
the Negro's favor. There is still an undertone implying that if Quork had
been the defendant's slave, the physical chastisement would have been
legal. Two other lawsuits sprang out of this same incident.[153] In the
latter, decided in 1783, the Supreme Court of Massachusetts held that
slavery no longer existed in the state. The decision comes in the form of
Chief Cushing's charge to the jury. It is worth quoting at length,
because it is typical of a movement which accompanied the
Revolutionary War, and then subsided, to rise again with the Civil War.
The jury were told in 1783:

> Fact proved. Justification that Quork is a slave, that Mr.
> Jennison . . . was entitled to Quork as his property and
> therefore he had a right to bring him home when he ran
> away . . . And the defendant's counsel also rely on some
> former slaves of the Province, which give countenance to
> slavery. As to the doctrine of slavery and the right of
> Christians to hold Africans in perpetual servitude—that

(if it is true) has been heretofore countenanced by the Province Laws—but nowhere is it expressly enacted. It has been a usage, but whatever sentiments have formerly prevailed in this particular or slid in upon us by the example of others, a different idea has taken place with rights of mankind, and to that natural, innate sense of Liberty, with which Heaven (without regard to color, complexion, or shape of noses, features) has inspired all the human race.

And upon this ground our Constitution—by which the people of this Commonwealth have solemnly bound themselves, sets out with declaring that all men are born free and equal—and that every subject is entitled to liberty—as well as life and property—and in short is totally repugnant to the idea of being born slaves. This being the case, I think the idea of slavery is inconsistent with our own conduct and Constitution; and there can be no such thing as perpetual servitude of a rational creature, unless his liberty is forfeited by some criminal conduct or given up by personal consent or contract.[154]

Connecticut used the lash like the other colonies. Although she had no statute until 1750, the first legislative recognition of whipping imposes it both on the Negro or Indian servant who stole, and on the white man who bought or received goods (whether stolen or not) from a slave.[158-160] The slave was given up to thirty stripes as against a maximum of twenty for the white offender. Likewise, a slave abroad after 9 PM without orders from his master, was subject to not more than ten stripes.[161] This law, however, provides for corporal punishment only at the hands of officials. The lack of any provisions either empowering or restraining masters in their conduct toward their slaves, indicates the small extent of slavery in Connecticut.

But whipping as a punishment survived to the last. While Connecticut enacted gradual emancipation in 1784,[162] two years later whipping, up to 40 stripes, was made the punishment for defamation[163] by a Negro or Mulatto, and whipping up to 30 stripes the punishment for breach of the peace.[164] No case involving corporal punishment of a slave is reported from any Connecticut court—again signalling the feeble development of slavery in that state.

Rhode Island in her early days was indistinguishable from the general pattern of the colonies. The master's right to chastise his slaves was recognized by limiting it. In 1688 the royal instructions to Sir Edmund Andros directed him to:

> . . . pass a law for the restraining inhuman severity, which by ill masters or overseers may be used toward the Christian servants or slaves, wherein provision is made that the willful killing of Indians and Negroes be punished with death, and a fit penalty imposed for the maiming of them. [165]

In 1704, whipping had already been imposed for slaves wandering off their masters' premises without a pass after 9 PM. [166-7] Whipping was retained, though with dwindling emphasis, to the end of the period closed by Whitney's cotton gin. [168]

New Hampshire was the northernmost colony at the time of the Revolution. The disinterest in slavery is reflected by the paucity of slave laws. The master's right to inflict physical punishment on his slaves was, however, recognized by the standard royal instructions to the governor, commanding him to pass a law restraining abuses. [169-172] In 1694, the colony complied with this directive to the extent of enacting a law that if a master knocked out an eye or a tooth of a manservant or maidservant, the servant should go free, and imposing the death penalty for killing an Indian or Negro. [173]

But this was evidently not thought sufficient since the King's admonition was repeated in 1698, [174] and again in 1702. [175] The colony's reaction to this tells the story of the master's power over his slaves perhaps better than any direct narrative. In 1706 the colonists addressed a petition to the Queen complaining of the existing (1694) "Act for Restraining Inhumane Severities."

> This Act as it is drawn, is too large, in that the wilful killing a man's own Negro Servant is to be punished with Death; for that is not the Description of Murder (which is killing with Malice). He that do's it in his own defence, do's it wilfully. Therefore, it ought to be said in the Act without Provocation, or malice. [176]

By 1706 New Hampshire was not yet convinced that slaves would be of no value to her. In the light of hindsight furnished by New England's later moral indignation over slavery, this petition is hilarious. Its fine objections to phraseology go both too far and not far enough. So doing, they reveal the colonists' attitude toward the master–slave relation. The proviso that killing must be without provocation could easily have been implied.   This verbal objection is, however, raised only on the background of killing "a man's own Negro". It was in dealing with their own slaves that the colonists felt that they might have to defend themselves. In 1706 they took care that no master should suffer from such a predicament; they did not then bewail the lot of the Negro. Morals shift with economics.

New Hampshire evidently continued to balk at the King's orders. In 1715 identical instructions were issued to Governor Elizens Burges, with the proviso, "if not already done".[177] But the King must have been far from sure that it had been done, for in the following year he issued the identical order to the new governor.[178]

Meanwhile, whipping as a punishment inflicted by officers of the law had been instituted in 1714 for slaves found at large without a pass after 9 PM and unable to give a good account of themselves in any town which had no house of correction.[179] It may be inferred that New Hampshire had no acute labor shortage at this time. Imprisonment was made the primary punishment for slaves, and whipping was imposed only where confinement was mechanically impossible. There was no such pressure to keep the slaves working every moment as would make the colonists unwilling to lose the time of their imprisonment.

Since the opposite condition prevailed in colonies further south,[180] it must be inferred that little work was done by slaves in New Hampshire. This accords with the disappearance of slavery there. Another act, "for Restraining Inhumane Severities", varying only slightly from earlier ones, was passed in 1718.[181] No further legislation appears on the subject, until the repeal of such provisions in 1792.[182]

Pennsylvania gives one of the sharpest illustrations that high principles can lead nowhere until times are ripe. Though the colony was a Quaker stronghold, and the Quakers had begun agitating against slavery early as 1693, slavery was a flourishing institution in Pennsylvania. And so was its corollary—the right of the master to physically chastise his slave. The Duke of York's Laws of 1676[183] prohibited "abuse and cruel treatment of servants" and also decreed emancipation in cases where the master has maimed or disfigured a servant, or has struck out an eye or a tooth. In 1683,

> The Governor put ye Question to the Colonial Council whether a Proclamation were not convenient to be put forth to Impower Masters to Chastise their Servants and to punish any yet shall Invegle any Servant to goe from his master. They unanimously agreed and Orded it accordingly.[184]

The following year the Council enacted a blanket formula for corporal punishment: wherever the number of stripes is unspecified, it shall not exceed twenty-one.[185] So even among the Quakers there was an overall recognition of the right of corporal punishment.

Whipping and branding, to be executed by the sheriff, were the punishments imposed on all Negroes for grand theft (apparently without distinction as to whether slave or free) by the law of 1706.[186] Attempted rape or carrying weapons without a license from the masters were similarly punished.

Differences in punishment depended upon whether the servant was bound for a term of years or for life. White servants, bound only for years, could be forced to make restitution by an extension of their term; for the same offense, black slaves for life had to be whipped.[187] So the practice of whipping Negroes, either directly by the master or through a public agency, continued in the Quaker stronghold up to the Revolution and the act for gradual abolition of slavery in Pennsylvania in 1780.[188] While there are no new statutes on the subject after 1770, neither are there any repealers before 1793. There are no judicial decisions on slavery from Pennsylvania prior to 1786.[189] Of the few that have been reported, none involves corporal punishment.

In Jamaica and Barbados the master's right of corporal punishment was not only recognized, but enforced more ruthlessly than in the colonies on the continent. Not only was a master authorized to whip his slave, but the master was himself punished if he did not exercise his rights.[190] Contrary to the colonies on the mainland, which recognized the right of corporal punishment by curbing its abuse, Jamaica gave slaveowners carte-blanche to maim or kill their slaves if they felt like it:

> If any slave by punishment from his owner for running away or other offense suffer in Life or Limb, none shall be liable to the law for the same . . .[191]

> If any person kill a slave Stealing or Running Away, or found by night out of his Owner's Ground, Road, or Common Path, such person shall not be subject to any damage, or action for the same.[192]

The same law imposed three months' imprisonment on anyone who should kill the slave of another "out of wilfulness, wantonness, or bloody mindedness".[193] But while this provision was later expanded to include assaults as well as killings, no one seems to have taken it very seriously, and there was general surprise, when in 1777, a man was convicted for violation of this act. Nothing is more indicative of the relations

between master and slaves in Jamaica than the incredulous report in
REX v. FELL [194] as given in Mrs. Catterall's collection:

> This is a remarkable case of an indictment against a
> white man, for beating a Negro slave, and for taking from
> him a piece of meat, bought in the public market, for his
> master, Mr. Welch. The facts were proved by white wit-
> nesses, with many circumstances of aggravation. . . . It
> was questioned, whether an indictment could lie in the
> case of a slave? The affirmative was satisfactorily
> established. Fell was convicted, and though a refractory
> and turbulent man, on account of his poverty, fined only
> L 20. Mr. Pinnock (formerly Chief Justice) told me after
> this trial, that he remembered two attempts of the same
> kind which had failed.

As will be seen later, the slaveholders on the continent expressed no
astonishment when they caught themselves enforcing their own laws for
the protection of their slaves. This, as well as the Jamaican laws already mentioned, accords with de Tocqueville's view that the slaves in
the American states were generally treated better than elsewhere.[195]

Three other cases involving physical chastisement are mentioned in
the Jamaica reports up to 1787. Two involve assault on slaves, REX v.
DAVIS, referred to without citation in REX v. NEPTUNE,[196] and REX v.
NEPTUNE itself.[197]

REX v. DAVIS apparently resulted in a conviction, the report in the
Neptune case saying, that "the traverser appeared to have acted otherwise barbarously, which doubtlessly weighed against him with the jury."
But while REX v. FELL and REX v. DAVIS furnished legal authority for
the indictment against Jones for the assault against Neptune, whereby,

> . . . he cut him through the ear to the pericardium, and
> afterward dragged him to his house . . . where he flogged
> him, . . . yet the jury, governed probably by the generally
> received notions of slavery, returned their verdict of not
> guilty. [197]

REX v. PRICE,[198] decided six years later, shows the modicum of
protection which the West India colonies gave their Negroes, and also
shows that flogging was used to punish whites as well as blacks. This
puts the practice of whipping slaves into its true perspective—whipping
was a punishment in general use which happened to suit the needs of a
slave system on a newly settled continent. In a society desperately short

of labor, it imposed discipline with a minimum separation of the laborer from his work. The court's opinion in REX v. PRICE, tells its own story:

> These men were indicted for feloniously taking from two Negroes baskets containing roots and vegetables the property of Robert Gouttie, of the value of 40 or 50 shillings. No white person was present when they robbed the Negroes, but they were convicted on circumstantial evidence of two men who detected them on their coming to Kingston, in consequence of the information of the Negroes. On the recommendation of the Court, the jury reduced them to be imprisoned for a few days, and to receive each twelve lashes on the bare back in the public market place.

The history of Barbados is almost identical with that of Jamaica. Masters were not only authorized to whip slaves belonging to them or to others, but were penalized if they did not do so.

> And if any Master of a Plantation, etc., finds any Negro or Slave on his Plantation without a ticket or Business from his Master, and doth not punish him with a moderate whipping, he shall forfeit ten shillings.[199]

So "any person" might "apprehend" and "correct with moderate whipping" any Negro found off his master's plantation without a pass, "especially" on weekends and holidays.[200] And Barbados had any number of other provisions for whipping slaves or inflicting even more severe physical punishment.[201]

While North Carolina was never fully at home in the institution of slavery,[202] the corporal punishment which it inflicted on its slaves was perhaps more severe than that of most other colonies on the American continent.[203] As elsewhere, the master was sometimes allowed to decide whether he preferred to pay a fine and keep the slave untouched, or save the fine and forego the slave's labor to the extent that whipping might interfere with it.[204] Also, as in other colonies, the master's right to chastise his own slaves privately was recognized by seeking to curb its abuse.[205]

The first and last recorded case from North Carolina during this period concerning corporal punishment metes it out to the master's son and servant for conspiring to keep a "slave from the deserved punishment due him for former Roguerys of this Kind"—the son getting thirty-nine lashes and the servant, twenty-nine.[206]

South Carolina, with her slave system still expanding at the time of the constitutional convention,[207] necessarily used flogging as a means of discipline. Here, too, the right to inflict physical punishment was confirmed by laws seeking to prevent its abuse. In 1691 the Grand Council was authorized to emancipate any servant where it found that "any master or mistress or overseer shall under pretext of correction unreasonably abuse his, her or their servants."[208] In 1717 an act dealing solely with white servants provided that:

> . . . to prevent the barbarous usage of servants by cruel masters . . . the master shall not exceed the bounds of moderation in correcting them beyond the merits of their offenses.[208a]

As early as 1686 corporal punishment by public authorities was clearly indicated by the statute which imposed on slaves trading with freemen or servants "such punishment or censure, not extending to the taking away of life or limb as the Grand Council shall think fit".[209] Persons apprehending slaves who strayed from their master's plantations, were authorized "reasonably to chastise and correct, and cause to be sent home to his or their several owners."[210]

In 1690, "An act for the better ordering of slaves"[211] provided whipping for the first offense of violence toward a white person, whipping plus splitting the nose and burning the face for the second,[212] and whipping up to thirty-nine lashes on any servant who killed a slave.[213] The act of 1712 "for the better ordering and governing of negroes and slaves" prescribes whipping for slaves straying from their masters' plantations or for carrying weapons in "Charlestown" on Sundays or holidays, and fines the master twenty shillings for failure to whip.[214] Under this law also, slaves (except children) committing petty larceny received up to forty lashes for the first offense, had their ears cut off and were branded on the forehead for the second offense, and had their nose slit for the third.[215]

Forty lashes was also the punishment for a Negro who enticed a slave away.[216] The penalty of whipping was continued for slaves behaving violently towards whites;[217] and forty lashes were given to slaves over sixteen who ran away and stayed away for twenty days. For the second offense the slave was branded with the letter "R", and the owner was fined twenty pounds if he neglected to inflict this punishment;[217a] for the third, the slave received forty lashes and had one ear cut off; for the fourth offense, he was castrated if a man, and if a woman, she was "severely whipped and branded on the left cheek with the letter R and had her left ear cut off."[218] This policy was continued throughout the period ending in 1793.[219]

Delaware used corporal punishment where many other colonies imposed death for attempted rape. A law of 1721 resorted to an otherwise familiar punishment for this offense—standing in the pillory, with the ears successively nailed to the pillory and then cut off.[220] If a slave was convicted of stealing, his master had to make good the loss; if he did not, the slave was whipped.[221] This was the standard option to the master, depending upon whether he preferred to stand the direct pecuniary loss, or any loss in the slave's efficiency resulting from the whipping. In this way the master himself had the ultimate decision about whether or not corporal punishment should be inflicted.

So in 1740, free Negroes dealing with slaves were bound to make restitution of any goods taken, and to be whipped with not more than twenty-one lashes.[222] Up to thirty-nine lashes were given when one slave assaulted another.[223] Nor was corporal punishment limited to Negroes. Thirty-nine lashes was the penalty on all persons for slave or horse-stealing.[224] This provision, appearing as late as 1779, shows again that the system of corporal punishment for slaves was the adoption of a punishment previously imposed on freemen, to a situation where the labor shortage was so acute that the colonists felt compelled to maintain a form of discipline which involved a minimum separation of the slave from his work. In 1793 the same penalty was enacted for kidnapping free Negroes.[225] There are no Delaware cases before 1794 dealing with the substantive law of corporal punishment.[226]

Once Georgia established slavery, she used flogging as a penalty. As in several other colonies, the first statutory recognition of corporal punishment was an effort to curb its abuse.[227] But Georgia, which had begun with complete prohibition of slavery, also had the unusual institution of a workhouse for Negroes.[228] Having originally done without slaves, however reluctantly, the province did not immediately feel that it had to keep them working every moment of their lives. Specific provisions of the act are likewise ambivalent on this matter. The master of the workhouse was authorized to punish slaves in his custody by whipping them or by putting them in irons.[229] Whipping accords with the pattern of extreme labor shortage, but putting a slave in irons removes him from his work.

Controlled corporal punishment was again approved by the Acts of 1765[230] and of 1770[231] which authorized anyone apprehending a slave who refused to submit to examination, "moderately to correct such slave" and elsewhere provided for corporal punishment "not extending to life or limb." Slaves drafted into the militia were punished corporally rather than by fine.[231a] There are no judicial decisions from Georgia up to 1793, dealing with corporal punishment of slaves.

Louisiana developed under the French and Spanish law until the time of the Lousiana Purchase in 1803. From 1762 to 1802, the territory was under Spanish rule, being governed from Havana.[231b] Flogging and other corporal punishment was used as much as in the English colonies, but under Spain there was more. One is struck by the comparative mildness of the French and American administrations, as contrasted with the medieval cruelty of the Spanish regime. The Louisiana Code Noir provided for corporal punishment in essentially the same way as the English laws. There were artistic and patriotic differences. Whereas the English colonies branded their slaves with letters of the alphabet, Louisana used the fleur-de-lys as its brandmark. But otherwise punishments were the same.[234c]

Under French rule there is a whole series of cases beginning in 1723 where flogging was authorized, either by a court or by the master directly. Some of these cases involved slaves, others free Negroes.[232] In Louisiana this period may theoretically be carried to 1803, instead of 1793. Because Louisiana was a sugar colony and a non-English possession, the invention of the cotton gin had little or no effect upon it. The distinction is only academic, however, as there are no decisions between 1780 and 1809.

The Spanish system was less utilitarian than that of the English colonies. While the latter used corporal punishment on both whites and Negroes, making it the sole punishment for slaves because it did not withdraw them from work, the Spaniards differentiated between punishments more from the standpoint of appearances and outward prestige. Whipping was not used on whites at all, evidently considered a degrading penalty reserved for slaves; on the other hand, slaves were imprisoned, thus making them temporarily unavailable to their masters.[233]

Otherwise the basic pattern of inflicting corporal punishment on slaves was different in French and Spanish Lousiana from what it was in the Lousiana Territory.

While a master could punish his slaves directly, the slaveowners did not rely on sporadic action. Discipline imposed on all members of a group by force resembled a war. As in a war, chosen individuals had to fight for the society as a whole. In most of the states, the slaveholders met this problem by organizing slave patrols—a sort of anti-slave militia and military police force combined. These patrols were recruited from among the slaveholders themselves. They were under patrol captains and served for specified terms; they had power both to search the houses of slaves and to administer corporal punishment.

In Virginia, slave-patrolling was originally a function of the militia.[234] This arrangement continued until after 1732.[235] Up to that time, patrols appeared only to retrieve runaways. But in 1757, the duty of continued forcible supervision of slave quarters was prescribed; and slave patrols became a special branch of the militia, not merely an occasional function. [236] This was confirmed by the amendment of 1766.[237] Three years later the system already tended towards over-production. A claim was made for compensation paid to a detachment of thirteen armed militiamen ordered to apprehend a group of slaves suspected of insurrection. The claim was allowed though the suspicion of insurrection was held unfounded.[238] No further changes appeared in the Virginia patrol law before 1793, nor are any private laws on record. This is undoubtedly due to the changing character of the institution in Virginia. The state was then already making the transition from an area which had employed slaves, to an area which supplied them to the colonies further south.

No cases involving patrols found their way into the Virginia courts during this period. Nor are there records either of legislation or judicial decisions on patrols in Maryland—a consequence of the light concentration of the slaves there. New York, like most of the northern states, seems never to have had slave patrols or patrol laws. (Patrols were associated with large plantations which the northern colonies never had). The same was true of New Jersey, Massachusetts, Connecticut, Rhode Island, New Hampshire and Pennsylvania. Jamaica, like the other plantation colonies, apparently operated patrols, though they were recognized indirectly rather than specially set up.[239] None of the Jamaica cases up to 1783 deal with patrols. Barbados required every owner of slaves worth 200 or more, to furnish a militiaman if he himself was unable to serve. [240] It may be inferred that the militia did patrol duty. [241]

Although slavery never reached full development in North Carolina, the state copied its neighbors in maintaining limited slave patrols. These were detailed particularly to search for weapons.[242] Like other features of slavery, patrols never worked smoothly in North Carolina. Those who controlled the legislature were determined to force the state into the image of her sister commonwealth, but the rest of the people hung back. In 1779 the legislators complained that under the "act concerning servants and slaves, passed at Newbern in the Year 1773,"

> the encouragment given to the searchers or patrollers,
> the penalty inflicted on them in case of noncompliance

with their duty, and the times appointed for searching are insufficient.[243]

In an effort to make the system operate as in South Carolina or Virginia, the Act of 1779 resorted both to the carrot and the stick. Patrollers expenses were henceforth to be paid out of the public funds[244] and the fine for refusal to serve was raised to £100.[245] Monthly searches were ordered for guns and other weapons; searchers had to apprehend any slaves whom they found wandering loose.[246] Upon that note the period came to a close. It sets the tone for all phases of slavery throughout its history in North Carolina.

South Carolina, with the fastest growing slave population, also saw the most rapid development of patrols. While its statutes do not go back further than 1682, by 1704 the colony already had a patrol law.[247] The impetus came from the distrust of the slave population during foreign wars. In 1704 the War of the Spanish Succession was in progress, and South Carolina was then the southernmost English colony. So military commanders were given authority to detail slave patrols from the army.[248] The patrols did not fully serve their purpose, according to the acts of 1722 and 1734.[249] Another comprehensive patrol act was passed in 1746.[250] The need for a new law was said to stem from the need for greater security—not as in North Carolina, from the laxity of the patrols.[251]

This law divided the state into patrol districts, provided in elaborate detail for the drafting, duties and pay of patrollers, and for the exemption of certain classes. At one stroke it lays bare the cost of slavery to the community—the necessity of maintaining a military force to control the labor force. As long as no other large-scale enterprises were possible, slavery put the southern states in the vanguard. When population pressure should have increased sufficiently to provide an almost automatic mode of disciplining wage labor, slavery would become hopelessly inefficient by comparison, and obsolete.

In South Carolina, the difficulty with patrols was not that the patrollers failed to attend, but that they treated patrol-riding as an occasion for a spree.[252] At the same time the garrison-state character of South Carolina is manifested by the law of 1743 which penalized the white inhabitants for not going armed to church.[253]

The fact that the men tended to get drunk while patrolling shows how much they took the military or quasi-military life as a matter of course. To be armed in the saddle must have been second nature to them. Here we glimpse the affinity of the South Carolina slave-owners to the cavalry-aristocracy of feudal Europe.[253a] Only small changes in the patrol laws appear to have been made after 1746.[254] Though South Carolina long continued to be hungry for slaves, the pattern of her society had crystallized by the middle of the 18th Century. It was a military caste engaged in large-scale agriculture, thus reproducing some of the main characteristics of feudal Europe.[254a] Up to 1793 there were no extant judicial decisions dealing with patrols. In later years, as will be seen, such cases did arise, and throw an extremely interesting light upon the state's social organization.

Delaware, never having had a large concentration of slaves, did not develop a patrol law. Georgia, on the other hand, followed the general pattern of South Carolina. The state had been opened to slavery in 1750. By 1757 it had enacted its first patrol law,[255] obviously modelled on those of South Carolina.[256] These laws continued with small modifications[257] until the invention of the cotton gin. Sec. 7 of the Act of 1768[257a] provided, "And in order to prevent the nightly disorders and riots in the town of Savannah,"that jurisdiction of patrols was extended to white persons as well as Negroes. One may infer from this that in Savannah there was something akin to an unruly urban white proletariat, which for police purposes, at least, the ruling classes treated as in the same category as the slaves.

Georgia differed from South Carolina in not having the same highly developed cavalry aristocracy. Patrollers had to furnish only whips and firearms; servants were sometimes ordered to ride patrol, and when they did the master had to furnish the horse.[257b] The alleged tendency of patrols to get drunk on duty is something which Georgia seems to have taken on hearsay rather than from experience.[257c] Of the very few judicial cases recorded from Georgia prior to 1793, none concerned patrols.

A case arising under the French domination of Louisiana indicates that while slave patrols never crystallized as separate units, the regular army sometimes did the work of searching slave houses.[258] This however, is an isolated instance. Patrol riding was not an integral part of the slave system in Louisiana. The French Code has no provision on the subject. Nor was there a change under the Spanish regime.[259] This survey shows that patrolling was an extraordinary institution developed in the English colonies which had the largest slave populations. It was superimposed on the methods used by all the colonies to maintain control over their slaves.

The counterpart of the master's control over the slave's person was his duty to care for him. A slave society poses the problem of what to do with the slaves when they are seasonally not working, or when they cannot work because of disability or old age. There are only three choices: 1) turn the slaves loose, and let them fend for themselves; 2) throw their support on the community at large; 3) make each slaveholder responsible for his own slaves.

Allowing slaves to operate for themselves was basically contrary to the slave system. We have already dealt with the efforts expended to suppress "outlying" slaves; similar measures were taken against slaves trading for themselves. [259a] To throw the burden on the community at large would merely mean that the large and rich slaveowners would sometimes have to support the incapable slaves of small and poor slaveowners.

So it was in the interest of the largest slaveowners that every slaveholder be made responsible for his own slaves. As a result, the slave states had a full-fledged system of what a later era would call "social legislation". Maximum hours, though long, were fixed by law in several states; the principle was recognized that the maximum work period could be regulated by law. So the laws also required masters to furnish their slaves with a minimum of food and clothing. In a slave society where slaves did not buy their means of subsistence, this was the equivalent of a minimum wage law. The requirement that masters care for superannuated slaves is the equivalent of old age pension laws in a capitalist society; it was reinforced by laws forbidding emancipation of slaves above a certain age.

Physical protection of slaves fell into two categories: protection against injuries by persons other than the master, and protection against the master himself. An injury to a slave by a third person was considered an injury to the master's property and therefore to the master. It forms a part of the relations between the master and third persons. On the other hand, the protection which the law gave the slave against violence or cruelty by the master is properly part of the relations between master and slave.

Maximum hour laws were the least developed phase of the legal protection which the system afforded the slaves.[259b] Comparatively few of the colonies had such laws. While the maxima seem long by present day standards, it must be remembered that during the period 1865-1937 the principle of maximum hours was repudiated entirely.

Virginia, New York, New Jersey, Massachusetts, Connecticut, Rhode Island, New Hampshire, Pennsylvania, Jamaica, Barbados, North Carolina and Delaware did not bother with maximum hours for slaves. Maryland enacted a "reasonable limits" law. An overseer of slaves could be fined not over 1000 pounds of tobacco if he should "unreasonably labour them beyond their strength or debar them of necessary Rest and Sleep . . . ."[260]

This section, directed specifically at overseers, was designed first of all to protect the master. The overseer—a hired employee—could not abuse the master's property; the master himself is not subjected to any restraints. In 1715 that was changed, and overworking a slave at the master's order was made criminal.[261] From then on Maryland seems to have protected her slaves (rather than their masters) from overwork.[261] While the prohibition was vague, it is broad enough to include overlong working hours. As already indicated, this principle was to disappear after the Civil War, not to revive until later.

Of all the colonies, South Carolina had the most explicit maximum hour law for her slaves. The great revised slave law of 1740[262] provided "That if any owner of slaves, or other person who shall have the duty and management or overseeing of any slaves shall work or put to labour any such slave or slaves more than fifteen hours in four and twenty hours from the twenty-fifth day of March to the twenty-fifth day of September, or more than fourteen hours in four and twenty hours from the twenty-fifth day of September to the twenty-fifth day of March, every person shall forfeit any sum not exceeding twenty pounds, not under five pounds current money for every time he, she or they shall offend herein, at the discretion of the justice before whom such complaint shall be made." Inordinately long maxima perhaps, but after the Civil War the principle of legislative maximum hours for men was rejected entirely.[263] This law remained in effect throughout the period preceding invention of the cotton gin.

Georgia instituted a maximum hour law of sixteen hours in 1757. The Louisiana decisions under French rule likewise show that the state placed a ceiling on slaves' working hours. In D'AUSSEVILLE v. CHARPENTIER,[264] decided in 1730, an overseer was charged with "cruelty . . . in . . . exhausting the slaves by long hours and vile fare."[265] Here maximum hours were enforced to protect the owner of the slave against misuse by servants or overseers. The Code Noir makes no special reference to length of working hours, but this limitation is probably comprehended in the command that masters should treat the slaves "en bons peres de famille",[266] and by the prohibition of Sunday work.[266a]

While maximum hour laws were not widespread, most of the colonies, including all which had slaves in large numbers, compelled the master to furnish adequate food and clothing, and to support the slave in sickness and old age. As states, these laws correspond to capitalistic "social legislation" embodied in minimum wages and old age and disability pensions.

Laws requiring masters to furnish their slaves with adequate food and clothing were general throughout the colonies. The constitutional inhibitions which were later thought to forbid similar laws[267] for wage earners, were one of the advances of capitalism.

By 1749 Virginia had laid down the law to its slaveowners to the effect, "that all masters and owners of servants by act of Parliament, Indenture, or Custom, shall find or provide for them, wholesome and competent Diet, Clothing and Lodging. ... "[268] Reenacted in 1753,[269] this provision remained in force until after 1793. Failure to provide adequate food and clothing was claimed as a ground of emancipation in GWINN v. BUG,[270] but not sustained.

Maryland provided severance pay in kind for its indentured white servants,[271] and required adequate food and clothing, enforcing the requirement by a fine.[272] No special laws along these lines were enacted to protect slaves—perhaps because they were first not thought worth the protection, and later (as slavery became attenuated), did not give rise to situations which demanded such legislation. Needless to say, this state of affairs continued throughout the period preceding the invention of the cotton gin.[272]

In New York a law requiring adequate food and clothing for servants was enacted only eleven years after the final cession of the colony from the Dutch. No similar provision was enacted for slaves.[273] Thus, while in principle New York recognized the feudal equivalent of minimum wage laws, unlike colonies further south, she never applied this principle to her Negro slaves. Presumably, because slavery was dying on the vine, the problem did not arise often enough to demand legislation. New Jersey, Connecticut, Rhode Island, New Hampshire, Pennsylvania and Delaware had no laws on the subject during the period antedating the cotton gin.[273a]

Massachusetts, like Maryland, provided severance pay for her white indentured servants. The Body of Liberties of 1641, containing some of the colony's earliest and most fundamental legislation, decreed that faithful servants should not be "sent away empty."[274] There were no general laws guaranteeing adequate food and clothing for slaves, doubtless because the question did not arise often enough. But in isolated instances the courts made orders for care of slaves. Thus in 1676 the slave Jethro was recaptured after having been taken prisoner by the Indians. On his recapture, the court ordered "that said Negro do forthwith betake himself to his former service . . . until two years . . . from the date hereof . . . during said term . . . they do find him meat, drinke, and apparell fitting for one in his degree and calling, and at the end of his said service, that he go forth competently provided for in reference to apparell."[274a]

Jamaica required its slaveowners to furnish their slaves with sufficient clothing and to maintain one acre planted with provisions for every five slaves.[275] Fines of five and forty shillings were imposed for violations, though as has already been pointed out, these laws were apparently not enforced as thoroughly as they were on the mainland. Barbados was peculiar in legally requiring the master to furnish adequate clothing, but saying nothing directly about food, except where runaways were in custody of the sheriff.[276] Violations were punished by fines of five shillings.

Barbados did have an indirect way of making masters supply adequate victuals to their slaves, but it took effect only in the extreme situations where the slave had committed a capital crime. As in many other colonies, masters were paid compensation by the state for slaves executed under legal process. But

> The Condemners of such Negro or Slave shall also enquire what allowance of Provision and other necessaries such Negro had from his owner, and if it shall appear that such Negro or slave might have been induced to the Offences committed for want of reasonable and accustomed provision, the owner shall not be paid anything out of his value as aforesaid.[276a]

North Carolina, like most of the colonies where slavery survived the American Revolution, obligated masters to give their slaves adequate food and clothing. But it began with legislation which probably applied only to white indentured servants,[277] enforcing the duty through compulsory sale of the servant to another master.[278] In 1753 this requirement was expressly extended to slaves.[279] The same provision, supported by the roundabout and feeble mode of enforcement of allowing a person from whom a slave has stolen, to recover damages from the master, was continued throughout the era prior to the cotton gin.[280]

South Carolina, having been colonized from Barbados, immediately adopted the West Indian legislation requiring adequate clothing, but said nothing about food.[281] Apparently no direct sanctions were provided. As in Barbados, there was the indirect and attenuated sanction that if the slave had committed a capital crime, the master was denied the

usual compensation if lack of food or clothing had incited the slave to
the offense. On the other hand, if a runaway slave was in the hands of
the sheriff, the law required the sheriff to provide food and lodging
under a penalty of forty pounds for neglect to do so.[282] At about the
same time a statute was passed making masters responsible for
furnishing their white indentured servants with food, clothing and
lodging. In case of violation, such servants were set free.[283]

Subsequent acts continued this protection for white indentured
servants,[284] but punishment was by admonition alone for the first and by
fine for the second offense. Only for the third, was the servant sold to
another master.[285] In a chronic labor shortage, such as the colonies
experienced during their early years, the South Carolina employers
evidently considered releasing a servant too drastic a remedy for general
use.

The very fertility of the land, which made slavery the only means of
conducting large-scale operations, also forced South Carolina
slaveowners to insist that slaves be furnished with adequate food. For if
they did not get enough food, they often ran away. So in 1722 the
obligation of furnishing adequate food, enforced by a fifty shilling
fine,[286] was added to the requirement of sufficient clothing which the
South Carolinians had copied from Barbados.

It is not remarkable that the same system of laws was continued by
the act of 1735.[287] But the act of 1735 contains another provision
unique in the history of American slavery. Section XXXVI of this act
recites that "many of the slaves in this province wear clothes much
above the condition of slaves", and forbids masters to allow their slaves
to wear anything "finer, other or of greater value than Negro cloth".
Constables and even private citizens were authorized to seize and keep a
slave's clothes if of too good quality.[288-289]

This law delineates three features of the South Carolina slave
economy during the eighteenth century. In the first place, it is
medieval, with sumptuary laws regulating classes, both upward and
downward. The fluidity of early capitalism has not touched it, despite
the fact that it is a rising colony. In the second place, its prosperity is
so great that even the lowest classes share in it. In the third place, the
conditions underlying such a law illustrates the paradox of South
Carolina society which will confront us again and again until the
abolition of slavery. While the preamble says that slaves acquire their
good clothes by "sinister and evil methods" (unspecified), the act
postulates that everything is done with the master's connivance and that
the master will step in to defend the slaves's condition and prevent any

seizure of his clothes. While South Carolina was organized as a garrison-state, for continuous warfare between masters and slaves, the personal relations between masters and slaves were perhaps closer than in any other colony. Side by side with the armed garrison, is a casual familiarity based on the notion that everyone knows and accepts his respective position in the stratified society, and that no force is needed to maintain statu quo.

(This combination of looseness and strictness undoubtedly contributed to the slave revolts which occurred in South Carolina during the eighteenth century.)[289a]

Laws guaranteeing adequate food and clothing to slaves were reenacted in 1740. Now they could be enforced, not merely by justices on their own motion, as in 1722, but through complaints lodged by outsiders.[290] The prohibition against slaves wearing too good clothes was likewise reenacted in 1740.[291]

The law of 1740 remained unchanged until 1793.[292] At least one decision[292a] in this period recognizes the master's duty to furnish adequate rations.

Georgia, which first permitted slavery in 1750, waited only until 1755 before imposing legal coercion to make masters supply their slaves with sufficient food and clothing.[292b] Eight years later, the same obligation was imposed on wardens of workhouses.[293]

Louisiana, as indicated by judicial decision under French and Spanish rule, placed owners and overseers under obligation to furnish slaves with wholesome food,[294] and sufficient clothing.[295] This was enforced in part by forbidding masters to work their slaves on Sundays,[296] the idea being that this day should be reserved not for rest, but for work which the slave might do on his own account to clothe and feed himself.[297]

Just as the slave system imposed on the master the burden of feeding, clothing and housing the slave, it imposed on him the duty of supporting the slave when he was unable to work, either because of old age, or physical or mental infirmity. A corollary of these laws were the restrictions on emancipation: high minded grants of freedom were (as they would again be after the XIIth Amendment) one of the ways to escape from the necessity of caring for slaves who had ceased to be profitable.[297a] This was an old Spanish custom. Cervantes makes Don Quixote say that old soldiers should not "be treated like blacks, whose masters release them and grant them their liberty when they are old and cannot work, and by casting them out of the house with the title of freemen make them the slaves of hunger from whom they can only hope to be freed by death."[297b]

The colonies met the problem either by prohibiting emancipation of aged and infirm slaves, or by making the master put up a bond to guarantee that the emancipated slave would not become a public charge. There were only two exceptions to these requirements. The necessity of a bond was abolished in some of the northern colonies just before they abolished slavery entirely. And in South Carolina the community at large gallantly assumed the obligations of small slave owners to support slaves who had become insane.

Virginia placed her first limitations on the emancipation of aged slaves in 1691. The act stated:

> And forasmuch as great inconveniency may happen to this County by ye Setting of Negroes and Mulattoes free, either by entertaining Negro slaves from their masters service, or receiving stolen goods, and being grown old bringing a charge on ye Country, for prevention whereof, Be it enacted by ye authority aforesaid, and It is hereby enacted that no Negro or Mulatto be after ye end of this present session of Assembly set free by any Person or Persons whatsoever unless Such Person or Persons their heirs Exrs or Admrs pay for ye transportation of such Negro or Negroes out of ye country within six months after such setting them free, upon penalty of paying ten pds Sterl. to ye Church wardens of ye parish where such Person shall dwell with, which money, or so much thereof as shall be necessary ye said church wardens are to cause ye said Negro or Mulatto to be transported out of ye country. And ye remainder of ye said money to imploy to ye use of ye poor of ye parish. [298]

Similar precautions were continued throughout the period ending in 1793; in 1748 owners were obligated by law to care for and maintain sick servants and not emancipate them, under a penalty of ten pounds if the servant became a charge on the community.[299] The same provision was reenacted in 1753.[300] When the wave of anti-slavery sentiment engendered by the revolution[301] broadened the masters' opportunities to emancipate their slaves,[302] the law still compelled former masters to support emancipated slaves who could not support themselves.[303] An identical provision appeared in the act of 1792.[304]

Maryland had the same experience as the other colonies: emancipation was a glamorous avenue of escape from the obligation to furnish support. The colony forbade the manumission of disabled slaves in 1752, describing the existing situation in a preamble:

> Whereas sundry Persons of this Province have set disabled
> and superannuated slaves Free, who have either perished
> through want, or otherwise became a burden to
> others . . . [305]

This was the state of law until 1793.

New York was no different from the colonies further south, and dealt with "emancipation" in the same way. Gifts of freedom were recognized as an escape from responsibility which would force the public to support disabled slaves. Consequently masters who attempted manumission had to give security for continued support of the slave if he proved unable to earn his living. [306] A rather unusual illustration of the master's inclination to throw off sick or disabled slaves is reported in the case of the slaves Sam and Robin. [307] Sam had been emancipated by his master's will and had also been bequeathed money and the slave Robin. His petition complains that the executor puts Robin to his (the executor's) own use when Robin is well, and throws him on Sam's care when Robin is disabled or sick.

Late in the year 1717 the legislature required only that the manumitted slave should not become a public charge. [308] These laws were reenacted in 1730. [309] Yet on the eve of the American Revolution, New York found it necessary to devote not a section but an entire statute to this problem. In 1773 the colonial legislature passed "An act to prevent aged and decrepit slaves from becoming burdensome within this colony". [310] The preamble recites:

> Whereas there have been repeated Instances in which the
> owners of slaves have obliged them after they are grown
> aged and decrepit to go about begging for the common
> necessities of Life, whereby they have not only been re-
> duced to the utmost distress themselves, but have be-
> come burthens on the Humanity and Charity of others;
> and sometimes also such owners by Collusive Bargains,
> have pretended to transfer the property of such slaves to
> persons not able to maintain them, for which the like,
> evil consequences have followed; for the prevention
> whereof and effectually to suppress such unjust and in-
> human practices.

The act imposes a fine of £10 on owners who do not support their overaged slaves, and of £20 on owners who try to get rid of such slaves by selling them to persons who are themselves unable to support the slave.[311] After the Revolution when the confiscated estates of United Empire Loyalists were sold at public auction, the state as the master's successor undertook to support incapacitated slaves.[312] In 1792, however, the state anticipated the benefits of general emancipation by shedding its slaveholder's responsibility to care for incapacitated ex-slaves. It dumped their support onto the town's pauper relief.[313] Feudalism was breathing its last; capitalism was on the march.

New Jersey, in 1713, required masters emancipating their slaves to give bond in the sum of £200 to pay each emancipated slave £20 a year.[314] Manumitted slaves, it was said, "are an idle, slothful People, and prove very often a charge to the place where they are". The New Jersey law made this requirement in all cases, not merely for overage or incapacitated slaves. This law continued on the books throughout the period ending in 1793. But after the Revolutionary War, New Jersey wanted to free her slaves and several cases of emancipation were reported where the necessity of posting bond does not seem to have been required.[315]

Massachusetts took the same precautions against great-hearted emancipation which would throw incapacitated slaves on the towns for support. In 1703 manumission was forbidden unless the master gave bond in the sum of fifty pounds that the slave would not become a public charge.[316] The same restrictions on emancipation continued until the total abolition of slavery in Massachusetts in 1781.[317] Judicial decisions begin and end with the case of Negro Jones,[318] who was ordered manumitted in accordance with his late master's will, "Provided security be given . . . to indemnify the town of Boston from any charges that may arise from the Petitioner's freedom".

Connecticut dealt with the same problem in 1750. In that year "An act concerning Indians, Mulatto and Negro Servants and Slaves",[319] said that:

> And for preventing Disorder, and Insolences from being Committed by Indians brought back from Other Plantations; and for Preventing Charges coming upon Towns by Negro, Indian and Molatto Servants, and Slaves, Coming and being made Free.
>
> And that all Slaves Set at Liberty by their owners; and all Negro, Mulatto or Spanish Indians who are servants to Masters for Time, in case they come to want after they shall be so set at Liberty, or the time of their said service be expired, shall be relieved by such Owners, or masters respectively, their Heirs, Executors, or

Administrators; and upon their, or either of their Refusal so to do, the said slaves, and servants shall be relieved by the selectmen of the Towns to which they belong; And the said selectmen shall recover of the said Owners, or Masters, their Heirs, Executors or Administrators, all the charge and cost they are at for such Relief, in the Usual Manner as in the case of any other Debts.

The provision was re-enacted in 1782, but with the modification that the master could petition for leave to emancipate, which, if granted, relieved him and his personal representatives of the obligation to support.[320] Leave to emancipate was authorized if a majority of the selectment, "shall be of the opinion that it is likely to be consistent with the real advantage of such servant or slave, and that it is probable that the servant or slave will be able to support his or her own person . . . "

This same statute sets gradual abolition in motion: no persons born in Connecticut after March 1, 1784, shall be slaves after age 25. The juxtaposition of the two clauses shows the halting transition from an agricultural to an industrial society: the same law which limits present emancipation makes it general for the future. In 1792 the requirement of a certificate was limited to slaves under 25 or over 45.[320a] Legislation prohibiting the emancipation of aged or incapacitated slaves is surprisingly uniform throughout the colonies.

Rhode Island passed her act in 1728.[321] Masters about to free a slave had to give bond of at least a hundred pounds to "indemnify the Town or Place from all charge for or about such Molatto or Negro, to be manumitted and set at Liberty in case he or she by sickness, lameness, or otherwise, be rendered incapable to support him or herself." As elsewhere, this was the state of the law to 1793.

New Hampshire never tried to regulate emancipation. Slavery there was feeble and died a natural death.[322] While it lasted longer than in Massachusetts,[323] its abolition demanded no act of government. Emancipated slaves likewise took care of themselves without legislation.

Pennsylvania limited emancipations in 1725.[324] Like New Jersey,[325] another state in which slavery hardly survived the eighteenth century, the Quakers felt obliged to slave their consciences by shifting the blame to the alleged idleness and slothfulness of the free Negroes.[326] (None of the states where slavery was an essential part of the economy resorted to this subterfuge.) The law continued until 1793. The only case reported on the subject is RESPUBLICA v. BETSEY,[326a] which, while dealing specifically with the emancipation of children born before or after the date of gradual emancipation, has language which touches the master's obligation not to free slaves over the age of 28.

Unlike the colonies on the continent neither Jamaica nor Barbados had laws designed to guard against the freeing of slaves unable to support themselves. Here it must be inferred that the concentration of slaves was so high (at present blacks form about 99% of the population), that no master thought of freeing a slave merely to turn him loose. Everyone felt that the resulting number of freedmen would be too large. Although there are some Jamaican court cases on free Negroes,[327-8] none involves emancipations to escape from obligations toward the slave.

North Carolina first made a special provision for the support of disabled white servants. Without regard to emancipation, they were to be cared for by the church-wardens at the master's expense for the balance of the term of servitude or until the servant recovered.[329] Masters were sternly forbidden:

> Upon any pretext whatsoever to remit to such servant
> or servants any part of his, her, or their time, to be
> cleared of them, whereby the said servant or servants
> may perish or become a charge to the parish.[330]

Violators were fined five pounds for every servant so turned loose, which the parish used for the servant's support.

On the other hand, North Carolina never seems to have enacted such legislation for her Negro slaves. The reason may perhaps lie in the rudimentary development of slavery in this colony. In other words, slaves in North Carolina were half-independent anyway, and sudden emancipation of those unable to support themselves was neither much sought by masters nor much feared by the community. There are no North Carolina decisions on this phase of emancipation during the period now under consideration.

South Carolina forbade the emancipation of incapacitated white servants.[332] But a different policy was followed with respect to slaves. South Carolina was at the opposite pole from North Carolina. Paradoxically, both extremes led to the same result. While slavery in North Carolina was always underdeveloped so that there was small opposition to emancipation, South Carolina was developed in the highest degree, and emancipation was not tolerated.

Both systems dispensed with the special laws against emancipation of disabled slaves. In South Carolina, masters were required to send manumitted slaves out of the state within a year.[333] If they did not leave they were returned to slavery unless the particular manumission was approved by the assembly. Once the freedman had been sent out of the state, South Carolina was no longer interested. If he remained within the state, he was not free, and his former master was still responsible for him.

In 1735 the period of grace before departure was shortened to six months.[335] But the law covered only manumissions for meritorious conduct. Manumission to escape supporting the slave was as good as impossible; the state went out of its way to make it unnecessary. It was tacitly assumed that well-to-do slaveowners would take care of their own disabled slaves; but after 1751 the counties supported lunatic slaves of poor owners.[336] The fact that this legislation was enacted only for poor slaveowners, shows that the affluent ones raised no problem. The South Carolina caste-society was prosperous and well organized. Probably without much effort, the governing classes exercised the minimum noblesse oblige of not shirking their cast obligations. South Carolina decisions are on record only up to 1692 and again after 1784. None deals with emancipation for purposes of evading support of disabled slaves.

Delaware first followed the general routine of requiring security on manumission.[337] Only testamentary manumissions are mentioned. Like other northern or border colonies, Delaware justified this legislation with the claim that: "It is found by experience that free Negroes and Mulattoes are idle and slothful and often prove burdensome to the neighborhood wherein they live".[338] The act of 1740 limited the bond to emancipations of slaves over 35; in 1767 the requirement was extended to all ages.[339] In 1781, when slavery was on the wane, the necessity of giving bond was again confined to emancipations of slaves under 18 or over 35.[340] Prior manumissions without bond were also validated if the slave had reached 21 by the time the statute was passed, or was not over 35 at the time of manumission.[341-2] During this period there are no Delaware cases arising from emancipations to evade responsibility.

Georgia up to 1793, was still a frontier community, and had no laws requiring masters to suport overaged slaves, or forbidding emancipations intended to evade a duty to support. Even by 1793, Georgia had had slavery for only 43 years and the problem of overaged slaves had presumably not arisen often enough to receive legislative attention.

Louisiana specifically required masters to support their overaged slaves on penalty of a fine.[343a] Restrictions on emancipation were not, however, tied to this problem. Louisiana recognized freed Negroes as part of the structure of its society.[344] Emancipation had to have the approval of the Upper Council.[345] Slaves freed in an effort to escape supporting them, did not form a separate legal category. The same situation obtained under Spanish rule where an act of emancipation had to be passed in each case.[346] In only one instance was such a problem specifically presented, and there emancipation was granted by the governor.[347]

Prohibition against cruel treatment of slaves took two forms. One was strictly restraint on the master with respect to the slave as a person. The other was restraints on third persons (including hirers and overseers) with respect to the slave as the property of the master. Both have already been noted as part of the basic law which permitted masters to inflict corporal punishment. The present section, dealing with the obligations of the master to the slave, will consider the restraints placed on the master with respect to the slave as a person.

The first restraint on slaveowners against abusing their own slaves in Virginia was an unwillingness to destroy their own property. Laws had to be passed and enforced where universal self interest was an insufficient brake. This depended partly upon the personal characteristics of the master, upon the price of slaves, and upon the social relations between masters and slaves. The inclination toward excesses was greater on the frontier and less in more stable communities. So all the colonies had to face this problem early in their history.

Virginia's first law was against cruel treatment of servants, presumably white servants. On November 1st of 1693 the Virginia House of Burgesses passed "a bill prohibiting masters' Cruelty to their Servants"[348] and sent it to the Council of Colonial Virginia on the same day.[349] In 1748, as already noticed,[350] masters were forbidden to "give immoderate correction".[351] While this act was repealed by royal proclamation in 1752,[352] the laws protecting slaves against their masters continued in force through 1785.[353] The provision against immoderate correction has disappeared from the law of 1792, however.[354] Presumably legislation was thought to have become unnecessary.

The only judicial case touching this subject before 1793 is DANDRIDGE v. LYON,[355] decided in 1791, and already referred to. There the court said that "No danger of a Negro child perishing by the cruelty of the mother's owner, in not allowing her time to nurse and cherish it, for the benefit of another, is to be apprehended".

Maryland prohibited excessive punishment for servants in 1715. But since the governing section mentions servants only, and makes emancipation the sanction for a third offense, the law was evidently only for white servants.[356] No similar statute appears to have been enacted regarding slaves, but some judge-made law grew up. ATTORNEY GENERAL v. OVERZEE, [357] decided in 1658, was a prosecution for cruelty to a slave. While the record of the case is not clear, the defendant apparently was the slave's owner. The jury, however, acquitted. In the long line of Maryland decisions reported from 1658 to and including 1793, there is not another case of this type. One may infer that the problem did not often arise in Maryland.

New York enacted a law for the protection of servants against abuse as early as 1684. [358] In 1702 slaves as such received a limited protection—masters were authorized to impose punishment "not extending to life or member". [359] No similar act appears after 1733, nor is such a provision to be found in the general slave laws of 1788 [360] or 1790. [361] The problem evidently became obsolete. The records of judicial decisions in New York are interrupted between 1682 and 1800; in the short period before 1682 there are no cases involving chastisement of slaves.

King George I instructed the governor of New Jersey that, "you shall endeavour to get a law past for the restraining of any inhuman severity which by ill masters or overseers may be used towards their Christian servants and their slaves." [362] These royal orders differed from several of the early colonial statutes (especially among the northern colonies) in expressly covering slaves as well as white servants. In 1713 New Jersey enacted the standard authorization that masters could inflict punishment on their slaves, but "not extending to life or limb". [363] This law continued until after 1793.

The Massachusetts Body of Liberties of 1641 dealt with possible cruelties by masters to white servants. A servant fleeing his master because of claimed mistreatment was entitled to the protection of the law in the interim, until final disposition had been made of his case. If the master's cruelty extended to mayhem like knocking out an eye or a tooth, a bondservant was set free. [364] Massachusetts had Negro and Mulatto servants, as distinguished from slaves. [364a] The original charter made no such provision for Negro slaves. None was made later, doubtless because slavery in Massachusetts never developed to a point where the colonists felt they had to meet the problem. The courts of Massachusetts never dealt with limitations on a master's right to chastise his own slave. The question comes up like a momentary flash in QUORK WALKER v. JENNISON. [365]

The action is for assault and battery, and the defense is that the plaintiff is the defendant's slave and therefore the defendant had a right to inflict physical punishment. But it was now 1781. The court did not pass on the master's right to inflict corporal punishment on a slave; instead it held that Quork Walker was a free man, and granted him £50 damages.

Connecticut never enacted any laws regarding masters' corporal punishment of slaves. Nor are there any judicial decisions dealing with the subject. Rhode Island had neither statutes nor judicial decisions on mistreatment of slaves by masters. Slavery was evidently sparse enough that the problem did not arise.

In New Hampshire the King instructed the governor to have a law passed restraining the severity of masters and overseers.[366] As has already been noted the King issued similar subsequent orders in 1688[367] and 1692.[368] In 1694 the colonial legislature finally complied to the extent of freeing white servants if the master put out an eye or a tooth, and imposing the death penalty for killing a Negro.[369] Nevertheless, the royal instructions were again repeated in 1698,[370] and again in 1702.[371] And, as also said above,[372] four years later, the colonists complained that the punishment for killing a Negro was too rigid. By 1715, the King once more repeated the directions to pass a law protecting servants and slaves, but with the modifier, "if not already done". Yet in the following year they were reiterated to the next governor.[373]

New Hampshire bears the questionable distinction of having drawn more royal admonitions against cruelty to servants and slaves than any other colony. The warning of 1716 was, however, the last. In 1718 the colony passed another at imposing the death penalty for the wilful killing of Indian or Negro servants,[375] which apparently satisfied the Crown. After that slavery in New Hampshire steadily diminished, and the subject of cruelty to slaves does not arise again before 1793. During this period there are no judicial decisions on the subject.

Pennsylvania protected white servants against mistreatment by masters as early as 1676, granting emancipation where the master had disfigured the servant or struck out an eye or a tooth.[376] Pennsylvania never enacted any parallel legislation for Negro slaves. But with gradual emancipation already under way, an act was passed to prevent the separation of members of slave families.[377] Evidently no other precautions were found necessary in the undeveloped state of Pennsylvania slavery. The statute of 1788[378] is itself a striking illustration of how slavery in the northern colonies simply failed to grow. Several of the colonies in their early history had Negro servants for terms of years.[379] They did not introduce lifetime bondage until further development of large plantations when shorter terms of servitude fell into disuse. Pennsylvania on the other hand retained the institution of indentured Negro sevants until after the close of the Revolutionary War. No Pennsylvania judicial decisions deal with mistreatment of slaves by masters.

As had already been seen, Jamaica had some legislation for the protection of its slaves. But while some statutes expressly dealt with mistreatment, they did so chiefly by exempting the owner from liability. [380] As already noted, even such safeguards as existed were so rarely enforced that a jury verdict against the person injuring a slave caused surprise. [381] The West Indies were much harsher towards their slaves than the continent. Among the statutes available to this writer, there was no Barbados legislation designed to shield slaves from mistreatment.

North Carolina only had one act to prevent the malicious killing of slaves. [382] There were no safeguards for anything short of homicide, doubtless because in North Carolina's anaemic slave system there were few cases of excessive corporal discipline, and still fewer in which society took any interest. No North Carolina cases deal with the subject up to 1793.

South Carolina, in 1717, decreed that "to prevent the barbarous usage of servants by cruel masters . . . every master . . . shall not exceed the bounds of moderation in correcting them beyond the merits of their offenses."[383] This applied to white indentured servants; the ultimate sanction was release from the term of service. Five years earlier a fine of £50 had been established for the killing of a slave by his master. [384] At this time masters were not penalized for inflicting anything less than death upon their own slaves. In 1740 the penalties for killing a slave were greatly increased, and injuries also were punished.[385] Besides more direct penalties, murdering a slave now entailed disqualifications from office—another manifestation of South Carolina's caste-society. This was the state of the law to 1793. No judicial decisions touch the subject.

Delaware had no statutes dealing with cruelty of masters toward slaves, nor are there any cases. Georgia authorized slavery in 1750, and simultaneously passed her first act to protect slaves from their masters. [386] The act of 1755 introduced a presumption to facilitate prosecution where a slave had aparently been mistreated on remote plantations out of the presence of white witnesses.[386a] A more explicit general act was passed in 1765. [386b] In general, Georgia modelled her legislation on that of South Carolina; the laws against cruelty by masters to slaves paralleled those of the northern neighbor through 1793.[387] There are no Georgia cases on the subject during this period.

Louisiana apparently had the system of indentured Negro servants, which existed in the early days of the English colonies. As in the English colonies, the ultimate remedy for harsh treatment was release from service.[388] With a slave for life it was confiscation.[388a] In Louisiana, as in Barbados, ill treatment of a slave was held against the master if the slave ran away.[389] Cases of more direct remedies are not always clear as to whether they concern injuries to the slave by the master or by third persons.[390] After Louisiana passed under Spanish rule, there is one case of a runaway slave asking another master to buy her because her original master had mistreated her;[391] and another which is unclear about whether the injuries were done by the owner or a third person, but which, in any event, ended with an acquittal.[392]

After a little hesitation, the colonies adopted the Roman law rule that the status of a child follows that of the mother. Children of free mothers were free. Children of slave mothers were slaves.[393] This rule acknowledged the unenforceability of another one—that sexual intercourse between masters and slaves was forbidden.

Sexual relations between masters and slaves were one of those things, always forbidden and always done.[394] The race castes might be separated by barriers of steel or social imperative, but not enough to keep from getting into bed together. The firmer the caste lines, the easier they were to cross.

Since the slave had no civil rights, there could logically be no marriages between slaves and freemen. All the English colonies were logical on this point, except Maryland,[395] as well as Louisiana and the Dutch regime in New York.[395] (Louisiana, under the Spanish regime, did not allow its governors to marry, and recognized and encouraged a system of concubinage not found in the English colonies.)[396]

Logic would permit sexual relations at least between masters and female slaves. Children would be slaves and would not disturb the caste structure. But the early colonists were bedevilled by the fortuitous coincidence of caste and race. They undertook to forbid all sexual unions which were "unnatural" or "forbidden by the laws of God."[397] On the other hand, the caste basis of such legislation sometimes showed through in statutes which punished the white partner only.

Mulatto children of white women constituted a special problem. Since status followed the condition of the mother, they were free. And since they were born to inhabitants of the colony, they could not be deported like free Negroes who had come from the outside.

Emancipation involves both the relations of master and slave and of the freed Negro to society as a whole. For convenience it will be considered in its immediate aspect of master-slave relations. Emancipation confronted the colonists in two ways: as involuntary and voluntary.

Involuntary emancipation was not so much a reality as a foreboding which sprang from the history of the institution. Slavery had been confined to non-Christians. Did baptism then operate to emancipate the slave? The colonists soon reconciled their slave system and their missionary zeal by providing that baptism or conversion to Christianity should not emancipate a slave.[397-407]

Here we see how the later identification of color with caste was purely fortuitous. Forced immigration into North America was feasible only if it satisfied certain postulates. There had to be a population (1) sufficiently numerous, (2) capable of being forcibly enslaved and, if necessary, transported en masse, and (3) in a condition to survive the operation.

The population of Europe was not sufficiently numerous, and only a fraction of this population could be transported as indentured servants. The countries of Asia and North Africa were populous enough, but, in the 17th century, as far advanced as the Europeans, and well able to defend themselves against slave raiders. On the other hand, peoples who were too primitive tended to die out on contact with civilization.[408] Only an advanced person can be enslaved. Civilized and defenseless Indians did, indeed, exist in Mexico and Peru. But these regions had inconveniently been preempted by Spain during the previous century.

Black Africa was populous, and presented the golden mean: at the pastoral or at the agricultural level, its inhabitants were sufficiently advanced not to die out on contact with civilization and sufficiently backward not to be able to defend themselves. And no other power had preempted the territory. Needless to say, in going to Black Africa for their slaves, the Europeans were following the beaten paths. In 1377 Ibn Khaldun wrote:

> To the south of this Nile, there is a Negro people called Lamlam. . . . The people of Ghanah and Takrur invade their country, capture them, and sell them to merchants who transport them to the Maghrib. There, they constitute the ordinary mass of slaves.[409]

So Black Africa became the source of forced-draft settlement of North America. Negroes had two basic characteristics: (1) They were not Christians.[410] (2) They were black. When the colonists sought a moral justification for New World slavery and the slave trade, they found it in the paganism of the Africans. But as this proved an impracticable criterion, the caste identification shifted to the Negroes' physical characteristics. So there developed the identification of race with caste—in its origins wholly apocryphal.

Some colonies also applied the converse rule. Christians alone were entitled to hold slaves. The privilege of slaveholding was part of the Christian state of grace. Barbados underlined the inferior status of Jews by allowing them only a limited number of slaves. One of the earliest colonial salutes to religious tolerance and the brotherhood of man was a New York law of 1730 granting Jews as well as Christians the unrestricted right to hold slaves.[413] So free Negroes were generally (but not always) disqualified from holding slaves.[414]

In a few situations the possibility of involuntary emancipation was real. The English colonists tried to protect themselves against any emancipation which might result from a slave's having been in England.[415] On the eve of the American Revolution and the first abolition, the English courts, in SOMERSET'S case, held that presence on English soil freed the slave. Under French law, presence on French soil originally did not work for emancipation,[417] but the French Revolution changed this.[418] Some of the colonies also forbade their slaves from listening to Quakers.[419]

Voluntary emancipation was generally reserved for meritorious services, including services in the Revolutionary Army in the Revolutionary War.[420] Here we see the contestants arming up for what was to become the "moral issue" of the Civil War. The North glorified the Negro, but shunned him personally; the South glorified slavery, but granted emancipation as a reward.[421]

Injury or mistreatment of a slave by the overseer, the life tenant, or a third person, gave rise to a cause of action by the owner, or the remainderman.[422] If serious enough, it also subjected the wrongdoer to criminal penalties.[423] This both sprang from and emphasized the character of the slave as valuable property. In later years, slavery fell behind wage capitalism because the slave was not expendable, while the wage laborer was.[424]

The price of a slave in the period ending with 1793 was usually from $300 to $600.[425] Other aspects of relations between slaveowner and slaveowner had little or no bearing on the rise and fall of the institution in America. Mortgages and other credit transactions,[426] ownership of children as between the mother's life tenant and remainderman,[427] or the descent of slaves as personality or realty,[428] were not much affected.

When crimes committed by slaves were too serious for whipping, they put the master into a position antagonistic to the rest of society. If society punished the crime, the slaveowner would lose his slave, either temporarily or permanently. So where a slave had to be executed or imprisoned there was a problem of balancing interests. The slave society met this problem, first, by working out a compromise with its members. If a slave was executed for a crime, or died in jail awaiting trial, the state usually paid compensation to the master. But this compensation had a statutory maximum generally below the price which slaves brought on the market. And during certain periods after the Revolutionary War, when the colonies were short of money, some suspended compensation altogether.

Second, many of the colonies provided that where slaves were tried for crimes, they should be tried before a jury of slaveholders, or before panels of justices of the peace and freeholders, a tribunal always mindful of both the public and the private interests of the ruling class.

Third, in some colonies penalties were imposed on slaveholders who secreted their slaves to prevent prosecution. Slaves doing business for themselves presented another situation in which the master's interests were considered adverse to those of the rest of the community. The reasons for this attitude varied. In the more developed colonies, there was the fear that the slave would get his stock in trade by stealing. North Carolina sought to protect laboring whites from slave competition.

Virginia passed its first compensation act in 1691, granting the owner 4,000 pounds of tobacco for any slave killed in the execution of the act for suppressing outlying slaves.[429]

During the century which followed, Virginia had a standing provision for compensating owners of executed slaves,[430] under which owners were paid on presenting certificates of execution and valuation.[431] Petitions for compensation were also entertained and sometimes granted where slaves had otherwise been lost in the course of legal proceedings.[432]

Maryland was more generous than most of the colonies. Having allowed three-fourths of the value as compensation in 1717,[433] in 1737 it provided for payment to the owner of "the full value" of an executed slave. It likewise included under the general law all cases of condemned slaves dying before execution—situations which gave Virginia so much trouble.[434] These provisions continued as the law of the colony throughout the period ending with the invention of the cotton-gin.[435]

New York had a statute which evidently left the matter of compensation for executed slaves in doubt. After the executions following the slave insurrection of April, 1712, the legislature passed an act "for the Enforcing and better putting in Execution the aforesaid act whereby the Petitioners owners may be relieved".[436] Before that, the death penalty had been imposed on slaves escaping to Canada and the owner granted £30 pounds compensation if the slave was 15 years old or over, and fit for service.[437] In 1708 the colonial assembly extended the compensation to all cases of slaves executed by law,[438] but with apparently ambiguous results. The act of 1712 followed. In 1745 the upper limit of compensation for a slave was raised to £35 in case of fugitives to Canada.[439] Presumably this higher ceiling also applied to slaves executed for other reasons, though the statutes are not explicit on that point. The law then remained unchanged until 1793.

New Jersey passed its first compensation law in 1713, holding it better to compensate owners than to risk having them conceal or take away their slaves to avoid punishment. Compensation was limited to £30 each for men slaves, and £20 each for woman slaves.[440] This provision, however, was repealed in 1768.[441] After that there was no state compensation to owners of executed slaves.

Massachusetts had no general compensation law for executed slaves. But there is one case where value was paid for a slave "impressed into and dying in the King's service".[442] In one other case the colony (rather than the slave's owner) paid damages to a woman who had been wounded by a slave.[443] And in 1733 Massachusetts paid £41 5s compensation for an executed slave.[444]

Connecticut had no provisions for compensating owners whose slaves had been condemned to death. Nor were there any decided cases. Apparently the problem never arose. There are neither statutes nor decisions in Rhode Island granting compensation for executed slaves. The closest approach was payment for slaves enlisted in the army of the Revolutionary War, and lost as battle casualties. These instances will be considered in connection with the abolition of slavery in the northern colonies. It is clear that there were too few cases of executed slaves to require attention: one such instance is reported, but nothing is said about compensation to the master.[445] New Hampshire had neither cases nor statutes dealing with compensation for executed slaves.

At first Pennsylvania did not compensate masters for executed slaves. The act of 1700 imposed the death penalty on slaves for murder, rape and buggery, but left the master to bear the loss.[446] But by 1725 the colony came to realize that individual slaveowners could not stand such losses, and the community would have to assume them. So the act of 1725 provides for compensating owners of executed slaves.[447] This continued to be the law until 1793.

Jamaica showed how reluctant a slave society was to lose its slaves under whatever circumstances. If several slaves were condemned to death for the same crime, only one was executed—as an example. The owners of the others had to make proportionate reimbursement to the owner of the executed slave. [448] The same reluctance to destroy "slave property" comes out in the remarkable case of REX v. SLEATER, [449] "an indictment against a Deputy Marshal for refusing to execute two slaves condemned in a court of magistrates and freeholders. He was fined £20". When an individual slave was executed, the owner was entitled to a flat £40 compensation. [450]

Barbados granted 30 pounds for a slave lost in the militia. [451] This was both the maximum which the colony paid for an executed slave and the maximum which an owner could receive. Anyone whom the slave had injured, had first call upon the colony's compensation money. If there was no injured party, the owner got the entire compensation payment. [452] There was the further qualification that if the master's refusal of adequate food or clothing had driven the slave to commit the crime, the master received nothing. [453]

North Carolina had a compensation statute until 1786, [454] when it was repealed because the state could no longer carry the expense. [455] This is one of several such repealing acts which followed the Revolutionary War, when the states were in financial trouble. [456] The preamble to the repealer recites the cruelty of masters, allegedly driving slaves to crime.

It is amusing, and quite in the spirit of the times (continuing through the Civil War), to see purely economic questions obfuscated by the placing of "moral" blame. When the states are short of money, masters are suddenly discovered to be cruel, and their cruelty is said to contribute to slaves' crimes, so as to deprive masters of a moral right to indemnification.

South Carolina was a border colony until the organization of Georgia in 1733. Florida to the south was Spanish. So South Carolina was more exposed to foreign invasion than the other colonies. As early as 1719 she adopted the system fo enlisting and arming slaves in military service, and indemnifying the owners for those killed. [458] The absence of any controversy over this measure again attests to the solidity of South Carolina's caste society. [458]

South Carolina followed the law of Jamaica respecting slaves executed for crime. Where a group committed a capital offense, only one was executed, the owners of the others making proportionate reimbursement to the owner of the executed slave. [459] In 1712 the proportionate contribution was limited to one-sixth the value of the slave executed.[460] In 1714 (the end of the War of the Spanish Succession), South Carolina restricted the recovery for executed slaves to £50, because the colonial treasury was then already feeling the strain of paying indemnities.[461]

For the same reason, capital punishment was thereafter withheld from most crimes.[462] But the treasury was no better off by 1717. In that year the legislature repealed compensation in murder cases, and imposed a special levy on slaveholders to pay the compensation when a slave of one of their number was executed.[463] At the same time the provision for transportation, instead of execution, for offenses less than murder was repealed, as supposedly having encouraged slaves to commit crimes. [464]

By 1722 the colony's finances must have improved, and the emphasis shifted again toward compensating owners in order to relieve them from any temptation to hide slaves who had committed serious crimes. The maximum indemnity was raised to £80. But if a slave was executed because of an escape, the loss fell on the owner[464] (presumably on the theory that the loss would have fallen on the owner had the escape been successful).

A higher compensation (£100) was also granted retroactively for slaves executed under preceding acts for anything other than wilful murder. [465] In 1740 the limit was again raised, this time to £200, but coverage was withheld not only in murder cases, but for "slaves taken in open rebellion". The motivation was still "that owners of slaves may not be tempted to conceal the crimes of their slaves to the prejudice of the public".[456] The same act restored indemnity for slaves killed while running away. [467] (The colony clearly was prosperous again). The state of affairs continued unchanged despite the Revolutionary War, until 1793.

When Georgia was chartered, she became the new southern border colony and followed South Carolina's example in arming the slaves and compensating owners for slaves killed, maimed, or freed for meritorious service.[468] She also provided compensation for owners of executed slaves,[469] but like the other states which found themselves in financial trouble after the Revolutionary War, repealed her compensation statute in 1793.[470] Louisiana, under the French domination, compensated owners whose slaves were executed for crimes. [471] We have no available record under Spanish rule, but the law was undoubtedly the same.

Slaveowners were by definition, "the dominant forces of the community"[472] in a slave society. Where balancing of interests was a delicate matter, they handled that problem themselves. The community at large demanded punishment of slaves for crimes, but the slaveowners wanted to keep slave property for which they had paid. Many colonies

and states did not allow the general populace to meddle with this
balance. Slaves had to be tried before panels of commissioners appointed by the governor, or by justices of the peace and freeholders, or
before juries of slaveholders.[473] A strange variant of this problem appears in the penalty which Jamaica and South Carolina imposed on mar-
shals and constables who refused to execute condemned slaves.[474]
Reluctance to destroy slave property appeared even in rape cases, where
the community would be most excitable.

The West India colonies, South Carolina and Georgia imposed sanctions on masters who tried to conceal or spirit away slaves charged with
crime.[475] Compensation for executed slaves was designed to remove
any temptation to do so; this group of colonies added the stick to the
carrot.

All the colonies forbade slaves to trade for themselves. The only
exceptions were granted as rewards in Jamaica and South Carolina as a
kind of partial emancipation.[416] Most of the colonies grounded the prohibition on the danger that slaves would steal to get the goods which
they traded.[411,465]If the master received the profits of the slave's
business, no objection was made,[475a]presumably because the master
would then himself be responsible and would see to it that the slave did
not trade in stolen goods. North Carolina forbade slaves in business for
themselves as undesirable competition with free laborers.[477] Georgia
forbade employing slaves in handicrafts for the same reason.[480]

Free Negroes and Mulattoes were generally treated like slaves.
They had the right to own property, and in some colonies to transmit it
to their heirs or legatees. But, they could not be sold, nor held to life-
long servitude. A person held in slavery but claiming to be free could
sue for his freedom. Heavy penalties were imposed on any one selling a
free Negro or Mulatto as a slave. Otherwise free Negroes had no civil
rights.

In general they were subject to corporal punishment like slaves; for
some offenses they were sold into slavery either for a limited period, or
for life. Emancipated slaves had to leave the jurisdiction within a short
period. If not, or if they returned, they were sold into slavery. They
could not intermarry with whites. As a rule, free Negroes could not hold
slaves. Louisiana constituted an exception to nearly everything that has
been said. Under Roman law free Negroes had many more rights than
under English-colonial law. A table of free Negroes' rights and liabilities
is given in the Appendix for each of the colonies.[481]

The events which closed the Eighteenth Century etch the paradox of
North American slavery. The Industrial Revolution brought with it the

American Revolutionary War, the prohibition of the slave trade, and abolition of slavery in the northern states. It also brought the British cotton spinning industry and invention of the cotton gin which together gave slavery a new, last heyday. Termination of the slave trade and abolition in the northern states were well under way by 1793. Expediency and morality coalesced, so action came quickly. It soon became evident that a wage economy operated more efficiently than a slave economy.[482] When this began to be felt, the first to go was the slave economy's source of supply. And when the regions where slavery was unprofitable had the population necessary for a wage economy,[483] those regions abolished slavery itself.

Hand in hand with these practical considerations went the emotional appeal of the Revolutionary War. Having fought for our own freedom, how could we keep others in bondage?[484] All colonies but Georgia prohibited the slave trade.[485] Abolition, on the other hand, was confined to the northern colonies where slavery did not pay. Statutory preambles recite practical and idealistic motivations in about equal parts.

The first move in this direction had come from the mother country, where the Industrial Revolution was in full swing. The high ideals and philanthropy expressed in England at that time happened to coincide with the economic needs of an industrial society. Slaves were "freed" if upon English soil; but any service which they had rendered was still that of a slave and not of a free laborer, so that when they became destitute in England, they were not entitled to any public support. In 1772 Lord Mansfield decided the famous case of SOMERSET v. STEWART,[486] holding that slavery "is so odious that nothing can be suffered to support it but positive law", and that a slave brought to England became automatically free.

The court went back to the 1569 decision of CARTWRIGHT'S CASE,[487] which had held, "That England was too pure an Air for Slaves to breath in". CARTWRIGHT'S CASE had come up before any English settlement in North America (except Newfoundland). In SOMERSET v. STEWART, Lord Mansfield observed that "'the last confession of villenage extant, is in the 19th of Henry the 6th'". (1440). Yet in between, in 1729, Sir Philip Yorke, then Attorney-General, delivered an opinion,[488] "that a slave, by coming from the West Indies, either with or without his master, to Great Britain or Ireland, doth not become free ... " Here we see the contra-capitalist current induced by the colonization of North America, and then beginning to yield before the Industrial Revolution.

SOMERSET v. STEWART was followed a few years later in KNIGHT v. WEDDERBURN. [489] But when the question arose whether these free Negroes should get public support as free laborers if they became paupers, the answer was "no". They were left to starve. In KING v. INHABITANTS OF THAMES DITTON, [490] Lord Mansfield, who had decided SOMERSET v. STEWART thirteen years before, limited the effects of his earlier decision, saying:

> The case of Somerset, the Negro slave, goes no farther than to determine that the master of such a servant shall not have it in his power to take him out of the kingdom against his will; to give this pauper a settlement, she must come within the description of a positive law. Her being black or a slave is no objection, but the statute requires a hiring; there is none here, and therefore, the case is not within the statute.

Turning the slave out to starve is precisely what the slave system had sought to avoid. The Industrial Revolution was about to progress beyond that stage. [491]

In America the Continental Congress, with all states but Georgia concurring, resolved on October 20, 1774, to end the slave trade. [492] Over the ensuing years the states implemented this resolution with their statutes. Virginia ended the slave trade in 1778 [493] and broadened the masters' rights of manumission in 1782. [494] This was foreshadowed by complaints about the bad condition of tobacco culture—a complaint beginning in 1710 and running to the eve of the Revolution. [495] Virginia tobacco planters were suffering from crop surpluses. [496]

Maryland prohibited the importation of slaves in 1783. [497] New York, in 1785, [498] New Jersey, in 1788. [499] Shortly after the Revolution, New York manumitted all slaves who had been confiscated from the British or British sympathizers, and forfeited them to the state. [500] Massachusetts abolished slavery outright in 1781. [501] This action was preceded by the qualms of conscience which ran through so many of the colonies during and after the Revolutionary War:

> Mr. Wheeler brought into Congress a letter directed to Doct. Appleton, purporting the propriety, that while we are attempting to free ourselves from our present embarrassments, and preserve ourselves from slavery, that we also take into consideration the state and circumstances of the Negro slaves in this province. The same was read and it was moved that a committee be appointed to take the same into consideration. After

some debate thereon, the question was put, whether the matter now subside, and it passed in the affirmative.[502]

The final decision, however, did not come until after uncertainty and hesitation. In 1775 slaves were excluded from the Massachusetts army on the ground that to include them would be inconsistent with the high purposes of the revolution.[503]

Massachusetts, the most advanced industrial state, having abolished her own slavery by judicial decision in 1781, already began thinking of general abolition. The post-revolutionary twinges of conscience apparently could be quieted by nothing less. At the state constitutional convention of 1788, we find the blunt statement:

> Thompson: Shall it be said, that after we have established our own independence and freedom, we make slaves of others?[504]

The slave trade was forbidden to residents of Massachusetts in 1788.[505-6] As will be seen later, this crusading spirit died out with the excitement of the Revolutionary War. It was not to be revived until an expanding industrialism again made it expedient. In fact, as early as 1795, John Adams said that expediency was the real cause of the post-revolutionary abolition.[507] Abolition in Massachusetts sprang from the confluence of abstract idealism and current expediency.

Connecticut flatly declared that the slave trade had to be terminated because additional slaves were obnoxious to the white population and that "sound policy" required abolition. This occurred in 1784.[508] Rhode Island abolished her own slave trade in 1774 and enacted gradual abolition in 1784. But she was reluctant to abolish either slavery or the slave trade in the country as a whole. The following exchanges took place at her Constitutional Convention in 1790:[509]

> 'Jona. Hazzard argues Southern states should be left to handle problem themselves. Geo. Hazzard says he has been in the slave trade.'

> 'If we totally abolish Slavery it will Ruin many persons.— Will not be possible to effect the Abolition of Slavery at present—after all the Reflection.'

> 'Mr. Marcht. The Slaves in South Carolina Equal to Half their Real Estate. This property was obtained when it was not supposed not lawful even in this state. They acquired a right which they supposed to be equal in their Real Estate.'

Rhode Island had been torn by such doubts for years. Importation of slaves into the state had been prohibited as early as 1774,[510] directly after the resolution of the Continental Congress to that effect. This action was prompted by the inconsistency of demanding liberty for one's self while imposing slavery on others. In 1778, over some opposition, Rhode Island adopted the system of allowing slaves to enlist and freeing those who had, with compensation to the owners.[511] But then the state almost immediately changed her mind, and decreed that there should be no more such enlistments or emancipations once the existing act had expired.[512] Vacillation appears once more in the act prohibiting Rhode Island slaves from being sold out of the state: the legislature again looks forward to general abolition.[513]

Here we see emotional excitement gripping the state before the Revolutionary War actually began and fading before the fighting had ceased. Rhode Island did not feel that expediency required freeing such slaves as she then had;[514] for that, "some favorable occasion" still lay in the future.

When gradual abolition was enacted in 1784,[515] it proceeded on grounds of principle, but as in Connecticut, did not actually free a single slave. The act merely provided that no persons should be slaves if born after March 1, 1784. Gradualism was likewise applied to prohibition of the slave trade. The act of 1784[576] closed some loopholes in the 1774 law.[493] Another statute passed in 1787 "to prevent the slave trade and to encourage the abolition of slavery"[575] imposed penalties for attempted evasion of existing laws. But even these measures were stronger than the stand which Rhode Island took with regard to national abolition or general termination of the slave trade. The state was much more anxious to limit its own slavery than that of the nation. Rhode Island vessels were undoubtedly among the carriers for the southern states.[494a-519]

New Hampshire was agricultural but not suited to slavery, and the institution slowly died out.[495-520] There was no sudden abolition like that which pressure of incipient industrialization produced in Massachusetts. This caused the Massachusetts constitutional convention to complain that New Hampshire had an advantage, since in New Hampshire the Negroes were still slaves, while those in Massachusetts were free.[486-521] New Hampshire, having very few slaves,[497-522] took no steps to abolish the slave trade.

In 1780, Pennsylvania passed an act for the gradual abolition of slavery[493-523] along the same lines as those of Connecticut and Rhode Island. Nothing brings out the practical aspects of abolition better than to contrast this statute with abolition in Massachusetts. The preamble of the Pennsylvania act is full of high sentiment,[499-524] which were, undoubtedly genuine. Pennsylvania was the state of the Quakers, who had been agitating for abolition since the previous century.[500-525] Yet, despite all high principles and noble sentiments, there was no freeing of slaves. That took place only in Massachusetts, the most advanced industrial state. The Pennsylvania act for gradual abolition also prohibited the importation of slaves,[501-526] which had been curbed as early as 1712.[502-527]

"As to North Carolina," declared Patrick Henry at the Virginia Constitutional Convention of 1788,[503-528] "it is a poor, despised place." Despised or not, it was certainly poor. We have already seen how far the slave system remained undeveloped in this state.[504-529] Abolition never gained much momentum because there never was much to abolish. To a large extent slavery could be disregarded.[504a-530] And the slavery which did exist was mostly a reflection of the systems in the state's two powerful neighbors—Virginia and South Carolina. No move was made to abolish slavery, nor even to curtail the slave trade within the period ending in 1793.[505-531] The only sign of awareness was a reaction against the revolutionary fervor, in the form of an act restricting the right of emancipation.[506-532]

After having insisted on the slave trade at the Constitutional Convention,[507-533] South Carolina went along with the general trend to the extent of prohibiting the trade in 1792.[508-534] There was, of course, no thought of abolition. Georgia, undeveloped, with a rapidly increasing population, and ever hungry for more slaves, neither forbade the slave trade by 1793[509-535] nor took any steps toward abolition. The same was true of Louisiana under the stagnant Spanish regime.

After the fires of Independence had cooled, the sentiment for abolition died down, not to reappear until the Civil War. In the meantime, it was remarked, Negroes had never been treated as citizens or as the equals of white men since the Revolutionary War.

Here the country's laws reflected the historical process. Schopenhauer divides mankind into four categories: 1) Those who inflict pain on others for their own satisfaction; 2) those who practice "justice"—i.e., follow self-interest, but without harm to others; 3) those who treat others as they treat themselves; 4) those who sacrifice themselves for a group or for a cause.[158] [509c] In common speech the second and third groups are sometimes called the "practical men" and the "idealists."

The idealists we have always with us. They operate as if in a void, except that they agitate in terms of current concrete problems. Their ideals[158a] [509d] lead nowhere until changing circumstances move the practical men over to the idealists' point of view. In mathematical terms, any particular group of idealists are a constant, the self-interested practical men are a variable. Thus the Quakers agitated for the abolition of slavery as early as the 17th century, but for the time being they were a voice crying in the wilderness.[159] [538C]

By the Treaty of Utrecht, in 1714, England's interest in the slave trade was expanded to the extent of securing a monopoly of the Spanish carrying trade.[539] [159a] But as slavery became wholly unprofitable in certain colonies, the "practical", self-interested doers suddenly came over to the views of the Abolitionists, who worked for the benefit of the slaves rather than for their own interests.[159b] [540]

It is when such a confluence takes place that a society accomplishes great things. When the time is ripe, and the "practical" men have adopted the views of the idealists, it is still the latter who give the final push which brings about change. In the colonies which were ready to abolish slavery, it was the excitement of the Revolutionary War for their own liberties which induced the colonists to decree abolition.

After the new order has been achieved, the confluence breaks, thermidor[159C] [544] sets in, and society returns (on a new level) to its pedestrian, if not sordid norm.

From the Invention of the Cotton Gin to the Missouri Compromise (1793-1820)

The wielder of the lash gets very tired of his job in the end, but the white man's heart is brimful of the hope of power and wealth, and that doesn't cost anything; not a thing. Let's hear no more about Egypt and the Tartar tyrants In the supreme art of getting the two-legged animal to really put his back into his work, these classical experts are the merest conceited amateurs.

Celine, Voyage au Bout de la Nuit

Capital further developed a coercive relation, which compels the working class to do more than the narrow round of its own life-wants prescribes. As a producer of the work of others, as a pumper-out of surplus labor and exploiter of laborer-power, it surpasses in energy, disregard of bounds, recklessness and efficiency, all earlier systems of production directly based on compulsory labor.

Marx, Kapital

Whitney's invention of the cotton gin in 1793 was like the strawberry atop the sundae. It capped off half a century of inventions which had turned British cotton cloth production into a mechanized industry.[2] Before being mechanized, the European cotton cloth industry had not been capable of utilizing such a machine. In 1742 Durbrueil put forth a similar invention, but it fell flat because at that time there was an insufficient demand for cotton.[3]

The invention of the cotton gin in 1793 however, dove-tailed with the inventions which immediately preceded it. Now an industry which could use much more cotton than it was getting, would be supplied by a source which could furnish much more cotton than it had in the past.

Upon the invention of the saw gin, exports of cotton from the United States to England increased from 487,600 pounds in 1793 to 1,600,000 pounds in 1794, and to 10,000,000 pounds in 1796. When the British cotton goods industry had been unable to process a large amount of raw cotton, (before 1790) the United States only supplied 1/636 of what the British processed. Sixty years later, from 1846-1850, the United States furnished 4/5 of what was manufactured in England. In other words:

> From 1786 to 1790, the average amount of cotton imported by Great Britain from the United States was 100 bales; from 1816 to 1820, 166,310 bales; from 1846 to 1850, 1,297,230 bales; from 1876 to 1880, 2,589,070 bales.[4]

The area of cotton production in the United States was almost identical to the area in which slavery had previously been profitable. (Only Virginia and Kentucky, the tobacco states, were excluded). The question then was, with what system would the existing slave states meet the new demand for cotton? Three factors tended to make a simple expansion of the slave system the most likely method:

1. Using the slave system for the new crop made use of social and economic machinery already in existence.

2. In the southern states the slave system was relatively free from economic objections. Slaves had to be kept on when not working. But the cotton crop insured that there would be only a short part of the year when the slaves did not work. In the Gulf states, preparation of the soil began about February 1, and picking was completed by December 1, or at the latest by December 15. This left only six weeks or two months out of the year in which the slave was not engaged in cotton raising. In South Carolina, the date to begin preparing the soil was one month later, March 5, and picking was likewise completed by December 1.[5]

3. The change to cotton following the invention of Whitney's saw gin implied a one-crop, or nearly one-crop economy. It was to one-crop economics that the methods of slavery were best suited and those of wage capitalism the least suited. For the sanction of wage capitalism is the lay-off. If a worker does not obey the rules, he is fired. Hand in hand with the lay-off as discipline goes the right to lay-off the worker when he is not working. In an industrial society, different groups of workers will be employed at different times. There is not one period when everybody is unemployed. In a one-crop economy, on the other hand, any seasonal lay-off will affect virtually all workers at once. To have the whole laboring population suddenly dumped into unemployment

carries at least the danger of rioting. At most it invites revolution. The lay-off under such circumstances is not the same flawless expense-cutter which it is under a system of varied industries.

Consequently, the "cotton kingdom" employed the already existing slave system. The Industrial Revolution, basically anti-slavery, fostered slavery in the American southern states. For a second time since the discovery of America, the growth of capitalism in Europe promoted the growth of an anti-capitalist society in North America.[5a]

This trend marked in England by SOMERSET v. STEWART[5b] was reversed. The Industrial Revolution, like the anti-feudal discovery voyages, started a current counter to the main stream.

But while the first period of capitalist development in Europe coupled with non-capitalist development on the North American continent had stretched over almost two centuries, the second period was compressed into less than seventy years. And while the second upswing of slavery was merely a repetition of what had gone before, the development of capitalism which lay ahead was built upon what had already been done; i.e., the Industrial Revolution was an advance on the developments which had preceded it.

It followed that the second impetus to slavery in North America came under much less favorable circumstances than the first. Parodoxically, the Industrial Revolution furthered slavery, but was at the same time bringing slavery to an end. In North America the Industrial Revolution engendered a late and fleeting bloom of the agricultural economy. The cotton kingdom was both its product and its victim. To the cotton kingdom, the Industrial Revolution was Saturn who devoured his children.

So in the period following 1793, two interrelated features characterized the parallel existence of slavery and the capitalist wage system in the United States. First, the slave states, despite the push given by the cotton gin, fell behind the wage states. Secondly, the characteristics and efficiency of the latter became more and more marked as they alone attracted new immigration from Europe.

Thomas Hart Benton thus describes the relative standing of the sections before and after the American Revolution:

> In the colonial state, the southern was the rich part of the colonies, and expected to do well in a state of independence. They had the exports and felt secure of their prosperity; not so the north, which expected privations from the loss of British favor. But in the first

half-century after independence this expectancy was
reversed.   The wealth of the north was enormously
aggrandized: that of the south had declined.   Northern
towns had become great cities.   Southern cities had
decayed or became stationary; and Charleston, the
principal port of the south, was less considerable than
before the Revolution.   The North became a money-
lender to the South, and southern citizens made
pilgrimages to northern cities to raise money upon
hypothecation of their patrimonial estates. [6]

The changed relative conditions of the two sections of
the country, before and since the union, was shown in
their general relative depression or prosperity since that
event, and especially in the reversed condition of their
respective foreign import trade.   In the colonial
condition, the comparison was wholly in favor of the
South; under the Union wholly against it.   Thus in the
year 1760, only sixteen years before the Declaration of
Independence, the foreign imports into Virginia were
850,000 pounds sterling, and into South Carolina
 555,000; while into New York they were only 189,000;
into Pennsylvania 490,000; and into all the New England
colonies collectively only 561,000.

Thus in the year 1821, the imports into New York had
risen to $23,000,000, this being about twenty times its
colonial import at about an equal period before the
adoption of the Constitution; and those of South Carolina
stood at about $3,000,000, which for all practical
purposes may be considered the same as they were in
1760. [7]

As the members of the Constitutional Convention had foreseen,[8] an
active slave system tended to keep out new immigrants.[8] Almost the
entire immigration after 1793 went to the states which had no slavery,
or where slavery was being allowed to die a natural death.   The
immigrant to a slave state was subject to the necessity of underselling
the slave. By going to a non-slave state he was under such compulsion to
a much more limited degree.[9]

As soon as the population presssure became great enough in the
northern regions, it also became possible to begin to organize large scale

business enterprises based on a wage system. From now on Merriwells' dictum that "slave labor is dearer than free labor wherever abundance of free labor can be procured" [10] would hold true.

So J. B. Cairias, The Slave Power,[10a] said in 1862:

> Since the settlement of the Southern States a vast change has taken place in the American Continent. Free labour, which was then scarce and costly, has now in many of the large towns became superabundant, and it is quite possible that even with external conditions so favorable as the southern half of North America undoubtedly presents, free labour would now, on a fair trial, be found more than a match for its antagonist.

As soon as the population of the non-slave states beame sufficiently dense, the population pressure became great enough that firing and the threat of firing could be used as a mode of discipline.

> There are no words in the language which throw so much terror into the ears of workers as 'slack season' and 'fired.' Other words might conjure up the fear of death, but they do not plunge a man into the same dank prison of worry and care. At least they can be fought against. But the fear of hunger, of finding one's self without a roof over one's head, thrown out on the sidewalk, is greater than the fear of death.[11]

Firing the employee cost nothing and tired no one. Besides, the employer does not support wage laborers when they are not working.[12] As the population became dense enough for wage enterprises to be operated on a large scale,[13] their superiority to slave operated enterprises became evident. The use of slave labor by the cotton belt was therefore handicapped by the same Industrial Revolution which brought it into being, and made it inefficient by comparison and obsolescent from the start. The cotton kingdom was born afflicted with progeria.

In addition, the wage-system developing in the north had the stimulus of moral superiority added to its practical advantages. In 1820, the Massachusetts legislature resolved, that:

> The United States were the first nation to provide by law against the slave trade. And now when other nations are awakened, perhaps by our very example, to the enormity

of this practice, when a rapid and almost universal change in public opinion has taken place in Europe, shall Republican America, by opening a new market for slaves, give a new stimulus to that traffic? [13a]

Two new states—Kentucky and Vermont—were added to the Union before 1793. [14] And between 1793 and 1820, Tennessee, Ohio, Louisiana, Indiana, Mississippi, Illinois, Alabama, Maine, and Missouri were also granted statehood.

THE COURSE OF SLAVE LAW 1793-1820.

There was little change in the laws of slavery during the period 1793-1820. The far most noteworthy occurrences have already been mentioned. These were the shift of the balance of population from the slave states to the non-slave states, and the repeated efforts of the Indiana Territory to be relieved of the anti-slavery clause in the Northwest Territory Ordinance. These were non-legislative changes. Legislation, if any, followed patterns already set, with the exception of South Carolina's re-opening of the slave trade in 1803, [23a] and the final legislative closing in 1808. [23b]

By the early 1800's, it was an established tenet of slave law that while slaves were tied to their masters, they were not tied to the soil. The master could move them about, or sell them. This became especially important after the invention of the cotton-gin. Kentucky and Virginia both lay north of the cotton belt. They cultivated tobacco, which they produced in surplus quantities. [25]

Thus the surplus of slaves in those states coincided on the one hand with the invention of the cotton-gin, causing an increased demand for slaves in the new cotton states, and on the other, with the outlawing of the slave trade, turning Kentucky and Virginia into slave breeding states. The legal principle that a slave should not be tied to the soil, but could be sold from one state to another became a key to slave state economies after 1808.

The fugitive slave clause in the Constitution and a federal Fugitive Slave Law passed in 1793, [26] tended to crystallize control over fugitive slaves. During the period ending in 1820, this form of control was generally accepted and caused no noticeable controversy. There was almost no legislative change on the subject between 1793 and 1820.

The first mention of fugitive slaves after 1793 was in New Virginia Justice, which gave the acts in force in 1795. These provided that no slave could leave the tenements of his master without a pass, and gave the nearest justice of the peace discretion whether to punish or not. [27]

A slave found on another plantation without a pass might receive up to ten lashes from the owner or overseer of that plantation.[28] Any two justices could direct the sheriff of the county to bring back two or more outlying slaves and put them in jail. A posse could be raised if necessary.[29] The master of a vessel carrying a slave out of the state without the owner's consent was fined $300.00.[29a]

In 1819 the Virginia legislature passed "An Act to reduce into one act, the several acts for apprehending and securing runaways."[30] Here the law is pretty well crystallized and beyond its formative period. The bulk of the act dealt with the mechanics of bringing back fugitive slaves and with rewards for their apprehension. Only a small part was concerned with the basic right of recapture.

The country was still sufficiently open that slaveowners had the problem of outlying slaves. "Many slaves run away and lie outside, hide, and lurk in the swamps, killing hogs and committing other injuries to the inhabitants of this commonwealth."[31] The right of recapture was made as broad as possible. "Any person may apprehend a servant or slave suspected to be a runaway, and carry him before a justice of the peace."[32] But once the supposed runaway had been taken, the owner was held to strict proof to show that he really had lost the particular slave and was really claiming a runaway.[33] This last shows the care which the law took to regulate relations among slaveholders, and one old problem was set at rest by statute. If the apprehended runaway died in jail before being delivered to his master, the state compensated the master.[34]

Otherwise, the statute provides for having the runaway brought either directly to the owner,[35] or to a jailer and a justice of the peace.[36] Advertising in case the owner did not come forward to claim the slave,[37] and rewards to the taker-up, varied with distance, and the slave's chances of escaping permanently at the spot where he is taken.[38] Ferry or bridge-keepers were made criminally liable if they allowed a slave to cross the Potomac.[39]

The paramount right of the master to retrieve his slave continued in a new form after the Revolutionary War. When a British ship had taken slaves, and was herself captured, with the slaves going as prize with the ship, the original slaveowner's claim was held paramount to that of the purchaser from the prize court.[39a] However stealing a slave while he was a runaway was not considered an offense.[39b] There was a clash of tendencies in these rulings, but the underlying cause seemed to be loss of interest in the fugitive slave problem in Virginia. Only one other case touched the situation at all. In a will dated 1774, Dr. Nicholas Flood authorized his executor, on behalf of his widow, to sell any slaves who proved to be runaway.[39c] The executor's actions in this respect were confirmed by the court. Virginia was making the transition from a slave-using to a slave-breeding state. Slaves were being quickly transported from the Commonwealth, and the fugitive slave problem was fading from the legal horizon.

Maryland with a waning slave system, felt that it was up to masters to see that their slaves did not become fugitives. Unaffected by the upswing caused by the cotton gin, her first action after 1793, was to impose additional penalties on masters for permitting their slaves to wander around freely.[40]

In 1802 Maryland revised her law on runaways,[41] which indicates how American society was slowly changing. The short statute deals entirely with advertising and disposing of runaways,[42] except for section 4, which imposed a fine of $100.00 on any sheriff refusing to comply with the provisions of the law.[43]

The disappearance of slavery in Maryland tended to conflict with the remaining slave interests. Fraudulent certificates of freedom began to turn up in the hands of runaway slaves. In 1805, the state legislature tried to counteract this tendency by tightening the requirements for such certificates.[44] Two years later, certificates of freedom could be issued only by clerks or registrars where deeds of manumission were recorded.[45] Later, the act of 1810 provided that a judge had to be satisfied that a Negro was not a fugitive before he could release him.[46] But fugitive slaves continued to be a headache.

Maryland's experience was the direct opposite of Virginia's. The reason was that Maryland was not a slave-breeding state, but rather a border state. The tensions which eventually led to the Civil War were beginning to be felt. In 1816, the Maryland legislature took note of "the encouragement given to Negroes running away from their owners in this state, and the harbouring of the same by sundry citizens of the Commonwealth of Pennsylvania and the State of Delaware, has become a serious unconvenience to the owners of slaves."[47] Another sign of growing tensions was found in the 1817 statute which set up special procedures for selling slaves out of the state and procedures for determining whether alleged runaways were actually slaves or were free.[48] That same year the Maryland legislature renewed its complaints that Pennsylvania was not only harbouring, but also inviting fugitive slaves from Maryland.[49]

Thus the whole nature of the fugitive slave problem had changed since pre-Revolutionary days. Then, slave owners had to cope with the desires of slaves to escape. By the early 1800's it became necessary to deal with the efforts of nascent industrial states to induce slaves to escape, and the efforts of slave states to kidnap free Negroes to make up for the lost slave trade.

As we have already seen, the right of the master to retrieve his slave, was the linchpin of the slave system. It made the plantation economy possible when the continent was almost uninhabitated. And when an industrial economy moved to replace the plantation economy, the fugitive slave law became the focus of attack. That these factors appeared so markedly before 1820, shows that Maryland, a border state, did not yet know which way she was going to jump.[50]

The 1816 and 1817 resolutions by the Maryland legislature were fruitless, but they were followed by another one in 1820.[51] But after 1817, the lines began to harden. The Maryland Resolution of 1820 no longer asked for action by state governors, but rather by Congress, and it referred to Pennsylvania alone, omitting any mention of Delaware.

Despite pressures to bring slaves into Pennsylvania, there were only four Maryland cases between 1793-1820 which remotely touched the subject of fugitive slaves. LOWE v. BOTELER[51a] involved the sale of a slave who was a fugitive at the time of the agreement of sale. It was provided that if he were not recovered, the agreement of sale should be void. In BOARMAN'S CASE[51b] a slave belonging to a lunatic was ordered sold because he had made several attempts to escape and might become totally lost. In HAY v. CONNOR[51c] the hirer of a slave as a ship's cook was held liable, when after transferring him to another ship, the slave escaped when the second vessel was forced into an emergency port.

New York passed a law for the gradual abolition of slavery in 1799.[52] She retained fugitive slave laws to the extent of penalizing those who harbored the slaves of another without the owner's consent.[53] But by 1813 the law was more concerned with freeing towns to which slaves had escaped from possible obligations to support them, than with the returning the fugitive slave to his master.[54]

The Industrial Revolution was just reaching New York, which had developed an attitude similar to the New England states against making the public support unemployed slaves or freedmen.[55] Three years later, this viewpoint was also frequently expressed in towns which were saddled with the support of slaves formerly belonging to estates which had been forfeited.[56] In 1817, the 1813 law was repealed but the question of supporting unemployed fugitive slaves was apparently left up in the air.[57] Presumably, New York was industrializing so fast that "unemployed fugitive slaves" were found not to constitute a problem. All that remained of the fugitive slave law was a provision for returning slaves stowed away on New York vessels while the latter were lying in the harbors of slave states. [58]

FISH v. FISHER, [59] decided in 1800, indicates that the New York courts were by then looking for reasons to declare escaped slaves free. The plaintiff (originally a slave) had escaped from New Jersey to New York, where his master let him to a New York merchant for 20 years. This contract of lease was held to be an approval of the slave's escape, in effect a sale, therefore an importation into New York. The slave was accordingly declared free.

There were only two other New York cases on fugitive slaves in the period ending in 1820.   GLEN v. HODGES[61] followed the orthodox existing law, and decided that the federal fugitive slave act of 1793 could not be thwarted by an attachment in Vermont where a slave had escaped from New York to Vermont. This was a new aspect of the fugitive slave situation. It was no longer so much a contest between the master and the slave, as a contest between the master and those who wanted to give the slave a new status as a wage employee. From 1793 until the outbreak of the Civil War, there was an unremitting assault on the keystone of the slave system; the right of the master to retrieve his absconding servant.

New Jersey adopted a wage economy with much less hesitation. In 1795, employing or harboring slaves without their masters' consent was punished only by a fine of four dollars a day.[63] The reward for picking up fugitive slaves was only one dollar and transportation expenses.[64] Former fugitive slave acts were repealed, [65] and there were no further laws passed in New Jersey through 1820.

In 1813 the New Jersey courts showed their basic attitude toward fugitive slaves by holding that the statutory penalty of $30 for enticing away a servant did not apply to slaves.[66]   The same act had separate provisions regarding slaves, but since prosecutors did not rely upon this part of the act, defendants usually went free. So a charge of enticing "black servants into Pennsylvania" was held too vague to sustain recovery.[67] The states north of the Mason and Dixon Line were steadily getting into the fugitive slave business. Fugitive slaves were prospective employees in wage-operated enterprises.

Massachusetts, perhaps because it was too remote, had no laws encouraging escaping slaves prior to 1820. However, these were soon to come. Also, there were no Massachusetts cases relating to fugitive slaves during the period 1793-1820.

Connecticut, in 1797 repealed her entire fugitive slave law dating back to 1750. [69] In the following year, a three-year statute of limitations was placed on collection of penalties for violation of what remained in the act.[70]   The fugitive slave business, as it was now developing in the northern states was summarized by the editor's comment to the Revision of 1821. "The consequence has been that there are now very few slaves and in a short time, slavery will no longer be a reproach to this state.   The number of Negroes however, is rather increasing, than diminishing like the Indians."[71]   There was only one Connecticut case on escaped slaves during this period, RICHARDS v. STEWART[72] in which a citizen of Connecticut attempted recapture of alleged fugitives in answer to the owner's advertisement.

Rhode Island imposed a fine of $300.00 for concealing slaves to help them escape.[73]   Otherwise there was nothing relating to fugitive slaves. New Hampshire had no laws nor cases on fugitive slaves during the period 1793-1820.

Pennsylvania likewise had no new fugitive slave laws during this period.[74] In judicially decided cases, the state still recognized that "as soon as it was proved the Negro was a slave, that not only his master had a right to seize and carry him away, but that in case he absconded or resisted, it was the duty of every magistrate to employ all the legitimate means of coercion in his power for seizure and restoring the Negro to . . . his owner." [75] So it was said in COMMONWEALTH v. BECK[76] that "Negroes often desert their masters, and find protection among their friends. On a habeas corpus directed to such patron, if the Negro fails to establish his claim of freedom, he is delivered to the owner."

Southern Congressmen bringing their slaves with them were safe in Pennsylvania. If the slave escaped before the master actually went to Washington, the slave was returned to the owner.[77] The same was true for slaves escaping from other states to Pennsylvania.[78]

North Carolina enacted only three new statutes dealing with fugitive slaves,[79] and these were of a minor nature. The state did not have a slave system of her own. She merely followed the powerful states which bordered on her. In 1812 North Carolina prohibited Negro pilots on boats.[80] This act alone suggests the northern activity of hiring away slaves from their masters—actually recruiting a wage-labor force from among slaves—had begun. Also, reward to the taker-up of a runaway slave, though no reward had been offered, was authorized where the slave was recaptured in a county other than that of the master's residence.[81] In the previous year the sheriff had been empowered to sell slaves held as runaways, after a specified time and public notice.[82] The cases during this period reflect the precariousness of slavery in North Carolina.

STATE v. HALL[82a] was an indictment in which the court took occasion to observe that "the act of assembly was passed in turbulent times, when a practice prevailed of carrying slaves away under the pretense that they belonged to the public as confiscated; or that they were owned by disaffected persons: they were sometimes carried off . . . by stealth, or other times openly and by violence; the former case is embraced by the word steal. To the latter case, the words of intention expressed in the statute must be exclusively referred."

ESTES v. LENOX[83] was an action of debt to recover the statutory penalty imposed on those who harbored or maintained runaway slaves. Likewise in McALLISTER v. SPILLER,[84] one inhabitant of North Carolina induced the slaves of another to run away. The same is true in CUTLAR v. BROWN.[85] North Carolina, with a loose slave system was evidently a poaching ground for those who sought to entice slaves away. In JORDAN v. JORDAN,[87] the defendant knowingly stole and sold a runaway.

South Carolina had almost no new fugitive slave laws in the period 1793-1820. The state was far enough away from the non-slave states so that northern efforts to seduce slaves into wage-earning jobs was hardly felt. The structure of its feudal society was unbreached and under iron control. For the time being the economy was prosperous. At the beginning of this time South Carolina was like T. S. Eliot's Church, which "can sleep and feud at once."[87a] Everything put together offered little incentive for slaves to escape. The only law even hinting at this problem came in 1817.[88] In Section X it provided that slaves lodged in jail and not claimed within three months may be sold. One may infer that this includes fugitives. The status of South Carolina slaves at this time, itself operating as a deterrent to escapes, is indicated by BOOTH v. L'ESPERANZA,[89] which says that "most of our coasters are navigated by slaves, and frequently commanded by a slave."

There is however, a noticeable swing in the South Carolina cases from 1793-1820, growing more and more conscious that northern industry was seducing slaves. In 1798 it was held non-actionable for the defendant to say that the plaintiff had harbored his (defendant's) Negro.[90] By 1807 the only case of actual runaways involved slaves hired away by the British in the Revolutionary War.[91] But in 1812 a slave was sold at a reduced price because he was a notorious runaway.[92] In 1816 a runaway slave appeared among the crew of a ship hauled in for salvage.[95] In 1818 a suit for breach of warranty was grounded on the claim that the slaves sold were runaways and thieves.[96] In 1818 also, the country "had been in a state of alarm in consequence of the depredations of runaway Negroes."[97] The following year the slave stealing act was held to apply to all slaves, even though "his labor is voluntarily dispensed with by the owner . . . or when he has run away, and cannot command them."[98]

Here we see the parallel operations of the Industrial Revolution and the cotton gin, one of its products which reprieved the slave system. While the life of the latter was prolonged, the slave areas were becoming the poaching ground of those recruiting labor for the new industrial enterprises of the north.

Delaware, in 1816 provided that slaves taken as fugitives should be advertised by the sheriff for six weeks and if not claimed, "the sheriff is hereby directed to discharge such servant or slave from his custody, nor shall such servant or slave be liable to any of the costs and charges of his apprehension, commitment or prison fees."[98a] Strict rules of proof were now enacted to insure that anyone claiming a slave as a fugitive was really the owner. Without such proof the sheriff could not deliver the slave.[98b]

Georgia, likewise had no new fugitive slave laws after the invention of the cotton gin, nor were there any cases on the subject. Georgia was an anomaly among the states. In the 18th century, as the southernmost colony, Georgia had the problem of slaves escaping into Florida, which was then Spanish territory. But Spain was losing her energies and as the southernmost state, Georgia was the furthest removed from the new northern raids upon the slave areas to fill the demands of a budding industrial society.

There was no change in Louisiana during the remainder of the Spanish regime and the year (1802-3) when she was French again. In 1803 Louisiana became a territory of the United States,[99] and in 1812 a, state.[100] As might be expected, when Louisiana became U.S. territory, she had never heard of the Industrial Revolution. Outside of the cities, the country was still partly bush. Fugitive slaves still escaped there, rather than being enticed into a competing economic world by labor recruiters for northern infant industries. The law of 1804 recites "that whereas many times slaves run away and lie hid and lurking in swamps, woods, and other obscure places, killing hogs and committing other injuries to the inhabitants of this district etc. . . . "[101]

The Black Code of 1806[102] was almost wholly out of the 18th century. If a slave ran away, a master could denounce him and relieve himself of responsibility for the slave's acts.[103] The county judge had to keep a record of runaway slaves.[104] The jailer had to pay a reward for runaway slaves brought in [105] and then transfer them to New Orleans for employment and advertisement.[106] If the owner did not claim a slave within two years, he could be sold.[107]   Citizens were authorized to fire upon runaway slaves,[108] with or without an order from a justice of the peace.[109]

But by 1819, Louisiana, too, began to feel the effects of the incipient industrialization of the north. In that year the state imposed a penalty of from two to twenty years on all forms of slave stealing and aiding or concealing runaways.[110] The slave states were no longer faced with the simple desire of the slaves to runaway, but with demands of another economy to use them as wage laborers.

Quite consistent with the legislative history, fugitive slave cases begin in 1810.   The first involved a fugitive from Maryland to Louisiana.[111]   But in the same year McCARTY v. BAQUIERES[112] concerned a habitual runaway. In BAYON v. PREVOT,[113] decided in 1815, the slave escaped when taken out of prison for reasons of health.   In GUILLOR v. DOSSAT,[114] the slave escaped from jail where he was held pending litigation.   In LABRANCHE v. WATKINS,[115] the contest was between the slave's owner and the sheriff who had picked the slave up as a runaway, insufficiently advertised him, and used him as his own servant. In ZANISO v. HABINE,[116] the old regime still showed through. A slave was not presumed to be a runaway merely because he ran off to avoid being with a new master.

Vermont had been admitted as a state in 1791.[117a] She had no fugitive slave laws, nor were there any Vermont cases on the subject.

Kentucky was separated from Virginia and admitted as a state in 1792.[118]   Her constitution carried over the laws of Virginia.[119]   Her first general fugitive slave laws were passed in 1798.[120] While grandly entitled a compendium of all acts then in force, it consisted of only four sections providing: (1) a reward of ten shillings for taking up a runaway; (2) that, a runaway may be committed to jail and advertised; (3) that he may be hired out in the meantime, and that he may be sold one year after the last advertisement.   There was also provision for recovering the reward and a provision for jailer's fees.

At this stage, Kentucky was a clear example of pioneering slavery. The slave owners had gone into relatively unsettled country bringing their slaves with them.   However they were not confronted with a jungle, or anything approaching it. So the comprehensive law of fugitives said nothing about outlying slaves. On the other hand, they had not yet become the targets of agents raiding for northern industry. The comprehensive law merely deals with the mechanics of returning escaped slaves. It says nothing about stealing or enticing. The law of servants enacted the same year, was concerned only with slaves meeting together, and going from one plantation to another. The plantation economy[121] was newly developed in Kentucky at the time, (later 18th century) and was then without competition.

By 1807 the trend was still the same. The Kentucky pioneers were hungry for slaves. An act was passed imposing criminal penalties for stealing a free person and selling him as a slave.[122] So strikingly enough, the period closed in 1820 with a law for giving up fugitive slaves fleeing from other states to Kentucky.[123] Clearly, Kentucky was still a frontier slave state. She still had so few slaves, that despite her border location, the labor raiders from the northern industries did not find it worthwhile to operate there. On the other hand, being a frontier community, slaves from more concentrated slave areas escaped to Kentucky. This picture is borne out by the fact that up to and including 1820, there were no Kentucky cases dealing with fugitive slaves.

Tennessee was admitted to the U.S. in 1796.[124] In 1799 she imposed criminal penalties on persons persuading any servant or slave to absent himself from his master, or who harbored a runaway under any pretense whatever.[125] This was a full-fledged statute against enticing slaves away from their masters. It is not clear why this should have begun earlier in Tennessee than in Kentucky. One can only surmise that Tennessee was settled earlier, and consequently, there were enough slaves for northern industrial poachers to find it worthwhile to operate there.

By 1803, the tug-of-war for colored labor was in full swing. The legislature passed a law imposing penalties for uttering any words tending to induce slaves to insurrection, "or to absent himself or herself from the service of their masters."[126] The statutory law remained in this form until 1820.

In 1817 the courts clearly recognized the competition of wage labor, and sought to meet it by the measure used in the 18th century—excusing a runaway who has been mistreated.[127] The Supreme Court of Tennessee said in YOUNG V. FORGEY,[128] "the temporary owner shall operate with the care of preserving the life . . . of the slave committed to his charge . . . the evils to be apprehended from a different rule will be prevented . . . the slave will not be wantonly exposed to hardships which generate disorders. He will be furnished with food and raiment needful to such preservation, and cruelties which force him to absent himself will not be practiced upon him. It is because of this obligation of the temporary owner, that the price fixed for a year, is not much, if at all greater than the half price given for a day laborer for whom the employer is not bound to provide."

In 1820 it was held that a person could not be punished for harboring a runaway slave unless it was alleged that the harboring was without the owner's consent.[129]   This was a reversal of a judgment of conviction. The governing class was still inclined towards a strict construction of the anti-harboring laws when they impinged upon residents of Tennessee.

Ohio was admitted to the Union in 1803.[130]   Here for the first time was a new, non-slave state, which had not taken part in the revolutionary war. She was also the first westerly non-slave state. Ohio was part of the Northwest Territory, and therefore came under the Ordinance of 1787, which prohibited slavery but authorized the return of fugitive slaves from other parts of the union.[131]   Mrs. Archbald Dixon, in her book "The Missouri Compromise and its Repeal" said, "The new states formed out of this territory were peopled with unexampled rapidity, and at the time of the Missouri difficulty the northern states had such an increase in population over the Southern states as to give them a majority in the House of Representatives."[132]

When first admitted to statehood, Ohio tried to be very righteous about Negroes coming to reside in her territory. Those who came had to have certificates of freedom from some other states.[133]   Penalties were imposed for employing, harboring or secreting fugitive slaves.[134] Procedures were outlined for returning fugitives from other states,[135] but removal of alleged "fugitives" without going through all legal processes was severely punished.[136]   There were no Ohio cases on fugitive slaves between 1803 and 1820.

Indiana, admitted as a state in 1816,[137] had slavery before being acquired by the United States in 1778.[138]   While the area was sparsely settled,[138a] it is quite clear that there were slave holders among the French settlers.[139]   The Northwest Territory Ordinance made slavery illegal in Indiana after 1787. The first reaction was to petition for a suspension of the Ordinance in Indiana. The reasons were precisely those given at the time of the original settlement of the continent. The introduction of slaves would increase the rate of population, and speed up settlement.[140]   This was essentially the argument that slave labor was still much cheaper than free labor.

The language of the first (1796) petition to suspend the anti-slavery provisions of the Northwest Territory Ordinance said in part, "Your petitioners do not wish to increase the number of slaves already in the dominions of the United States. All they hope for or desire is, that they be permitted to introduce from any of the United States such persons, and such only as by the laws of such states are slaves therein." The Ordinance, they said, was "contrary not only to the interest, but almost to the existence of the country they inhabit, where laborers cannot be procured to assist in cultivating the ground under one dollar per day, exclusive of washing, lodging, and boarding; and where every kind of tradesmen are paid from a dollar and half to two dollars per day. Neither is there, at these exhorbitant prices, a sufficiency of hands to be got for the exigencies of the inhabitants, who, attached to their native soil, have chosen to encounter these and many other difficulties, rather than avoid them, by removing to the Spanish dominions, where slavery is permitted, and consequently the price of labor much lower."[141]

Similar petitions were repeated in 1800, 1804 and 1806, but always denied.[142] The adverse report in 1803 by John Randolph of Roanoke has already been quoted in Ch. I.[143] Taking a longer view based on the sad experiences of Virginia, he opposed starting the same process anew in Indiana. After 1807, such petitions ceased.[144] The territorial legislature had, however, gone ahead and enacted slave laws of its own. These were copies of ready-made statutes in states having a denser population and more slaves.[145]

Under the law of 1802, justices of county courts were empowered to hear complaints of masters against servants for desertion without good cause.[146] This assumed that the servant had already been brought back. Throughout this act it is also assumed that service was for a fixed term of years, not for life. In 1806, twenty-five stripes (welts) were imposed on any slave or servant found ten miles from his master's residence without a pass.[147] If the slave were found upon another's plantation, the latter could inflict ten lashes.[148] Those harboring a fugitive slave were fined $100 and those aiding an escape, up to five hundred.[149] The penalty for entertaining the slave of another without his permission was continued at $1 a day in 1807.[150]

Runaways were condemned to two hours in the pillory.[151] Stripes for straying more than ten miles from the master's plantation were raised to thirty-five.[152] By 1810, however, the personnel of the legislature had changed.[153] The Indiana Constitution of 1816 expressly forbade slavery.[154] By 1820, the only remaining fugitive slave law dealt with fugitives from other states coming into Indiana.[155]

Mississippi was the first newly admitted cotton state (1817).[157] She had all the strengths and all the weaknesses of the new slave system which the cotton gin, as part of the Industrial Revolution, engendered. But Mississippi's weaknesses far outweighed her strengths. Mississippi and Alabama constituted the wild South, almost exactly analogous to the wild West, but since its growth was cut short by the Civil War, the tradition was lost. The people of Mississippi were at the opposite pole from the sophisticated South Carolinians of the 18th century. They were cruel to their slaves, reflecting the cheapness of life on the frontier, but not necessarily racial hostility. To a large extent they had moved to Mississippi to escape creditors, taking their slaves as the most movable property and leaving everything else behind.[159]

On the eve of the civil War, Mississippi alone among the slave states had almost no bank capital.[160]   Before Mississippi became a state, twenty stripes were inflicted on a slave going from home without a pass. Anyone might apprehend such a slave.[161] Seditious speeches by a slave were punished with 39 stripes.[162]   Yet the threat of slaves being induced to run away was not thought very serious. A fine of twenty dollars was imposed on any white person harboring or entertaining a slave without the owner's consent.[163]   Mississippi was still largely unsettled and out of contact with the Industrial Revolution. The territorial code of 1807 was still concerned with "outlying slaves."[164]

Only five years later though, in 1812, the territory imposed the death penalty on any free person assisting slaves in rebellion.[165] In the same year the legislature passed an act pertaining to slaves charged with treason.[166] The gulf coast South was obviously getting nervous about the activities of northern raiders who might use former slaves as factory hands. Almost from the beginning, the burgeoning cotton kingdom was faced with its own destruction. An 1809 law provided that slaves be held as runaways if they were more than eight miles from their master's plantation without a pass, or if they had "lain out" for more than two days.[167] There were no Mississippi cases of fugitive slaves up to 1820.

Illinois was admitted as a state in 1818.[168]   Like Indiana, Illinois was formerly French territory. Its relatively few French inhabitants had held slaves under French law,[169] but American immigration—almost all from non-slave states—tipped the balance in favor of actual enforcement of the prohibition of slavery contained in Article VI of the Ordinance of 1787.[170]   The increase in population of the non-slave states, where nearly the entire stream of European immigrants went, had already begun to make itself felt.[171]

When Illinois first passed her own laws as a territory in 1812, she simply incorporated the Indiana laws as of 1809.[172] This included limited fugitive slave laws.[173] Still, before it was admitted as a state in 1818, Illinois tried to devise ways to bring in slaves as laborers in manufacturing establishments. The preamble to the Act of 1814,[174] says: "Whereas the erection of wells and other valuable improvements are greatly retarded in this territory from want of laborers, and whereas experience has also proved that the manufacture of salt in particular, in the United States cannot be successfully carried on by white laborers, and it being in the interest of every description of inhabitants to afford every facility to the most extensive manufacture of that article, so necessary to them all, as the most natural means of obtaining a certainty of the necessary supplies thereof at the lowest price."[175]

The Illinois Territory was not yet abreast of the times in its maneuver. Slaves could still be imported as slaves for use in industry. The territory simply had not yet hit upon the brilliant idea of "freeing" slaves in order to employ them in manufacturing.

The Illinois Territory laws authorized justices of the peace to punish fugitives with not more than 35 stripes. Any person was authorized to bring before a justice of the peace any slave found more than 10 miles from his master's "tenement". The justice then had power to inflict the stripes at his discretion.[176] A slave at another's dwelling without a pass was subject to ten lashes, without court order,[177] and the person harboring the slave was fined up to $100.[178] Anyone assisting a servant to abscond was fined $500.[179] These laws merely reproduced the statutes of Indiana.[180] After admission as a state, Illinois honored the Fugitive Slave Act of 1793,[181] but nothing more. There were no Illinois cases up to 1820.

The next year, 1819, saw the admission of Alabama as a state.[182] While still a territory, Alabama imposed up to 20 stripes on any slave wandering off the master's tenement without a pass,[183] and up to ten stripes on any slave found on the plantation of another.[184] The slaveowner was likewise penalized for allowing his slaves to wander or for permitting on his plantation more than five of another's slaves.[185] This was the same basic code originally introduced in Illinois and Indiana.

Like Mississippi, Alabama was largely a wilderness, and had the problem of "outlying" slaves. They could be seized by anyone, who then became entitled to a $30 reward. This was payable out of the public treasury. The owner had to reimburse the territory for only 3/4.[186] A slave jailed as a runaway and not claimed by the owner for six months, could be sold at public auction.[187] The owner could redeem the purchase price but not the slave.[188] There were no Alabama cases on fugitive slaves up to 1820.

Maine was admitted in 1820,[189] as the non-slave state paired to the contemplated admission of Missouri as a slave state. The fact that this "rule" had been introduced showed the direction of events. Although the Industrial Revolution had brought the cotton gin, and with it the cotton kingdom worked by slave labor, its impetus to industrial, non-slave regions was greater. The cotton kingdom could not depend upon events to take their course. The foreboding was already there, that if left to run their course, events in the wake of the Industrial Revolution would destroy the very cotton kingdom which that revolution had produced. So, from the moment of its birth, the cotton kingdom had death staring it in the face.

Before being admitted as a state, Maine had been a part of Massachusetts.[190] There were no separate statutes for Maine up to the time of her admission, nor were there any cases on fugitive slaves.

Missouri was part of the Louisiana Purchase, and had slavery before becoming part of the United States.[191] The laws of the District of Louisiana governed the territory at first, empowering overseers to give 10 lashes to slaves visiting other plantations without a pass.[192] These laws likewise provided for the apprehension of outlying slaves on warrants issued by justices of the peace.[193] The act of 1817 provided for taking before a justice of the peace, slaves travelling without a pass, and that a reward of $5 plus expenses be given for apprehended runaway slaves, unless the owner offered a flat $10. Runaways were to be sold if no owner claimed them.[194] Missouri had no further statutes covering fugitive slave matters before her admission as a state in 1820.

The Missouri Compromise of 1820 marked the point where the non-slave states had gained a numerical preponderance in the House of Representatives. Not even the political device of admitting slave and non-slave states in pairs had been enough to check the population growth of the latter. Less then thirty years after the invention of the cotton gin, the impetus it first seemed to give to the slave system proved to be delusory. The same developments which gave the slave economy a second wind, now forced it to fight for dear life.

The situation lasted thirty years longer, until the admission of California in the Compromise of 1850. When California was admitted by itself and unpaired as a non-slave state, it broke the Missouri Compromise and gave the non-slave states a majority in the U.S. Senate. The attempt to admit additional slave states through the Kansas-Nebraska bill[195b] was merely "idealization of an ephemeral technique."[196] The cotton kingdom was doomed to extinction by the same forces which had brought it into being, because they induced a far faster growth in the competing industrial and wage economy.

DISCIPLINE

The methods of discipline over slaves and the patrol system became crystallized in the early part of the 18th century. Discipline had to be administered so that it caused the slaves to lose as little time as possible from their work. This necessity, if anything, became aggravated with the ending of the legal slave trade in 1808. The patrol system, like the laws against fugitive slaves, had to cope with the same problem; the systematic recruiting of slaves as wage employees in northern industries.

Virginia continued her old system of enforcing corporal punishment by prohibiting its abuse. Thus, castration of slaves was forbidden except for an attempt to ravish a white woman.[197] In other instances, Virginia retained direct provisions for corporal punishment, as the infliction of a maximum of 30 lashes against any Negro (slave or free) lifting his hand against a white person, except in his own defense.[198] Riots, routs and unlawful assemblies of slaves were punished with stripes under the general slave act of 1819.[199] The use of abusive language toward a white person by either a free Negro or slave was also punished by a maximum of 30 lashes.[200]

Captains of vessels were sometimes slaves. If any slave captain received on board or traded with another slave without the consent of the latter's master, the skipper-slave was subject to 39 lashes.[201] Slaves found guilty of hog stealing received 39 lashes for the first offense. For the second they had to stand for two hours in the pillory with both ears nailed thereto and then cut loose from the nails.[202] For a third offense the slave as "adjudged a felon".[203] A slave attempting to ravish a white woman was castrated.[204]

There was not a single Virginia case on the corporal punishment of a slave in the period 1793-1820.[204a] Virginia thus demonstrates its transition from a slave-using to a slave-breeding state. Slaves who required severe measures of control were sold south. The most tractable were kept at home.

Maryland likewise retained her laws inflicting corporal punishment but gradually ceased to use them. Slavery fell into disuse and with it the problem of disciplining slaves. Slaves were given up to 39 lashes if they carried a gun or other weapon without the owner's consent.[205]

The Maryland law of 1809 seemed to express revulsion against corporal punishment on the one hand and reasons for retaining it on the other, i.e., not to take the slave away from his work for any considerable length of time. For all crimes ranging from robbery to rebellion, the judge hearing the case was given discretion to impose either imprisonment or flogging up to 100 lashes.[206] The third choice given the judge, that of sentencing the slave to banishment, shows the simultaneous pull of the old institutions of slavery on the one hand, the new urge to get rid of it entirely, plus the nineteenth century tendency toward milder penalties.[207]

Maryland took a step backward in 1818, when all laws authorizing confinement of slaves in the penitentiary were repealed, and flogging up to 40 lashes was substituted.[209] Maryland, as a border state could not make up its mind whether to continue with the slave system or attempt to industrialize, an ambivalence which continued until the passage of the XIIIth Amendment. There were no Maryland cases on corporal punishment of slaves between 1793 and 1820. As in Virginia, this reflects the declining importance of slavery in a tobacco growing state.

Not only did New York have no corporal punishment for slaves between 1793 and 1820, but the punishment for serious crimes was transportation out of the state.[210] This is a good illustration of the policy of keeping slaves who were easily manageable and selling the troublesome ones out of the state.

New Jersey at first imposed whipping at the master's option,[211] but later established workhouses for slaves.[212] Enough laborers were by then available so that imprisonment could be used as punishment. It was no longer necessary to keep a slave at work while he was under going punishment. Now the northern states were beginning to make effective use of the principle that "slave labor is dearer than free labor whenever abundance of free labor can be procured."[213] In 1800, New Jersey, like New York a few years later, underlined the nature of the changed situation by providing that slaves convicted of a crime could be transported out of the state.[214] The wage ("free") states were already getting more docile labor, but the cotton states were short of workers so they were willing to use convicts from the north.

Massachusetts had liberated all her slaves in 1781.[215] There were accordingly, neither statutes nor cases on corporal punishment of slaves after 1793. Connecticut passed a series of statutes repealing the corporal punishment of slaves before the 18th century came to an end. The laws of 1797 abolished corporal punishment for defamation,[216] stealing[217] by slaves, their being at large after 9 PM without an order from their master,[218] and for disturbing the peace.[219]

Repeals of this kind make clear what was happening. The population of New England had already become sufficiently dense so that discipline could be maintained by the effortless and cost-free device of firing an employee. There was no longer any need for time consuming and expensive corporal discipline. The abolition of corporal punishment also had the appearance of being more humane, so the practical advantages happened to coincide with humanitarian concerns.

In Rhode Island corporal punishment had been falling into disuse before 1793.[220] There were neither new statutes nor judicial decisions on the subject during the period 1793-1820. In New Hampshire, slavery, and with it corporal punishment, had disappeared between 1793 and 1820. Pennsylvania had no new laws on corporal punishment for slaves, but did not repeal existing laws.[221]   There were however, no Pennsylvania cases on corporal punishment of slaves during this period. North Carolina continued corporal punishment. An Act of 1818 inflicted 39 lashes on any Negro convicted of selling spiritous liquors.[222]   As in the past, the exercise of force was allowed but had to be reasonable.[223]

South Carolina also continued to impose corporal punishment on slaves. The patrol law of 1800[279] authorized patrollers to inflict up to 20 lashes on members of any unlawful Assembly. Interestingly enough, there were no South Carolina cases directly involving physical chastisement of slaves in the period 1792-1820. This indicates that South Carolina was still a caste society in which everyone pretty much accepted their place. The only cases touching the subject were actions for undue correction, usually civil.[226]   The charge was invariably sustained, except once, where it was held barred by limitations.

Delaware continued corporal punishment. Slaves attempting to commit rape on white women received 39 lashes and had to stand in the pillory for one hour with ears nailed to the posts. The soft part of the ears were then cut off.[227]   For assault and battery, they received 39 lashes.[228]   Nevertheless imprisonment also began to appear as a penalty showing that Delaware was not pressed for slave labor. In 1798 the state imposed a jail sentence of 48 hours on slaves coming into town from outside on the day of annual elections.[228a] There were no cases on corporal punishment of slaves. So while the state followed the old pattern in her statutes, the institution was dying out.

Georgia retained corporal punishment by limiting its abuse. Persons other than the owner were fined or imprisoned (or both) for beating, whipping, or wounding a slave.[229]   Fine or imprisonment at the discretion of the court was meted out to owners who "brutally beat" their slaves by "unnecessary and excessive whipping."[230] As in the past, and as in other states, corporal punishment was prohibited if excessive. Article IV, Section 12, of the Constitution in force in 1817 penalized killing of a slave unless it happened by accident in the course of giving moderate correction.[231]   There were no Georgia cases on the subject during the period 1793-1820.[232]

Louisiana was acquired by the United States in 1803. During the following year, the territory enacted laws empowering a justice of the peace to order stripes or lashes for a slave straying from his master's plantation without a pass,[233] for entering the plantation of another owner without a pass,[233a] for carrying weapons,[234] and for riots, routs and unlawful assemblies.[235]   Both white persons and free Negroes were lashed if they were unable to pay the fine for harboring or entertaining a slave without the master's consent.[236]

Any person was liable to 39 lashes if he could not pay the fine for selling to, or buying or receiving from a slave.[237] A slave was given up to thirty-nine lashes for lifting his or her hand against "any person not being a Negro or Mulatto," except in cases of self-defense against wanton assault.[238] The "Black Code" was enacted in 1806.[239] It imposed twenty-five lashes on a slave found on horseback without a permit.[240] Any slave absent from his usual place of work or residence, if resisting arrest, was subject to any physical penalty short of death.[241] Insubordination against an overseer drew twenty-five lashes; and fifty lashes if it resulted in bloodshed to the overseer.[242]

This statute, which could also condemn slaves to work in the fields two to four years with chains around their legs, emphasized the need of the plantation system to devise punishments which did not withdraw the slaves from their work. In 1807, punishment was placed at the entire discretion of the judges.[242a] Striking a white person was punished at the discretion of the judges for the first or second offense,[243] and usually included corporal punishment.

Cases under the American regime begin in 1809.[244] OGDEN v BLACKMAN,[245] decided in 1814, imposed corporal punishment on the slave for larceny, and fined the master. This was the only Louisiana case involving physical punishment during the period 1793-1820, except MARTINEAU v. HOOPER,[246] where the slave was said to be rebellious, and attempting to escape. The inference to be drawn, is that Louisiana, like South Carolina, had up until this time, a caste society in which everyone tended to accept his or her caste.[247]

Vermont had no slavery,[247a] and no laws for the physical punishment of slaves.

During the 1793-1820 period, Kentucky became important as a new slave state. Her chief crop, however, was tobacco, not cotton. Since Virginia had already overproduced tobacco, this foreshadowed the incomplete establishment of slavery in the state. Nevertheless at the beginning, the state seemed to have all the characteristics of a frontier slave state which took its legal code ready-made from an older state, Virginia. Slaves straying from house without a pass were punished with stripes;[248] those coming on to the plantations of others received 10 lashes;[249] those carrying arms up to 39 lashes;[250] riots, routs, etc., drew stripes at the discretion of the justice of the peace.[251] A fine of 15 shillings or twenty lashes was inflicted on anyone present at an unlawful meeting of slaves.[252] Slaves offering to sell any commodity without their master's leave received ten lashes.[253] Lifting a hand against any person not a Negro was punished with 30 lashes,[254] giving false testimony with 39 lashes.[255]

In 1802 all non-capital crimes were made punishable by not more than 39 lashes.[255a] Since the same law provided that only free persons should be confined in the penitentiary, this again revealed the basis of all slave punishments—to punish without removing the slave from his work. An 1807 law decreed that all crimes punishable with stripes should be deemed misdemeanors.[256] Another act of 1807 also revealed the labor shortage problem which the slave system was intended to meet. The preamble states that "considerable inconvenience has resulted to slaves and slave holders in this commonwealth, from the length of time for which slaves accused of certain crimes have under present law been confined in prison." For which reason the owner was given the right to bail out his slave.[256a]

In 1811, up to 100 stripes were imposed for advising murder.[257] In 1815, thirty-nine lashes were given for stopping salt water or filling up wells.[258] SMITH v. HARRIS,[259a] an unsuccessful civil action by an owner against a third party for shooting a slave claimed to be in a rebellion, was the only case on the subject during this period. Probably many more never got before a court, because of the frontier nature of the community.

Tennessee was much the same as Kentucky, with the difference that the western part of the state was suitable for cotton. She therefore developed as a conventional slave state on the frontier. Trading on a forged pass drew up to 39 lashes;[260] riots, routs, unlawful assemblies, seditious speeches or insulting language to any white person, received stripes at the discretion of the court.[261] In this provision one sees the reaction of one of the northernmost slave states against activities designed to recruit slaves as wage laborers in northern industry. The same law imposed fifteen stripes on slaves found in "Negro houses and suspected places," or off their own plantation without a pass in the nightime.[262]

In 1813, five to thirty lashes were inflicted on a slave selling liquor without a written permit from his "master or controller".[263] In the town of Greenville, the constable was authorized to apprehend and the chairman or board of commissioners to give not more than ten lashes to any slave living in the country but found strolling in the streets of the town "after night or on sabbath days," unless with a pass, or going to or attending church services.[264]

The North Carolina Act of 1741,[265] providing for capital punishment was changed in 1815 to give the three-judge trial court almost unlimited authority to fix sentences.[266] This unquestionably included corporal punishment, so specified penalities in other laws were expressly continued in force.[267]   There were no Tennessee cases on corporal punishment of slaves through 1820.

Ohio, being part of the Northwest Territory from which slavery was excluded, had no laws imposing physical punishment on slaves, nor were there any Ohio cases on slavery through 1820.

We have already shown how Indiana was the product of the original, sparse French settlement, combined with later mutually antagonistic immigration from the south and from the east.   The result was a temporary system of slavery, despite the prohibitions of the Ordinance of 1787. As physical punishment existed for free persons,[268] there was no difficulty in applying it to slaves. The territorial law of 1802 inflicted stripes on disorderly "servants."[269] Persons (evidently white) dealing with slaves received 39 lashes[270] and generally, where free persons were punishable by fine, "servants" were punished by whipping— twenty lashes for every $8, but not more than 40 lashes all told.[271]

In 1806, being ten miles from "the tenement of his or her master" without a pass brought up to twenty-five stripes;[272] being upon the plantation or in the dwelling house of another master entailed ten lashes;[273] riots, routs and unlawful assembly, up to 39 stripes.[274] The following year, a servant assaulting a master was given ten stripes.[275] The number of stripes inflicted on lazy or disorderly servants, or servants refusing to work was put exclusively at the discretion of the trial judge.[276]   The penalty of up to 39 lashes on white persons for dealing with servants was continued.[277] Runaways using a forged pass were pilloried for two hours, if unable to pay the fine of $30, and given 39 lashes on failure to pay the fine or give security therefore.[278]

The punishment meted out to slave or servant for being ten miles away from his master's plantation was later raised to 35 stripes.[279] The punishment for being on another master's plantation without a pass and for riots, routs and unlawful assemblies were continued.[280]   As the compiler notes, the composition of the Indiana territorial legislature had changed by 1820,[281] and there were no further laws of this kind. In 1818, Indiana repealed her existing apprentice laws. [282] The Constitition of 1816, on which the State was admitted, forbade slavery.[283]   There were no Indiana cases during this period.

Mississippi was a frontier state, but also a heavily populated slave state, and as such, it enforced corporal punishment on its slaves. In 1807, the territory, for all non-capital offenses, prescribed burning in the hand, or such lesser corporal punishment "as the court shall deem fit."[284] The punishment for perjury "without further trial" was having one ear nailed to the pillory for an hour and then cut off. Then the other ear was nailed to the pillory for an hour and cut off,[285] and the victim then received 39 lashes besides.[286]   This kind of terror, aimed at the testimony of slaves,[287] was clearly designed to make them say what the judge and jury of slaveholders wanted them to say.

Slaves away from home without a pass received twenty stripes;[288] those on the plantation of another without a pass, ten lashes;[289] thirty-nine lashes for carrying weapons illegally;[290] and for riots, routs and unlawful assemblies;[291] ten lashes for trading illegally;[292] slaves keeping dogs, twenty-five lashes;[293] up to twenty lashes for lifting his or her hand in opposition to any white person,[294] and up to 30 lashes were given for petty larceny.[295]   One hundred stripes was made the limit on all offenses not capital.   More than 39 lashes were to be given only with the concurrence of the two slaveholders[296] trying the case with the justice of the peace.

Stripes or burning could be inflicted on a slave tried for a capital offense but found guilty of something less.[297]   Selling articles without the master's written consent brought ten lashes,[298] and patrols were authorized to administer not more than fifteen lashes to slaves found "assembled or strolling without a pass."[299]

The one Mississippi case of this period repeats the old colonial pattern.   Corporal punishment was recognized by curbing its abuse.   "In vain shall we look for any law passed by the philanthropic legislature of this state, giving even the master, much less a stranger, power over the life of a slave."[300]

Illinois, with no slavery of her own,[300a] originally duplicated the laws of Indiana Territory.   Corporal punishment was prescribed for free Negroes or Mulattoes immigrating into the territory,[301] or those convicted of stealing or "harbouring runaway Negroes or Mulattoes or slaves belonging to persons either in this territory or elsewhere".[302] Persons trading with "servants" and unable to pay the fine received 39 lashes. [303]

Before Illinois' statehood, the Indiana statutes were in force, providing that where free persons were punishable by fine, servants should be punished by whipping at the rate of 10 lashes for every eight dollars, but with forty lashes as the maximum.[304]   Runaways using a forged certificate of freedom had to stand two hours in the pillory,[305] but came away with their ears. Section 13, of the Act of 1815, gave up to 35 stripes to any servant or slave found more than 10 miles from his master's tenement without a pass, Section 14 inflicted up to 10 lashes for being on another's plantation, and Section 15 gave up to 39 stripes for riots, routs or unlawful assemblies.   These were the only provisions attempting to punish slaves directly as such.[306]

The Act of 1808 continued the punishment for unlawful assemblies.[307]   Even after the state's admission in 1818 with a constitution forbidding slavery,[308] the law retained stripes for lazy or disorderly servants, or servants guilty of misbehavior, [309] and also kept the provisions that allowed free persons to be punished by fine, but made servants and slaves punishable by whipping.[310]

Alabama, like Mississippi, was a frontier slave state, and used corporal punishment on slaves. The Constitution of 1819 recognized corporal punishment by restricting it. "The general assembly . . . shall have full power . . . to obligate the owners of slaves . . . to abstain from all injuries extending to life or limb, and in case of their neglect or refusal to comply with such laws to have such slave or slaves sold for the benefit of the owner or owners."[314]

Territorial statutes had followed the line of burning the hand,[315] or "such other and corporal punishment as the Court shall think fit to inflict". Also the punishment for perjury was the same as in Mississippi, "without further trial" to have an ear nailed to the pillory for an hour and then cut off. Then the same for the other ear, and 39 lashes to boot.[316]   Hunting with fire drew 39 lashes,[317] wandering off the master's tenement without a pass, 20 stripes,[318] being on the plantation of another, ten stripes;[319] carrying a gun, powder, shot or club up to 39 lashes,[320] as did unlawful assemblies, riots or routs.[321]   Keeping dogs was punished with twenty-five stripes. [322] Lifting a hand against a white person got up to 20 lashes. [323]

As in Mississippi, there was no exception for self-defense, but the maximum penalty was less than in the more settled states.[324]   This provision was repealed in 1814.[325] First offense could be punished by branding in the face or breast.[326] Patrols were authorized to administer up to fifteen lashes to any slave found assembled or strolling without a pass.[327]   There were no Alabama cases on corporal punishment up to 1820.

Maine had been split off from Massachusetts, which had no slavery since 1781, and had no laws for corporal punishment of slaves, nor were there any cases.

Missouri, part of the Louisiana purchase, and admitted as a slave state by the Missouri Compromise, had the conventional slave statutes, including corporal punishment. At first the territory was governed by the laws of the District of Louisiana.[328]   These included stripes for being at large without a pass,[329] ten lashes for visiting another plantation without a pass;[330] up to 39 lashes for carrying arms,[331] and stripes at the discretion of the justice of the peace for riots, routs, unlawful assemblies or seditious speeches. [332]

White persons, free Negroes or Mulattoes were given up to twenty lashes if found at an unlawful meeting of slaves, and unable to pay the fine.[333] A maximum of 39 lashes was meted out to persons trading with slaves without the owner's consent, and unable to pay the fine.[334] Lifting a hand against a white person drew 39 lashes, but was excused in case of self-defense.[335] Missouri here followed Kentucky and Virginia rather than the pioneer gulf states.

PATROLS

Patrols were an adjunct of large plantations. They moved in where cotton was established and tended to disappear in the states which became slave-breeding states or which slowly abandoned slavery.

Virginia revised and re-enacted her patrol laws in 1819.[336] Patrols were appointed by the Justices of the Peace and had to report to them.[337] Actual patrol riding and visitation of slave houses was done only "once in every month, or oftener (if thereto required by such officer)."[338] They were always obligated to take slaves before a Justice of the Peace to receive punishment. The patrollers were not authorized to administer it themselves.[339] The court receiving the report could also authorize payment of the patrol at the rate of seventy-five cents for every twelve hours.[340] Fines were imposed on officers and sergeants for failure to appoint patrollers.[341]

The condition that only the Justices of the Peace, and not the patrol itself could chastise slaves, shows the contraction of the patrol system in Virginia. Characteristically, there were no Virginia patrol cases during this period. The only case even remotely touching the subject, holds that where the right to visit slave quarters was given by the owner to one person, it could not be delegated.[342]

Maryland had had no system of patrols before 1793[343] and introduced none afterwards. In 1806 the constable was authorized to "visit" suspected places in raiding against illegal dogs and guns.[344] That was all. The same was true of New York, New Jersey, Massachusetts, Connecticut, Rhode Island, New Hampshire, Vermont and Pennsylvania, Delaware, Maine, Ohio, Indiana and Illinois. They had no patrols before 1793,[345] and none after.

North Carolina continued on her difficult path of trying to keep up with the other slave states. In 1794 it tried to tempt patrollers with exemption from jury duty, roadwork, the payment of all county and parish taxes of forty shillings, and fees in addition to regular compensation of one-half the penalties recovered.[346] They could directly inflict up to fifteen lashes "on slaves found off owners' plantations, or travelling on Sunday or other unreasonable times."[347]

This provision showed that the governing class in North Carolina was borrowing from the states to the south rather than from Virginia.[348] Patrols of militia were also used to oppose possible slave insurrections.[349] In 1802 another act was passed,[350] levying a tax per slave to pay the patrollers.

The only case on patrols during this period was RICHARDSON v. SALTAR[351] which showed a tendency to keep patrols strictly within their legal limits. The defendant was a member of a patrol, but he involved himself with a posse, none of whom were patrollers. They beat and injured the plaintiff's slave allegedly for exhibiting an insufficient pass. The court held that:

> Saltar had not the right to exercise the powers of a pa-
> troller by himself, and as the other defendants were pre-
> sent aiding and abetting him in an unlawful act, they
> were all guilty of trespass.[352]

South Carolina, keeping her old status as a large plantation state, also kept the patrol system. In 1800 the Legislature found that existing laws were insufficient to keep slaves, free Negroes and Mulattoes and Mestizoes in subjection. [353] The patrol was authorized to inflict direct punishment, according to the patrol laws, on members of any religious meeting before sunrise or after sunset. [354] However there was now a noticeable reluctance to ride patrol. The Sourth Carolina cavalier society of the 18th century was not what it used to be. It was assumed that those liable for patrol duty might send substitutes. If they neither sent a substitute nor came themselves, they were fined two dollars;[355] failure to make out a list of patrol detachments resulted in an $8 fine. [355a]

Patrollers were exempted from legal responsibility for exceeding their authority.[356] In 1802, however, religious meetings after 9 PM were again withdrawn from patrol jurisdiction if the majority of the meeting were white.[357] Here is a return to 18th century South Carolina with all of her paradoxes. Some of the ruling element wanted to put late religious meetings under patrol authority, evidently suspecting that religious meetings were a cover for rebellious meetings. But a contrary current prevailed.

Late religious services were allowed if the majority of the congregation was white. Master and slave were evidently present at the same church service. The caste lines were still so strong that there was no segregation. Unsegregated gatherings were therefore promoted to the status of a legal requirement, avoiding the more drastic measure of patrol supervision. The ruling class in conflict with itself, and the conflict between the ruling class and other sectors of the community were mirrored in BELL v. GRAHAM,[358] one of the most interesting of all American cases on slavery.

A patrol broke up a mixed church meeting. Some years before, a Methodist society had established a church at Shady Grove. They had regular meetings, numerously attended by the black population as well as the white. For some time preceding the occurrence which gave rise to this action, the patrol, or persons assuming that character, had frequently come on the days of worship, for the purpose of exercising their office on slaves who were without passes, and on some occasions, conducted themselves in such a manner as to produce the greatest disturbance during public worship, in consequence of which the regular travelling preachers had refused to attend it, and it was left in charge of defendant, the class leader who continued the regular meetings.[359] "It was impossible to ascertain from the evidence whether the congregation which consisted of thirty or forty persons, was constituted of a majority of blacks or whites."[360] The defendant became informer against the patrol members before the grand jury. On the grand jury's refusal to return an indictment, a patrol member sued the defendant for malicious prosecution. "The jury, contrary to the express charge of the presiding judge, found a verdict for the plaintiff for $56.25."[361] The Supreme Court of South Carolina unanimously reversed the judgment.

Here we see the conflict between the judges—members of the ruling class—on the one side, and other citizens of South Carolina on the other. Since no slave was a party to the proceedings, the jury did not have to consist of slaveowners. But the conflict between the judges and the jury was not the whole story. While the patrol was raiding the meeting:

> They also caught several othes slaves near the house whom they threatened and prepared to whip, but dismissed, on the entreaties of the defendant, and the tears of a lady who interceded for them. [362]

And it must be remembered that the patrol was itself an instrument of the rulers of the state.

Yet where the various elements clash, the final decision by the Supreme Court is in favor of free association of the castes. For the judgment of malicious prosecution was reversed even though the court could not determine whether the majority of the meeting was black or white. The comments of the Supreme Court merit quoting at length:

> But feeble indeed, would be the protection of our inestimable constitution, which professes to secure to us this privilege freedom of worship if a petty patrol

officer was permitted to mar and disturb our devotions at his pleasure, and with impunity.

There is no question about the propriety of the policy which has been adopted, in a long series of legislation, in relation to this unfortunate class of the community, and that it daily becomes more and more necessary to keep them in proper subjection by a strict enforcement of the laws relating to them, and that it is the indisputable duty of the patrol to carry them into execution; but they are not at liberty to overleap the bounds which these laws prescribe to them, and particularly where such a stretch of power is productive of injury or inconvenience to the worthy citizens of the state.

A subsequent act, in 1803 (260, sec. 26, 2 Faust 505) reciting that certain religious societies had petitioned for a repeal of a part of the above clause, provides that it shall not thereafter be lawful for any person or persons to break into any place of meeting, wherein should be assembled the members of any religious society, at any time before nine o'clock in the evening, provided a majority of them should be white persons; or otherwise to disturb their devotions, unless by a warrant from a magistrate, if one resides within three miles.

In the case under consideration, the meeting was at a public meeting house, the doors of which were open, and in the midst of day. But it was strongly argued, on the trial below, that the act of 1803, gave that power, where a majority of the congregation consisted of persons of colour. That act was intended to remedy a supposed severity which grew out of the act of 1800, and was founded on the well-known custom of the Methodist Society to hold their class meetings with closed doors, on some occasions, after night; and it would indeed, be a strange anomaly in legislation to legalize an evil which it was their avowed intention to prevent. The act itself warrants no such construction.

It follows, therefore, that the prosecution against plaintiff, so far from being devoid of probable cause, and fraught with malice, was well founded; and I have no hesitation is saying that the plaintiff ought to have been

> convicted, if the Grand Jury had found the bill. The
> congregation had suffered a series of insults from a
> particular class of persons assuming to themselves the
> right of disturbing their assemblies, and upon being
> advised that they were amenable to the laws, the
> plaintiff, the head of the little flock, reluctantly
> consented to take upon himself the office of prosecutor;
> the object of which was to shield them from further
> molestation.

The court's language sharply portrays the caste nature of South
Carolina society at this time. Patrols had evidently been downgraded to
a more special employment, from the position which they had occupied
in the middle of the 18th century.[363] Nothing brings out the caste-
structure of South Carolina better than three of the court's
expressions: The supercilious reference to "a petty patrol officer", the
solicitude for the situation "where such a stretch of power is productive
of injury or inconvenience to the worthy citizens of the state," and the
paternalistic finale:

> The congregation had suffered a series of insults from a
> particular class of persons, assuming to themselves the
> right of disturbing their assemblies; the plaintiff, the
> head of the little flock, reluctantly consented to take
> upon himself the office of prosecutor.

And all this was said on behalf of an unsegregated church service. But it
marks the end of an era.

HOGG v. KELLER[364] likewise is stricter against the patrol than
against the slave or his owner. If the slave had a pass it was construed
liberally in favor of sufficiency.[365] But the fear of slave insurrection
was gradually creeping upon the South Carolina slaveholders. It had
been foreshadowed by the ominous words in BELL v. GRAHAM[366] "that
it daily becomes more and more necessary to keep them in proper
subjection by a strict enforcement of the laws relating to them, and that
it is the indispensable duty of the patrol to carry them into execution."

Two years after BELL v. GRAHAM, the South Carolina Supreme
Court said in GIST v. COLE[367] that:

> the patrol law ought to be considered as one of the
> safeguards of the people of South Carolina, for the
> protection of their dwellings, and as security against
> insurrection, a danger of such nature that it never can or

ought to be lost sight of in the southern states. It may justly be considered as a branch of our militia system.[368]

This ended the period 1793-1820. South Carolina, though nowhere near the non-slave border, had begun to take notice of the northern slave raiders. Gone was her haughty and complacent self-confidence. For the first time in her history, South Carolina had become scared.

Georgia, having modeled her patrol system on that of South Carolina,[369] found her citizens shirking such service.[370] An attempt was made to get the patrol law working, with more severe penalties on patrollers and captains of patrols.[371] Louisiana established contingents for the policing of slaves, but not as they were known in the states of English origin. Interestingly enough, these contingents included bodies of free Negroes. Inclusion of free Negroes in the militia was begun in the War of 1812,[372] and later spread to the policing of slaves.

In 1815, after the war with England was over, it was observed "that the policing of slaves was extremely neglected in the counties for want of persons to oversee these plantations where there are a great number of slaves".[373] Henceforth, the owner was obligated to keep on the plantation one white man for every thirty slaves.[374] The duty of periodic visitation was assigned to the parish judge.[375] (This makes visitation and inspection much more civilian functions than in the garrison state of South Carolina or the other originally English states).

Violations were punished by a fine ranging from $100.00 to $500.00.[376] In 1815 "an auxiliary troop of free men of color" was set up in Natchituches. It was "to be employed in maintaining a good police;" was under the immediate orders of the commanding officer of the militia, and was not to exceed 80 men.[378] There were no Louisiana cases involving patrols or their equivalent during the period 1793-1820. The state was far enough away from the northern manufacturing states, that unlike Carolina, she had yet to become aware of the activities of northern business to recruit slaves as wage laborers.

Kentucky adopted the sparse patrol laws of Virginia.[379] In 1813 county courts were empowered to fix patrol districts.[380] Otherwise there was no legislation, showing that in Kentucky, patrols were of little importance. Tennessee maintained patrols, having them appointed by captains of militia.[381] Towns also were obligated to appoint patrols, who had the usual duties of inspecting slave houses and had to ride nightly.[382] (Contrast this with the Louisiana system where the duty of making inspections was given to a judge, and had to be performed only once a month.)[383] The justice of the peace decided whether a patrol was necessary.[384] There were no Tennesssee cases on patrols during this period, indicating either that the subject was not of much practical importance, or that Tennessee was still enough of a frontier state that few cases got to court.

Mississippi, a flat country in the Mississippi Valley, one of the most important of the new cotton states, with large plantations, naturally adopted the system of patrols. They were established by the Act of 1809.[385] Mississippi followed the new trend which was almost opposite to that of the South Carolina cavaliers in the 18th century. Patrol-riding was now a burdensome duty imposed on the lower orders. Persons of the rank of captain or above were exempted. Those who are not, were permitted to send a substitute if they could.[386]

Lesser offenses could be dealt with by the patrols directly. For more serious ones they had to take the slaves before a Justice of the Peace.[387] They were also authorized to kill dogs kept by Negroes.[388] Lists of persons eligible for patrol duty had to be furnished by militia captains[389] who also had to get the patrol together.[390] These duties were enforced by penalties on the members of the patrols[391] as well as on the patrol captains.[392] Here we see again the enormous chasm between the new cotton states and South Carolina.

Eighteenth century South Carolina was much like feudal Europe, with a military caste engaged in large scale agriculture. But Mississippi had an essentially commercial population eager to make money out of cotton, adopting the slave sytem because it was at hand, ready made, but whose individual members had to be forced to take the quasi-military measures necessary to make that system work.

Alabama set up a patrol system essentially like that of Mississippi. Like the Mississippi statutes of 1809,[393] the Alabama law of 1812[394] required militia captains to make lists of those eligible for patrol duty and imposed penalties both on members of the patrol and patrol captains for failure to attend or perform.

MAXIMUM HOURS OF LABOR

States which had no maximum hour laws for slaves before 1793,[395] had none after that date. States which did not have slavery felt themselves free from such annoying obligations. The problem of maximum hour laws for wage workers was not to come up again seriously until the 20th century. In the meantime, those states which had maximum hour laws earlier in the 18th century continued them. Maximum hour laws were clearly relics from the 18th century.

Maryland had no new maximum hour laws for slaves. The old "reasonable limits" formula[396] was retained. South Carolina likewise kept her 18th century fifteen hour act[397] in force, while Georgia left her sixteen hour law[398] in force, but also penalized masters for working their slaves excessively.[399]   Louisiana, after acquisition by the United States, first passed a law guaranteeing that slaves should have Sundays off, or be paid for their labor on that day.[400]   In addition, the usages of the French territory were expressly kept in force, and legislative provision was made for breakfast and dinner hours.[401]

Vermont, and Maine, admitted as free states, never adopted laws fixing the maximum working hours of slaves nor did the slave states Kentucky or Virginia. In fact, during the entire 19th century there was not a single law passed in the U.S limiting working hours. Humanitarian arguments were put forth to stop the slave trade and to further abolition, but "humanity" did not restrain an employer from working employees for interminable hours. In this respect the new slave states were more like the "free" states rather than the old slave states. Ironically, prisoners, presumably even slaves, were protected by a maximum hour law.[401a]

Ohio and Illinois, being "free" states, had no laws limiting maximum hours of labor, and Indiana copied her laws from Virginia[402] which also had had no maximum hour laws.[403]   Mississippi, one of the leading new cotton states in the deep south followed the pattern of the northern industrial states. There were no statutes limiting the slaves' hours of labor. Alabama followed the same pattern as Mississippi. The new slave states, however far south or given over to cotton they might be, had no maximum hour laws protecting their slaves. Missouri as a territory and a state, followed the new slave states. Slaves like "free" employees could work interminable hours.

Laws requiring the master to furnish adequate food and clothing also became relics of the 18th century. But since they were more obviously a part of the mutual obligations which the slave system imposed on master and slave, they were more widespread than maximum hour laws. This had been true in the 18th century, and was also true in the 19th. Virginia kept her old laws[404] in force guaranteeing adquate food and clothing to slaves.[405]   The only Virginia case on this subject during the period is WOODDY v. FLOURNOY[405a] decided in 1820.

There five slaves were hired to work in a coal mine. The contract stipulated that they should "be cloathed as usual," but when they were sent back to their owner "they had been returned naked."   It is significant that this problem, however infrequent, came up when an attempt was made to use slaves in a non-agricultural enterprise. Here we see two forces working together; the decline of the plantation system and the ruthlessness of the new industrial economy.[405b] In COREY v.

MACON[405c] the hirer was "to pay the expense of feeding and clothing the slaves, their levies and taxes, and the doctor attending them."

Maryland having had no statutes assuring slaves adequate food and clothing before 1793,[406] enacted none afterwards.   Probably the question did not assume much importance.   In McDONOUGH v. TEMPLEMAN[406a] maintenance was included in hire; in FISHNICK v. SNELL[406b] the cost of maintaining a suckling mother is considered a loss; in MOORE v. WHITE the costs of maintaining infant slaves is held to be an expense of trusteeship which cannot be charged against the estate. The same was generally true in New York, Connecticut, Rhode Island, New Hampshire, Pennsylvania, Delaware and Massachusetts, Vermont, Ohio and Maine.   None have either statutes or cases.

In New Jersey there were no statutes after 1793, as there were none before.[407]   HEIRS OF POTTER v. POTTER'S WIDOW[408] however, indicates that an obligation to furnish a slave with food and clothing had once been recognized, but that it was falling into disfavor. The widow supported an old and infirm slave and then sued the heirs for the support. The court held that she could not recoup her expenses, though it gave no inkling as to who, if anyone, had the obligation to support the slave. We are clearly in the 19th century.

North Carolina continued her old laws without change, guaranteeing slaves adequate food and clothing.[409]   In STATE v. SUE,[410] the dissenting opinion recalls the practice of denying compensation to masters whose slaves had been executed for crimes induced by denial of adequate food and clothing.[411]

South Carolina continued her Eighteenth Century laws without change. In FABER v. BLADRICK,[411a] the family physician attended a sick slave. In McDOWELL v. MURDOCK,[411b] the testator expressed the wish that the legatee treat the slaves well.   GAYLE v. CUNNINGHAM[411c] holds that sound policy as well as sentiments of humanity favor keeping mothers and infants together.   Georgia, in FORBES v. MOREL,[412a] is the one case during the period illustrating this solicitude.   A sheriff levying on slaves was held entitled to recover subsistence money from the owner even though the slaves may have been left with the owner. It was feared that any other rule would fill the jails "with miserable victims."

Louisiana had a special law requiring adequate food and clothing to be furnished to Negroes coming from Haiti (Hispainola) but detailed as undesirable.[413] The general provision for slaves was part of the Black Code of 1806.[414]   Third persons could lodge a complaint that insufficient care was being given a slave.[415] So persons emancipating slaves were required to maintain them, even after emancipation, in sickness, want, old age, infancy, "or any other proven infirmity". [416]

In 1799, Kentucky guaranteed servants "sufficient food, clothing and lodging".[417] This statute speaks of "servants" but evidently means indentured servants, since it elsewhere refers to the term of servitude.[418] But during their term of servitude it deals with indentured servants as if they were slaves, providing among other things, that free Negroes, Mulattoes and Indians could not purchase any servant except of their own color.[419] There do not seem to be any statutes directly requiring adequate provision for slaves. This was apparently included in the Virginia statutes taken over en masse.[420] In RUMSEY v. MATTHEWS[421] decided in 1808, the hirer of slaves agreed "to find the said Negroes in clothing suitable to the seasons". Similarly, in REDDING v. HALL [422] the hirer was required to furnish medical care to the slave, mere feelings of humanity being feared "too weak to stimulate active virtue".

Both these cases concern hirers, which in two ways reflects the frontier condition of the state at the time. In the first place, there is evidently considerable (absentee) ownership; the working of slaves was done by persons other than the owner. In the second place the court's skepticism of the overseers' humanitarian instincts discloses the violence of the frontier.

Persons who were undoubtedly slaveholders before, have achieved governmental positions, carry over the noblesse oblige of their former states, and are sensitive to dictates of humanity toward their slaves. But there were many more, in a frontier community, who had advanced far enough that they are able to hire slaves. These, the judges feel, must be restrained by law since their feelings of humanity (if any) were not enough "to stimulate to active virtue."

There was no Tennessee law requiring masters to clothe, feed or house their slaves. As in North Carolina, slavery never got going smoothly in Tennessee. There was a strong tendency to adopt the ways of wage labor rather than the patriarchal practices of slavery. This is emphasized by the counterpart provision that emancipated slaves unable to support themselves had to be supported by the county,[423] and not by their former masters. As in Kentucky, another frontier state, the law seems to offer protection only against the neglect of hirers.[424]

Indiana, mechanically patterning her laws on those of Virginia, guaranteed adequate food, clothing and lodging to servants.[426] Since Indiana at the time was disguising her slave law as a law for servants, there is an anomalous provision for slaves, authorizing complaints to a magistrate,[427] but only from servants who were also citizens of one of the states. The net effect of this law was undoubtedly to deny the right of petition to most of the few Negroes in the territory.[428] Since the original purpose of these laws was to disguise slavery forbidden by the Ordinance of 1787, the provisions were continued under the apprentice laws[429] enacted after the admission of Indiana to statehood under a constitution which forbade slavery.[430]

Mississippi, as a new slave state was more in step with the northern industrial states than with the slave states of the 18th century. The general slave law of the territory[431] contained no section obligating a master to furnish his slaves with adequate food and clothing. Nor are there any such laws up and including 1820, although the Constitution of 1817 had authorized the legislature to pass such laws.[431a]

Illinois originally followed Indiana.   In 1807 the territory had adopted the laws of England where not merely local,[432] and in 1812 the laws of Indiana, where not merely local.[433] So the territory followed Indiana in requiring masters to furnish adequate food and clothing to servants[434] and to apprentices.[435]   These laws remained in effect through 1820. There are no Illinois cases up to that date.

The constitution of Alabama,[436] like that of Mississippi, empowered the legislature to enact laws guaranteeing slaves sufficient food, clothing and lodging. No such laws had been passed while Alabama was a territory, and none were enacted by the state to and including 1820.[437] Nor were there any cases. Missouri had no laws guaranteeing slaves adequate food, clothing or lodging up to the time of her admission in 1820.

Virginia continued her policy of making the former master suport emancipated slaves who could not support themselves.[438-439] UPSHAW v. UPSHAW[440] illustrates the problem and the duty of the master to support unprofitable slaves. Since Virginia was passing from a slave-using to a slave-breeding and slave-selling state, the problem did not arise very often. There would be no point in emancipating slaves whom the master intended to sell. Similarly, they would be sold before growing old.

Maryland preserved her Eighteenth Century laws to guard against emancipated slaves becoming public charges. She added no new ones except the single private act of 1816, permitting William Gibbons, a free Negro from Delaware to live in the State of Maryland, but making him give bond not to become a public charge.[441]   In MCDONOUGH v. TEMPLEMAN,[442] the hirer agreed to furnish the hired slaves with food, clothing and lodging during the time of hiring. SCRIVENER v. SCRIVENER[443] notes that two slaves about 60 years of age are "of course rather an expense than a profit." BURROUGHS v. NEGRO

ANNA[444] annulled the attempted testamentary emancipation of a woman slave over 45.

In short, the duty of supporting over-aged slaves and the corresponding limitations on emancipation were recognized, but seldom came up for practical application. Maryland's slaves in general were being sold south, so the problem infrequently presented itself.

New York had no laws limiting emancipation or providing for the care of over-aged slaves. On the contrary, the advance of industrial economy and the gradual disappearance of slavery showed itself in a series of laws which relieved masters of any such duties. In the original law for gradual abolition, passed in 1799,[445] there were still limited requirements that masters support slaves incapable of supporting themselves, particularly child slaves. The act of 1801 continued this practice, but by the same act, the state itself undertook to support "certain poor persons, formerly slaves,"[445a]and imposed penalties on persons suffering their slaves to beg,[445b]or selling incapacitated slaves to persons unable to support them.[445c]

By 1802 the state provided a maximum of $2 per month to the overseers of the poor to pay for each abandoned slave child,[446] and in 1804, the state took over the support of child slaves whose masters had abandoned the right to their services. Masters were thus freed of all responsibility for the support of slaves whom they had abandoned. Free enterprise was taking shape.

However, there were still tricks by which employers sought to combine the advantages of slavery with the advantages of wage labor. Slaves owned in neighboring states were manumitted, brought into New York as indentured servants, and later "freed" from bondage when too old to work.[448] Since this involved public support of slaves introduced from outside New York, the state could not let it pass unnoticed. Instead, it made all such contracts of indenture void,[449] directly increasing the market of free labor. At the same time masters of slaves born after July 4, 1799, were compelled to educate them.[450] This completely reversed the policy of slavery and illustrates how the new industrial economy had need of literate employees.

In the same year (1810) immigrants from Virginia and Maryland who had brought their slaves with them were allowed to hire them out for seven years more. After that the slaves would be free, but the masters were still liable for their support if the former slaves were not able to support themselves.[451] Evidently, there was a demand for labor in New York which did not exist in Maryland or Virginia. Instead of selling their slaves into the cotton belt, some Virginia and Maryland masters put them into northern industry, but New York found it more profitable to employ "free" labor for this purpose. So the state made a compromise with these immigrant slaveholders. They might hire out their slaves for seven years, the common law period for indentured servants. After that the slaves would be "free", but the immigrant masters were still liable for support—a duty no longer imposed on native New York slaveholders. Persons owning real property both in an adjoining state and in New York, and bringing in slaves to cultivate their New York lands, were shortly thereafter excepted from these provisions.[452]

A testamentary emancipation likewise left the estate free of any obligation to support if the testator procured a certificate that the slave was capable of supporting himself.[453] Such a certificate was made conclusive of the facts which it recited, again making emancipation easier and more certain, and leaving the emancipated slave to swell the wage labor force. Each slave so thrown on the labor market necesarily depressed wages. On the other hand, if the certificate was refused, the owner had the right to make a new application to the sessions. Quaker emancipations were validated, but the Quakers remained liable for the support of emancipated slaves unable to support themselves.[454] Quakers had long since jumped the gun on manumissions, for which they were subjected to harsher rules than the community at large.

Sale to owners too poor to support the slave was prohibited by the act of 1813.[454a] The same statute also provided that the state should support destitute slaves who had formerly belonged to persons whose property had been confiscated.[455g] In 1816, the overseers of the town were made liable for the support of the former slaves of F. Philipse, whose slaves had been forfeited, presumably in the war of 1812.[456] In 1817, masters manumitting slaves over 45 years of age were again made liable for their support unless they procured a certificate of the slave's ability to support himself, in which case they were exonerated.[457]

The trend to free the former master of all obligations is shown in HOPKINS & MUDGE v. FLEET & YOUNG,[458] where the trial court had rejected a certificate signed by the Overseers of the Poor reciting "We do hereby certify that the bearer, named Jordan, the property of William Hopkins & Co. appears to be under the age of fifty years, and of sufficient ability to get his own living. We do hereby manumit the same." On appeal the certificate was held not only admissible but conclusive, and the decedent's estate free of any obligation to support the former slave. The court said[459] "the certificate . . . was conclusive evidence of the age and ability of the slave and sufficient to charge the town with his subsequent maintenance as a pauper." The new policy was clearly to create cheap labor by increasing the wage-labor force, and to take the chance that occasionally a town might have to support an ex-slave who could not fit himself into the new economy.

In OVERSEERS OF THE POOR OF THE TOWN OF CLOVERACK v. OVERSEERS OF THE POOR OF THE CITY OF HUDSON[460] the court enforced the law forbidding transfers of overaged slaves to persons too poor to support them. The sale was held void. But the parties to the suit announce a new era. The litigation was solely between the Overseers of the Poor of two towns. Both masters (and all later masters) were out of it. The voidness of the sale of an aged slave to a pauper is important only in fixing residence and determining which town is saddled with the duty to support. Although the law was framed under slavery, application shows that not only slavery, but the whole obligation of the master to care for the servant was a thing of the past.

New Jersey followed the same practice as New York. Slaves between 21 and 40 could be emancipated on the strength of a certificate that they were sound and able to support themselves.[461] If the slave was under 21 or over 40, the owner could manumit upon posting a $1,500.00 bond.[462] This illustrates the transition from the Eighteenth Century paternal system to the wage system of the 19th century. When the latter reached its full flower, employees would simply be "fired at 40". Even if a slave was not emancipated according to the requirements of the act, his former owner had to support him only "if able".[463] If not, the township supported the pauper ex-slave. These statutes were obviously drawn up with an eye to increasing the wage labor force, and to resolving possible doubts in favor of throwing workers onto the labor market.

As in New York, masters were required to teach their slaves to read and write,[464] as the new industry found more use in literate than in illiterate employees. In 1804, legal means were provided for abandoning (the statute uses this word) children born to slaves after "the Fourth of July next".[465-8] They were to be supported by the mother's owner until one year old, then considered paupers and bound out by the Overseers until age 25 if male, and age 21 if female. Apprentices formed a pool of low-wage labor. That this process was made to begin when slave children were one year old shows the extremes to which the industrial economy was already going in its hunt for cheap wage-labor. In the same year, the signature of one overseer of the poor was made sufficient on a certificate or deed of manumission, and the statute specified the instruments of manumission which could be received in court.[469]

But by 1809, the sums paid by the state treasury for maintaining abandoned black children became so great that the state decided to place a limit on them. The act of 1809[470] states that "whereas large and unusual sums of money have been drawn from the treasury last year by the citizens of this state for maintaining abandoned blacks, which has caused suspicions that they have misconstrued the law and thereby obtained drafts upon the treasury which are not strictly just and according to the letter and the spirit thereof".

Henceforth:

> No warrant (should) be paid for keeping any abandoned black child, except the same is accompanied with a certificate from the clerk of the township or the clerk of the board of trustees of the poor-house of the county in which the said abandoned black was born, as the case may be, setting forth said abandonment, to have taken place agreeably to law, likewise a certificate from the trustees of Overseers of the Poor of said township or county under his or their oaths that the award set forth in said warrent for the maintenance of said abandoned black is consequence of a bona fide agreement entered into by the said trustee, or trustees, Overseer or Overseers of the Poor with the person who has maintained the said black, provides to any demand or charge against the state in said warrant.[471]

But exactly the same complaint was again recited in the preamble to the Act of 1811,[472] with the added spice "that in some instances the money drawn for their maintenance amounts to more than they would have brought if sold for life", so state payments for abandoned Negro children were cut off altogether.[473] History has clearly progressed into the Nineteenth century and the industrial age. There is on the whole, little litigation on the subject. VOLTER v. VOLTER'S WIDOW[474] illustrates this phase of development, too. The slave was old and infirm. The court did not say who was responsible for her, but merely decided that her master's estate was not responsible.

ANONYMOUS,[475] decided in 1809 represents a vestige of the old practice. The court denied manumission of a slave, after the Overseers of the Poor had similarly denied it. The designation of the case as "Anonymous" however is significant. The case must have been really aggravated, otherwise the court reporters would not have gone out of their way to conceal the names of the parties. On the other hand, while the reports conceal the names, they do not express any moral indignation at what the owner must have attempted. The public sympathy was with the owner who wants to get rid of the burden of an unprofitable slave and throw him on the street.

This case also shows the hypocrisy which underlay the assumption of moral superiority by the "free" states. Corporal punishment was something which had to be imposed while the slave was still subject to the master. If it is cruel, it can be charged against the master. But the severest blows of the wage system—unemployment and starvation—come precisely after the employee had been separated from his work and from his employer. Thus the resulting cruelty is not the employer's and he can act as if it did not exist. The industrial employer could thus sit back with folded hands and cast a holier-than-thou look on the slaveowner.

Massachusetts, having had no slaves since 1781, had no laws prohibiting the emancipation of overaged slaves or requiring their master to support them. But the problem of supporting indigent ex-slaves remained, and Massachusetts handled it by including them among free paupers guarded in the house of correction. In 1796 the Town of Bylston was paid for the support of a Negro; the Town of Great Barrington for one; the Town of Ipswich for one; the Town of Lincoln for the support of one Negro woman and her child, including doctor's bills; and the Town of Norton, for the support of one Negro, including doctor's bills.[476] In the following year there was a similar entry,[477] as there was in 1798,[478] 1799,[479] 1800[480] and straight through to 1818.[481]

While the slave states kept their laborers in slavery, they also supported them as such when unable to work. If former slaves did not fit into the industrial system of the "free" states, they were put into the House of Correction, i.e., in jail. Cases in which towns fought over the duty of supporting indigent "freed" slaves occurred in Massachusetts, throughout the period 1793-1820.[482] Before the abolition of slavery in Massachusetts "a practice was prevailing to manumit aged or infirm slaves, to relieve the master from the charge of supporting them".[483]

This foreshadows the expendability of wage labor as against slave labor. Writing in 1856, Frederick L. Olmstead reports the following conversation which he had at one of the Alabama River ports: "Negro hands were sent to the top of the bank, to roll the bales to the side, and Irishmen were kept below to remove them, and stow them. Upon asking the mate the the reason for this arrangement, the mate replied:

> 'The niggers are worth too much to be risked here; if the
> Paddies are knocked overboard, or get their backs broke,
> nobody loses anything.'[484]

As the United States Supreme Court observed almost a century later, the policy of the new economy was to encourage industry by insulating the employer from its risks. What the court said in 1943 about assumption of risk applies equally well to the burden of maintaining overaged or otherwise incapacitated workers. "Perhaps the nature of the present problem can best be seen against the background of one hundred years of master-servant doctrine. Assumption of risk was a judicially created rule which was developed in response to the general impulse of cannon law courts at the beginning of this period to insulate the employer as much as possible from bearing the human overhead, which is an inevitable part of the cost of doing of industrialized business. The general purpose behind this development in the common law seems to have been to give maximum freedom to expanding industry." [485]

Yet while "insulating" themselves from disabled and overaged workers, and leaving them to starve or be supported as paupers in houses of correction, the new industralists could parade great moral superiority over the slaveholders who held their employees in bondage. In 1820 Massachusetts eulogized herself in the Missouri controversy:

> The Committee of both Houses, who were appointed to consider 'what measure it may be proper for the Legislature of this Commonwealth to adopt, in the expression of their sentiments and views relative to the interesting subject now before Congress of interdicting slavery in the new states, which may be admitted into the union beyond the River Mississippi.'

> Slavery has always been considered by our wisest and ablest statesmen as the great moral and political evil, and necessity has been thought the only justification for its continuance.

> The United States were the first nation to provide any law against the slave trade. And now, when other nations are awakened perhaps, by our very example, to the enormity of this practice, when a rapid and almost universal change in public opinion has taken place in Europe, shall Republican America, by opening a new market for slaves, given a new stimulus to that traffic?

> It is no less than whether those vast regions, spreading from the Mississippi to the Pacific Ocean, shall be a land of slaves or of freemen; and this not for a single state, but for a country, which is to furnish many states of the Confederacy, not for a day or a year, but forever.

> Independent of any right as a member of this
> confederacy, this commonwealth has a deep interest in
> the establishment of the principles of natural law and
> civil liberties, and in the honor, prosperity, and happiness
> of every part of the nature. It may justly be expected
> that Massachusetts, which was among the first to extend
> the blessings of liberty and equal rights to all her
> inhabitants, should now lift her voice to prevent the
> extension and perpetuity of slavery.[486]

Here is the new situation in a page of print. In a single resolution, wage labor was held good not only from the standpoint of policy and prosperity, but much more loudly, morally far superior to slave labor. As the chess commentators say, "The rest is only a matter of technique." Although the Massachusetts legislature still protested that they had no intention to interfere with slavery where it existed[487] slavery was doomed. And this was less than thirty years after the Industrial Revolution, which spawned the cotton gin, and seemed to give a new lease in life to "the peculiar institution."

Connecticut, like New York and New Jersey, permitted masters to emancipate their slaves, free of all liability for support, either if the slave was between 25 and 45, or if the slaveowner procured a certificate of exemption.[488] This system was continued through to 1820.[489] Where no certificate was granted, the town was primarily liable for the support of ex-slaves who became destitute, but could recover over against the master.[490] Otherwise, the towns themselves were liable, as in Massachusetts.[491]

Rhode Island had a special problem in the field of slaves emancipated to escape support. Ever since the slave trade was forbidden, slaves imported into Rhode Island became free. But it turned out that this rule could be used to free slaves whom the master no longer wanted. So a penalty of $300 per slave was imposed for slaves imported for the purpose of freeing them.[492] There are no Rhode Island cases during this period.

Pennsylvania had the same problem and handled it in the same way as the other "free" states. The statute of 1803 defines which township is liable for the support of all ex-slaves, adding that if the slave has not been liberated after age 28 in accordance to law, then the township may recover over against the former master.[493] But masters were entirely freed of the administrative problems of care. Pennsylvania, like Massachusetts looked morally down her nose on advocates of slavery.

Her resolution on the Missouri Compromise[494] read in part:

> A measure was ardently supported in the last Congress of the United States, and will probably be as earnestly urged during the existing session of that body which if adopted would impede the march of humanity and freedom throughout the world, and would affix and perpetuate an odious stain upon the present race: a measure in brief, which proposes to spread the crimes and cruelties of slavery, from the banks of the Mississippi to the shores of the Pacific.

The adaptability of the wage system in a populated country to large scale operations without the costs of the slave system, was combined with a moral and emotional excitement which overlooked the shortcomings of the wage economy and emphasized those of the slave economy. The "practical men" and the "idealists" therefore drew together to oppose slavery and favor a wage economy, or in other words, a "free" system. There were still complications to disentangle, but as observed in the case of Massachusetts, from here on it was only a matter of time and technique. Slavery was on its last lap, despite a last backward look.

Two cases arose on this subject from 1793 to 1820. They show on the one hand the shifting of the <u>administrative</u> burden of care from the employers (owners) to the towns; on the other, the lengths to which owners were willing to go to shed the responsibility of caring for slaves who were no longer profitable.

In one case, Chief Justice Tilghman said:

> The pauper is not to be left starving, until the representative of Arndt (the former owner) can be compelled to maintain them. The township in which the master resides is in the first instance bound to support him in case he falls into distress. By the old laws of the former province, the person maintaining was obliged to give security to indemnify the township. They may take their remedy against the estate of Arndt.

In the other case, OVERSEERS OF FERGUSON v. OVERSEERS OF BUFFALO,[497] the owner tried to manumit a slave when the latter had reached the age of 78. The master was held still responsible for his upkeep, but the litigation was between the two towns. The master was not even a party. Cruelty of the individual masters toward their slaves was to be a major propaganda point to the end of the Civil War. The kind of cruelty depicted in this case on the part of northern slaveowners on becoming industralists was never mentioned. This focusing of moral indignation on the misdeeds of the slaveowners was itself part of the process of abolition.

In 1798 North Carolina got around to protecting slaves whom masters liberated to escape having to support them.[498] This act states that "it is represented to this General Assembly that slaves rendered incapable of serving their owners from advancement in years and other disability, are often neglected by such owners, and by them permitted to go at large and become a common nuisance."

This preamble once more reflects the undeveloped nature of slavery in North Carolina. And where even that undeveloped institution becomes inconveniently burdensome on the masters, they meet it by measures which are equally those of an undeveloped society.

For the preamble does not say that masters formally emancipate incapacitated slaves, but that they simply turn them loose. The institution in North Carolina was hardly skin deep. The act follows that of the states where slavery was fully developed and required masters to support overaged and otherwise incapacitated slaves. At the same time the act also provides that if the master did not care for the slave, the county shall do so. Thus, North Carolina, primitive during the 18th century, entered into both the slave system and the industrial system almost at the same time.[499]

In 1801, North Carolina adopted the device of obligating owners to give a bond when they emancipated a slave.[500] The preamble observes that "it frequently happens that slaves or Negroes emancipated by their owners became a county charge." If the bond was not put up within 6 months after the emancipation, the former owner was fined 300 pounds.[501]   The only case touching the subject, however, is LITTLEJOHN v. UNDERHILL'S EX'RS,[502] decided in 1816. There the testator set up a trust to care for one of his slaves who was too old to work. The court held that the trust takes precedence over the other bequests in the will. "For we consider this as a kind of a charge upon the assets in favor of the community, which in case of a deficiency of assets is entitled to a preference against the claims of individuals."[503]

With the dawn of the new century, South Carolina found herself modern to the extent that slaveowners now emancipated overaged slaves to escape supporting them. The old noblesse oblige had passed away. The law of 1800, regulating patrols "and to impose certain restrictions on the emancipations of slaves,"[504] recited in its second preamble, that "it has been the practice for many years past in this state for persons to emancipate or set free their slaves in cases where such slaves have been of bad or depraved character, or from age or infirmity, incapable of gaining their livelihood by honest means."[505]

A complicated procedure was set up by which a master proposing to emancipate a slave had to submit himself to examination before five freeholders concerning the slave's character and ability to earn his own living. The five-man jury was empowered to impose conditions on the emancipation, but upon their approving it, the master received a certificate which authorized him to manumit the slave.[506] In 1820 the question became moot, when all manumissions were prohibited except upon act of the legislature.[507] Despite the note of alarm in the preamble of 1800, the problem seems to have been relatively mild, since there were no cases on it.

In Delaware the law of 1797[509] continued the policy of having the master give security on manumission. This seemed to apply to all manumissions, not merely testamentary ones.[510] But the practice of informal emancipations became so widespread that in 1819 the state recognized them even if no security had been put up, making the owners liable to the county for support, and they remained liable if the slave had been liberated when over 35.[510a] There were no Delaware cases on the subject.

Georgia made emancipation dependent on an act of the legislature in 1801,[511] but this does not seem to have solved problems, as the state became more settled precisely when a wage economy was taking shape in the northern states. In 1815 the first Georgia law obligating owners to support aged or infirm slaves was passed.[512] Courts were given power to conduct inquiries on receiving any sworn information that debilitated slaves were being neglected. Georgia, like North Carolina, was a frontier community in the process of becoming settled. When masters found that a slave counld not work they did not bother to emancipate, but simply abandoned him.

So the statute deals directly with abandonment rather than emancipation. But the only sanction seems to be the right of the governing officials to recover from the owner money spent for the slave's care. In this respect the Georgia statute resembles the poor laws which were used to handle destitute ex-slaves in the northern states. There were no Georgia cases on the subject during this period.

Louisiana went further than most other states. The first slave law after the territory became American[513] permitted emancipation but required masters to support all slaves over 45 at the time of emancipation, or below 21 if males and below 18 if females. If the master did not furnish support, the sheriff was authorized to seize them summarily. [514] The Black Code of 1806 [515] imposed a fine on the owner for failure to support incapacitated slaves. [516]   In 1807, emancipations were limited to slaves over 30, [517] and the obligation to support disabled emancipated slaves was made absolute. [518]   There are no cases on the subject showing that incapacitated slaves were generally cared for.

Vermont, admitted in 1791 without slaves, had no laws guarding against responsibility-shirking emancipations.   However, there is one case [520] in which one of the judges of the Supreme Court of Vermont bought a slave outside of the state; used her as such while she was capable, and then, "when she became infirm, sick and blind", discarded her.   She became a public charge.   It was held that the municipal corporation which took care of her could not recover against the defendant, her former de facto owner. Vermont was unquestionably on the forefront of nineteenth century progress.

The Kentucky constitution of 1792 adopted the Virginia laws which were in force during this period. [521] At the same time it commanded the legislature to pass laws permitting owners to emancipate their slaves; "saving the rights of creditors, and preventing them from becoming a charge to the county in which they reside." [522] In 1799 the Virginia laws were repealed and counties in which emancipation took place were authorized to demand a bond against the slaves becoming a public charge because of age or infirmity. [522a]

In 1799 a specific law was enacted requiring the master to maintain to the end of their term, bond servants who had become disabled, [523] and a similar law was enacted for slaves. [524] The master had to support all freedmen who were unable to support themselves. Kentucky was taking her place among the old line slave states.

Tennessee provided for the giving of security by the master on emancipation in 1801. [525] But where the freedman actually became destitute the county where the emancipation took place had to provide him with necessities in accordance with the poor laws. [526] Tennessee follows the trend of the northern industrial states. The picture given by Kentucky and Tennessee seems incongruous, since Tennessee ultimately seceded, while Kentucky did not. The reason may be in the divergence between eastern and western Tennessee, and a struggle for control within the state.   Sometimes the security was apparently given by volunteers, or at least by persons having some independent interest in the slave's freedom. [527]

There are no cases directly on an ex-master's duty to support incapacitated freedmen.   But KEEBLE v. CUMMINGS [528] shows that

Tennessee, as a border state, was within the range of the "emancipation" movement which sprang from northern industrialism. There the complainant charged that his father, "being in his dotage, and possessed of very little property except six slaves worth at least fourteen hundred dollars, was induced by the slaves to express a desire of liberating them."[529]

Ohio being admitted as a free frontier state, had neither laws limiting the manumission of slaves nor laws such as existed in New England placing destitute ex-slaves under the general poor law. There are no Ohio cases through 1820.

Indiana, attempting to introduce slavery under the guise of bond servitude, took a middle course for protecting "servants" against emancipations which were nothing but a device for the master's shirking responsibility of support. Where the responsibility fell directly on the county, the master was subject to a fine of thirty dollars, besides having to reimburse the Overseers of the Poor.[530] In 1807 the territory tried to be consistent with its own theories and provided that masters had to maintain servants for the balance of their indenture if the servants became disabled.[531] Making the master responsible only for the remainder of a fixed term brought Indiana laws abreast of theory, and also took partial advantage of the new wage system under which the master was not responsible for anything. This is true even though the law of 1807 also mentions slaves.[532] There were no Indiana cases on the subject, indicating that it rapidly declined in importance.

Mississippi, from the first, limited emancipations to cases of meritorious service.[533] Even so a bond had to be given that the slave would not become chargeable to the public. Here, Mississippi's earliest legislation foreshadowed her position throughout the slave period. She was a thorough-going plantation state, not depending on industry at all. But since the methods of northern industrialism were borrowed in other fields, the total effect was that Mississippi, as the outstanding new cotton state, combined all the cruelties of slavery with all the cruelties of the wage system.

In 1814, the meaning of these provisions was made clear, when a bond of $10,000 was fixed for the emancipation of the slave Elizabeth and her twelve children, who were also the children of the emancipating owner.[534] Occasionally however, emancipations were allowed without security.[535] In one of these cases, the reason evidently was that the emancipated slave was married to a free man of color.[536] In the other, the reason is not clear.

Illinois adopted the Indiana laws in force in 1809,[537] among which was the law forbidding emancipation of indentured servants to escape responsibility.[538]   Slaves brought into the territory were accommodatingly transformed into bond servants.[539]   Masters had to give a $500 bond that the servant would not become a public charge at the end of his time, if the servant (former slave) was in poor health or over forty at the time of emancipation.[540] This statute again suggests the device of having one's cake and eating it, too. Dispensing with the bond would tempt the owner to early emancipation, after which the ex-slave would nevertheless be thrown on the general labor market at lower wages by reason of being overaged.

Here, again, it can be seen how the Abolitionist movement gained impetus by concentrating on the moral wrongs of slavery, and glossing over those of the wage system.   White bond servants had to be maintained until the end of their term, if disabled when "liberated".[541] In 1819 the required bond for slaves was raised to $1,000.   The introduction of slaves into Illinois for the purposes of liberating them was forbidden entirely on penalty of a $200 fine.[542]   Masters were similarly obligated to maintain disabled bond servants until the end of their terms, upon penalty of a $30 fine. [543] There were no Illinois cases through 1820.

The Alabama constitution of 1819 authorized emancipation but expressly gave the legislature power to pass laws to prevent emancipated slaves from becoming a public charge.[544] There were no Alabama cases on the subject through 1820.

Maine, having been carved off from Massachusetts, had the same legal history. There were no Maine statutes through 1820. However short the legal history, it does include one case of contest between communities over the obligation to support a destitute Negress. Although the pauper in question was the daughter of a free black woman, this fact was disregarded. Rather, the liability of the community was decided on the theory that "a slave (the father) can neither acquire nor communicate a settlement, like a free man." [545] Maine, like the rest of New England, was in the vanguard of industrialization in 1820, and discarded the liability for support on grounds not recognized by the slave states themselves.

Missouri began development as a conventional slave state. While yet a territory, she required former masters to support incompetent ex-slaves. If they did not, the sheriff was authorized to take action directly against the former master.[546] In other words, the burden of maintaining freemen unable to maintain themselves fell on the former master, not on the county. In this, Missouri followed the law of the Louisiana Territory. This provision was continued in the Missouri constitution adopted on her admission as a state. [547] There are no Missouri cases on the subject up to her admission as a state.

PROHIBITION OF CRUELTY TO SLAVES

After 1792,[548] as already noted,[548a] Virginia prohibited castration except for an attempt to ravish a white woman. With one possible exception, there were no cases of mistreatment of slaves by the master. On the other hand, there were four in which the master went out of his way to avoid the separation of slave families upon sale.[549] In COMMONWEALTH v. CHAPPLE[550] the defendant was convicted of stabbing a slave. The opinion says nothing about whether it was the defendants' own slave. The same is true of COMMONWEALTH v. COHEN[550a] (second degree murder of a slave). FITZHUGH v. FOOTE[550b] goes to the length of holding that with respect to the separation of families "humanity forbids and will not be countenanced in a court of requite."

Maryland retained her 18th century system of not having any laws prohibiting cruelty of masters toward slaves. Doubtless, this was for the same reason. There was not enough to make legislation worthwhile. There are no cases of cruelty from any master to a slave during this period. The only case is the opposite. The refusal of a master to dispose of his slaves to a slave dealer, or to separate a family.[551] New York continued the policy developed before 1793 when there were no laws restraining masters' treatment of slaves,[552] nor are there any cases. New Jersey revived the policy of the Act of 1713[553] in the Act of 1798.[554] Persons treating their slaves inhumanely were fined up to forty dollars.[555] There are no New Jersey cases on the subject, indicating that it was not a practical problem.

In Rhode Island there was no legislation and no cases on mistreatment of slaves by masters. As in the 18th century, there were no indirect problems. The same is true of New Hampshire. By 1820 there were no slaves in the state.[556] Pennsylvania had no new laws against mistreatment of slaves. The old rule against separation of families[557] continued.

North Carolina continued her statute against the malicious killing of slaves.[558] In 1817 killing a slave was made homicide for all purposes.[558a] Up to 1820 at least one case, WALKER v. MEBANT[559] shows a disinclination of masters to inflict cruelty on their slaves. There the slaves' original owner "agreed to keep the Negro girl at his own expense during his life . . . not wishing to separate her from her parents during his life." There is no other case of relations between master and slave, but as will be seen, there are two significant cases on killing of slaves by third parties. The stunted character of the North Carolina slave system apparently led to slaveowners not bothering their slaves much. By the same token, new slaveowners carried a chip on their shoulder toward slaves. The caste lines were sufficiently uncertain that it was feared that a more relaxed attitude might obliterate them.

There was no new legislation[560] in South Carolina regulating the conduct of masters toward slaves. There are no direct cases of mistreatment of slaves by masters during this period. But the issue arose indirectly several times, and the attitude was always paternalistic. There was severe condemnation of mistreatment on the one hand, and care to the extent of not separating families on the other.

In FAIRCHILD v. BELL,[561] a physician sued the master in quasi-contract for medical services volunteered to a slave whom he saw "not far from his residence . . . belonging to the defendant, in the road, in a miserable condition, almost naked, shockingly beaten, and having on her leg an iron of fifteen pounds weight." The plaintiff-physician:

> Was induced from motives of humanity to take her to his house, where she was carefully attended, clothed, nourished and cured. It was clearly proven at the trial, that the defendant exercised towards the slave, a continued series of cruelties, and that she would have perished but for the humane assistance of plaintiff. When the woman was brought to the plaintiff's, he informed a justice of the peace, who advised him to keep the Negro, and administer relief to her.

The trial court charged the jury that "The slave lives for his master's service. His time, his labor, his comforts, are all at his master's disposal. The duty of humane treatment, and of medical assistance, when clearly necessary, ought not to be withholden. That assistance was denied by the master in this case, and denied from the worst of motives. The plaintiff rendered those services and gave that assistance which the master ought to have procured; and therefore, ought to be compensated." The jury returned a verdict for the defendant in the teeth of the charge. A new trial was granted and affirmed.

In TEASDALE v. INSURANCE CO.,[562] the sale of a cargo of slaves at Havana rather than Charleston was approved because "considering the deplorable condition of the Negroes, humanity dictated a sale of them at Havana." So in GAYLE v. CUNNINGHAM[563] the court said that "sound policy as well as humanity, requires that everything should be done to reconcile these unhappy beings to their lot, by keeping mothers and children together."

Finally, in STATE v. HUDNALL [565] the execution of a slave for murder was halted because of several irregularities in the trial. [566] "Every feeling of humanity and justice revolts at the idea, that any other mode of trial, less formal . . . than what the act has prescribed, should be sanctioned." [567] For the most part, South Carolina still exercised noblesse oblige with regard to her slaves. Delaware had no variation from the pattern formed in the 18th century. After 1793 there are neither statutes nor cases on cruelty by masters toward slaves.

Through 1820 Georgia prohibited cruel treatment of slaves by masters. [568] The compiled laws of that year impose fine or imprisonment at the court's discretion on any master "who shall cruelly beat such slave or slaves by unnecessary and excessive whipping." The state constitution of 1798 provided generally that maiming a slave should receive the same punishment as maiming a white person. [569] There were no cases, probably indicating that Georgia society was still in a formative state. The country was still half-frontier, and although there were statutes protecting slaves, no case under them reached a court.

In Louisiana the code guarded against mistreatment of slaves by tenants with the general provisions that these should "govern said slaves as good and honest men." [570] As to masters, the laws of the French territory were kept in force, [571] and a limited prohibition was introduced against the separation of families on public sales. [572] Special permission was given to fire upon armed runaways, [573] indicating that otherwise it was forbidden to fire on a slave. At the same time a presumption was enacted making the master criminally liable for mutilation of a slave when no one else was present, unless the master is able to prove the contrary or takes an exculpatory oath. [574]

There are no cases during this period directly on mistreatment of slaves by masters. It may be inferred that the problem did not often arise. BAYON v. PRIVOT [575] approves the removal of a slave from prison because of ill health. The owner had to bear the loss if the slave later escaped. JOURDAN v. PATTON [576] holds that where a defendant who has blinded a slave has made full indemnity to the owner, the defendant is entitled to take the slave. "The principle of humanity, which would lead us to suppose that the mistress, whom he had long served, would treat her miserable, blind slave with more kindness than the defendant cannot be taken into consideration. Cruelty ought not to be presumed." [577]

Vermont had no slaves under her first constitution,[578] so had no laws governing the conduct of masters toward slaves. But in spite of the state's enthusiasm for liberty and the rights of man, there was one case in which a Negro was tortured.[579] The court held that there was no statute covering the offense, and levied a fine.[580]

The Kentucky constitution of 1792 authorizes laws to protect slaves from mistreatment by their masters.[581] No such statute was, however, passed through 1820.[582] While Kentucky copied the laws of the eastern states, it was probably still too much on the frontier to put them into practice, so there were no cases.

Tennessee, though also on the frontier, gave some protection to slaves from the outset. The statute of 1799[583] punishes wilful and malicious killing of slaves. It clearly applied to the slaveowner, inasmuch as the second section makes special provision for the case where "the slave so killed shall be the property of another and not of the offender."[584] YOUNG v. FORGUY[585] expresses the philosophy that if temporary employers of a slave are subjected to the same obligations as the master, it will tend to prevent cruelty at their hands. There were no other cases.

When Indiana first became American territory there was a minimum inclination to treat Negroes with humanity. Phillbrick, in his Introduction to the Laws of Indiana Territory, 1801-1809, refers to a case in 1779 where a Negro was ordered burned at the stake, though the punishment was actually commuted to hanging.[586] The law of 1802 however, gave a summary (but unspecified) remedy against any master "guilty of injurious demeanor towards his servant."[587] The state constitution on admission in 1816, declared "that all men are born equally free and independent," which put an end to the de facto slave laws.[589] In 1818 however, the law still provided for the discharge of apprentices who had been mistreated.[590]

The Mississippi constitution of 1817 empowered the legislature to pass laws "to oblige the owners of slaves to treat them with humanity."[591] No such laws had been enacted by 1820. But Mississippi revived the pattern of the old colonies in the 17th century: the law was framed in judicial decisions before being explicitly put into statutes.

In STATES v. JONES,[592] decided in 1820, the Supreme Court of the new state held a white person guilty of the murder of a slave. The court said "The question in this case is whether in this State, murder can be committed on a slave. In vain shall we look for any law passed by the philanthropic legislature of this state, giving even to the master, much less to a stranger, power over the life of a slave. The motion to arrest judgment must be overruled. The defendant was sentenced to be hung on the 27th July, 1821."

This case illustrates one of the several trends which existed in Mississippi then and until the Civil War. In many other instances, one would hesitate to apply the term "philanthropic" to the cheapness attached to human life, in what was essentially a frontier community.

As already noted,[593] Illinois first continued the laws of Indiana Territory. The Act of 1807 provided that apprentices might be discharged by a Justice of the Peace if mistreated by the master.[594] Similarly, "An act concerning servants"[595] dealing entirely with Negro servants,[596] contains a clause that if any master "shall be guilty of injurious demeanor towards his servant, it shall be redressed on motion, by the court of common pleas of the county wherein the servant resides."[597] There was no further legislation, nor are there judicial decisions.

Alabama's constitution on her admission as a state, gave the legislature power to pass laws "to obligate the owners of slaves to treat them with humanity, to abstain from all injuries to them extending to life or limb, and in case of their neglect, or refusal to comply with the directions of such laws, to have such slaves sold for the benefit of their owners."[598]

Previous to that, the territory had enacted a statute imposing a fine up to $2 on any owner who inflicted cruel or unusual punishment on any slave within the territory, or even permitted subordinates to do so.[599] This measure was grounded in the fact that "it has been the humane policy of all civilized nations where slavery has been permitted to protect this useful but degraded class of men from cruelty and oppression."[600] The principles of humanity which the Alabama settlers tried to bring with them were laudable. But, as will be seen, the realities of the frontier got the better of good intentions, and the lives of slaves soon became as cheap as the lives of everyone else.

Aside from the laws of Louisiana, which Missouri took over in 1804,[601] there are no laws regulating the conduct of masters toward slaves up to the time of her admission as a state. There were no cases during this period.

SEXUAL RELATIONS

Harriet Martineau described the wife as but "the chief slave of the harem."[602] After the closing of the slave trade in 1808, slave children were at a premium and it became profitable for the slaveowner to act as his own stud. Here the rule that status follows the female line was pushed to its limits.

After 1793, Virginia continued the rule that free or slave status descended through the female line.[603] The fact that castration, while generally forbidden, was allowed for an attempt to ravish a white female [604] indicates a growing uncertainty of caste lines and a corresponding tightening of the rules designed to keep the race-castes apart. This clearly reflects the pressure to "free" slaves and bring them as employees into northern industry. The same tendency was still at work in 1819. Slaves were given the death penalty for rape.[605] At the same time, castration was made the punishment for a slave's attempt to ravish a white woman.[606]

Maryland generally continued the policies which had been developed up to 1793. Descent of status through the female line was put into practice by a statute of 1796, providing that immigrants into Maryland might bring their slaves with them as long as the slaves or their mothers had been residents of the United States for three years previously.[609]

But children of Negro men and white women were made free from birth, rather than from age 31, as they had been under the old law.[610] When slavery became unprofitable in Maryland, it was discovered that the Christian religion forbids visiting the sins of the parents on the children.[610] This doctrine was not immediately extended to children of slave mothers. In 1801, there is a record that one John Crist had his marriage annulled because his wife "had prostituted herself with a Negro man, and after her intermarriage with said John Crist was delivered of a Mulatto child." [611] Statutes of 1808 and 1809, take every combination of Mulatto for granted. [611a]

No other Maryland statutes touch the subject during this period. In 1794, one Shorter was held free on a jury verdict, as being descended from Elizabeth Shorter, a free white woman married to a Negro man. [612] This case is an interesting illustration of the shift of opinion in Maryland. The original ancestors were both servants of the same master and were married in 1681. Up to that year, marriage of white women servants to Negro slaves was a ground for enslaving the white woman, and therefore, encouraged by the masters.[613] A little over a century later, when the tobacco business had gone to pot and slavery was fading out in Maryland, marriage of a white woman servant to a Negro was grounds for freeing her descendants.

The same result ensued in ROBERT THOMAS v. REV. HENRY PILE. [614] In NEGRO MARY v. VESTRY OF WILLIAMS AND MARY'S PARISH [615] however, where the female ancestor had been imported from Madagascar, it was held incumbent to prove her freedom, since Madagascar countenanced slavery. MAHONEY v. ASHTON, [616] decided in 1797, profers another variation of the problem, and set the limits to which Maryland courts were willing to go in decreeing freedom on the ground of descent from a free female ancestor. In that case, the female ancestor had been in England. But while it was said this might make her free in England, it did not do so in Maryland, consequently her descendants were slaves.

The bunching of Maryland cases in which freedom is claimed on the ground of descent from a white woman is no doubt the result of the concurrence of the trend toward emancipation, and the desire to find reasons for it at the end of the 18th century, and the practice of 17th century masters to marry their white woman servants to slaves in order to enslave them. So a tendency to limit this ground of freedom seems to appear in HIGGINS v. ALLEN[617] where a judgment of freedom was magically reversed. It may be noted that THOMAS v. PILE[618] (1798) is the last case on record of emancipation. After the invention of the cotton gin, Maryland slaveholders apparently decided it was more profitable to sell their slaves south.

In 1808 however, SHORTER v. BOSWELL[619] was reversed for refusal to admit hearsay evidence of the freedom of the plaintiff's female ancestors several generations back. In WALLS v. HELMSKY,[620] decided in 1817, the Court of Appeals of Maryland reversed a judgment on a verdict for freedom. Here the testimony was both that one white man wanted to marry the petitioner's mother, and that she had another as husband in Virginia. In 1817 New York established slave marriages.[621] This was merely an intermediate step toward general abolition.

In OVERSEERS OF THE POOR OF CITY OF HUDSON v. OVERSEERS OF THE POOR OF TOWN OF TAGHKANAC,[622] decided in 1816, we find a white woman who delivered a "black" child. The only legal point which the case decides is that since the child is reported as "black" rather than Mulatto, there is no liability for support on the defendant township. Otherwise, as before 1793, there are no statutes or cases in New York on sexual relations between slaves and masters. There are neither statutes nor decisions in New Jersey, Rhode Island, nor New Hampshire after 1793 on sexual relations between whites and blacks.

In 1804 Massachusetts executed a Negro for murder and rape on a white woman.[622a] The defendant offered to plead guilty, which the court at first refused to accept. The defendant's sanity was then tried. He was found sane, and then executed. INHABITANTS OF DIGHTON v. INHABITANTS OF FREETOWN,[623] indicates again that as slavery disappeared, slave marriages became recognized as a legal institution. DUNBAR v. MITCHELL[624] records an Indian-Negro marriage.

INHABITANTS OF ANDOVER v. INHABITANTS OF CANTON[625] gives the interesting picture of intermarriage among whites, Indians and Negroes. The opinion says:

> Caesar was, at the time of Lewis's birth, and long before, a Negro slave of Charles Wentworth and so continued till his death in March, 1780. Abigail, who was the daughter of an Indian father of the Punkapug tribe. Her mother was a white woman but admitted by the guardian of the tribe as one of their number. In 1803 he married Hannah Richardson, the daughter of a Mulatto father and a white mother. On the 17th of November, 1763, the general court passed a resolve that John Billings, guardian of the tribe, be directed to take the same care of the Mulatto children of the said tribe, as of other Indians, and to bind out the said Mulatto children as other Indians. There is no doubt that Abigail was a Mulatto, within the meaning of the legislative acts, providing for the care of this tribe of Indians, and for those who mixed with them.

Lewis' "mother was free, being the daughter of an Indian and a white woman, both of whom were free. We think there is no doubt that, at any period of our history, the issue of a slave husband and a free wife would have been declared free."

In INHABITANTS OF MIDWAY v. INHABITANTS OF NEEDHAM,[626] was an assumption for expenses incurred in the support of Ishmail Coffee and his wife. "He was a Mulatto, and his supposed wife a white woman. They were inhabitants of Massachusetts Bay at the time of the supposed marriage, which was previous to 1770. As the laws of the province at that time prohibited all such mariages, they went into Rhode Island, and were there married, such marriage not being then prohibited by the laws thereof. It was objected that this marriage was void in law, but the judge overruled the objection."

In Massachusetts all these cases of intermarriage arose in contests between towns over the support of paupers. The cases were too few to point unmistakeably to the conclusion that the children of mixed marriages were a depressed class in "free" Massachusetts but they certainly suggest so.

Connecticut has one pauper case in the period 1793-1820. In TOWN OF WINDSOR v. TOWN OF HARTFORD,[627] "Fanny was born in Hartford, in the year 1785, and was the illegitimate daughter of Sarah, a slave of Jonathan Butler." She was held free. This case must mostly be read between the lines. The date of Fanny's birth was one year after 1784, the time from which all Negroes were born free.[628] That Fanny was the "illegitimate" daughter of a slave woman belonging to a named master suggests that she was the child of the slave and the master.

Pennsylvania, enacting the statute for gradual abolition of slavery in 1780,[629] had no further legislation on sexual relations between whites and Negroes. But the old laws persisted. In COMMONWEALTH Ex Rel SUSAN STEPHENS v. CLEMENTS,[630] decided in 1814, the Pennsylvania Supreme Court held a slave marriage in Maryland void without the master's consent. This is the only case. North Carolina has no new statutes on sexual relations between masters and slaves. Throughout, the subject seems to have been taken quite casually.

In CUNNINGHAM'S HEIRS v. CUNNINGHAM'S EXECUTORS,[631] it was held that the testator could not devise real property to the children of one of his woman slaves. One is left to infer that the devise was made because the children were the testator's. Another case decided the following year, emphasizes the same casual attitude. It is held that there is no presumption of slavery "in relation to persons of mixed blood." Such persons may be descended from Indian, or from a white mother. The emphasis which this case puts on individual liberty shows again how little importance North Carolina attached to slavery as an institution.

In STATE v. DICK,[633] on the other hand, one sees at once a certain affirmative tolerance toward sexual relations between slaves and owners, and the reluctance of a slave society to execute its slaves. The defendant, the property of a woman, was convicted of assault with intent to commit rape upon a spinster. Judgment on the conviction was arrested because the indictment did not contain the words "contra formam statuti". Such technical decisions are made when the court is looking for reasons to reach a desired result.

South Carolina had no new legislation on sexual relations between masters and slaves during the period 1793-1820. The state's caste-system was so well and firmly fixed that there was no need for legislative changes. Nothing shows this better than the matter-of-factness with which the state's highest court treats the phemonenon of racial blending in STATE v. WILSON:[634] "Everyone knows that there are persons of this color, Mulattoes, that are free and that among the subjects of slavery are found all the various shades of color between European and African."

A Mulatto slave is mentioned in BRAILSFORD v. HAYWORD.[635] JILINEAN v. JILINEAN[636] says that connections between master and female slave were not "disgraceful" in Haiti, notwithstanding the suggestion which this makes. Other cases hardly seem to consider them "disgraceful" in South Carolina. One of the most interesting cases is STATE v. McDOWELL[637] where the child of a white woman and a Negro was sternly held free, and qualified to testify as a witness. We shall return to this on the subject of free Negroes.

In 1795, Delaware repealed the provision making Mulatto children of white women women subject to servitude through age 31.[638] It was evidently becoming more profitable to employ these people as wage laborers. An amusing sidelight on the sexual relations between white and black is the law of 1799,[638a] permitting free blacks and Mulattoes to give testimony in certain instances, but never to charge a white man with being the father of a bastard child. There are no other Delaware statutes or cases during the period 1793-1820, but the laws of 1816 and 1819 speak of "Mulattoes," as a matter of course.[638b]

There are neither new statues nor decisions in Georgia regarding sexual relations between masters and slaves during the period 1793-1820. The state was evidently not yet sufficiently developed to bring this subject within the range of law, beyond the original limitations of the sister colonies.

After Louisiana was acquired by the United States in 1803, the American statutes are almost barren of any reference to sexual relations between masters and slaves. The pattern existing at the time of the Louisiana purchase was simply allowed to continue. The first available[639] notice is in the law of 1816,[640] which prohibits the importation of slaves convicted of rape. The first such statutory reference within the state itself was the law of 1818, imposing the death penalty on "any slave, free Negro, Mulatto, or Indian," convicted of raping a white woman.[641] In the same year Joseph Leblanc was granted $300.00 compensation for a slave executed for rape.[642]

The Louisiana cases begin with MITCHELL v. COMYNS,[643] decided in 1810, in which a fugitive Negro girl from Maryland was living with the defendant in New Orleans. The slave was returned to the original owner, her purchase from a slave dealer in New Orleans being held no defense. There is no comment on the fact that the defendant was living with a slave. ADELLE v. BEAUREGARD[644] in the same year held that mixed color carries no presumption of slavery, "although it is in general correct to require the plaintiff to produce his proof before the defendant. It is otherwise when the question is slavery or freedom. The law cited by the plaintiff is certainly applicable. We do not say that it would be so if the plaintiff were a Negro. Persons of color may have descended from Indians on both sides, or from a white parent or Mulatto parents in possession of their freedom. Considering how much probability there is in favor of liberty of those persons, they ought not to be deprived of it on a mere presumption." [645]

In TONNE v. MAURIN, [646] the plaintiff 'a person of color' lived with the defendant's testator as his ménagère." It is left ambiguous whether she was the testator's mistress. The court holds she has no claim against the estate since "it must be presumed that the parties joined their stock for their mutual support." In PIREAU v. DUVENAY [647] the white father of a deceased woman of color, his natural daughter, is denied her estate on the ground that he never acknowledged her during her lifetime. The estate went to the natural brothers and sisters of the decedent, also persons of color. Sexual relations between the races were here taken in stride and no preference was given to a white father over his unacknowledged Mulatto bastards.

BERE'S EXECUTORS v. QUIERRY'S EXECUTORS, [648] perhaps indicates the lines which were drawn in holding that a colored woman's living in public concubinage with a white man for 30 years did not create a general partnership affecting the man's property. So in TRUDEAU'S EXECUTOR v. ROBINETTE, [649] it was held that a slave could not be emancipated before age thirty. When she was 24, any deed of emancipation was void as against a purchaser even though the original owner had given her freedom de facto, lived with her and had "three or four" children by her.

GIROD v. LEWIS [650] lays down the general policy that while slaves may marry with the consent of their masters, it does not produce any civil effects. On emancipation however, a previously dormant marriage springs into effectiveness. It may be remarked here that nowhere does any case come to grips with the real issue which underlay the question of whether slave marriages could exist, or how much effect they should have. Marriage is the social machinery for taking care of mother and children. Where the slaveowner cares for mother and children, marriage becomes a fifth wheel.

The matter-of-fact acceptance of sexual relations between the race-castes appears again in MARIE v. AVART, [651] where the decedent's mistress was the slave of another. The decedent directed the purchase and emancipation of both the slave and his natural son by her. Since her owner did not oppose her suit to determine values, it was held she could maintain it, though herself a slave. In a later stage of the case [652] however, the heirs opposed the emancipation on the ground of the testator's insanity at the time of making the will. They were upheld both by the jury and the higher court, and freedom was ultimately denied.

In LIVANDAIS' HEIRS v. FON,[653] the testator bequeathed his property to his bastard son by a slave. The child having predeceased its master, she, as a slave, could not inherit its share.

Vermont, denied the existence of slavery by her constitutions of 1777 and 1786,[654] had no laws regulating the sexual relations of white and Negro, either before or after her admission as a state in 1791.

Kentucky generally adopted the existing Virginia statutes,[655] presumably those governing sexual relations between the race-castes.[656] In 1799 the new state recognized the presence of Mulattoes by making them incompetent as witnesses except against other Negroes, Mulattoes or Indians,[657] and by formulating the usual rule that the status of slavery is traced through the mother.[658] Another statute prescribes death for rape on a white woman.[659] Here the feelings of the non-slaveholding community get the better of the slaveholder's desire to preserve their property. There are no further Kentucky statutes on the subject. Kentucky was still too near the frontier, and the frontiersman had other things to do besides fix caste-lines by law. As might be expected, there were no judicial decisions. Tennessee, likewise on the frontier, also had no legislation nor cases of her own on sexual relations between the race-castes.

There are a few District of Columbia cases on sexual relations between whites and Negroes, generally reflecting conditions in Maryland and Virginia. In WOOD v. JOHN DAVIS,[660a] we find "Duvall, J., stated that in all the petitions for freedom which he filed in Maryland, in the cases of the Shorters, the Thomases, the Bostons, and many others, he always stated their title at large, tracing it up to a free white woman."

Ohio, while under the Northwest Territories Ordinance, forbade marriages "prohibited by the laws of god."[661] From past models,[662] one may infer that this meant interracial marriages. The Constitution of 1802[663] and an act of 1803, "to regulate black and Mulatto persons,"[664] takes Mulattoes as a matter of course. The same is true in 1807.[665] There are no Ohio cases during this period.

Indiana took Mulattoes as a matter of course, and specifically defined them.[666] Like Ohio, she disallowed marriages, "prohibited by the laws of God."[667] In 1818, after the trend had already been away from the original attempt to organize Indiana as a slave state,[668] the state enacted a clear-cut caste-law, punishing the white partner only for sexual intercourse with a Negro, and explicitly prohibiting interracial marriages.[669] There were no Indiana cases.

Mississippi from the outset recognized the existence of Mulattoes by referring to them in the various laws.[670] Death was given for rape on a free white woman[671] indicating an insecurity of the caste status which overrode slaveowners' objections to losing their property. Here we see the contrast between a frontier society and a settled aristocracy like that of South Carolina.

Illinois began by adopting Indiana laws in force in 1809[672] which included the definition of Mulattoes and the prohibition againt mixed marriages. [673] In 1807 the prohibition against marriages "prohibited by the laws of God," was made explicit.[673a] In later legislation, Mulattoes were taken for granted.[674]   Except for the prohibition of mixed marriages, no specific attention is given to sexual relations between the race-castes. There are no cases during this period.

Alabama likewise took Mulattoes as a matter of course. [675] There were no cases to 1820. Maine, part of Massachusetts till 1820, had no statutes nor cases on the sexual relations of race-castes. Missouri was governed from Indiana before admission as a state. Mulattoes were taken for granted.[676] There are no cases through 1820.

EMANCIPATION

In the period 1793-1820, emancipation began to take two courses. In the southern states things remained about what they were during the 17th and 18th century, but barriers began to be set up against outside emancipation drives. Emancipation was granted either as a reward or as a sanction to enforce the prohibition of the slave trade. On the other hand, in states where abolition was under way, emancipation became an adjunct of abolition.

There is one English case in this period, which reveals the economics underlying "emancipation" and abolition. If an emancipated slave worked for agreed wages, he could recover only the agreed wages— not on quantum meruit. [677] This is a decision which can arise only where the quantum meruit—the reasonable value of the work—is higher than the agreed wages. Under nascent capitalism, all the noble sentiments of "freedom" and "emancipation" were dragooned into service to secure low-wage labor. [677a]This movement later culminated in a paragraph of the Emancipation Proclamation:[677b]

> I hereby enjoin upon the people so declared free to abstain from all violence, unless in necessary self-defense; and I recommend to them that in all cases where allowed, they labor faithfully for reasonable wages.

Free enterprise evidently did not extend to "emancipated" slaves. Understandably, the Emancipation Proclamation is a document which is celebrated but not quoted.

Virginia enacted her first new emancipation statute to enforce the prohibition of the slave trade.[678] If a slave was freed, the former master was required to give him a certificate of emancipation.[679] Emancipation by will was expressly authorized.[680] But emancipated slaves had to leave the state within a year,[681] unless emancipated for acts of extraordinary merit and expressly granted permission to reside in Virginia.[682] The permission was in turn subject to defeasance if the slave was afterwards convicted of any crime.[683]

A tendency to in some quarters look favorably upon emancipation was suggested by SHELTON v. BARBOUR,[684] decided in 1795. There the trial court refused to admit a prior judgment against the freedom of the plaintiff's mother. The jury found the plaintiff free. The judgment was reversed on appeal and the case remanded with directions to find against emancipations unless the plaintiff could show that either he or his mother was freed since the previous judgment. The same trend appears even more pronounced in PLEASANTS v. PLEASANTS[685] where the court of last resort declined to apply the strict rule against remoteness of vesting where it would prevent emancipation by will.

WYTHE'S WILL[686] shows that Chancellor Wythe had freed slaves living on his estate at the time of his death. The same willingness to support emancipation prevailed in CHARLES v. HUNNICUTT.[687] By a will made in April of 1781, the testator provided that certain slaves should be free "on or before the first month next 1782." No fitting emancipation statute existed at the time, but one was passed in May, 1782. While the trial court held the attempted manumission void, the court of appeals took the view that such a provision could validly be made in anticipation of a change in the law. "Devises in favour of charity, and particularly those in favour of liberty ought to be liberally expounded." The same result followed a fortiori where freedom coincided with the policy against importing slaves.

Virginia, surfeited with slaves, would not stretch a point to prolong the slavery of one who had been removed and brought back. This happened in WILSON v. ISBELL,[688] where Isbell was taken to Maryland, kept there for 2½ years and then brought back to Virginia. She was declared free. Another case in the same year (1805) though holding against manumission, nevertheless shows how much steam there was behind the emancipation movement in Viriginia at this time. WOODLEY v. ABBEY[689] did not permit a husband and wife to manumit slaves which she had received from her previous husband, on suit of the first husband's heirs. The Negroes were returned to slavery by a divided court, though they had been free de facto for 12 years.

There is a whole string of Virginia cases on manumission about this time, and most of them grant decrees of freedom. The plaintiff in

PARISH v. GRAY[690] was finally declared free by a court in a sixth trial after five juries had disagreed.   There followed HUDGINS v. WRIGHTS,[691] holding Indians not subject to slavery in Virginia since 1691; WHITING v. DANIELS[692] where an attempted emancipation by will was held defeated, by a previous deed to the slaves inter vivos, and PATTY v. COLIN[693] which did not allow slaves to be taken on execution, if it could possibly be avoided, where their former owner had sought to emancipate them by will.

DAWSON v. THRUSTON,[694] decided in 1808, dealt with a deed of trust executed in 1797, "intended to provide for the gradual emancipation of slaves therein conveyed." In HUGHES v. HUGHES[695] the testatrix, by will dated 1804, emancipated all her Negroes. Similarly, MURRAY v. McCARTY,[696] decided in 1811, and GRIFFITH v. FANNY,[696a] decided in 1820, grant emancipation through a narrow interpretation of the rule allowing a master to leave the state with his slaves and bring them back on his return. In KENDALL v. KENDALL[697] the testator originally emancipated his slaves by will, but revoked the emancipation clause by a codicil executed on the day of his death.

The current policy in favor of emancipation receives strong expression in WILLIAM & MARY COLLEGE v. HODGSON[698] where an annuity in kind to William & Mary College was held not chargeable against the entire estate "lest it might deprive some or all of the manumitted slaves of the testator of the liberty secured to them by his benevolence and humanity, which is supposed to have been an act no less meritorious than the establishment of a free school."   BUTT v. RACHEL[699] invoked the rule that Indians were free—even if brought from Jamaica in 1747.

The number of emancipations seems to fall off after 1811. Virginia, still surfeited with slaves, was undoubtedly finding her new role as a slave supplier to the cotton states. Maryland's first law again emancipation was a reflection of the state's movement away from agriculture. The "Patowmack Company," building Washington, found it could operate best if allowed to move slaves freely across the Potomac and back. But this was hindered by the rule that a slave imported into Maryland became free. So the existing law was modified to the extent of permitting slaves to be brought in for 12 months without resulting emancipation.[700] In 1804 the legislature allowed the "Patowmack Company" to keep slaves outside of Maryland for an indefinite period, repealing the 1-year limitation of 1794.[700a]

For the last time, and on a minute scale, the advance of industry here gave a paradoxical impetus to the non-industrial slave economy. But the trend away from slavery undermined the caste system based upon it. That was now to be replaced by a new caste system based entirely on color.

In 1796, Maryland explicitly enacted a law that emancipation of a slave does not entitle him to vote.[701] The previous statute against emancipations by will was repealed.[702] An elaborate procedure was set up for trying claims to freedom before a jury.[703-4] What this adds up to is the creation of a new depressed caste of wage laborers. Yet, no one was permitted to jump the gun. Slaves entitled to future freedom had to serve out their entire term, if they left their master prematurely.[705-6]

An indication of the state of flux in which slavery in Maryland found itself at this time were the laws prohibiting the transfer of certificates of freedom,[707] and the vacillation of laws which follow. Various individual exceptions were granted from time to time to the rule that slaves were freed if brought into Maryland from another state.[708] The right of emancipation was extended to children born to female slaves between the date when future emancipation was declared and the date when the mother was actually free.[709] In 1810 previously inadequate deeds of emancipation were validated.[710] On the other hand, the right to move slaves across state lines and back again without manumission was made general.[711]

The drive underlying the "emancipation" movement comes to light again in the law of 1818 authorizing the judges of the Orphans' Court to bind out the children of free Negroes if not already working.[712] The great movement for "freedom" was nothing more than the systematic creation of a class of low-paid wage earners. Following the laws of this period, one has the impression of watching a pendulum. In the same year, 1818, in which the foregoing law was passed, there was also a law guaranteeing that persons who inherited slaves could bring them into the State of Maryland without fear of emancipation.[713] In the two succeeding years, we find private acts validating deeds of manumission of 1806,[714] and 1812,[715] respectively.

The same urge toward "emancipation" appears in the Maryland cases during the period 1793-1820. While the first two are claims to freedom because of descent from a free white woman,[716] the fact that the claims were upheld is indication of the trend. Minors, however, could not emancipate,[717] nor were slaves free if brought by refugees from Santo Domingo in 1791[718] (though in this latter case the trial court had granted freedom). Slavery was still presumed for all persons descended from an ancestor imported from a country where slavery was legal.[719]

In MEHONEY v. ASHTON, decided in 1797[720] however, Maryland seems to react to the rise of the cotton kingdom. It has been remarked that SOMERSET v. STEWART[721] signified the impact of the industrial revolution on the slave system in showing new ways to emancipation. If the cotton kingdom was a second counter-current, it logically should have brought about limitations on SOMERSET v. STEWART, and produced new rules that taking a slave to free territory did not necessarily emancipate him. MAHONEY v. ASHTON illustrates this new tendency.   At first sight it may seem ironical that this should have arisen in Maryland, where there was also a strong current in favor of emancipation. But litigation brings opposing social tendencies to a head when the conflict is mild enough to be settled in court. MAHONEY v. ASHTON limits the operation of SOMERSET v. STEWART so far as Maryland is concerned and rather ingeniously turns the language of the English case against emancipation. The opportunity of selling slaves to the cotton states seems to have gained the upperhand for the time being.

In NEGRO PLATO v. BAINBRIDGE,[722] the court in 1799 found a bona fide intention to emigrate from South Carolina and settle in Maryland. Consequently, the slave whom the master brought along did not become free. In NEGRO DAVID v. PORTER,[723] decided the same year, the slave had been brought from Maryland to Pennsylvania, and back again to Maryland. His presence in Pennsylvania was held to free him under Pennsylvania laws, and this status continued in Maryland. But in NEGRO HARRY v. LYLES,[724] importation from Virginia did not mean emancipation. In JENNINGS v. HIGGINS,[725] absence of a bond was used to deny wages to a slave[726] first held free but whose judgment was later reversed.   Here the interests of the dying slave system and of rising industrial capitalism coincided. The new industrialism was not going to pay any wages which it could avoid.

In NEGRO JAMES v. GAITHER [727] manumission by deed and will were held insufficient.   On the other hand, in NEGRO CATO v. HOWARD,[728] an agreement to manumit at the end of seven years was held binding even as against a bona fide purchaser.   But BURY v. NEGRO GRACE [729] was another link in the new chain against emancipation: a testamentary gift over was held to override an intervening testamentary manumission by an intervening life tenant. Likewise, SPRIGG v. NEGRO MARY,[729a] where two years in the District of Columbia did not emancipate when the slave was brought back to Maryland.

The pendulum took a swing in the opposite direction in STARTER v. BOSWELL,[730] giving the widest scope to proof of a free female ancestor and in STEWART v. OAKES [731] granting freedom under the laws of Virginia because the slave had been taken to Virginia.   QUEEN v. NEALE[732] is on the other side of the line, holding that a plaintiff claiming freedom from slavery cannot ask a change of venue on the ground that he could not get a fair and impartial trial in the original court. But here the owner brought the slave to Baltimore when a refugee from Santo Domingo, kept him for two years, then sold him in Maryland and returned to Santo Domingo, and the slave was held to have been freed; [733] so with immigrants from New York who had not complied with the Maryland laws for the registration of slaves brought in with an immigrant master. [734]

Here the rules against importation and in favor of emancipation were strictly applied two years later. [736a] The act in question (Stats. 1783, ch. 23) had later been repealed. [735] In the following year however, the opposite result was reached under the same statute, [736] and again two years later. [736a] In another swing back, however, JOHNSON v. NEGRO LISH [737] allowed emancipation by will, over the objection that the slave had been transferred to the testator by a defeasible gift. The gift was held absolute, the attempted defeasance void.   In the same year however, a deed of manumission was held void for not having been recorded in time. [738]

In 1820 we are back at the opposite pole from SHORTER v. BOSWELL. [739] Evidence of reputation of the freedom of the petitioner's female ancestors was not allowed: [740] "general reputation of the neighborhood, that the petitioner, or his maternal ancestors, were free Negroes," was inadmissible. "In the cases referred to in the reports of Harris and McHenry such evidence was received by the court. It was, however, refused by the Supreme Court of the United States. So where the widow elected to renounce her share under the will in favor of her third as widow, emancipation clauses in the will were ineffective, the slaves being needed to round out the widow's third. [741] NEGRO CLARA v. MEAGHER, [742] closes the period. It finds defective the signature of an attesting witness to a deed of emancipation. The emancipation is consequently held void.

New York has a steady though slow movement towards emancipation. The period after 1793 begins with an act validating previously doubtful emancipation by Quakers. [743] As in other states, no slaves were manumitted, but those born after July 4, 1799 were declared free, but bound to serve the mother's master until 28 if men, until 25 if women. But in the interim the institution of slavery was otherwise maintained. In 1801 the New York legislature once more declared that baptism shall not free a slave. [745] Importation of slaves was carefully regulated and slaves brought into the state in disregard of regulations became "free." [746]

What happened to them after "freedom" may be inferred from what already been said. They probably became the lowest paid laborers. As a last resort, the state supported "poor persons formerly slaves."[747] While children of slave mothers were bound to service until the ages of 28 and 25, the "right" to service could be abandoned under restrictions in 1801,[748] and unconditionally after ages 21 and 18 in 1804.[749] Here we see how "emancipation" was the emancipation of the master from the burdens which encumbered the slaveowner.

In 1807 only residents of ten years (instead of one year) were permitted to remove slaves from the state without losing them.[750] At the same time consequences of emancipation were tardily accepted, and the faint beginnings show themselves of a movement to make emancipated slaves part of the general community. In 1809 they were granted the right to inherit.[751] In 1813, slave marriages were declared valid, with the stern proviso that they did not manumit.[751a] In 1810 persons coming into the state to reside permanently were prohibited from bringing their slaves; any stay of nine months was permanent residence.[752]

The abolition movement brought a new variation of the old problem of "freeing" slaves incapable of working. Slaves were "freed" by owners outside New York state, indented to citizens of New York, who then abandoned them in New York.

> And whereas, to evade the existing laws of this state concerning the importation and transfer of slaves, persons residing in adjacent states have manumitted their slaves and afterwards induced them to indent or bind themselves for a term of years to certain persons, citizens of this state, receiving at the same time for such term of service, a price or consideration equal to the full value of the slave, whereby the persons so manumitted are not only reduced back to a state of virtual bondage, but after having grown too old in service as to be incapable of gaining a subsistence, are turned out to become a charge on the community, to the great burden of the public and against the true intent of the laws of this state.[753]

Indentures for personal service of individuals who had been slaves in other states were henceforth made void.[754] The master was now required to "use all proper and reasonable means" to teach reading and writing to children of slave mothers born after July 4, 1799.[755] This illustrates again how the rising industrial society had greater use for literate than for illiterate employees.[755a]

Later in that same year a compromise was reached. Slaveowners who had brought their slaves from other states were permitted to hire them to citizens of New York for periods of not over seven years, provided the slaves were free at the end of that time, and the original owners still liable for their support if they were unable to support themselves.[756]   As in Massachusetts, "freed" slaves brought with them the problem of where their settlement should be counted for purposes of pauper relief. [757] The new and old systems continued side by side, with industrialism and emancipation slowly advancing and slavery and the agricultural economy slowly receding.   The right to use slaves on land stretching across state lines without risk of emancipation was confirmed once more,[758] two weeks after free Negroes and Mulattoes had been given the right to vote.[759]

Four years later, manumitted slaves were given standing in court, but with the explicit reservation that they had no cause of action against their former masters.[760]   Marriages were made valid, as between former and even present slaves.   But in the latter case the statute carefully confirms the rule that the marriage does not emancipate.[761] Slaves still could not be witnesses, except against another slave,[762] yet they had to be taught to read. If not so taught, they became free at age 18, to be bound out by the Overseers of the Poor.[763]   Exportation of slaves was not forbidden,[764]   which contrasts with the policies of Kentucky and Virginia, which became slave-exporting states.   The unspoken policy of New York was evidently to keep slaves at home for possible future freedom, and low wages. So persons coming into the state could bring slaves born before July 4, 1799, but such slaves became free at the ages of 25 and 28. In the interim they had to be taught to read.[765]

But even employment as wage laborers did not come all at once. An intermediate stage was created in which slaves emancipated under this act were put into the position of apprentices with their former masters.[766] As both a link with the past and a forewarning of troubles to come, New York enacted her own law against fugitive slaves.[767]   In 1819, the penalty for exporting slaves was increased.[768]   The period comes to a close without even notice of the Missouri Compromise by the New York legislature.

The New York cases of this period begin in 1800, and records had doubtless been destroyed due to the fact that New York was the theatre of so much fighting early in the Revolutionary War. Like the statutes, the judicial decisions show the slow exit of the institution of slavery. The prohibition against sale of slaves was held intended to defeat importation, and to apply only to voluntary sales, not to sales by executors to pay creditors of the estate.[769] But a New Jersey master's hiring out his slave in New York, after the slave had escaped to New

York, was held a consent to the entry into New York, so the slave was freed.[770] A claim of manumission by the seller before transfer was upheld against the buyer, though made for the first time after the seller's death.[772] So a covenant to emancipate after 8 years was enforced against a buyer who took without notice in the meantime.[773]

WELLS v. LANE[774] upheld a Quaker manumission and holds a slave free who was treated as such for over twenty years by her former master. "After such declarations and such a lapse of time, to authorize the plaintiff to claim her as a slave would be extremely unjust; and unless she was a slave there is no ground upon which he could maintain his action." In the next case—HOPKINS & MUDGE v. FLEET & YOUNG,[775] the true operation of "emancipation" becomes apparent. Support of an indigent ex-slave was saddled on the town rather than the former owner. So EXECUTORS OF ROGERS v. BERRY[776] holds manumission by an infant, approved by the infant's guardian, valid until disaffirmed. The cases find particular grounds for emancipation almost continually until the general abolition in New York in 1827.

CEASAR v. PEABODY[777] holds a slave imported from Virginia, not freed by a sale on execution, but freed by a subsequent resale, because the latter was voluntary. While the master's attainder for treason was strictly construed, and not permitted to emancipate a slave in a doubtful case,[778] in 1815 the New York Court of Appeals, expressed the view that "I rejoice that an instance has occurred, by which the law will operate in favor of personal liberty."[779] A few vestiges of the old system remained. Selling a slave during a master's lifetime defeated an emancipation clause in his will.[780]

In New Jersey, the act of 1798 expressly recognizes emancipation.[781] But there was as yet no great pressure in this direction. Persons bringing slaves into the state were fined, but their slaves were not freed.[782] Significantly, the general slave law already held the town liable for support if a manumitted slave became a pauper.[783] In 1804, twenty years later than the New England states, New Jersey passed her law for gradual abolition.[784] All slaves born after "the 4th of July next" were declared free. But they would remain servants until the ages of 25 if male, and 21 if female,[785] unless sooner abandoned according to law.[786]

The process was speeded up by making the signature of the Overseer of the Poor sufficient on the deed of manumission in certain cases.[787] In New Jersey, as elsewhere, emancipated slaves were placed under the jurisdiction of the Overseers of the Poor. This legislation says what everyone knew, but what was drowned out by the lyrics of abolition; that slaves were being freed to furnish rock-bottom cheap labor. The next step was to emancipate slaves taken out of the state, which was done in 1818.[788]

The few New Jersey cases which arose between 1793 and 1820, upheld emancipation at age 25. STATE v. FREES[790] holds the evidence insufficient to emancipate, but refuses the master's request to assess costs against the Abolition Society of Salem, on the ground that "was a laudable and humane thing in any man or set of men to bring up the claim of these unfortunate people before the court for consideration." STATE v. MOUNT[791] denied freedom where conditional emancipation had been granted, if the slave had no children for ten years, but this condition was not fulfilled.

In STATE v. HEDDON,[792] a slave who had joined the British in the Revolutionary war and was then taken prisoner, was held free. STATE v. McDONALD & ARMSTRONG[793] held an oral declaration of freedom with acquiescence by the master to be effective. STATE v. VAN WAGGONER[794] went contrary to states further south in holding that Indians could be slaves. Paradoxically, the cases after 1797 show a trend away from emancipation.[795]

Massachusetts had no slavery after 1781. The only legislative expression on emancipation is the ringing resolution of February 13, 1820, against permitting slavery in new territories.[796] SHELBURNE v. GREENFIELD[797] indicates that in practice, the Declaration of Independence was taken as freeing the slaves in Massachusetts. INHABITANTS OF WINCHDON v. INHABITANTS OF HATFIELD,[798] says that while slavery existed in Massachusetts, emancipation was frequently granted for faithful service, usually by will. In general, suits for freedom were not resisted, "for such was the temper of the times," that a dissatisfied slave was of little value while emancipation freed the master of the obligation of support. INHABITANTS OF STOCKBRIDGE v. INHABITANTS OF WEST STOCKBRIDGE[799] seemed to hold that manumission was accomplished by the simple purchase of a slave with intent to make him a servant; but when the case came up on a second appeal,[800] this suggestion was definitely rejected.

Connecticut had decreed gradual emancipation in 1784, by directing that all persons born after that date should be free. But slavery continued during the lifetime of the last slave. Masters were permitted to emancipate, subject to the restriction of supporting indigent former slaves or of having obtained a certificate freeing them (the master's) from this obligation.[801] The state salved its conscience by declaring piously:

All born since the first of March, 1784, are free. Death

and emancipation will soon abolish a practice which is equally repugnant to the dictates of sound policy and the voice of humanity. But it ought to be remarked that those who are yet slaves, are treated with proper kindness and are in general much happier, than those who have obtained a liberty, which they know not how to use as not abusing it.[802]

This solicitude for the happiness of slaves and fear of their abusing freedom was experienced only in states whose industrialization was less advanced than that of Massachusetts. Although "free" persons born after March 1, 1784 were subject to servitude until reaching the age of 25, this was cut down to age 21 in 1797.[803] The end of slavery was hastened by accepting almost anything as an effective emancipation. "The declaration of the mistress made to the servant that he should be free at twenty-five years of age amounted to a manumission."[804] Apparently the institution of slavery died quietly in Connecticut: there were almost no cases on emancipation from 1793 to 1820. Persons born after 1784, were on the same footing as apprentices or minors until they became free.[805]

Rhode Island forbade importation of slaves and enforced the prohibition by providing:

> that if any slave shall hereafter be brought in he or she shall be, and hereby is rendered immediately free, so far as rights, personal freedom, and the enjoyment of private property, in the same manner as the native Indians.[806]

There was no further legislation and no cases.

New Hampshire had neither legislation nor cases on emancipation during the period 1793-1820. Pennsylvania did not have any new legislation, and the judicial decisions show the same tendency to decree emancipation wherever legally possible,[807] but with a tenderness towards persons from other states travelling with their slaves.[808]

As early as 1795, North Carolina showed a tendency opposite to that of the northern states where slavery was on its way out. In that year the slave trade was forbidden,[809] but slaves illegally imported did not become free.[810] In 1801 owners liberating their slaves were required to give bond for their support if they became indigent.[811] In 1796 however, emancipations were confirmed as granting freedmen the same rights as freeborn Negroes.[812]

As might be expected, North Carolina was vacillating in her attitude towards emancipation. As also might be expected, interest in

the subject waned as the Revolutionary War faded into the past. There
was no further legislation to 1820. The same vacillation appears from
the cases.   Perhaps the clearest instance is ADMINISTRATOR OF
ALLEN v. PEDEN, [813] in which the North Carolina Supreme Court held a
private act of emancipation to be unconstitutional. The opinion is like a
still photo of all the effects of the Revolutionary War combined with the
uncertain status of slavery in North Carolina from the first.

The Supreme Court of the state said:

> The administrator was, in law, the owner of the persons
> emancipated by the General Assembly.   The act of
> emancipation passed not only without his consent, but
> against it.   However laudable the motive which led to the
> act of emancipation, it is too plainly in violation of the
> fundamental law of the land to be sanctioned by judicial
> authority. We are compelled to pronounce it a nullity.

In   other   cases   the   judiciary   were   generally   reluctant   to
emancipate.[814]   Although North Carolina was never fully at home with
slavery, the attitudes which took shape after the Revolutionary War
foreshadowed   North   Carolina's   secession   in   1861,   just   as   their
counterparts foreshadowed the contrary position of the northern states.
Northern agitation for emancipation was probably reflected in the
decision of 1819[814a] imposing the death penalty for slave stealing.

In keeping with her Eighteenth Century history, South Carolina
showed no movement toward general emancipation, but granted a
number of individual emancipations for meritorious service. The caste
system was so firm, and the ruling caste so confident of themselves that
they could grant occasional manumissions as a generous bounty.   The
very fact that emancipation was kept on an individual basis, again
indicates the feudal character of the South Carolina slave system.

The first private act of emancipation which appeared during the
period 1793-1820 was the liberation of Abraham in 1804.[815]   The
preamble states "Whereas a certain Negro man named Abraham
belonging to Mr. William Kirk has rendered certain meritorious services
to this State, for which he ought to be rewarded," and the state treasury
paid twelve hundred dollars to the owner to emancipate the slave
completely. In 1817, the legislature passed an act[816] appropriating:

> the sum of $1,100 . . . at the disposal of the Governor, to
> purchase freedom of the servant who gave information of
> the projected insurrection in the city and neighborhood of

> Camden; and also that the sum of fifty dollars per annum,
> out of the public treasury be allowed to said servant,
> until otherwise directed by law.

This enactment encapsulates the South Carolina social system. It is not assumed that the emancipated slave will be able to make his own living, so apart from compensation voted to the master, the freedman himself is granted an annuity of $50 a year. But this annuity was not without strings. It ran "until otherwise directed by law." The legislature retained the right to cut it off. However far it may extend, it remains a bounty.

Not until 1820[817] was there a general law touching emancipation, and then it was restrictive. There was enacted "An act to restrain the emancipation of slaves and to prevent free persons of color from entering into this state."[818] The preamble states:

> Whereas, the great and rapid increase of free Negroes
> and Mulattoes in this State, by migration and
> emancipation renders it expedient and necessary for the
> legislature to restrain the emancipation of slaves, and to
> prevent free persons of color from entering this state . . .

The act then provides flatly "that no slave shall hereafter be emancipated but by act of the Legislature."[819]

By 1820, slave raiding from the Northern states, for cheap wage labor, was making itself felt. But at the same time, South Carolina was at the beginning of a decline. The soil had been used up, and the cotton belt was moving into the states of Georgia, Alabama and Mississippi. It was becoming unprofitable to hold slaves, and despite the law of 1800, emancipations were occurring for that reason.[819a] Again, the northern demands for cheap wage labor were now being implemented by insurrections for "freedom." So, along with the total prohibition of emancipation except by legislative act, fine and imprisonment were imposed for circulating written or printed material with intent to disturb the slaveholding peace or security of the state.[820]

South Carolina's economic hegemony was no more. It is usually in decline that societies enact measures of repression. There are some instances of voluntary emancipation in the court cases. In SNOW v. CALLUM[821] the testator provided that "Minda and her increase" should be free after ten years. The children were held free at the end of that time, though the mother had died in the meantime. CARPENTER, GUARDIAN OF SUNDRY FREE NEGROES v. COLEMAN[822] gives a broad interpretation to the statutory requirement to produce a slave and treat him well during a suit for freedom. BYNUM v. BOSTWICK[823] in 1812, says that emancipation by a testamentary trust is void.

> Many cases of beneficient provisions for slaves are allowed to take place subsilentio, by the humanity of those interested. But when the law is appealed to, it must take its course.

STATE v. BALDWIN,[823a] decided the following year, notes that petitions against pardon of slave stealers had been circulated. There are no other cases on emancipation during this period.

Delaware saw the tendency toward manumission in 1797, and bent with the wind by enacting a law regulating the procedure.[824] This was further refined in 1810, when statu liberi, were definitely declared slaves in the meantime,[825] but their children slaves only until age 25 if males, and age 21 if females.[826] In 1819, the state confirmed the emancipation of all former slaves whose masters had failed to put up the required bond at the time of emancipation.[826a] There are a few private acts during this period allowing importation or exportation of particular slaves.[827] The rule emancipating slaves if illegally exported or imported was enforced virtually without qualification, showing that slavery had had its day in Delaware. This was subject only to narrow exception in favor of stateline plantations.[828]

The constitution of Georgia of 1798 forbade the Legislature from passing laws emancipating slaves without the owner's consent.[829] Three years later the legislature prescribed that an application to the legislature should be the only mode of manumission.[830] Georgia here is embarked on another segment of her strange course of development. The last of the original thirteen colonies, she was the only one which prohibited slavery. But because of her location, slavery was still profitable. Yet by the time she permitted slavery, the Industrial Revolution was already under was in the North. So she restricted emancipation drastically as soon as she expressed herself on it.

In 1818 further restrictions were placed on manumission, inasmuch as:

> the principles of sound policy, considered in reference to the free citizens of this state, and the exercise of humanity towards the slave population, imperiously require that the number of free persons of color within this state should not be increased by manumission, or by

the admission of such person from other states to reside therein.[831]

The solicitude expressed for the happiness of the slave population[832] sounds like a guarded suggestion that free Negroes, or slaves assuming the rights of free Negroes might incite slaves to revolt. Specifically, manumissions by will were abolished.[833] There are a few individual emancipations on record,[834] and no Georgia cases on emancipation during the period 1793-1820.

Louisiana became part of the U.S. in 1803. There had been no French or Spanish cases on slavery since 1780. The Code of 1804 expressly authorized emancipation by formal written instruments.[835] But a subsequent condition was imposed on emancipation. If a liberated slave did not thereafter pay all taxes he could be sold back into slavery to pay delinquent taxes.[836] In 1807 an entire act was passed "to regulate the conditions and forms of the emancipation of slaves."[837] Compulsory emancipation was allowed only if made for compensation by the Commonwealth. Voluntary emancipation was authorized by deed or will for slaves at least 30 years of age upon a showing of the slave's good character during the past four years. Of the cases from Louisiana in this period, STATE v. CECIL[839] is notable because it qualified a freedman as a witness. Otherwise the majority of cases upheld emancipation where it was claimed.[840]

Vermont, admitted in 1791, liberated all slaves coming into the state.[841] SELECTMAN v. JACOB,[842] decided in 1802, held that "though the bill of sale may be binding by the laws of another state or dominion, yet when the master becomes an inhabitant of this State, his bill of sale ceases to operate here" and the slave was freed.

Kentucky, by her constitution of 1792, already showed the impact of the Industrial Revolution. The legislature was forbidden to pass emancipation laws except with the owners' consent, or for his compensation.[843] At the same time the legislature was commanded to set up machinery for voluntary emancipation.[844] The separation of Kentucky from Virginia came as Kentucky was settled. The settlement was done primarily by slaveowners, mostly from Virginia. However, at the same time the slave area expanded, it also felt the effects of the Industrial Revolution. The Kentucky constitution of 1792 shows that its framers were torn between fear of involuntary emancipation, and the desire to facilitate voluntary emancipation, which the framers knew many Virginia slaveowners wanted. This schizophrenia would haunt Kentucky even after the end of the Civil War.[845] But the interests of the newly arrived slaveowners soon gained this upperhand. As pioneers, they were not too attentive to legal formalities, and did not register their slaves as required. So in 1788, the provision freeing unregistered slaves was suspended for three years.[846]

A private act of emancipation appeared in 1817, freeing a slave whom his master intended to free, but did not before he died.[847] However, the general trend continued. The pioneers brought their slaves into Kentucky, without much regard for legalisms, and the registration law was again softened to meet their needs.[848] Kentucky cases on emancipation began to reach the Court of Appeals about ten years after the state was organized, and continued to occur until 1820. The great majority deny emancipation,[849] showing that while the state was experiencing qualms of conscience, the overriding tendency was to set up a new slave area.

Tennessee passed an emancipation act in 1801,[850] and county courts were given the power to emancipate. The act was mainly aimed at stemming a flood of indigent freedmen, indicating that slavery was not working well in Tennessee. There are a few private acts of manumission.[851]

There are only two cases on emancipation during this period: EDWARDS v. MCONNELL[852] dealt with the effect of the French Revolutionary decree of 1794, freeing slaves in Haiti, while MCUTCHIN v. PRICE[853] says that a direction to an executor to emancipate will be enforced if there is a legal way for the executor to carry it out.

The District of Columbia, torn between opposing forces, generally favored emancipation. In ROSE v. KENNEDY,[853a] the correctness of the Virginia oath taken on importation from another state was held a jury question; bequeathing a slave by will for a term of years was held to emancipate at the end of the term.[853b] Transportation from Maryland to Alexandria (Virginia) or Virginia to Maryland, likewise effected emancipation,[853c] and "a hiring from Alexandria to Washington was considered the same as from Virginia to Maryland."[853d] Where a Negro had conducted himself as free for many years, it was taken as prima facie evidence of freedom.[853e] If the required oath on an imported slave was not taken within 60 days after importation, the slave was free[853f] as was one not registered according to the laws of Maryland.[853g]

The clause in a will manumitting slaves was enforced where there was enough in the estate to satisfy the widow's share without recourse to the slaves, and the widow elected to take her legal share rather than under the will.[853i] Once acknowledged and recorded, a deed of manumission dated back to the time of its execution.[853j] The will of a <u>statu</u>

libera was free.[853k] If a slave was imported into Virginia, no presumption that his master took the necessary oath arose against him before the slave was of age.[853l] So in the same way, procedure generally supported the cause of the petitioner for freedom.[853m] Decisions against emancipation generally were cases where the court permitted a certain amount of moving between different states, principally Maryland and Virginia.[853n]

Ohio, once part of the Northwest Territory where slavery was prohibited, continued this prohibition in her first constitution[854] and had no statutes on emancipation. There were no Ohio cases to 1820.

Indiana which originally condoned slavery under the pretense of indentured servants, provided that their freedom should be recorded at the end of their term.[855] For failing to register, the master lost all claim to services from the slave, but the slave apparently did not become free.[856] Children born to indentured colored servants became indentured until the ages of thirty and twenty-eight years, for males and females respectively.[857]

There is a suggestion that "indentured servants" might be liberated before their term from ill-treatment. In such cases the court hearing the complaint might make "such orders thereupon, as in their judgment will relieve the party injured in future."[858] These statutes were, however, repealed in 1810, saving rights under existing indentures.[859] After that the legislature's attention was turned to false certificates of emancipation.[860] This shows the substitution of the wage system for the slave system and the employment of illegal devices to secure cheap wage labor.

When Indiana was admitted as a state in 1816, the state constitution provided, "that all men are born equally free and independent."[861] For the first time there was express provision that apprentices could be discharged if mistreated.[862] There were no Indiana cases on emancipations to 1820.

In 1805, Mississippi prohibited the liberation of slaves otherwise than for meritorious conduct.[863] Since this is the first enactment of the new territory, it shows the paradox of its coming into being. Expansion of the slave area was profitable because of the cotton gin, and necessary because of soil exhaustion in the older, eastern states. But at the same time, industry was growing in the North and making demands for emancipation to supply cheap wage labor in new industries.

Mississippi therefore emerged as a new form of garrison state. It fought not against the slaves, like 18th century South Carolina, but against the efforts of other regions to "emancipate" them. In 1817, the state constitution was adopted in contemplation of Mississippi's admission as a state. The general assembly was forbidden to pass emancipation laws except for distinguished service.[864]

There are, however, a series of emancipations by special act[864a] HARRY, ET AL. v. DECKER & HOPKINS[865] is the only case on emancipation to 1820. It upholds the freedom of slaves brought from Virginia into the Northwest Territory (Vincennes) and then to Mississippi. It is interesting that even the Supreme Court of Mississippi says, "In matters of doubt . . . courts must lean in favorem vitae et libertatis." Perhaps nothing illustrates conflicting cross-currents better than this.

Illinois, bent on circumventing the Northwest Territory prohibition of slavery, had no provision for emancipation. The closest thing to it was a law freeing apprentices when they completed their terms.[866] Otherwise, Illinois during this period has nothing but enactments that slaves shall not become free if working in the state.[867]

The preamble of the law of 1814[868] spells out the demand of new industry for cheap labor, which was obtained from the slave areas. At this time Illinois still tried to accomplish its ends by not emancipating slaves who were drafted into industry:

> Whereas the erection of mills and other valuable improvements are greatly retarded in this Territory, from want of Laborers, and whereas, also experience has proved that the manufacture of salt in particular . . . cannot be successfully carried on by white laborers . . .

There were no Illinois cases through 1820.

Alabama enacted a constitution modeled on that of Mississippi. But the constitution of 1819 was even stricter against emancipation than that of Mississippi two years before. The legislature could pass no laws for emancipation without the owner's consent.[869] Even the authorization for meritorious conduct was eliminated. Before statehood, Alabama sought to curb the owners' push towards emancipation. Owners were not allowed to emancipate except for meritorious conduct.[870] This again shows the cross-currents which were in motion in the new slave states. These states represented new slave settlements at the very time industry was gathering steam in the north. There was both the tendency to be caught up in the "emancipation" movement which such industry generated, and the tendency of the slave sytem as soon as established, to dig in its heels against emancipation. There were no Alabama cases on emancipation through 1820.

Maine, being part of Massachusetts until 1820, had no slavery and no emancipation laws. There were neither statutes nor cases.

Missouri as a territory authorized emancipation by writing (particularly by will) in 1804.[871] Suits for freedom were expressly authorized.[872] These statutes clearly reflect the northern location of Missouri, with the tendency toward emancipation overriding any urge to hold the slave system intact. There are no cases through 1820.

RELATIONS BETWEEN SLAVEOWNERS

Most relations between slaveowners continued as they had been before invention of the cotton gin.[873] States where slavery was disappearing show paucity of both statutes and cases. Otherwise, there were only two noticeable changes. Slavery now presented the paradox of being practically dependent upon the soil but legally divorced from it. The slave system was now an instrument mainly in the hands of pioneers. But that brought a new problem. Pioneers are people who have broken away from old restraints. Enjoying their new freedom, they were largely engaged in selling defective slaves to one another.[874] The prices of slaves went up in relation to the currency,[874a] but this was undoubtedly due to the inflation after the Revolutionary War. Later, the price range was $139.51 on an execution sale, up to $1200.[874b]

Abolition of the slave trade underlined a practice which had existed in Louisiana previously,[875] (and to a small extent in other colonies) namely the requisitioning of slaves for public works. When slaves could no longer be imported, there was greater inclination to requisition. Slaves were requisitioned to destroy a house encroaching on a street,[876] to build a canal[877] or to repair a broken and inundated levee.[878] Other states, however, did not use slaves in this way after 1793.

Virginia, Maryland, New York, New Jersey, Pennsylvania, and Connecticut continued their former practice of compensating the owners of slaves condemned to death, who were either executed or died while awaiting execution. Maryland[880] added a provision for compensation where the death sentence had been commuted by the Governor. Except for Virginia and Maryland, these states did not even have new statutes. There were no cases whatever.

North Carolina restored compensation for executed slaves in 1796, but only for the counties of Bladen, Halifax, Granville, Cumberland, Perquimans, Beaufort and Pitt.[881] It was apparently thought that there were not enough slaves in the other counties to raise the question. North Carolina then adopted the device used by Barbados in the 18th century.[882] If the master did not furnish the slave with adequate food and clothing, he was not entitled to compensation if the slave was executed for a capital crime. [883]   Compensation was limited to two-thirds the value of the slave,[884] and was paid when necessary by a tax "on all black polls,"[885] meaning both slaves and free Negroes.   The following year these provisions were extended to include the counties of Warren, Onslow and Chatham.[886]

In South Carolina, the general acts for granting compensation continued in force.   Specific accounts paid appear in the appropriation acts, beginning with 1799.[887]   The standard compensation was $122.40 per slave.   This was only a little more than one-tenth of what a good slave brought on purchase.[888]

Louisiana enacted her first general compensation statute under American jurisdiction in 1806.[889]   The law was quite generous; it set a maximum of five hundred dollars, but allowed the court to award part of this as damages to the injured party.   A maximum of $300 compensation was authorized for a slave killed while running away.[890]   Louisiana had another feature not found in the states of English origin: public compensation to a person maimed in the pursuit of a runaway.[891]   Both as respects rights and obligations,[892] Louisiana made slavery slightly more a public institution than did the English colonies.   There were also some private acts granting compensation in situations not exactly covered by the general law.[893]

Kentucky gave compensation for the full value of the slave.[894] Tennessee did not until 1820, restore the North Carolina compensation act which had been repealed in 1786.[895]   Indiana, though she tried to set up de facto slavery under the guise of apprenticeship (and sometimes openly used the word "slaves") never went so far as to speak of executed slaves or to grant compensation for them.

Until 1820, Mississippi, Alabama and Missouri did not grant compensation to masters for executed slaves.   Illinois, which started by adopting the laws of Indiana,[896] had the same subsequent history.

PROTECTION OF SLAVE PROPERTY VS. PUNISHMENT OF SLAVES

After 1793, the drive toward emancipation (and the transformation of the slave into a wage laborer) makes itself felt in more frequent provisions that slaves charged with crime shall be tried before a jury, the same as free persons. It was forgotten that the requirement of trying slaves before slaveholders was a protection of slave property, and therefore incidentally, of the slave himself.   The trend from 1763-1820 was to give slaves charged with crime the mechanical safeguards of freemen, though it is doubtful whether this put them in a more favorable position as defendants.[896a] States which continued the classical system of letting slaveholders mete out punishment to slaves are given in the footnote. [897]

The states which recognized the new era of industrialism by giving slaves the "right" to be tried by a petty jury were New York,[898] (replacing the master's right to opt for a jury,[899] which treated the slave more as a chattel, but was probably more favorable to him in practice); New Jersey, (continuing the law of 1768)[900] and North Carolina (repealing the law which had set up special courts for the trial of slaves). [901]

Connecticut and New Hampshire had no penal laws specifically defining the trial of slaves[902] and introduced none after 1793. Vermont came into the union without slaves and had no statutes for the trial of slaves.[902a] Louisiana, (after the Louisiana purchase in 1803) followed the pattern of the English slave states which tried slaves before a justice of the peace or before a judge and freeholders.[903]

Kentucky first continued the laws of Virginia. [904] But in 1799, the "right" of jury trial was accorded.[905] Tennessee followed the North Carolina procedure until 1815,[906] in which year the number of freeholders trying slaves was increased from four to nine.[907] Ohio having no slaves, had no laws for the trial of slaves. The same was true of Indiana, though the territory flirted with slavery for a few years.

Mississippi tried slaves before three "justices of the quorom" and two justices of the peace.[908] In 1812, slaves charged with treason were made triable before three justices of the quorom or two justices of the quorom and one justice of the peace.[909] In 1814 offenses punishable by not more than 100 stripes were tried by a single justice of the peace; offenses punishable by 39 lashes or more, before a justice of the peace and two "respectable slaveholders".[910] Other more serious offenses were still tried under the law of 1807, except that the panel now might consist either of justices of the quorom and justices of the peace, or entirely of justices of the peace.[911]

Illinois though a part of the Northwest Territory, and nominally without slavery, went as far as authorizing a justice of the peace to impose up to 39 lashes for "riots, routs, unlawful assemblies, trespasses and seditious speeches."[912]

Alabama first followed the lead of the other southern slave states in providing for trial of slaves before justices without a jury. All of the justices sitting had to concur in a finding of guilt.[913] But the act of 1819, the year of statehood, introduced jury trials for slaves.[914] This is characteristic of the new cotton states. They were pulled both ways; by

the social system of the old slave states on the one hand, and by that of
the emerging industrial North on the other. The cotton kingdom was
thus an anomaly from its first day to its extinction in 1865. Missouri,
went with the new trend in likewise providing jury trials for slaves in
capital cases.[915] There are no Missouri cases up to the time of her
recission.

The urge to secrete or spirit away slaves came into a new setting
with pressure from the new industrialized states to entice slaves into
"freedom" to serve as cheap wage labor.[916] The fear that masters will
secrete or take slaves away receded as a problem after invention of the
cotton gin. Neither South Carolina nor Georgia[917] had any new laws or
cases.

SLAVES TRADING FOR THEMSELVES

The prohibition against slaves trading for themselves continued, but
under new statutes which show that this activity was causing continuous
trouble. In Virginia, a person trading with a slave without the owner's
permission in 1795, was subject to a fine of four times the value of the
article plus twenty dollars.[918] The code of 1819 imposes an added
penalty for trading with a slave on the Sabbath without the master's
leave.[919] For the first time, extra penalties up to a $200 fine are
imposed on the master or skipper of any vessel dealing with a slave
without the slaveowner's written consent.[920] There are, however, no
cases during this period.

Maryland kept her existing laws[921] but added a special provision
forbidding slaves to be in any liquor store after sunset without the
master's written permission,[921a] and another that slaves might be
apprehended if caught selling liquor.[922] In 1818, another act was passed
regulating the sale of liquor by and to slaves, first in Kent County[923]
and then in Prince George's, Somerset, Dorchester and Talbot
counties,[924] without modification of any existing laws. The following
year this restriction was repealed for Talbot and Dorchester
Counties.[925] In 1819 however, the City of Annapolis was exempted
from the prohibition against slaves being in any liquor store after sunset
without written permission.[926] The institution of slavery loosens under
one's eyes.

New York continued to forbid trading with slaves; the penalty was
stiffened to treble the value of the articles and $12.50, payable to the
owner of the slave.[927] No judicial decisions are on record.[928]

New Jersey had no further laws or cases on slaves trading for
themselves. Perhaps the new order appears in a law of 1798 fining

masters who permitted their slaves to go begging.[929] Trade had become a more general occupation of free persons, and slaves could no longer make money by it. Where once they traded for themselves, they now begged.

Connecticut, Pennsylvania and Delaware had no new laws, but apparently retained their old ones.[930] The only case is in Pennsyvlvania, permitting slave members of a salvage crew to share in the salvage money.[930a] Rhode Island and New Hampshire had no such laws before 1793, and none afterwards.

In 1794 North Carolina imposed a fine of 20 pounds on owners allowing their slaves to hire themselves on their own time.[931] One may infer that in North Carolina, slavery was just undeveloped enough that slaves trading independently constituted a continuing problem, and just developed enough that the slaveowners wanted to suppress it. Apparently slaves made it a practice to offer wares for sale to crew members of vessels in port.   In 1805 the legislature passed a law explicitly forbidding this practice.[932]

The urge to trade with slaves however continued, showing the seriousness of the problem in the state. In 1819 the Legislature once more tackled the problem, for the first time imposing jail as well as a fine for "fraudulent" trading with slaves.[933] Although the legislative history indicates continued violation, no case under any of these laws ever reached the appellate courts.

In South Carolina, the laws against trading with slaves give evidence of an increasingly settled society. While the law of 1738[934] forbade "any hawker, peddler or petty chapman" from trading with a slave, the law of 1796 also prohibited shopkeepers from doing so.[935] But such dealing continued, and in 1817 the penalties were increased because:

> it was found be experience that the penalties heretofore
> imposed on shopkeepers and other traders who deal with
> Negroes without the permission of their owners are
> insufficient and have not answered the ends intended.[936]

The severity of the new penalties reflects the acuteness of the problem. Even feudal [936a]and hidebound South Carolina was feeling the impact of the trading generated by the Industrial Revolution.   The violent penalties also foreshadow the "fire-eaters" of the 1850s."[936b] South Carolina has begun to lose her sense of proportion, and the sun has begun to set over the feudal stronghold of North America. There was one case on the subject, "a conviction in 1805 for trading with a slave who was sent as an informer."[937]

Georgia, with the history of once having prohibited slavery, found herself confronted with owners who allowed their slaves to work independently. An 1803 statute[938] prohibited this except in the towns of Savannah, Augusta and Sunbury. The exceptions reveal that though slavery was "the one thing needful,"[939] that state had not completely assimilated the institution.

Louisiana forbade trading with slaves as soon as she was under American jurisdiction.[940] Interestingly enough, these laws provided for jailing slaves trading for themselves,[941] presumably on the theory that any master who allowed his slave to do so could not himself be urgently in need of labor.

Kentucky enacted a statute along the usual lines. Anyone dealing with a slave was liable to four times the value of the article involved, and the slave offering to sell the item received ten lashes.[942] This prohibition was based on the believed encouragement to theft if slaves were allowed to trade for themselves. According to the recital of the statutes, the practice was very common, showing incomplete establishment of slavery in Kentucky, and foreshadowing the state's staying with the union in 1861.[943] In 1807, the severity of the original act was relaxed, bespeaking an inner conflict and vacillation which was to continue until the close of the Civil War.[944]

ENDERMAN v. ASHBY,[945] decided in 1801, granted damages for violating the law against trading with slaves without the owner's consent. This was the only case up to 1820, but that even one case should have reached the appellate courts differentiates Kentucky from most of the older slave states. Conditions were less settled even when problems were resolve peacefully. From the start, agriculture based on slavery competed with commerce.

Tennessee followed the same pattern.[946] The statute expressly required a slave to have a pass. There were no cases. Even Tennessee was more stable as a slave state than Kentucky. In 1861 Tennessee seceded reluctantly, but seceded. Ohio, though flirting with slavery in contravention of the Northwest Territory Ordinance, had no statues on slaves trading independently, nor were there any cases. The District of Columbia cases are gathered in the footnote.[946a] Indiana, on the other hand, so far copied the pattern of the slave states as to include a prohibition of trading with a "servant".[947] These laws remained on the books through 1820, but there were no cases.

Mississippi, as might be expected, followed the general laws of the slave states,[948] but this fact sets off the uniquely severe penalties of South Carolina.[949] There are no cases through 1820. Illinois, like

Indiana, though part of this Northwest Territory, forbade trading with "servants."[950] There are no cases of any kind until after 1820. Alabama had the same group of statutes as Mississippi on slaves trading for themselves.[951] No cases came up by 1820. Missouri first adopted the law of Louisiana, that slaves permitted to hire themselves out should be sold, with 25% of the sale price being applied to the general revenue.[952] No cases arose up to the time of the state's admission.

SLAVE REVOLTS

There were relatively few slave revolts in the English continental colonies before invention of the cotton gin.[953] Even Aptheker, stoked by wishful thinking, puts little emphasis on slave revolts prior to 1793.[954] To this extent, Calhoun was right when in 1850 he blamed slave defections on agitators.[955] He did not understand that the agitation was itself the product of economics. As Aptheker observes,[956] slave revolts increased markedly after 1793. Legislation and court cases reflect the new state of affairs.

In 1794, the first signs appeared in a Virginia act designed to restrain Negroes and Mulattoes who pretended to freedom, but were in fact slaves.[957] Simultaneously it was made illegal for free Negroes to come into the state.[958] The law making insurrection a felony was continued.[959] By 1819, seditious speeches were punished with stripes.[960] There was a new special prohibition against teaching slaves to read and write.[961] The forebodings contained in the preamble to this section, "considerable evil to the community," tell the tale of what was taking place. On the other hand, there are no Virginia cases of slave revolts during this period.

The laws against teaching slaves to read was a final turning point in the relation between the two economic systems. The industrial revolution needed a literate proletariat,[961a] but education might lead slaves to demand freedom besides making them more suitable to the new wage economy. So the slave states went out of their way to keep slaves from learning to read and write, thus allowing themselves to fall further behind the "free" states.

The Industrial Revolution, which originally gave a new lease on life to the slave system in North America, was now helping it commit suicide. The Industrial Revolution had made slave revolts "a brooding omnipresence in the sky"[962] but concrete uprisings had in only one instance reached Virginia, already on her way to becoming a slave-breeding state. Gabriel's conspiracy[962a] was not reflected in the legal reports.

Maryland had no statutes or cases on slave revolts, but a dim reflection of passing events appears in Legislative Resolution No. 28, of 1820:[963]

> Whereas the owners of slaves in this state are frequently subjected to great imposition and serious inconvenience from the constant and ready protections afforded their runaway Negroes by the citizens of Pennsylvania, it is deemed necessary to call the attention to Congress to the subject. Whenever a runaway slave is pursued and found in Pennsylvania, every possible difficulty is thrown in the way, so as to prevent the recovery of such slave; there are persons always ready to lend every practicable aid in thwarting the just and legal efforts of the owner in the recovery of the Negro. If the legal proceedings fail, force is not infrequently resorted to.

New York had no laws or cases on slave revolts from 1793-1820. In states which were becoming industrialized, emancipation fed the wage-labor force. North Carolina passed laws against slave insurrection in 1795, 1798[964] and 1802.[965] The severity of the act of 1802 shows a pervading nervousness, and illustrates Aptheker's observation that:

> The dozen years following 1790 formed a period of more intense and widespread slave discontent than any that had preceded (with the possible exception of the much shorter period from 1737-1741).[966]

In 1819 the law was made still more stingent and savage by withdrawing the benefit of clergy from all its subdivisions.[967] But as in Virginia, there were no cases.

South Carolina reported a slave revolt[968] at Camden in 1817. An act was passed appropriating $1800:

> to purchase the freedom of the servant who gave the information of the projected insurrection in the city and neighborhood of Camden; and also that the sum of fifty dollars per annum, out of the public treasury be allowed to said servant until otherwise directed by law.

In the following year the town council of Camden was given the power of enforcing patrol duty.[969]

We are left in the dark as to he background and implications of STATE v. THACKMAN MAYSON,[970] in which the Supreme Court of South Carolina held in 1794 that "such a person was capable of committing a riot, in conjunction with white men." By 1820, the state Supreme

Court already seems to have been worried about insurrection.[971] There are however, no appellate reports of any actual uprisings.[972]

Georgia has no statutes and no cases on slave revolt to 1820. The situation probably reflects the frontier condition of the state—these matters were simply not brought before the law—as much as the total absence of such trouble. On the other hand, since Georgia was far removed from northern industry, there was probably relatively little proselyting for "emancipation".

Aptheker refers to slave revolts in Spanish Louisiana in 1791, 1792, and in 1795. After the province became American, a law was promptly enacted forbidding slaves to carry weapons of any kind,[975] and punishing unlawful assemblies and riotous speeches with stripes.[976] Masters were fined if they permitted slaves of another owner to remain on their plantation for more than four hours at a time without leave of the slave's owner;[977] and all free persons were fined for attending an unlawful meeting with slaves.[978] The lightness of this latter fine (three dollars) suggests that Louisiana was not yet much worried by persons from the industrial states who sought to proselyte slaves with "freedom".

In the following year however, there was a drastic reversal of policy; any one who should persuade slaves to insurrection suffered death.[979] Apparently, Louisiana was scared by the Haitian revolt, and in the same year, introduction of free persons from Haiti was forbidden.[980] The Black Code in the next year (1806) allowed civil damages to the owner of a slave who attended a meeting of slaves on another's plantation,[981] and repeated the prohibition against slaves going armed.[982] Slaves informing on rebellions were freed.[983]

But through 1820 there were no reports of slave revolts in American Louisiana. The only case even touching this subject was DORMENON'S CASE,[984] in which a lawyer was disbarred in 1810 for supposedly having aided the Haitian revolt, and then reinstated two years later (after having been elected to the House of Representatives) because the charge was supposedly unfounded.

The other states admitted after the American Revolution had laws against slave insurrections where a full-fledged system of slavery was contemplated. Such laws existed in Kentucky,[985] Tennessee,[986] Mississippi,[987] Alabama,[988] and Missouri.[989] They also existed where the new settlers intended to sneak in a slave economy in violation of the Northwest Territory Ordinance. So we find laws against slave insurrections, or "unlawful meetings" of slaves in Indiana[990] and Illinois.[991]

The Tennessee law is most indicative of the prevailing mood. It punishes speeches inducing slaves to defect, but almost takes away with its left hand what it lays down with the right. While speech is prohibited, the penalty is only a three dollar fine, and the scope of punishable speech is whittled away by definitions. It is as if the new slave states saw what was going on, but could not quite believe their own senses.

Two new trends showed themselves after the appearance of the cotton gin. Both were facets of the seemingly insatiable demand for cheap wage labor engendered by the industrial revolution, which was gaining momentum every day. On the one hand the slave states put more and more restrictions on emancipation and on the presence of free Negroes within their borders. To allow either carried the double threat of losing their slaves via emancipation, and of having free Negroes come in and stir up slave revolts.

On the other hand, the "free" states enacted a whole body of laws making free Negroes an inferior caste. [901] These laws gave away the purpose of "emancipation". It was designed not to make Negroes the equals of the white ruling class, but to create a stratum of low-paid wage laborers. Here and there, remnants of the old pattern survived in the slave states. South Carolina, even in decline, retained much of her self-assured caste system, and accorded free Negroes greater rights than they had in many of the "free" states.

Virginia opened the new era by forbidding the migration of free Negroes into the state. [992] Selling a free person as a slave took on new importance since the prohibition of the slave trade, and was punished with death.[993] Slaves could be freed by will,[994] but had to leave the state within 12 months after emancipation. [995] In allowing a year's leeway, Virginia was comparatively generous. Where emancipation was granted for extraordinary meritorious services, the freedman was permitted to petition for leave to reside within any one county of the state. [996]

Free Negroes were forbidden from migrating into Virginia at the end, as at the beginning of the period 1792-1820.[997] As in most states, both slave and "free", all Negroes and Mulattoes were disqualified as witnesses in court.[998] This disqualification was enforced even where the Negro blood came through the paternal line.[999] But emancipated slaves could take property by will. [999a]

The persistency of the emancipation forces is shown by PARISH v. GRAY[1000] already mentioned, in which a Negro was held free after six jury trials. However, vacillation not only as to original free status but even as to emancipation [1001-6] shows how far the state was uncertain in her own mind as to what she should do about free Negroes. Significantly, there are no cases of freedmen after 1811 except for violation of the interestate slave trade laws.

Maryland made sure that emancipated slaves remained a subordinate caste by expressly denying them the right to vote and other civil rights in 1796.[1007] But the same act made the children of Negro men and white women free from birth rather than from age 31.[1008] The pressure to have those people as low-wage laborers expressed itself in high sentiments of freedom. Elaborate machinery was set up for petitions to establish freedom.[1009] But free Negroes, whether free from birth or freed later were again put into a special lower caste by law.

First it enabled slaves to testify for or against them on charges of theft or receiving stolen goods, and then made the testimony of any slave available for or against any free Negro in all criminal prosecutions.[1010] Since the overriding interest was to create a supply of low-paid wage labor, many slaves mysteriously received certificates of freedom to which they were not entitled.[1011]

A whole series of special restrictions were placed on free Negroes. They were not allowed to sell corn or tobacco without a license;[1012] they were not allowed to emigrate into Maryland from another state[1013] and not allowed to keep dogs or weapons.[1014] Also, there was a special section on free Negroes in the law against slave rebellions.[1015] Masters could determine the status of the children of slaves whom they freed. If they made no such determination, the children remained slaves.[1016]

Yet the right of emancipation was strengthened and protected in 1817 by a law which prohibited the kidnapping and sale out of the state of slaves entitled to their future freedom in Maryland.[1017] The following year, however, brought the underlying purpose of emancipation to the surface once more in a law authorizing judges of the orphans' court to bind out the children of free Negroes.[1018] In addition, free Negroes could no longer be sentenced to the penitentiary, showing that Maryland was beginning to experience a shortage of industrial labor. Free Negroes as an inferior caste could, henceforth, be sentenced to corporal punishment in all cases, a step the legislators declined to take with white labor, regardless of any labor shortage.[1019]

Claims of freedom were frequent after the Revolutionary War, and were upheld by the courts through 1794, one year after the patenting of the cotton gin.[1020] The reluctance to grant freedom after this date indicates that the courts at least were persuaded that selling slaves south to the cotton states was more profitable than having them become wage labor.

The Maryland court at first could not agree on the competence as a witness of a Mulatto woman born free of a manumitted woman. Later it held both ways on the question.[1023] This indecision was the hallmark of a "moderate" slave state (which later did not secede, yet refused to emancipate her slaves against compensation). Maryland simply could not make up her mind about what to do with free Negroes.

New York, it must be remembered, continued to have slavery after 1820. In the meantime she validated those manumissions which had already been made,[1024] and passed the law for gradual abolition in 1799.[1025] Under this act all persons born after July 4, 1799, were declared free, except that children of slave mothers would remain servants of the mother's owner until 28 if men, and 25 if women. Ex-slaves who were paupers were maintained by the state.[1026] In the following year (1802), children abandoned by the mother's owner were granted two dollars per month.[1027]

In 1809, manumitted slaves were given the right to sue for property coming to them by descent and marriage. From now until the enactment of the 13th amendment, we see the vacillation of the northern states in their treatment of emancipated slaves. Three forces were at work simultaneously; the memory of slavery, the demand of the new industrialists for cheap labor, and against these, the demands of the idealists (Schopenhauer's class III) for human freedom.

Children born after July 4, 1799, and entitled to freedom in the future had to be taught reading.[1029] This provision served the idealistic Abolitionist and the new industrialist at the same time. Abolition of illiteracy increased human dignity and erased one of the hallmarks of American slavery, but literate employees were also more useful in industrial jobs. Of course, the competition for black labor worked both ways. Northern industries were glad to "liberate" slaves in order to employ them at low wages; southern slave holders and slave traders sought to supplement the number of slaves by kidnapping free Negroes. So in 1813, New York enacted a special law "to prevent kidnapping of Free People of Colour."[1030] Punishment was up to a $1000 fine and up to 14 years in prison. A second offense was punishable by imprisonment for life. The severity of these penal provisions shows the situation heating up to a point which was only resolved by the Civil War.

In 1814, New York took another step in the direction of making free Negroes citizens by passing "An Act to Authorize the raising of two regiments of color."[1031] This was a few months before the end of the war of 1812. It shows a remarkably swift advance from the position taken by Rhode Island in the Revolutionary War.[1032]

Commissioned officers however, were to be white.[1033] The inferior caste status was mitigated, but not removed. Nor was the law solely for the benefit of the Negroes. Slaves who enlisted were emancipated and their former owners exonerated from supporting them should they become indigent.[1034]   The change in attitude from the Revolutionary War was no doubt speeded by newly acquired insights into the needs and conveniences of an industrial society.

Not all freed slaves could be absorbed into industry, however. This seems to have been especially true of persons who had been slaves on estates confiscated from United Empire loyalists. In 1816, the state dumped the responsibility for supporting them onto the towns.[1035] Here we see the operation of the slave and wage systems side by side. Slaves were freed from slavery, but at least some were "freed" for pauperism. This side of emancipation was played down in abolition propaganda. Children of emancipated slaves were put into the same category as apprentices.[1036]

New York was inclined to give free Negroes more civil rights than many other states. In 1803, the court rejected an affidavit to show that a proposed witness was a slave and therefore could not testify.[1037] In 1806, the state decided that a free black man was competent to testify to events which had occurred while he was a slave.[1038] Again and again we meet with cases in which emancipation of the slaves freed the master from the obligation of support.[1039]

New Jersey began the new era by re-emphasizing the inferior status of the free Negroes. All Negroes, Indians and Mulattoes were made subject to corporal punishment for acts for which other persons drew a fine or jail.[1040] So not only rude slaves, but rude servants could henceforth be committed to the workhouse.[1041] Gradual emancipation was decreed in 1804,[1042] and immediately revealed that one of its chief objects was to free the master from the obligation of supporting the slave.[1043]

Interestingly enough the section allowing the abandonment of freeborn children of slaves was repealed the following year,[1044-47] showing that for the moment, the businessmen's anxiety to be rid of the duty of support had outrun the resources of the community. If anything, this underscored what "emancipation" really meant. New Jersey held free Negroes to be competent as witnesses.[1048] Otherwise there were no cases during this period.

Massachusetts, a completely free state, shows a long list of orphans supported by the towns as paupers.[1049] She also experimented briefly with the idea of making free Negroes and Mulattoes wards of the state like Indians,[1050] a device obviously not in keeping with the demands of new industries for low paid employment. The cases of this period show the same dreary line of contests as in other free states between towns, as to which had the obligation to support a free Negro pauper.[1051] There is also one case between private individuals over a similar disagreement. [1052] One case allows recovery of a money judgment by a free Negro,[1053] showing that the courts were open, if the colored litigant could find the necessary money. All the above likewise applies to Maine, a part of Massachusetts before 1820.

Connecticut enlarged the act for gradual emancipation in 1797.[1054] All slaves born after August 21, 1797 were to be free at age 21, rather than at age 25. There was therefore a class of statu liberi until the last child of a slave mother reached 21. The transition to an industrial wage economy was signalled by the repeal of the requirements which had existed since 1780, that free Negroes could not travel without a pass, and that any "servants and slaves" could not "be abroad" after 9 pm except on their master's business. Hand in hand with the metamorphosis of slaves to industrial employees went the repeal of some of the degrading indicia of slavery—like the punishment by stripes.[1055] Henceforth the most obvious caste marks would be the wage level and the jobs which were open (or not open).

The process of industrialization in Connecticut lagged behind that of Massachusetts and New York in one palpable respect. The acts of 1808 and 1821, retained the requirement of 1711 that made former owners liable to support emancipated slaves if they became destitute. [1056] This obligation was not, as yet, completely thrown on the public authorities. It was severely limited by the opportunity to secure a certificate that the slave was able to support himself. [1059] But its suvival indicates a slower movement in Connecticut than in her two neighboring states. So the first case of the period made the former owner liable to the selectmen of the town for such support.[1058] In the same way, there were fewer contests between towns as to which must support a colored pauper. [1059]

Rhode Island codified the subordination of free Negroes by continuing the law against miscegenation.[1060] Persons born after March 31, 1784, were declared free.[1061] They had to be supported by the mother's owner until they reached 21, if the mother's owner held her in slavery.[1062] Support of the children of other blacks was thrown on the towns, with the privilege of binding the children out as apprentices.[1063] Slaves emancipated before the age of thirty and destitute were supported by towns like other paupers. Slaves emancipated above that age were supported by their former owners.[1064]

Thus Rhode Island took a middle course between Massachusetts and New York on one side, and Connecticut on the other. The statute of

1798, also, re-enacted some of the old indices of inferiority on the part of free Negroes; namely, the act of 1770 for breaking up disorderly houses kept by free Negroes,[1065] and the act of 1750 against entertaining any Indian, Negro, or Mulatto servants or slaves.[1066]

There were no New Hampshire laws on free Negroes during this time, but two acts, both limiting the militia to free white males,[1067] show that the state made free Negroes an inferior caste.

The only Pennsylvania statute of this period was one dealing with paupers who were liberated slaves.[1068] Early in the period Pennsylvania insisted that free Negroes could be bound out as apprentices only until age 21.[1069] This too, was brought on by the Industrial Revolution. The system of minor apprentices belonged to an earlier era. The Industrial Revolution on the other hand, operated through public education and wage employment as soon as education was terminated. The reluctance to pay for services of free Negroes held as slaves continued however.[1070] In other words, the new industrial society played it both ways, whichever way gave it a better chance of getting something for nothing.

The trend away from the old apprentice system to the new wage system was expressed most forcibly in 1810 by the opinion in COMMONWEALTH v. STURGEON,[1071] where a free Negro of twenty-four tried to bind himself as an apprentice, but the court held that this had not been accomplished, adding:

> Cases of persons over age in this state becoming apprentices, are so rare, that the construction now given can be of little inconvenience, whilst on the contrary, to subject persons, who on equal terms become parties to the contract, to the power of the sessions by a disgraceful punishment for a breach of duty appears harsh and unexpedient.

Thus it was the employer who was relieved from the old "harsh" and now "inexpedient" sanctions of the apprentice laws. Emancipation freed the master!

The institution of apprenticeship staggered along until 1820.[1072] For no apparent reason, contests between towns as to which must support a colored pauper began late, and are few.[1073] (Perhaps the Quakers were less inclined to fight about charity.)

North Carolina inaugurated the era of the cotton gin by placing impossible conditions on the immigration of free Negroes. Any free Negro or emancipated slave entering the state by land or water had to put up a 200 pound ($1000) bond for good behavior. [1074] This was part of the picture outlined by nearly all slave states except South Carolina after 1793. Free Negroes were more and more restricted, and those not already in the state were kept out. Assemblies of free Negroes were put in the same category as assemblies of slaves and prohibited. [1075] Contrary to the trend in states where the Industrial Revolution was under way, masters who liberated their slaves had to give bond against their becoming a public charge. [1076] There are no further statutes on free Negroes in 1820.

North Carolina both retained much of her aristocratic tolerance toward free Negroes, and joined the movement of the other slave states in oppressing them. The first manifestation was the imposition of a $2 poll tax in 1795. [1078] In 1813 there was a swing back, and the poll tax on free Negroes was softened slightly. [1079] In 1800, Negroes bound for a term of years were forbidden to enter the state. [1080] In 1820 the legislature forbade all immigration of free Negroes. [1081] The preamble to this act says:

> Whereas the great and rapid increase of free Negroes and Mulattoes in this state by immigration and emancipation of slaves renders it expedient and necessary for the legislature to restrain the emancipation of slaves and to prevent free persons of color from entering this state . . .

The increase in emancipation indicates that slave labor was becoming unprofitable, at least in some parts of South Carolina. The increase in immigration indicates the same thing for other states. For until then, emancipated slaves moved into South Carolina, because the state had no restrictions on their entry. These freedmen probably came from the tobacco states of Virginia and North Carolina. [1081a] At the same time a contrary tendency was revealed in the new severe penalty on selling a free Negro as a slave. [1082] This was probably due partly to the continued demand for slaves in some parts of the state, and partly to the temptation to sell "slaves" to the new cotton states.

The beginnings of the decline of the slave system generated opposing currents in different parts of South Carolina. And in keeping with patrician beneficence toward the lower orders, the state allowed damages to free persons wrongfully held in slavery and made to work as slaves.

In STATE v. McDOWELL, [1083] we get almost a last view of Eighteenth century South Carolina's solid self-assured caste system. Slavery descended through the mother. Therefore the child of a Negro man and a white woman was free. Being free, he should be competent to testify as a witness in court. Against the great majority of the states, South Carolina did not boggle at this corollary of her own caste system.[1084]

> It was determined in this court by all the judges, that any person of color, if the issue of a free white woman, is entitled to give evidence in our courts.[1085]

The same serene self-certainty of a superior caste manifested itself in the rule:

> That no words, however, abusive used by a person of color, whether free or slave would amount to an offense, punishable by indictment.[1086]

This, too, was contrary to the law in other states.[1087] A freedman could not sue for occurrences which had transpired while he or she was a slave.[1088] But the rule selling free Negroes into slavery was rigidly enforced.

> The charge against those men was founded on the basest falsehood, fabricated by the defendant for the infamous purpose of enslaving them for life.[1089]

When the state's decline became steep, this aristocratic sense of superiority translated itself into Nullification, the South Carolina "fire-eaters" of the 1850's, the first secession, and finally, the bombardment of Fort Sumpter.[1089a]

Delaware established Negroes as "free" by repealing the law which imposed servitude until 31 on the child of a Negro man and a white woman.[1090] Otherwise, free Negroes were not allowed to set up sales booths on election day unless they resided in the town holding the election, [1091] and they were qualified as witnesses only to a limited extent.[1092] But Delaware vacillated (with regard to free Negroes) as might be expected from her location as a border state. In 1807, free Negroes were forbidden to enter the state, and resident free Negroes were declared non-resident if absent for two years. [1093] This was later shortened to six months,[1094] but non-resident free Negroes could not be hired.[1095]

In the same year, 1811, resale into slavery for a seven year term was enacted as a punishment for a free Negro convicted of larceny. [1096] Yet in 1819, the state validated all emancipations which had been made without giving the bond required to support the former slave if he became indigent.[1096a] The act contains the double-edged assurance that such persons "shall and may enjoy all the benefits and advantages that a free Negro or free Mulatto may or can do within this government."[1096b] Thus Delaware approached the time when she would not join the secession, but would keep, and expect to keep, her slaves.

As Georgia became settled, she proceeded to stamp out the vestiges of her early prohibition of slavery. In 1808, justices of the peace were given authority to bind out male free Negroes, and minors aged 8-21 to artisans and farmers.[1097] This was done because "the permitting of free Negroes and persons of color to roam about the country in idleness and dissipation has a dangerous tendency." Ten years later the state complained about slaves conducting themselves as free Negroes[1098] and placed further restrictions on manumissions and new burdens on "free" Negroes. Those not registered were to be sold as slaves.[1099] They were made liable to do roadwork,[1100] and forbidden to hold slaves or real estate.[1101] The prohibition against holding real estate was partly repealed the next year,[1102] as was the penalty for failing to register, providing they had registered after passage of the act.[1103]

In 1807, free Negroes within the limits of Savannah and Augusta were made subject to the same police regulations as slaves.[1104] A poll tax of 50 cents was levied on each free Negro, 21 and over.[1105] Individual emancipations during this period were made subject to express limitations placing a free Negro on a lower plane than free whites.[1106] Thus there was a legally established caste system, apart from slavery. EXPARTE GEORGE[1107] granted a free Negro the benefit of an appeal to the executive but expressly said that all Negroes whether free or slave had the same rights in this respect. "A Negro, whether he is a free man or slave is equally entitled to the benefit of an appeal to the executive."

Louisiana inherited the civil law under which free Negroes held substantially more rights than they did in the English colonies. They were permitted one gun, but could own more by special license if living "at any frontier plantation."[1108-1109] However:

> If any Negro or Mulatto, bond or free, shall at any time
> lift his or her hand in opposition to any person not being a
> Negro or Mulatto, he or she shall receive such punishment
> as the justice shall think proper not exceeding thirty
> lashes—except in those cases where it shall appear to
> such justice that such Negro or Mulatto was wantonly
> assaulted and lifted his or her hand in his or her defense.[1110]

Emancipated slaves had to carry their document of emancipation on pain of being throw in jail.[1111] If they did not pay poll taxes they could be hired out by the sheriff to work off the delinquent tax.[1112] In 1806, entry of free Negroes from Haiti was forbidden,[1113] but this came in the wake of the Haitian revolt. At the same time the outward symbols of subordination, which the French Code had imposed only on freedmen toward their former masters,[1114] were attached to all free Negroes.[1115] So the testimony of slaves was permitted in prosecutions against free Negroes, who were however, accorded a jury trial.[1116]

Free Negroes were bracketed with slaves for the purpose of capital crimes, and the stealing of a slave by a free Negro was made a separate offense.[1117] On the other hand, they were bracketed with whites as overseers of slaves,[1118] and Louisiana did not hesitate to arm free Negroes, provided that their commanding officer was white.[1119] A "colored corps" served in the war of 1812, and the pay of those who lost their lives was transferred to their parents.[1120]

Louisiana also reflects the problems raised by the requirements of many states that free Negroes leave the state. Where would they go? In 1816, Louisiana forbade the entry of free Negroes who had been convicted of crime.[1121] In 1820, peddlers were forbidden to sell spiritous liquor, arms or ammunition "to any Negro,"[1122] putting pressure on them to leave the state. The first United States case on the subject skirts the vexed question whether a person wrongly held in slavery should be awarded wages until the time that freedom is judicially declared. The Louisiana court avoided the question by holding that the service was rendered in return for the education which the plaintiff had received.[1123] So Louisiana went both ways on the question whether free Negroes were qualified as witnesses.[1124] Criminal and civil remedies for holding free Negroes as slaves not only existed but were enforced,[1125] and free Negroes could take slaves by will.[1126] Louisiana, like other states, saw freedman become paupers, though not nearly as often.[1127] While the Roman law greatly lightened the burdens of free Negroes in Louisiana, it did not do as much for them as the caste system of South Carolina.

Vermont, though enacting no special laws on free Negroes, expressed herself in favor "of colonizing the free people of color of the United States on the west coast of Africa."[1128] This was done:

> holding as sacred the great principle 'That all men are born equally free and independent and have certain natural, inherent and inalienable rights among which are the enjoying and defending of life and liberty, acquiring, possessing and protecting property, and pursuing and obtaining happiness and safety.'[1129]

The only cases on free Negroes show that in Vermont, the white population sometimes gave way to mob instincts against free Negroes, but the courts did not.[1130]

Kentucky inaugurated statehood by decreeing that free Negroes were not among the "freemen" who should be "armed and disciplined for its defense".[1131] The statutes consistently made free Negroes into an inferior caste. Free Negroes, Mulattoes, and Indians could own servants, but only of their own complexion.[1132] As in most other states, Negroes, Mulattoes, and Indians were disqualified as witnesses, except in cases between Negroes, Mulattoes, and Indians.[1133] They could not carry arms, unless living on the frontier and by license from a justice of the peace.[1134]

Slaves were punished with thirty lashes for lifting a hand against any person not a Negro.[1135] Stealing or selling a free Negro as a slave drew 5 to 10 years imprisonment, less than in many other states.[1136] In 1808, the state passed a law prohibiting the immigration of free Negroes with explicit reference to the laws of many states requiring emancipated slaves to leave the state.[1137] The question can be seen taking shape. Where were free Negroes to go?

Meanwhile, the laws continued to make a depressed caste of them in Kentucky. Whipping was imposed for stopping salt water or filling up wells.[1138] There was one private act during this period designed to safeguard a former slave intended to be free.[1139] As against the tendency to depress free Negroes, Kentucky allowed wages for the period that a free Negro was wrongfully held in servitude beyond the seven year period, after which, by agreement between seller and buyer, his slavery was to be terminated.[1140] The only other case on free Negroes during this period, while granting the subordinate rights, was firm about the rights it did grant.

> They are certainly in some measure parties to the political compact although they may not have every benefit . . . which the constitution secures . . . yet they are entitled to repose under its shadow and thus secure themselves from the heated vengeance of the government.[1141]

Like the other border states, Kentucky displayed the vacillation which would let her go with the North in the Civil War, but expect to keep her slaves.

Tennessee registered all free Negroes living within the state.[1142] A little later the poll tax on free Negroes in the town of Reynoldsburgh was fixed four times as high as that for whites. [1143] But beyond that the statutes did not go. Tennessee was evidently still on the frontier and not a developed slave state.

Virginia statutes were retained on the position of free Negroes in court proceedings. Slaves were disqualified against them in court proceedings, the same as against whites, [1145] but slaves were deemed competent witnesses for the government in criminal proceedings against free Negroes, [1146] but could not testify for the defendant. But Free Mulattoes were usually qualified to testify.[1146a] Selling liquor to assemblies of Negroes (apparently not necessarily slaves), constituted a disorderly house. [1148] Stripes were used as punishment against free Negroes in 1804.[1149] It should be remembered that though corporal punishment was used against whites in the 18th century, it began to become obsolete in the Nineteenth. It was retained for slaves because it did not interrupt their work, and became a caste mark, and was such when used on free Negroes.

Sometimes however the old caste system showed through and the assimilation of free Negroes from slavery worked to their advantage. Thus a freedman was not liable for money lent him as a slave to purchase his freedom—even where he had acknowledged the debt after emancipation. [1150]

The laws of the Northwest Territory revealed the true attitude of the North toward free Negroes. Slavery was forbidden, but so were interracial marriages thought to be "prohibited by the laws of God." [1151] Just before Ohio became a state however, this restriction was dropped. [1152] But the next legislature limited the militia to "free, able bodied white male" citizens,[1153] and enacted a general law "to regulate black and Mulatto persons."[1154] Ohio then admitted free Negroes only if they had a certificate of freedom from another state, required them to register in Ohio, and forbade employment to any who had not registered.

When Ohio was admitted as a state, members of the state legislature were chosen solely on the basis of the white male population. [1155-6] These provisions were coupled however, with the prohibition of slavery and involuntary servitude except for punishment of crimes. [1157] In 1807, entry of free Negroes into the state was effectively stopped by requiring a $500 bond for good behavior.[1158] This would change as the abolition movement gathered steam and Ohio became one of the chief havens for, and conduits of, fugitive slaves.

In 1818, the other side of the picture emerged. The slave states were kidnapping free persons to sell them into slavery.[1159] But at the time, the offense was only a high misdemeanor, punishable by 1-10 years imprisonment. [1160]

Indiana forbade all Negroes and Mulattoes from being witnesses, except in pleas of the United States against Negroes, Mulattoes or Indians, "or in court pleas where Negroes, Mulattoes, or Indians alone shall be parties." [1161] As in Ohio, marriages "prohibited by the laws of God" were made illegal. [1162] The militia was limited to free white males, [1163] and Negroes, Mulattoes, and Indians could not purchase any servant except of their own complexion. [1164]

In 1810, after there had been a change in the personnel of the legislature, [1165] the state took cognizance of the kidnapping of free Negroes for sale into slavery. At first, the offense was punished with the peculiarly aristocratic penalty of fine and disqualification from office. Later by a fine with the maximum raised to $5000. [1166] Likewise, the spirit of the slaveholding upper caste lingered in the law of 1818, punishing the white partner only for fornication between a white person and a Negro. [1167]

When Indiana was admitted as a state in 1816, the congressional act of admission granted the franchise to "all citizens of the United States," [1168] without making any restrictions about color. But the state constitution promptly removed ambiguities by restricting the franchise to white males over 21. [1169]

Mississippi made "Negroes, Mulattoes, and Indians and individuals of mixed blood" incompetent as witnesses. [1170] It is not clear whether the punishment of "any Negro or Mulatto for giving false testimony" refers only to slaves or also to free Negroes. The provision occurs in an act of the "Trial of Slaves," [1171] but witnesses included others besides the defendant. The first explicit mention of free Negroes puts the same poll tax on them as on whites. [1172] In 1816, selling a free person for a slave was made punishable by death, [1173] an interesting contrast to the much milder penalties in Illinois and Indiana. [1174] One must infer that in Mississippi, the temptation was so great that extreme measures were felt necessary to combat it.

One of the first laws which Illinois passed after being organized as a territory was an exclusion of free Negroes. [1176] Free Negroes who were already residents were required to register, [1177] and special penalties were imposed on them for harboring runaway slaves. [1178] Marriages "prohibited by the laws of God" had already been made illegal, [1179] and the militia limited to free white males. [1180]

Alabama gave qualified rights to free Negroes, permitting them to testify if their testimony could be corroborated. [1181] Sale of a free person as a slave was punishable by death,[1182] one of the consequences of the simultaneous mushrooming of the cotton kingdom and closing of the slave trade. There were no Alabama cases on free Negroes through 1820.

Missouri disqualified all Negroes and Mulattoes as witnesses except in criminal prosecutions against them, and "civil pleas where Negroes alone shall be parties".[1183] They were limited to one gun, and allowed more only on special license.[1184] Emancipated slaves travelling without a certificate of emancipation were put in jail.[1185] If they failed to pay taxes, they could be hired out to work off the account of the tax.[1186] As in the other new slave states, the penalty for selling a free person as a slave was death.[1187]

But Missouri was a border state which later not only did not secede, but alone accepted Lincoln's proposal to emancipate the northern slaves against compensation.[1188] So counsel was assigned to the petitioner in suits for freedom, and he could not be removed from the state pending suit.[1189] Through 1820, there were no Missouri cases on free Negroes.

The slave states and the free states alike restricted free Negroes but for almost opposite reasons. Without South Carolina's self-assured caste system, the other slave states denied rights to free Negroes somewhat in the spirit of De Gaulle's "I am too weak to compromise."[1189a] On the other hand, the rising industrialism of the free states depressed Negroes in order to get a pool of cheap wage labor. As with the abolition movement itself, profit rode the wave of popular feeling. But here the feeling which furthered profit was the underlying hostility to blacks.[1189b]

North Carolina prohibited her slave trade in 1794,[1190] Georgia in 1798,[1191] but South Carolina reopened hers for a last fling in 1803.[1192] The slave trade was abolished federally on January 1, 1808.[1193] New York passed her law for gradual emancipation in 1799,[1194] and in 1810 she prohibited the interstate importation of slaves by persons coming to reside six months or longer.[1195] In 1817, she accelerated the gradual emancipation by making all persons born of slave mothers before July 4, 1799 free on July 4, 1827.[1196] There were two federal prosecutions for slave trading during this period.[1197] New Jersey state law required a forfeit of ship and apparel if it was fitted out for slave trade.[1198] As already mentioned, the law for gradual emancipation was enacted in 1804.[1199]

Massachusetts had three federal slave trade cases during this period.[1200] In 1810, the Massachusetts courts were still willing to enforce payment on a contract to import slaves from Rio Pongas in

Africa to South Carolina, while the trade was legal in that state.[1201] A life insurance policy on a person who died on a slaving voyage was enforced. It was said that the beneficiary had no knowledge of where the insured was going.[1202] Business deals were strictly commercial!

Connecticut, like New York at a later date, accelerated gradual emancipation in 1797 by making all children of slave mothers born after August 1, 1797, free at the age of 21.[1203] In the following year, the statute of limitations for violation of the slave trade laws expanded to three years.[1204] In the one Connecticut slave trade case during these years, the prosecution was held barred by the statute of limitations.[1205]

In 1798, Rhode Island declared free all persons born after March 31, 1784. The owner of the mother had to support them until they were 21, if he held the mother in slavery.[1206] This is half way between the total emancipation of Massachusetts, and the laws of most states which declared free, children born in the future. In 1798, all children to and including fourteen were emancipated. The mother's owner had to support them until they were 21, but in the meantime they were not his slaves, nor even his bound apprentices. Rhode Island was industrializing fast. The only Rhode Island case during this period was a slave trade case. Parties in a venture for carrying slaves from Africa to the West Indies were held in pari delicto with none able to recover from another civilly.[1207]

By 1805, New Hampshire had evidently become convinced that slavery was unprofitable,[1208] and a resolution was passed in response to one from North Carolina memorializing Congress to enact a constitutional amendment prohibiting the importation of slaves from foreign countries.[1209]

Pennsylvania, in 1806, passed a resolution memorializing Congress against the slave trade. This followed similar resolutions from Maryland and North Carolina.[1210] At first, Pennsylvania was quite reluctant to enforce laws against the slave trade. In 1795, prosecution for kidnapping a Negro was instituted by the Society for the Gradual Abolition of Slavery. But the court refused to sustain it, holding that the Negro was a slave.[1211] A qui tam action for fitting out a slaving boat in New York was dismissed for want of jurisdiction.[1212] The federal laws against importation of slaves into any state which prohibited such importation were held not to apply to slaves brought as servants of French passengers from St. Thomas via Havana.[1213]

On the other hand, the law for gradual emancipation was applied with a vengeance. The courts pounced upon technical errors to accelerate emancipation.[1214] North Carolina prohibited the slave trade in 1784, effective May 1, 1795. The only case was GOVERNOR v. HORTON,[1216] a suit to recover a $100 penalty for bringing in a slave in violation of the act of 1794. North Carolina was no more concerned with the slave trade than with slavery itself.

South Carolina first passed a succession of laws prohibiting the slave trade for limited periods, and then reversed her policy in 1803. As might be expected, laws against the slave trade were not enforced if there was a way out. Delaware seems to have had no further statutes on the slave trade. Georgia abolished her slave trade in 1798.[1220] In 1818, the legislature attempted to strengthen slave trade laws by granting one-tenth of the prize to the informer.[1221]

Louisiana woke up to the prohibition of the slave trade in 1818. In that year the legislature made the sheriff of the New Orleans parish the receiver of slaves taken as imported in violation of the act of Congress.[1222] It also set up state machinery for condemning ships violating the federal act. [1223] Before that, a condemnation had been remitted under the Federal Act of 1803.[1224] The following year, 1810, the United States Supreme Court pointed out that the territorial legislature had never passed an act against slave trading, so the federal act did not apply.

In 1815, a Spanish slave trader was captured by a French vessel, which in time was captured by the Americans. The slaves were ordered returned to the Cuban owner on the grounds that the French vessel would probably have tried to smuggle them into the United States.[1226] There was enough demand for slaves so that the Louisiana Supreme Court went out of its way to say that slaves illegally imported were not emancipated, but remained slaves to be sold for the benefit of the state.[1228] In 1820, the United States Supreme Court upheld the condemnation of a slave ship as being actually bound for New Orleans, though ostensibly for Cuba.[1229] On the whole though, Louisiana would have preferred to continue the slave trade. Up to 1817, none of the newly admitted states apart from Louisiana had a seacoast, so they were not directly interested in the slave trade.

In 1805, Vermont seconded the North Carolina resolution that a constitutional amendment be passed authorizing Congress to prohibit the slave trade. [1230] Kentucky had an act prohibiting the importation of slaves from any foreign country or from any state to which the slaves had been brought since 1789. But the penalty was only a $300 fine, and the slave was apparently neither forfeited nor emancipated.[1231] Tennessee, Ohio, Indiana, Illinois, Missouri, and District of Columbia had no laws of their own or cases on the slave trade or general abolition.

Mississippi, admitted in 1817, was the first new state outside of Louisiana with a sea coast, but by that time the legal slave trade had already been closed. The federal law against the slave trade applied to the territory.[1232] This was followed by a territorial law in March, 1808.[1233]

From the Missouri Compromise to Foots' Resolution (1820-1830)

She carried a little carpet below her arm, which she then spread on the floor. Wilhelm said she might proceed. She thereupon brought four candles, and placed one upon each corner of the carpet. A little basket of eggs which she next carried in, made her purpose clearer. Carefully measuring her steps, she then walked to and fro on the carpet, spreading out the eggs in certain figures and positions, when done, she called in a man that was waiting in the house, and could play the violin. He retired with his instrument into a corner; she tied a band about her eyes, gave a signal, and like a piece of wheel-work set a going, she began moving the same instant as the music, accompanying her beats and the notes of the tune with the strokes of a pair of castanets.

Lightly, nimbly, quickly, and with hairbreadth accuracy, she carried on the dance. She skipped too sharply and surely between the eggs, and trod so closely down beside them, that you would have thought every instant she must trample one of them in pieces, or kick the rest away in her rapid turns. By no means She touched no one of them, though winding herself through their mazes with all kinds of steps, wide and narrow, nay even with leaps, and at last, half-kneeling.

–Goethe

From 1820-1860, the men who made America were dancing blindfold among eggs, but without the young woman's skill or accuracy. They not only did not know what they were doing, they usually thought they were doing something else. The only exception was Clay.[1]

After the Missouri Compromise of 1820, as the chess commentators say, "the rest is only a matter of technique." That the bloody denouement was without doubt inevitable,[1] did not change the fact that the technique was bumbling. Thomas Hart Benton was right in saying that the Missouri Compromise did not deserve the name of "compromise." It was an outright victory for the anti-slavery forces.[2] The "compromise" was that with the exception of Missouri, slavery should not in the future extend north of parallel 36° 30'.[3] Slavery could still be prohibited south of that line, although until the admission of California in 1850, the line was treated as working both ways.[3a] Nothing in the "compromise" made it do so.

Yet the anti-slavery forces raised a howl that the Missouri Compromise had been much too favorable to slavery.[4] This is the first instance in which the men who were guiding America's destiny showed that they did not know what was going on around them. Before going further, we may sketch the position of some of the chief figures from 1820 to the outbreak of the Civil War, and show that virtually all were blind to events.

Calhoun, one of the most perspicacious minds in American history, saw everything except the main point—that the South was outnumbered,[5] and that a rising society does not "will" a check to its economic ascent.[5a]

Webster dazedly affirmed that there was much agitation over fugitive slaves in Massachusetts which had few, and little in Pennsylvania, which had many.[6] Connecticut and Massachusetts were more industrially advanced than Pennsylvania.

With the Kansas-Nebraska Act,[7] Douglas stepped on an egg. Seward had his eyes open but he could not dance. Even as he called the positions of the eggs, he stepped on some. "But there is a higher law than the Constitution,"[8] could be said by a historian or by a revolutionary, but not by a senator exercising his office.[8a]

Jefferson Davis was grandly saying what he would or would not accept,[9] as if he had the choice, while Lincoln was saving the northern juggernaut from southern aggression.[10] (But unlike his colleagues, Lincoln never stepped on an egg.)[11]

Thomas Hart Benton was denying the earthquake, while the ground trembled under his feet.[12] After 1820 there was almost an about face from the clear and realistic thinking of Jefferson and John Quincy Adams.[12a] As we have said, Clay alone understood what was going on. His compromises were insufficient in degree rather than in kind.[12b] The fact that Clay's compromises were inadequate is the surest sign that the Civil War was inevitable.

Missouri was admitted as a slave state in 1820, with the proviso that there should be no other slave states north of parallel 36° 30'.[13] This compromise marked the first turning point in the relations between the slave and non-slave states. The latter now had a majority population and for the first time, a majority in the House of Representatives.[14] Nevertheless, it was enough of a compromise that it received the support of slave states in both Houses.[15] In the language of Thomas Hart Benton, "Mr. Clay has been often complimented as the author of the 'compromise' of 1820, in spite of his repeated declaration to the contrary, that measure coming from the Senate; but he is the undisputed author of the final settlement of the Missouri controversy in the actual admission of the State."[16]

This section will look at the brief period from the Missouri Compromise to Foot's Resolution[17] in 1830. The defeat of Foot's Resolution, followed by the uninterrupted advance of the Industrial Revolution in the northern states, was yet another milestone on the march toward destruction of the old agricultural by the new industrial society. The Resolution was an intended northern counterpart to the Fugitive Slave Act, but continuing immigration made it superfluous. (Senator Foot was another man who did not know what was taking place around him.) After the Missouri Compromise in 1820, no new states were admitted until after 1830.

The Missouri controversy resurrected an old problem in a new form. Exploration and settlement of the continent implied mobility and demanded that slaves be moved with the master. The point had been settled early, and during two centuries no problems flowed from it. But the Industrial Revolution brought a new problem, which impinged on the long dormant old one. Who should move with the settlement of the continent? For since the beginning of the Industrial Revolution there were two competing interests in America. There had been no such rivalry when the continent was first colonized. The proposal behind the Missouri controversy was for a limitation much more drastic than that known to feudal Europe.[18] The industrial part of America now wished that not only the slave but also the master not move beyond the soil he then occupied. [18a]

Ending the legal[19] slave trade in 1808 limited the supply of slaves. This had two necessary consequences. First, there were runaway slaves in Maine, New Hampshire, Massachusetts, Rhode Island, Connecticut, New York, Vermont and Canada.[24] Plainly, the movement to help slaves escape was coming from New England, which, as the growing industrial region, wanted low paid laborers. More severe punishment quickly followed for those convicted:

> enticing, persuading or advising any servant or slave away

from home, or from the employment of the owner or person properly in possession of such servant or slave, knowing the same to have been enticed away, or of harboring or employing any runaway slave or servant.[24a]

Again the telltale word "employing." This same statute gave masters the right to have a slave confined in jail as long as the public authorities were agreeable—evidently a preventive power.[24b]

A few days later another act required jailers to report to court all runaways in their possession for two weeks.[24c] The length of time before allowing action to be taken registers pressure in the opposite direction against which Virginia was also trying to guard. The hunger for slaves in the new-cotton states would have been appeased with a much shorter waiting period. In 1829 the penalty for enticing slaves away was increased from a fine of five to twenty dollars (with flogging as an alternative), to imprisonment from three to twelve months.[24d]

The only Virginia case during this period is DAVENPORT v. COMMONWEALTH,[24e] which upheld a conviction for stealing a free Mulatto child of eight. For the moment, Virginia was more plagued by southern attempts to compensate for the loss of slave trade than by northern attempts to get cheap wage laborers.

In Maryland the new trend, the "encouragement" of runaways by the free states is explicitly set forth in a resolution in 1821.[25]

> Whereas the encouragement given to Negroes running away from their owners in this state, and harbouring and employing of them by sundry citizens of the Commonwealth of Pennsylvania and the state of Delaware has been productive of serious inconveniences and of great injury to the owners of slaves ...
>
> Therefore, Resolved that the encouragement given to and the harbouring and employing of runaway Negroes from this state by sundry citizens of the Commonwealth of Pennsylvania and state of Delaware, has increased to so alarming a degree, and the inconvenience arising therefrom to the good people of this state has become so great and intolerable as to make longer silence on this subject on the part of the general assembly of Maryland, if not criminal, highly improper. The Governor of Maryland is memorialized to send this resolution to the Governors of Pennsylvania and Delaware, with request that they have their legislatures take countersteps.

One must not miss the word "employing" in this resolution. "Employing" in what capacity? Obviously in the lowest paid jobs and at a wage lower than that paid to white laborers for the same work. Otherwise the drive to "harbour and employ" runaway slaves would have been pointless.

In 1824, an act was passed prohibiting masters of vessels from receiving on board Negroes with no adequate identification from free states.[26]   The act is entitled "An act to prohibit the transportation of absconding slaves to Hayti or elsewhere." Apparently the propaganda for emancipation had reached slaves and led some of them to go even where they could not be employed as low paid wage laborers in new industries.   QUEEN v. STATE[27] upheld a penalty under the act of 1796,[28] where the defendant "did assist a Negro woman named Nelly in eloping and running away from (her master) by accompanying her a considerable distance, and showing her the road by which she might escape." Maryland was stretching old laws to meet new conditions, but was not yet increasing the penalties for enticing runaway slaves.

There are no other Maryland cases on fugitive slaves during the decade 1820-1830. Rhode Island, New Hampshire, Ohio, Maine, Missouri, Alabama and New York had no statutes or cases on fugitive slaves in these years.   New Jersey recognized the new movement, but with legislation strengthening the provisions for returning slaves escaped from other states.[29]   There were no cases directly on fugitive slaves, though several on abducting slaves.

Massachusetts had no new statutes, but in 1823 was faced with an attempt to reclaim a slave under the Fugitive Slave Act of 1793.[30]   For the first time the court was confronted with the argument that the act was unconstitutional. That such an argument should have been made was an impressive sign of the times.   In COMMONWEALTH v. GRIFFIN[31] the Supreme Court of Massachusetts still overruled the contention. This was the only case to 1830.

Connecticut had enacted only one statute on fugitive slaves during this period—apparently a move to nullify the federal Fugitive Slave Law.   Penalties of two to five years' imprisonment were imposed on kidnapping a free person "with an intention to have such person carried out of the state, or to be in any way held in slavery or service against his will."[32]   There were no Connecticut cases on fugitives from 1820 to 1830.

Pennsylvania expressed her awareness of what was going on by passing an act in 1826 entitled "An act to give effect to the provisions of the Constitution of the United States, relative to fugitives from labor, for the protection of free people of color, and to prevent kidnapping."[33] The title makes its bow to the Fugitive Slave Law of 1793. Actually the statute is designed to make enforcement more difficult, and to increase the risk of retrieving a slave otherwise than by meticulous legal process. No warrant could be issued for a fugitive slave except on application of the owner or an agent whose authority was exhibited in writing.[34] There had to be an affidavit of the claimant as well as of his agent or attorney.[35] Such affidavit could not, however, be used at the hearing before the judge on the application for rendition.[36]

At the same time, penalties for taking and carrying out of the state or seducing "by fraud or false pretenses" any Negro "with design and intention of selling and disposing of or causing to be sold, or of keeping and detaining, or of causing to be kept and detained, such Negro or Mulatto, as a slave or servant for life or for any term whatsoever" were imposed, running from $500 to $2000 fine and 7 to 21 years' imprisonment.[37]

The same penalty was imposed on "fraudulently" taking transfer of a Negro for the purpose of making him a slave in another state.[38] One can read between the lines. Any recapture of a slave which deviated in the least from the new burdensome procedure was likely to be held "fraudulent" and to be followed by the new Draconian punishments. The threat of such punishment deterred slaveowners from attempting to exercise any rights under the Fugitive Slave Act of 1793. So every fugitive slave case during this period refuses to return the alleged slave.[39]

Promptly in 1821, North Carolina provided "further punishment for harboring or maintaining runaway slaves."[40] In 1823 a minimum reward of $3.00 was fixed for those apprehending fugitive slaves in the county of the owner's residence.[41] Another law, aimed at taking away slaves on board of ship followed in 1825.[42] The Legislature of 1830-31 added still another: "An act providing further punishment for harboring and maintaining runaway slaves."[43] Profering the carrot with the stick, it also directed a reward of $10 for retrievers of fugitive slaves in the counties of Onslow, Jones, Craven, Lenair, New Hanover, Brunswick and Carforet.[44]

Yet the contract between this flood of legislation and the paucity of legal cases again shows North Carolina's indecision about slavery. At this time the legislature was more alarmed than the courts. There is only one case of fugitive slaves during this period—and it gives a narrow construction to the statute punishing concealment of a slave on board a vessel.[45]

South Carolina likewise followed the Missouri Compromise with a new law "to provide more effectually against the offense of harbouring

Negroes or other slaves."[46] But for the time being there was nothing further.

On the other hand, cases on runaway slaves begin to become frequent—much more so than in North Carolina which enacted statute after statute. Runaways were bought at reduced price.[47] There are cases of trover for fugitive slaves,[48] and several prosecutions for slave stealing or harboring runaways.[49]

Delaware fell in step with the now embattled slave states by enacting a fugitive slave law in 1826.[50] This covered both slaves fleeing to Delaware[51] and slaves carried out of Delaware.[52] Any Negro or Mulatto traveling without a pass could be picked up as a runaway slave.[53] Thirty lashes and sale into servitude for 7 years were the punishment for slave stealing.[54] In 1827, a new law was enacted to control runaway servants and apprentices,[54a] but none concerning slaves themselves.

Georgia responded to the new era by passing a fugitive slave law in 1826. The act prohibited carrying off by sea either free persons of color, or slaves falsely claiming to be free.[56] Abduction of slaves now extended to Georgia, and it necessarily extended to abduction on vessels. Three years later incoming free Negroes were quarantined on board of ship.[57]

> Whereas it has become highly necessary and essential to the welfare and safety of the good people of this State, that merchant vessels or ships coming by sea from other States or countries with free people of color acting as mariners or stewards, or in any other employment or capacity on board such vessel or vessels should perform quarantine, and that means should be adopted to prevent such persons of colour from coming into this State or from communicating with the coloured people of this State.

The sting is in the last clause of this preamble, "from communicating with the coloured people of this State." As will be seen, free Negroes were used as agents or instruments of the drive to recruit slaves into northern wage labor.[58] During this period, there were as yet, no Georgia cases of fugitive slaves.

In 1826, Louisiana lined up with the other slave states, enacting a new fugitive slave law.[59] Louisiana was far removed from the growing northern manufacturing centers, and at the moment, the need for the law was based only on:

> the difficulties attending the recovery of runaway slaves in this state, arising from their being detained for months

in prisons at a distance from the domicile of their masters, or from slaves changing their names or concealing
those of their masters.[60]

Fugitive slaves were collected in jails at New Orleans, Baton Rouge
and Alexandria.[61] Ascension was added as a slave depot the following
year.[62] There are no further acts during this period. Fugitive slave
cases which suggest systematic carrying out of the state begin only in
1830.[63]

Of the states admitted after the adoption of the Constitution, Vermont has no laws or cases touching fugitive slaves in the decade 1820-
1830.

Kentucky, a border state, almost immediately felt the pressure to
promote the escape of slaves. In 1821 the Legislature passed
"Resolutions having for their object the preservation of harmony
between this state and an adjoining nonslaveholding state."[64] The
preamble recites that:

> Whereas many cases have occurred, in relation to slaves
> who have escaped from their owners in this state, and
> have been found in the adjoining states, which do not hold
> slaves, calculated to disturb that harmony which it is in
> the interest of the citizens of those states and of this
> Commonwealth to cultivate and preserve towards each
> other; and it is the wish of the Legislature to use every
> means in its power to prevent the recurrence of such
> cases in the future; and it is deemed practicable, by a
> revision of the laws in this state in relation to slaves, and
> of the laws of the adjoining nonslaveholding states in re-
> lation to the people of colour, and to slaves who may
> come arriving there, escaping from their owners, so to
> frame laws of the respective states, as will in a great de-
> gree, if not entirely obviate the inconveniences which
> now exist.

Conferences were proposed with Ohio, Indiana, and Illinois.

In the next year the legislature turned its attention to slaves helped
to escape by water.[65] The act is aimed both at removal and employment on board of ship—again reflecting the wage-labor system of getting
fugitive slaves as employees. Needless to say they would be employees
at the bottom of the wage scale, thus enhancing the profit margin of infant industries. The Kentucky Court of Appeals observed "Free Negroes
and Mulattoes are almost everywhere, considered and treated as a degraded race of people."[65a] The scope of this act was enlarged in 1828.

In 1826 we see for the first time, slaves escaping to Canada. "A resolution requesting the president of the United States to call the attention of the British Government to the subject of slaves who make their escape into the provinces of Canada."[67]The preamble recites that "owing to our proximity to the possessions of His Britannic Majesty in the provinces of Canada, many of them are enabled to make their escape from the U.S. and enter the limits of these provinces." The words "Are enabled" suggests the work of third persons—which was undoubtedly true. Nothing similar had appeared before the Industrial Revolution was under full steam.

In 1829 the legislature tackled the subject once more, imposing imprisonment of from two to twenty years for enticing a slave away from his owner, or furnishing forged freedom papers.[68] Concealing a runaway gave rise to a civil cause of action by the slave's owner, and was made subject to a fine of $50-$500.[69] Litigation as yet is sparse and touches the subject only indirectly.[70] Kentucky was still too much of a frontier community to bring many cases to court.

The only Tennessee statute during this period spells out the existing provisions of dealing with fugitive slaves.[71] It does not seem to be directed against a newly arisen wave of escapee slaves. The only case tends to limit the act punishing the enticement and harboring of slaves.[72] The District of Columbia had few cases on fugitive slaves, and generally tended to apply laws against them narrowly.[73]

Indiana remembered her would-be slaveholding past with laws still facilitating the recovery of fugitive slaves.[74] But she also acknowledged the new era by reducing the penalty for giving a false certificate of freedom.[75] There were no cases between 1818 and 1845.

Mississippi, though on the Gulf coast, enacted one fugitive slave law after another. The Revised Code of 1824 extended the writ of habeas corpus to enable an owner to take a slave from the possession of someone who had seduced and taken him away.[76] Established machinery for recovering runaways came as a matter of course.[77] The need for labor was evidently too great to leave runaway slaves in jail. So in 1829 "all persons committed as runaways" were made available to counties "for work on streets, highways and bridges."[78] Even before the passage of this act, the pressure for such labor is clearly sketched by HUTCHINS v. LEE[79] which holds a county's title to a runaway slave which it has purchased unassailable, despite the failure to follow the statutory requirements. This was the only case on the subject through 1830.[79a]

Illinois prescribed that every black immigrant into the state produce a certificate of freedom from the state from which he came.[80] Every black in Illinois without such a certificate was deemed a runaway.[81] In the latter case however, the Negro was legally freed if no owner claimed him within a year after statutory advertising.[82]   There were no Illinois cases on fugitive slaves during this period.

DISCIPLINE-PATROLS

The slave states continued the old system of corporal discipline and patrols, only now these stood in a new relation to the overall economic picture. "Ruling classes decline inevitably when they cease to find scope for their capacities through which they rose to power."[83]   Or, where the exercise of those talents has become a hindrance rather than a help. From now on, corporal discipline, and even more so patrols, merely underlined the comparative inefficiency of the slave system as against the wage system, which could accomplish the same results by the cost-free device of firing or threatening to fire the employee.

Virginia reenacted the old punishment of stripes inflicted by a magistrate.[84]   The inference follows, obvious from the nature of the relations, that the same power continued in the master for lesser offenses. How far this method of discipline was becoming anachronistic may be seen from the fact that while it was still retained in 1825,[85]   for freemen (both white and black) too poor to pay a fine, it was abolished even as to them in 1828.[86]   The right of the master (though not its extent) to inflict corporal discipline on the slave was affirmed in COMMONWEALTH v. BOOK.[87]   COMMONWEALTH v. TURNER[88] seems to make it almost unlimited.

Maryland continued corporal punishment for slaves persuading another slave to run away from his master,[88a] and obstructing navigable rivers.   Faint streaks of the future however, may be seen in a law imposing a "moderate fine" on free persons of color engaging in religious assemblies other than between 7 A.M. and 5 P.M.[88c]

Indiana, Ohio, New Hampshire, Pennsylvania, Vermont, Connecticut, Rhode Island, Maine, New York, New Jersey, Massachusetts have neither statutes nor cases on corporal punishment of slaves.

In 1826, North Carolina imposed lashing on slaves trading for themselves,[89] as well as on free Negroes dealing with them.[90] Previously only the free Negro dealing with the slave had been punished, and then only by fine and jail.[91]   Lashes were likewise the penalty on free Negroes gambling with slaves.[92]

Patrols, as in the past, were given limited power to inflict corporal punishment.[93]   Slaves were also lashed for attending a muster or an election.[94]   But the courts now show a dislike of corporal punishment. In STATE v. ALLEN[94a] a slave was sentenced to be whipped and burned in the hand for grand larceny, but the judgment was reversed for want of jurisdiction.   In STATE v. YATES,[94b] the sentence of whipping (in addition to eleven months' imprisonment) was reversed in a conviction of a white man for manslaughter of a slave.   The court said that "the disgracing practice of burning in the hand" had been abolished by statute, and seems to conclude from this that whipping had also been abolished.

South Carolina however, continued the practice of corporal punishment.   In the period 1820-1830 it was imposed on slaves for killing or maiming livestock,[95] on free persons for receiving stolen goods from a slave,[96] on Negroes for harboring fugitive slaves,[97] and on free Negroes for coming into the state of South Carolina.[98]   STATE Ex Rel v. MARTINDALE[99] mentions infliction of corporal punishment as one of the usual tasks of patrol riders.

Delaware imposed lashes on white defendants for kidnapping free Negroes with intent to sell as slaves.[100]   Slaves were punished as in the past for non-capital offenses.[101]   There were no cases.

Georgia whipped free Negroes entering the state in violation of the laws quarantining them from slaves, and not departing within ten days.[102]   It also whipped those who taught slaves or free Negroes to read and write,[103] who kept a house of entertainment or sold goods or liquors in the towns of Clinton and Macon.[104]   There were no Georgia cases on corporal punishment from 1820-1830.

Louisiana had no new statutes imposing corporal punishment, and there were no cases.

Kentucky had no new corporal punishment laws.   In fact, a law of 1826 enlisting free Negroes in road and highway work subjects them to "the same fines and penalties that white persons are now by law."[105]

Tennessee lashed slaves selling liquor without their owners' permission,[106] or possessing liquor.[107]   But it also made the same provision as Kentucky.   Free Negroes made liable for road work were subject to the same punishment as whites.[108]   As in Kentucky, there were no cases.

There is one case in the District of Columbia during this period, in which a slave of 13 is found guilty of manslaughter for the killing of another slave, aged 15, and is sentenced to be burnt in the hand and whipped with ten stripes.[109]   On the other hand, a free Negro, for enticing away a slave belonging to Judge Washington, was only fined $50.[110]

Mississippi continued or adopted corporal punishment for slaves. Lashes were given for hunting,[111] and stripes for going from home without a pass;[112] there were lashes for furnishing a pass to a slave without the owner's permission,[113] for offering articles for sale without the master's permission,[114] and for keeping weapons or ammunition.[115] Free Negroes could be lashed for a second offense of keeping weapons without a license,[116] for rants and riots,[117] and for furnishing intoxicating liquor to slaves.[118] Any Negro could be lashed for using obscene language, assaulting white persons,[119] or for petty larceny.[121] Patrols were authorized to inflict up to 39 lashes at the discretion of a justice of the peace,[122] and to administer up to 15 lashes themselves on slaves found unlawfully assembled or strolling without a pass.[123]

Illinois inflicted whipping on either partner to an interracial marriage.[124] Previous corporal punishments were continued.[125] No Illinois cases during this period involve corporal punishment. Alabama, like Mississippi, instituted and continued the system of corporal punishment. Manslaughter by one Negro of another (either free or slave) drew 30-100 lashes at the jury's discretion.[126] Twenty-five stripes, in addition to fines, were inflicted on free Negroes and Mulattoes retailing spiritous liquors.[127]

Missouri authorized patrollers to inflict up to 10 lashes on slaves found strolling without a pass.[129] While corporal punishment was abolished generally in 1826,[130] it was retained for slaves.[131] There were no cases on corporal punishment.

As may be anticipated, patrols were made a regular institution in the cotton states. The prohibition of assemblies became more severe as the Industrial Revolution gained momentum and industrial employers became more and more interested in inducing slaves to break away from slavery into "freedom."

Virginia, New York, New Jersey, Massachusetts, Connecticut, Rhode Island, New Hampshire, Pennsylvania, Delaware, Vermont, Kentucky, Tennessee and of course the District of Columbia, Ohio, Indiana, Illinois, Alabama, and Maine had no new patrol laws.

Maryland passed patrol acts in 1822 and 1826.[132] In 1829 a new law forbade meetings for religious purposes in Prince Georges County of any colored persons whether slave or free.[133] As a border state, Maryland had just enough slave-operated agriculture to be discommoded by the activities of industrial slave recruiters. The key to all these acts lay in the complaint made by the preamble to the act of 1829; the religious meeting-house "tends to demoralize the slaves." There are, however, no cases under these statutes.

North Carolina continued her patrol laws. In Mecklenburg County patrol duty was limited to slaveowners, or persons who had an interest in a slave. All others were exempt.[134] This indicates at the very least, that slavery had become stationary in North Carolina. It was the opposite from the trend underway in South Carolina, where patrollers were now low-caste petty officers.[135] Various patrol acts were passed for individual North Carolina counties.[136] Some of these were then almost immediately repealed.[137] But in 1830 a general patrol law was enacted for all counties, and taxes levied to pay patrollers.[138] North Carolina finally followed South Carolina in making patrol-riding a job.

In TATE v. O'NEAL,[139-141] the jury found for the defendant patrollers in an action by the master alleging the excessive whipping of a slave. It was claimed that animosity existed between the family of one of the defendants and the plaintiff,[142] indicating that patrollers and slaveowners were still on the same social level. There were no other cases on patrols during this period, although the volume of litigation in North Carolina increased noticeably.

South Carolina had no new patrol legislation through 1830. But the state now seems to be having as much trouble with her patrols as with her slaves. In STATE v. COLE[143] we get the interesting information that "the prosecutor said he was actually obliged to remove his family to Charleston, to relieve them from the constant alarm in which they were kept by the turbulent conduct of the patrols." A patrol is not authorized to announce its approach with the firing of guns, to commence its operations by killing men's dogs, carry them on by beating his Negroes, and conclude with abusing himself." A conviction of riot was affirmed. The case indicates that "the times are out of joint." South Carolina's caste system is no longer running smoothly.

PARTEOUS v. HAZIL[145] again concerns lawlessness by a patrol, in this instance taking two guns from the plaintiff's house in a night raid when the plaintiff was absent and a colored man was acting as overseer of the plantation. The captain of the patrol was not even on duty. His son acted as deputy. The jury (not here confined to slaveholders) gave a verdict for one cent. A new trial was granted on the plaintiff's motion. STATE v. BLYTHE[146] was another prosecution under the patrol act where the conviction was set aside.

The requirement that a white person live on any plantation having more than ten working slaves was satisfied if this white person lived anywhere on the plantation, no matter how far from the slaves. And the low status of patrol riding is once more made clear when Justice William Johnson of the U.S. Supreme Court is held exempt.[147]

Georgia put the patrol law in the City of Savannah first at the

discretion of the mayor and aldermen,[148] and later at the discretion of
the mayor, aldermen and justices of the Superior Court of the
county.[149] Louisiana continued the patrol system, merely transferring
the appointment of patrols from the militia and police juries to police
juries alone.[150] The mayor and city council of New Orleans were given
authority to establish patrols for New Orleans should they should deem
them necessary.[151] There were no further statutes on patrols during
this period, and no cases.

The Mississippi Revised Code of 1824 included "An act to reduce into one, the several acts concerning patrols."[152] Patrol duty was
imposed first of all on slaveowners, but the statute leaves the door open
for a system of paid subordinate patrollers.[153] Doubtless learning from
the experience of the older slave states, Mississippi anticipated the
problem of disorderly conduct by patrollers.[154] There were no cases of
patrols during this period. Missouri enacted a new patrol law in 1822,[155]
but there were no cases.

No state enacted any further legislation between 1820 and 1830
regulating slaves' hours of labor. Here again, the newer slave states
were caught in the current generated by the "free" states of the industrial north. The "right" to work an employee unlimited hours was
doggedly asserted by employers of wage laborers, being formally
declared three quarters of a century later in NOCHUOR v. NEW
YORK.[156] As a matter of competition, the other states were doing the
same thing.

Virginia had no further statutes on requirement of adequate food
and clothing for slaves, and only one case directly on this subject.[156a]
Two other decisions of 1825 tell why. Virginia now exercised great care
over slaves as persons.[157]

Maryland had one case on the general subject, in which the hirer attempts to make an agreement with the master that the hirer will take
good care of the hired slave.[157a]

New York, New Jersey, Connecticut, Rhode Island, New Hampshire,
Pennsylvania, South Carolina, Georgia, the District of Columbia, Ohio,
Indiana, Mississippi, Illinois and Missouri had no new laws or cases on the
master's obligation to furnish his slaves with sufficient food and
clothing. Vermont, Massachusetts and Maine had no slaves.

North Carolina in 1826, extended to free Negroes[158] the
protections hitherto given to white servants and to slaves.[159] The same
statute required colored indentured servants to be taught a mechanical
trade.[160] Here North Carolina's undeveloped slave system again shows
itself—this time with a suggestion that it might later "overstep"[161] the

more developed slave states.   On the one hand, 19th century North Carolina still had colored indentured servants.   Elsewhere that institution had disappeared.[162]   On the other hand, by requiring a minimal education for free Negroes, North Carolina was responding to the Industrial Revolution. [163]   This was different from the states where slavery had taken a firmer hold, which set their faces against the Industrial Revolution by prohibiting slave education.   The act itself marks the contrast with South Carolina, which had no new legislation.

Delaware likewise has an act which is broad enough to extend such protection to apprentices.[164]   Two Louisiana decisions hold the master liable for medical attention furnished to the slaves. [164a]

Kentucky, new and headed toward becoming a full-fledged slave state, enacted a law in 1829 requiring masters to furnish slaves with adequate food and raiment.[165]   This followed a special law requiring adequate quarters for slaves in the hands of the sheriff.[165a]

SCOTT v. HUME[166] was a civil action by the owner against the pledge of a slave for "exposing him in inclement weather," so that the slave became sick, and then failing to furnish medical attention so that slave died.   Likewise, in CABINESS v. HERNDON[167] the purchaser of a slave "dismissed" her almost immediately upon receiving her.   It was January.   She wandered around half-naked, starved, and died.   Civil actions were available and were brought, yet in both cases cited, the defendant mistreating the slave was exonerated on one ground or another. Kentucky was very much on the frontier.   In GRUNDY v. JAMESON[167a] "physician's fees and expenses of sickness" of slaves were held chargeable against the hirer.

There were no new statutes in Tennessee.   The only case which touched the subject suggests that despite the state's frontier character, masters in Tennessee were inclined to take feudal[167b] care of their slaves.   In HOPE v. JOHNSON,[168] the court upheld a provision in a will emancipating the deceased's slaves and setting aside property in Indiana for their support after emancipation.   This foreshadowed the course which Tennessee was to take at the outbreak of the Civil War.   There was a strong current to emancipate slaves, so Tennessee seceded last. The slaveholders acted in the 18th century tradition, and unlike Kentucky, Maryland and Delaware, Tennessee did secede.   However, it may be added, Tennessee was without the savagery of the new cotton states.

Alabama had no direct provision requiring the master to supply his slaves with food and clothing.   She did however, apply the remote and indirect pressure of reducing compensation for an executed slave if the master had wholly or partly induced the slave's crime.[169]

The sparsity of legislation or court cases on the duty of the master to supply adequate food and clothing reflects the trends of the new industrialism. To compete with a wage economy, the slave states of the Nineteenth century instituted a system which superimposed the faults of wage labor upon the faults of slavery.

SUPPORT OF AGED OR INFIRM SLAVES

In 1824 Virginia enacted a new statute imposing a fine up to $50 on masters who allowed slaves "of unsound mind, or aged or infirm to go at large without adequate provision for his or her support." The Overseers of the Poor were given the duty of caring for such slaves, with the cost chargeable to the master.[170] This statute was a corollary to the new Virginia economy as a slave breeding state. Good slaves were sold south. Useless slaves were abandoned.

There were however, no cases, other than those refusing to enforce nonstatutory emancipation.[170a] Maryland found that "old and infirm Negro slaves belonging to deceased persons' estates which on settlement prove to be insolvent are frequently subjected to great suffering and want"[171] and gave the civil courts virtually unlimited discretion to care for them. This was a circumscribed variant of Virginia's problem. HAMILTON v. CRAGG[172] denied a testamentary emancipation to a two-year old slave, who "consequently was not able to work and gain a sufficient maintenance and livelihood." This was the only case. New York had one case which touched the subject indirectly. WARREN v. BROOKS[173] was a suit by Overseers of the Poor against a master who had emancipated a slave unable to support himself. The jury returned a verdict for six cents, which was set aside on the plaintiff's appeal. Legal brakes on emancipations did not stop them, and juries were disinclined to enforce laws which stemmed from the past.

In one case, New Jersey indirectly enforced the obligation to support a crippled slave. CHATHAM vs. CANFIELD[174] allowed a municipality to recover from the master, the money which it had expended for the support of a slave crippled from birth, and never able to earn his subsistence.

Massachusetts, Connecticut, Rhode Island, New Hampshire, Pennsylvania, North Carolina, South Carolina, Delaware, Georgia, Vermont, Kentucky, Ohio, Indiana, Maine, and Missouri had no new restrictions on emancipation, but for divergent reasons. In the northern states slavery was either gone or on its last legs. In South Carolina it had become static, because the state had passed its peak of development. In North Carolina, slavery never reached full development, and Georgia,

Kentucky and Missouri were still in a formative stage. From 1827 Louisiana permitted the emancipation of young slaves only under court supervision.[175] And the provision extended only to slaves native to the state.[176]

Tennessee granted a group emancipation in 1823 on condition that the former masters gave bond of $1000 so that the slaves named would not become public charges.[177] The same provisions were granted with an unlimited bond.[178] In 1829, emancipation by will was placed under court control and made generally subject to bond.[179]

Acting as a surety for the support of emancipated slaves appears as something which the master volunteers in HOPE v. JOHNSON[180] where he provided by will:

> that the plantation I now live on be sold and the proceeds laid out in land in the Indiana Territory, as well situated as can be procured, and the right thereof vested in my Negroes, with their increase, to above I give their entire freedom, and the settling of them on the above named land, under the direction of my executors.

The Supreme Court of Tennessee decided that "To provide for the subsistence of slaves now in being, who may hereafter become free is not against the law."

Mississippi does not seem to have approached this problem from the standpoint of the slave at all. Emancipations were restricted by the limitation that they could be granted only for meritorious acts, and not by any requirement that the slave be able to support himself.[181] Fining persons aiding an unsuccessful suit for freedom[182] $100 rounds out the picture of the controlling attitude. As usual, Mississippi—the outstanding new cotton state—combined the worst features of slavery with the worst features of wage labor. The condition that a former slave should not become chargeable to the public was however, inserted in some private acts of emancipation.[183] No Mississippi cases reached the appellate court during this period.

At first Illinois continued her previous law requiring a bond from slaveowners who brought slaves into the state for the purpose of emancipating them, but extended the time to put up such a bond and released past penalties.[184] However harsh the new industrial states may have been, Illinois here took the opposite position from Mississippi. Evidently, slaveowners from other states came to Illinois because they wanted to get rid of their slaves, but could not do so in the state from which they came. Illinois combined the beneficent aspects of wage labor with the beneficent aspects of slavery. No exception was made to the rule that slaves brought into Illinois became free, but the obligation of the former master to support them if they could not support themselves was borrowed from the slave states.

This paradise could not last. In 1829, Illinois generalized the occasional Mississippi insistence that the free Negroes themselves give bond not to become public charges.[185] It is true that this provision related to Negroes coming into the state, rather than to those brought in by their masters. Yet, the very provision parallels that of the harshest slave states. COLES v. COUNTY OF MADISON[186] upheld the 1824 remission of penalties under the Act of 1819 for bringing in slaves without furnishing bond for their support. It reflects the drive toward a society of wage labor in which the employee may be fired and left to starve without any obligation on the part of the employer.

Since Alabama had provided by her constitution of 1819 that the legislature might authorize emancipation of slaves, "preventing them from becoming a public charge,"[187] this precaution continued in force. Here we see Alabama lined up with the classical slave economy rather than with the industrial economy with which she was competing. Private acts of emancipation accordingly required the owner to give bond to protect the state against having to support the former slave.[188] Special acts were the only permitted form of emancipation. "Slaves could not be emancipated by will. It was essential, that the authority should be given either by general or special enactment."[189]

PROHIBITION OF CRUELTY TO SLAVES

Virginia had no new statutes protecting slaves against cruelty. At the same time the state first hesitated, then allowed great latitude to the master in chastising the slave.[191] There probably was comparatively little cruelty to slaves in Virginia after 1820; the state had gone into the business of breeding slaves and selling them south. She did not want to offer damaged goods. In those instances where the problem did arise, Virginia simply applied old law.

Maryland had no new statutes or cases on mistreatment of slaves. On the one hand, the institution was becoming attenuated. On the other, Maryland, like Virginia, was engaged in selling slaves south to the cotton states,[192] and was interested in offering sound goods.

New York, Massachusetts, Connecticut, Rhode Island, New Hampshire, Pennsylvania, Delaware, Louisiana, Vermont, Tennessee, Ohio, Indiana, Alabama, and Maine, had no new statutes and no cases on cruel treatment of slaves by masters. Here again, the reasons for the identical result were undoubtedly quite divergent. In most of the named states, slavery was a thing of the past, or on its way out. Louisiana probably had a fairly orderly society even in dealing with her slaves and cases did not arise to any great extent.[191a] Tennessee and Alabama were still too close to the frontier for such matters to get to court.

North Carolina had no new statutes protecting slaves against mistreatment, but several cases reached the Supreme Court in the 10 years from 1820 to 1830. They give a picture of a violent and turbulent society. The master was allowed all measures short of dismemberment or death.[193]

In 1821, South Carolina enacted the death penalty for the murder of a slave.[194] The intent of this statute was declared in STATE v. RAINES[195] which held that no judgment could be pronounced on a verdict of manslaughter of a slave.

> Under the old act (of 1740), the common law kind of homicide, technically called manslaughter, was intended to be abolished. For the citizen is only made amenable for three kinds of killings; murder, killing in sudden heat and passion, or by undue correction. No man has ever been adjudged guilty of manslaughter for killing a Negro.[196] . . . The professed object of the act of 1821, was to increase the punishment for murder and to omit the killing by undue correction.[197]

Apparently the object of the statute was to give the master greater latitude, while subjecting him to heavier penalties if he overstepped the bounds. Killing by immoderate correction was no longer a separate crime, and if the master was not found guilty of murder, he went scot-free. But he was taking his own chances. If the jury found he had committed murder, the penalty was death. This seemed to depend on whether the jury found that the master's actions implied malice. There are no other statutes, nor cases. Even the judicial glass leaves it unclear why the change of 1821 was made.

There were no new statutes in Georgia shielding the slave against abuse by the master. But the state had advanced far enough from the frontier that she severely punished extreme abuse. In STATE v. ABBOTT,[198] the prosecution of a master for killing his slave, bail pending trial was denied. This was the solitary case, however. Georgia was only slowly becoming a settled society which sought recourse to the courts.

In 1830, Kentucky provided that slaves who were mistreated by their masters should be transferred to another master.[199] This statute is interesting from several standpoints; all its features were characteristic of a state that was at once a new slave state and a border state, and foretell that Kentucky would not secede.

The remedy of pulling the mistreated slave out of the owner's possession was the remedy used for mistreated apprentices. The slave system was now being assimilated to the wage sytem. The statute also covered activity which "endangers" the slave's life and limb, not merely cases where the slave was actually killed or maimed. Thus Kentucky had a much milder system, than for instance, the Draconian law of North Carolina. [200]

Yet, in other settings, the Kentucky courts and slave owners showed a marked callousness toward their slaves. In CABANISS v. HERNDON, [201] the seller made a later delivery of a slave who was more sick than the buyer had suspected. The Kentucky Court of Appeals disposed of this problem in the following language:

> The Negro in this case was not delivered to Herndon until two or three days after the time when she was to have been delivered. This was about the tenth of January. And some time in the month of February following, she died in the kitchen of John Moss, into which she crept for shelter, half naked and starved, and where she remained four or five days. It was the option of Herndon whether to receive her or not, at the time she was sick.

> If he had received her, it would have waived her failure of the delivery at an improper time. This however, he does not appear to have done. Influenced by the discovery that the slave was more unsound than he had apprehended, and having it thus in his power either to accept or reject her, he determined on the latter. And as Cabaniss did not make the delivery in person, but did it by sending her, Herndon took the same means of sending her off. Although we cannot approve the want of humanity in sending her out when diseased at so inclement a season, yet as she was not his, and Cabaniss had taken that mode of sending her there, Herndon, however inhumanely he may have behaved towards the slave, we conceive, is entitled to a rescission of the contract.

A glimmer appeared in the qualification "as she was not his." A master might not have been permitted so to treat his slave. But the results of the case are what counts and nothing can be said where equitable relief is granted to the party whom the court upbraids for inhumane treatment.

Mississippi, a fully developed slave state under industrial conditions, followed the practice of the older slave states in shielding the slave against abuse by the master.[202] It is interesting to contrast Mississippi, still largely frontier, but rapidly becoming settled on large plantations, with a state like North Carolina, never developing under slavery, and remaining half-barbarous. Illinois authorized indentured servants to sue civilly for abuse.[203] There were no new statutes in Missouri protecting the slave from the master, but in MARNAN v. TRABUE,[204] the hirer of a slave was held civilly liable for "her death . . . occasioned by cruel and unusual treatment on the part of the defendant" even after acquittal on the criminal charge.

SEXUAL RELATIONS

With the illegalization of the slave trade, demand for American-born slave children skyrocketed. With slavery descending through the mother, it became profitable as never before for slaveowners to operate as their own studs.[205] At the same time, new fear of Negro independence, with consequent increased measures of suppression, was expressed in harsher penalties for rape of a white woman.

Virginia imposed an unconditional death penalty for attempted rape of a white woman in 1823.[206] Fear of Negroes' activities now served to outweigh the slaveowner's desire to protect their property, which had formerly restrained prosecutions for rape.

Previously free Negroes could not be indicted for rape, and where a defendant had been prosecuted as free, the court did not permit a third party to extricate him by claiming him as a slave. Under the law as it then stood, prosecution as a slave carried the death penalty. Prosecution as a free Negro did not.[208]

COMMONWEALTH v. ISAACS[209] disposed of a liaison between a white man and a free colored woman without regard to color. Further, it was held that though there might be violation of the law against "an act for the suppression of vice and punishing the disturbance of religious worship and sabbath-breaking" there was no common-law misdemeanor. Apparently Virginians were going through a stage of not knowing just what to do about sexual relations between Negroes and whites.

As in the past, Maryland took Mulattoes as a matter of course.[210] New York had no new statutes, but one case in these years likewise took Mulattoes as a matter of course.[211] From 1820-1830 New Jersey, Massachusetts, Rhode Island, New Hampshire, Vermont, Ohio, Indiana, had no statutes or cases on sexual relations between blacks and whites.

Connecticut was another state which took Mulattoes for granted.[212] The same was true of Pennsylvania.[213]

North Carolina punished assault with intent to commit rape on a white female with death, in 1823.[214] This kind of severity indicates that the general population of North Carolina was much more afraid of unruly slaves (and jealous of them) than the slaveowning section was anxious to preserve its property. It is again a sign of the weak hold which slavery had in North Carolina. Otherwise, North Carolina took Mulattoes for granted.[215] But there was a special new act against intermarriages in 1830,[216] revealing once more the insecurity of the caste structure in the state.

The legislature would not have to go out of its way to prohibit intermarriages unless there was such a trend among the population. The judges were drawn from the personnel of the slaveowners, so enforcement of the rape act of 1823 [217] encountered all kinds of technical difficulties. In STATE v. JIM, [218] judgment of conviction was arrested because the indictment had not charged that the act was committed "violently, and against the will of M.J." The Supreme Court of North Carolina philosophized, "The late act of Assembly, having elevated the offense to a capital felony, affords an additional reason for adhering to the established forms."[219] Furthermore the Supreme Court, disagreeing with the trial court, held that the jury should have been composed of slaveholders.

> That the master would have assurance of an equitable
> trial by persons who had property constantly exposed to
> similar accusations, and who would not wantonly sacrifice
> the life of a slave, but yield it only to a sense of justice,
> daily experience is a sufficient reminder.[210]

On retrial, a second conviction was reversed, this time because a witness who contradicted himself was held insufficient as a matter of law.[220a] In only one case was there a conviction for rape.[220b] It was slander to say that a white woman was pregnant by a Negro, but the plaintiff had to satisfy technical niceties to prevail. For instance, if the complaint charged words spoken by the defendant, that alone could be proven, but not words spoken by his agent at his instigation.[221] General reputation was enough to prove a marriage between a Mulatto man and a white woman. [222]

Apparently, sexual relations between whites and Negroes were accepted as existing. Minute examination of them in court was avoided. North Carolina had a very loosely structured caste system which only the top layers of society enforced in earnest.

Some of the South Carolina statutes refer generally to "Negroes and persons of color."[223] This general language was undoubtedly meant to include Mulattoes. A Mulatto slave was emancipated in 1823,[224] and a question is suggested by BROWN v. SHAND[225] where the testator "stated, that he meant to provide in his will for Mary (his slave) and his children." Were they <u>his</u> children?

In TABITHA SINGLETON v. ELIZA E. BRUNER,[226] every one understood that the issue was whether cohabitation was the consideration for notes given by the white decedent to the colored plaintiff. The Supreme Court held that the notes must rest on some other consideration. The trial court had held that even consideration of cohabitation was sufficient.

But REAL ESTATE OF MRS. HARDCASTLE v. PERCHER ESCHEATOR[227] gives a full view of the matter-of-fact attitude which the ruling class in South Carolina had towards sexual relations between whites and blacks:

> Free persons of color, and although they have not, like the freed men of Rome, or others, become incorporated in the body politic, it has no doubt been the result of the mark which nature has put upon him. For where this has been obliterated, some have obtained, and now enjoy all the rights of citizens. Some who have lost the distinctive mark, hold offices, as well as lands and even seats in the legislature.

STATE v. MARY HAYES[228] reaches the same result by the opposite reasoning (illustrating how "legal principles" are applied or not applied, to gain ends countenanced by society). A Mulatto woman, the daughter of a Negro father and a white mother, was convicted of keeping a disorderly house. The court refused to pass sentence, on the ground that she had been prosecuted under the wrong statute. Notwithstanding that her mother was white, she should have been tried under the statute and before a court having jurisdiction over free Negroes. Through reasoning from the degraded status of such offspring, she was freed of the charge.

STATE v. BENJAMIN SCOTT[229] presented the converse situation where the defendant was charged (with Negro stealing) "as a free person of color," and pleaded to the court's jurisdiction that he was white and should be tried accordingly. The defense was considered without comment on miscegenation and the defendant was given an opportunity to make his plea. In these relations, South Carolina retained her self-confident, eighteenth-century caste system.

Delaware, likewise took Mulattoes for granted,[230] but the state was far from calm and self-assured like South Carolina. Feelings of insecurity with respect to the Negro population showed themselves in a new law tightening the caste lines by forbidding intermarriage.[231] Among the extremely few Delaware cases on slaves and free Negroes during this period, only one involves sexual relations.

In 1821, Georgia made rape by a slave or free person of color on a free white female, a capital offense.[232] The caste system was insecure. That such a penalty was enacted betrayed a feeling that the colored population was not under control. It coincided with the Missouri controversy. The cases from Georgia during the decade, 1820-30, were largely slave trade cases, indicating that internal disputes never reached the courts. Louisiana not only took Mulattoes for granted, but specifically, intercourse between white men and slave women. In 1824, one Henry Hayes was authorized to emancipate a Mulatto slave named John.[233] If he was a Mulatto slave, his father must have been white and his mother a Negro slave. In 1827, a girl's color "rendering it doubtful whether she is a slave or not" was a ground of legislative emancipation.[234] Likewise, ENGLISH v. LATHAM[235] concerned "an indentured Mulatto man."

Two other cases present special variations. In CAPELLY v. DEVEREUX,[236] the plaintiff's godfather had bought him from his natural father. The plaintiff's mother was a free colored woman. The court also indicates clearly that the natural father was white.[236a] The petitioners in ULZIRE PAEYFERRE[237] were found to be free because they were descended from a free Indian woman. In GARDELA v. ABAT,[237a]it was mentioned collaterally that the natural daughter of the decedent was a woman of color.

Kentucky, recently settled and recently admitted as a state, took Mulattoes as a matter of course in the 1820's.[238] But it was actionable slander to say that a man kept a Negro woman and had a child by her.[239] After 1820, Tennessee shows her consciousness of the frequence of sexual relations between blacks and whites by forbidding children of free colored women to inherit, but permitting it if the father was also colored and apparently also if the mother herself was partly white.[240] In 1827 VAUGHAN v. PHOEBE declared that:

> Freedom in this country is not a mere name, and makes itself manifest by many . . . public acts . . . transfers its possessor even if he be black, Mulatto or copper colored, from the kitchen and the cottonfield to the court-house and the election ground. [241]

In 1823 a Negro was indicted for rape in the District of Columbia.

After selection of the jury, a juror was asked to be excused because he was a Quaker and felt he would not be able to vote to convict. He was not excused. [241a]In U.S. v. BIRCH, the District of Columbia lined itself up with the states taking Mulattoes as a matter of course.[241b] This continued to be the accepted point of view.

Mississippi was another state which took Mulattoes and Quadroons as a normal part of the population.[242] There are no cases through 1830. Illinois had accepted Mulattoes as a matter of course prior to 1820[243] and continued to do so.[244] Alabama followed the pattern of all the newer slave states. Mulattoes were considered a phenomenon of life, like the four seasons.[245] There was also a more specialized recognition of Mulattoes. Two statutes emancipated "descendants of the ancient creole population," some of whom are described as Mulattoes and some not.[246]

STATE v. PHIL shows that Alabama, though new, felt herself a sufficiently slave caste society to allow the slaveowners' property interest to override popular fears of independent Negroes, however strong this fear might be. On a charge of assault with intent to commit rape, the court had trouble getting a jury. In the proceeding court term, the judge had an illness in his family and adjourned the case. On appeal, the adjournment was held irregular and the defendant-slave was discharged by the upper court.[247] Missouri was like Alabama, taking Mulattoes as a normal part of life.[248]

As the laws reflect society from 1820-1830, we see two things. First, there was a substantial Mulatto population which aroused no comment whatever. Second, at the time of the Missouri controversy and demands from the industrializing states for "free" labor, there was an uneasiness about what "free" Negroes were likely to do. This was met by new Draconian laws punishing rape and attempted rape. But to a certain extent, the old order intruded itself because the death penalty deprives a master of his property. Consequently, technical reasons were sometimes found for avoiding a death sentence.

EMANCIPATION

The Industrial Revolution changed the whole picture of emancipation. The need for cheap wage labor suddenly inspired merchants, manufacturers and railroad men with the high ideal of "liberating" slaves. These gentlemen found themselves mysteriously transferred from Schopenhauer's Class II to Schopenhauer's Class III.[249] The slaveholders responded with frantic restrictions. Legal emancipation began to be abolished. It was gradually pared down to a few cases of special services, often that of betraying slave revolts.

Virginia continued her policy of permitting emancipation on condition that the emancipated slaves leave the state. Occasionally, they were allowed to stay by special legislation.[250] This group of acts included one allowing Thomas Jefferson's children to remain in the state.[251] There was a continuous stream of emancipation cases in Virginia during this period, showing the perilous state of the institution. BARNETT v. SAM[252] held that removal to North Carolina had not resulted in emancipation, after two lower courts had taken the opposite view.

DEMPSEY v. LAWRENCE[253] took care that a slave claiming freedom be adequately represented. A judgment against emancipation was reversed where the claimant was without counsel in the lower court. Working in Ohio on a single Sunday was held not to emancipate. "Such an occupation for a short time and even for the benefit of the master, and probably in his presence, could never operate an emancipation of a slave."[254]

The Virginia court formulated a doctrine to combat the "emancipation" activities of the northern states, the employers of wage labor:

> The lex loci is also to be taken subject to the exception, that it is not to be enforced in another country, when it violates some moral duty, or the policy of that country, or is inconsistent with a positive right secured to a third person or party by the laws of that country, in which it is sought to be enforced. In such a case we are told magis jus nostrum, quam jus alienum servemus. That third party, in this case, is the Commonwealth of Virginia, and her policy and interests are also to be attended to.

> These turn the scale against the lex loci in the present instance. For want of being emancipated agreeably to the provisions of our act on that subject, the duty of supporting their old and infirm slaves would devolve upon the Commonwealth. The burden is only to be borne by the master, in relation to slaves "so emancipated;" that is, emancipated agreeably to the provisions of the act.[255]

So Virginia vacillated in her attitude toward emancipation. A present right to future freedom was no freedom at all,[256] but a deed of emancipation once granted could not be revoked, even in the face of subsequent acknowledgments by the former slave.[257] If a master freed the mother, he could not reserve slavery over her afterborn children. They follow the status of the mother at the time of their birth.[258]

Indian slavery however, was revived.[259] A contract with a slave for future emancipation was void as slaves could not make contracts.[260] Yet a deed of emancipation by one son was held to take precedence over an earlier deed from father to another son, given possibly to defeat creditors, and superseded by a later family agreement.[261]

A deed of emancipation was held void in 1828, where it satisfied the requirements of the law in force since 1782, but not as of the time it was executed.[262] A grant of freedom, subject to service during the defendant's lifetime, was enforced.[263] A slave taken to Maryland became free, and was not restored to slavery upon being brought back to Virginia.[264] Slaves which the testator intended to emancipate were free if there was enough other property to pay debts. Otherwise they were not freed.[265] A measure of leniency was shown in respect to taking the oath on imported slaves,[265a] and in 1830 a divided court refused emancipation where there was no act of extraordinary merit, and the testator's will was construed as authorizing emancipation only if the freedman could remain in the state.[266]

Where a woman owner executed a deed of emancipation to take effect at a future date, but was married and died before the emancipation was to take effect, the divided Virginia Court of Appeals, reversing both lower courts, held that by her marriage, the grantor had lost her power to emancipate, and consequently, the deed of emancipation was void at the time when it was supposed to take effect.[267]

Where rules of emancipation were otherwise followed, Maryland did not try to defeat emancipation because of technical slips.[268] Statutes also appear allowing manumission of a slave over 45.[269] The jailer of Worcester County was compensated for taking charge of Negroes who had petitioned for their freedom,[270] and a free Negro from Virginia was given permanent residence.[271] On the other hand, statutes sometimes waived emancipation by removal in or out of the state.[272] So the decision also insisted on the 45-year age limit for emancipation, but the courts sometimes were willing to grant "freedom by implication."[273] A deed of manumission was enforced, though way late, by the terms of the will under which it was made.[274] Where a will expressly emancipated, even though personal property might be insufficient to pay debts, the emancipation was enforced.[275] Where there was no such express provision, the cases went both ways, with the later ones upholding emancipation.[276] A grant of freedom on condition of paying $10 a year to the testator's sister was operative immediately. The payment was not to be a condition precedent.[277] Thus, Maryland showed what may logically be expected of a border state in which slavery was fading out; a gradual swing toward emancipation.

New York had no new statutes on emancipation, but a few cases evince the kind of thinking which one would expect where the institution is about to disappear. Most of the decisions accomplish emancipation in one way or another; a few deny it. In PETRY v. CHRISTY,[278] the issue came up collaterally and the case was easy to decide. A ringing declaration for freedom could be made without actually deciding whether a Negro should be a slave or not. So all doubts as to the status of the children of a man slave and a free Negress were resolved in favor of freedom on consideration of "humanity."[279] A slave brought from Jamaica to Georgia was held to be free in New York.[280] The old system was preserved in that a master who had "emancipated" a slave unable to support himself, was held personally liable for his other support.[281] One case denied emancipation. Where the slave had agreed to pay a certain amount for his freedom and then did not pay it, the prospective emancipation was held conditional, with the condition unfulfilled.[282]

New Jersey was one of the states which played with the idea of emancipating the slaves and shipping them to Africa.[283] Otherwise there were no statutes; the cases maintained the rule that the master must support "freed" slaves who are unable to earn their living.[284]

Massachusetts, having long since abolished slavery, had nothing new on emancipation. In Connecticut "An act to prevent slavery" provided at the same time how masters might free their slaves and rid themselves of the obligation of supporting them, and that, if the procedure was not followed, former masters would continue liable for support.[285] Otherwise there were neither statutes nor cases. Rhode Island, New Hampshire, Vermont, Ohio, Indiana, Illinois, and Maine had neither new statutes nor any decisions on the emancipation of slaves between 1820-1830. Pennsylvania, like New Jersey, toyed with a plan for emancipating slaves and sending them back to Africa.[286] This was by resolution only however, and there were no statutes.

In the 1820's, Pennsylvania still respected slavery in other states. Slaveowners from outside the state were allowed to visit repeatedly, bringing their slaves. Their periods of stay could not be added together to make up the six months in Pennsylvania which would have freed the slave.[287] Of course, there may have been the consideration that any other position would have lost tourist business.

At the beginning of the decade, statutes on involuntary manumission were taken literally and freedom was granted or not, without suggestion of any policy beyond what was expressed in the statute.[288] Beginning around the middle of the decade, the cases indicate a great willingness to emancipate, even on minor excuses,[289] or shrug the matter off as about to become moot.[290]

At the end of the decade, North Carolina followed other southern states in severely restricting emancipation.[291]   Until then there was only one matter of emancipation, and that was legislative,[292] but North Carolina's unhappiness with the slave system came to the surface once more in a law restricting the issuance of "badges" to slaves to trade for themselves. [293] The only two North Carolina cases during this period both denied emancipation. In TURNER v. WHITTED,[294] a testamentary direction to emancipate was held void. In PRIDE v. PULLIANE,[295] a similar direction was held inoperative where the slave had been transferred before the testator's death.

South Carolina now freed slaves only by special act, and this mostly for the informers on the Denmark Vesey rebellion. The sole South Carolina case on emancipation during this period denied emancipation.[296a]

Delaware approached abolition with hesitant steps. No statutes deal with individual emancipation, or with any type of voluntary emancipation.   But emancipation through illegal importation or exportation was made definitive, [297] except that there was a whole series of private acts allowing specific slaves to be brought in from, or taken to neighboring states,[298] which in 1829 led to a general law allowing slaves to be taken to and from Maryland. [299]

In Georgia, new restrictions were put on the issuance of certificates of freedom.[300]   Presumably, forged certificates had been issued, or certificates issued to the wrong persons, or both. This suggests a certain looseness in the Georgia slave system, which however, was being tightened as a reaction to the northern industrial emancipation drive. The State Supreme Court held testamentary manumission ineffectual in 1822. [301] On the other hand, emancipation and return to Africa was permitted.[302] There were no other cases.

Louisiana continued her general emancipation law and also granted occasional special exceptions in favor of emancipation. The year 1827 even saw a general law for the emancipation of underage slaves.[304] In that same year, a slave illegally introduced into Louisiana and subject to sale on behalf of the state was emancipated on account of her youth, and because her color made it doubtful whether she was a slave at all.[305] The Attorney General was authorized to bind her out until age 18. There was evidently no great pressure to expel free female Negroes from the state. Otherwise there were no statutes in the decade of the 1820's. Emancipation had not become a problem. The cases generally uphold manumission in case of doubt.[306]

Kentucky, a border state, felt the pressure for emancipation almost simultaneously with the Missouri controversy. In 1823, the state required that certificates of emancipation carry a description of the slave, forbade duplicates and imposed up to 4 years' imprisonment on any "emancipated slave delivering such a certificate to another slave."[310] Kentucky generally upheld emancipation in cases of doubt.[311] The pull from the industrial north was stronger than that of the slave states who felt under siege. The Kentucky emancipation cases again foreshadow the state's option to stay with the union in 1861.

Tennessee went through a process which was the reverse of what was underway in most of the slave states. Until 1829 emancipation was by special act,[312] but that year saw a general law for testamentary emancipation.[313] There are only two Tennessee cases during this period. The earlier is generally favorable to emancipation.[314] The latter looks on benignly as freed slaves are sent out of the state.[315]

In the majority of cases, the District of Columbia held against emancipation.[316] This was especially true where freedom was claimed because of interstate transportation,[317] reflecting the fact that many persons came to the District for a temporary stay, and the District was inclined to be neutral as between slaveholders and non-slaveholders. In the year 1830, however, the proportion of decisions in favor of emancipation began to increase.

Mississippi allowed emancipation only for meritorious acts,[318] continuing the policy already in force. Aiders and abettors of an unsuccessful petition for freedom incurred a $100 penalty.[319] There were few private acts of emancipation,[320] and no cases. Emancipations were few, and special ones were managed by political wirepulling. In practice, slaves did not have sufficiently recognized rights to ever bring a controversy to court.

The Alabama constitution of 1819 gave the legislature power to authorize emancipation,[321] but no general law was passed by 1830. There were however, a substantial number of special acts for individual emancipation.[322] This incongruity reflects the way in which the new cotton states were torn between the ways of the old slave states and the ways of rising industrialism. In 1830, legislation was held to be the only way to emancipate,[323] showing the balance beginning to tip towards the ways of the old slave states faced with industrial competition.

Missouri had no new emancipation statutes during this period. The one case on voluntary emancipation was favorable,[324] but the cases on emancipation through removal into a free state tend to vacillate.[325] Missouri does not quite know which side she is on.

RELATIONS BETWEEN SLAVEOWNERS

Toward the end of the decade, in 1828, Virginia enacted a law allowing the real estate of a minor to be sold ahead of slaves when a sale was needed to pay debts. The surplus was to be invested in more slaves.[326] The state may have had more slaves than she could employ; but the business of breeding slaves to sell south was evidently thriving. Most of the cases during this period revolve around the question of whether an injunction should be granted to stop the sale of a slave, claimed to be unique, irreplaceable property.[327] This rounds out the picture of what was happening in the state. The bulk of the slaves were being sold south. Those who were kept, stood on special personal relations with the master.

Maryland went out of her way in 1823 to exempt from distress for rent, slaves not actually belonging to the person owing the rent.[328] In a suit for the conversion of slaves, the children born to the slaves pending suit went to the otherwise unsuccessful defendant. If the property increased in value between the conversion and the satisfaction of judgment, the defendant was entitled to the increase.[329]

Prices of slaves show pretty clearly that the Virginia case of CLAYTON v. ANTHONY [330] (man slave $253.50) was atypical. An 1825 public auction in Maryland resulted in the sale of "Sydney for $540, Louisa for $525, Eliza for $755, and Rachel and her two children for $1030." [331] The buyer of a slave could recover on a general warranty as slave for life, where there was an agreement by the previous master (seller) that she could "attend" a free husband in Baltimore whom she had married. [332] An owner who sold a slave at a reduced price upon an agreement not to sell the slave south, could recover damages when the buyer did sell the slave south of the Potomac. [333] Slaves were also relied on to pay an estate's debts.[334] As in Virginia, real estate could be sold ahead of slaves, where selling the slaves would leave the land unworked. [335] New York, Connecticut, Rhode Island, New Hampshire, Delaware, Vermont, Ohio, Indiana, and Maine had neither new statutes nor cases on relations between slaveowners.

New Jersey, even in her last days of slavery, imposed absolute liability on the owner of a ferry boat which carried away a slave. The slave here was valued at $200, which was taken as the measure of damages.[336] During this decade, Massachusetts in particular, was caught in a tug-of-war between slaveholders and Abolitionists. Abolitionists were white and free, and in their own minds working altruistically for the freedom of the slaves. It just so happened that their activities coincided with the demands of the Industrial Revolution.

COMMONWEALTH v. ROBINSON, [337] in 1827, led the way. Residents of Alabama had come with a colored child to Massachusetts, where they had themselves appointed its guardians. The defendants,

Abolitionists, took the child, and later it was taken from their possession by some colored people of Massachusetts. For one thing, the child's owners had voluntarily taken her to Massachusetts which made her free under Massachusetts law. So legally there was not even an attempt to rescue a slave. "Liberation" by Massachusetts Abolitionists was however, more apt to make the child a part of the Massachusetts economy. For another thing, the case shows how the Abolitionists worked through the Negroes, so much so, that the court held the facts to show collusion.

The respective performances of the Abolitionists and the Massachusetts colored people makes it clear how the colored people—a degraded class even in the north—were invested with speciously independent action, and used as tools for industrial abolition. It speaks for itself that this should have happened in Massachusetts, the most industrialized state in the Union, but not at all in New York, Connecticut, Rhode Island, or New Hampshire.[338]

By 1822, Pennsylvania was inclined to be lenient on those who interfered with the workings of the Fugitive Slave Act of 1793, at the same time giving that act a very narrow application.[339] Events were already shaping up for 1850 and beyond. In North Carolina, owners sometimes allowed their realty to be taken ahead of their slaves (and later complained about it).[341] The price of slaves gradually crept up from around $300[342] to over $500.[343] At the end of the decade North Carolina seemed to be definitely oriented as a slave-employing state.[344]

South Carolina had only one new statute governing relations between slaveowners, an act imposing a stiffer penalty on recipients of stolen goods.[345] This law was undoubtedly applied to slaveowners in a few cases. But as a settled society, South Carolina also resolved disputes between her citizens in court. There is quite a volume of litigation between slaveowners during the decade of the 1820's.

As elsewhere, the price of slaves, with some fluctuation, went steadily up after the closing of the legal slave trade in 1808. In 1821, a known runaway brought $350 as a reduced price.[346] A female slave was valued at $600.[347] In 1823, $500 was given for a lame slave, otherwise valued at $800-$1,000.[347a] While $725 was once assessed as the value of two slaves in 1825,[348] light-skinned slaves were sold for $2,640 that same year.[349] The following year, a slave skilled as a bricklayer, brought $800[350] and a slave lost in a canoe accident was valued at $1,000.[351] Remembering the way age reduced the slaves' value, it is significant that a woman slave bought for $339 in 1811 could be sold for $315 in 1824, when she was between 45 and 50.[352]

In 1823, slaves hired for $80 to $100 per year.[353] In 1826 hire brought $150 a year for a good carpenter, and an average of $70 plus, for others.[354] The cotton gin had also raised the price of manual hire. An old rule of thumb had been ten pounds ($42) a year. Now each case was to be estimated individually.[355]

Warranties in the sale of slaves covered only their physical fitness,[356] not their "moral qualities," proneness to escape,[357] or to crime.[358] Slaves were bequeathed by will,[359] and sometimes sold to facilitate division of the estate.[360] As in the past, injury to, or the killing of a slave gave rise to a civil cause of action on behalf of the master,[361] except that a carrier's strict liability for goods was not extended to slaves, on the ground that the carrier did not have the same control over slaves as over inanimate freight.[362] And on the theory that on large plantations the master had too little immediate control over his slaves, there was no respondant superior liability on the part of the master for the slave's acts.[363]

Three decisions give a glimpse of the de facto paternalism of the South Carolina caste sytem, which yielded to strict law when, but only when, challenged in court. Two hold that "horses belonging to slaves" could be sold on execution against the master.[364] Logically, the decision is impeccable. The significant and surprising thing is that the question should have arisen at all. One allowed leased slaves to keep their wages for themselves.[365] Georgia still appears to be a frontier state, in which peaceable legal process plays an unimportant part. There was no legislation whatever on the relations between slaveowners. The lone case, holding that upon sale of the mother, the children go with her, was by the United States Supreme Court.[367]

Louisiana, on the other hand, was a sufficiently settled community so that after the Louisiana Purchase, things went along in the good old-fashioned way. There was no new legislation concerning relations between slaveowners, but a considerable number of lawsuits. The prices of slaves during this period ranged from $227 and $300,[368] to $1,500.[369] There was almost every intermediate price.[370] Injury to the slave, or aiding a slave to escape, gave rise to a civil cause of action on the part of the master.[371]

Settled Louisiana was shown to be not much better than frontier Kentucky when it came to slaveowners' cheating one another. Freedom for fraud was a part of the spirit of the pioneers.[371a] There were quite a few cases on rescisions for selling defective slaves.[372] Inevitably, litigation arose from transfers of slaves—both inter vivas and by bequest or descent.[373] There was a scattering of cases arising from other situations.[374]

During the decade, Kentucky had several private[375] and one public act[376] governing the sale of slaves. A legislative divorce was also granted, on the ground, among others, that the husband had threatened to run off some slaves which had come to the wife from a former husband.[377] Kentucky was largely settled by slaveowners. Although moving to a frontier, the people who came were sufficiently acclimatized to civilization that they did not joyously shed it the moment they were beyond the reach of their old community.[377a]

Accordingly, Kentucky had quite a few cases on relations between slaveowners in the 1820-1830 decade. The spirit of the pioneers shows itself in their inclination to cheat one another.[377b] But where fraud was suspected, disputes over property were taken to court. Suits for rescission were familiar. Gentlemen were accusing one another of selling slaves with undisclosed defects.[382] Prices of slaves were, if anything, a little lower than in the older states.[378] The range however, was greater, going up to $1,750[379] and down to $160.[380] Hire ran from $60 to $250 a year.[381]

Injuries to slaves or abduction naturally gave rise to a cause of action in favor of the master,[383] as did an accusation of having children by one's slave, if not true.[384] Medical services to a slave or services in retrieving a slave raised a cause of action against the master.[385] Transfers led to a fairly substantial amount of litigation.[386]

Tennessee limited sales of slaves by personal representatives of decedents.[387] A couple of private acts authorized the sale of slaves in an idiot's estate.[388] That was all, during the two decades. Slaves were often less expensive in Tennessee than in the more developed slave states.[389] There was one other case of sale,[390] and one of adverse possession.[391] Tennessee did not have many cases between slaveowners, and generally, did not settle those few in the courts.

In the District of Columbia the commonest price for a slave was between $250 and $400,[392] with hire at $36 per year.[393] The highest price was $900,[394] but since that was for purchase of freedom, it may have been extortionate. From that, the prices range down to $25 for a group that was partially defective.[395] There were also a few miscellaneous cases arising out of relations between slaveowners, or a slaveowner to a free white man.[396]

Almost immediately after being admitted as a state, Mississippi repealed the common law rule and made slaves personal property.[397] This reflects the mobile character of American slavery, particularly in the new slave states. The same circumstances gave rise to the limiting rule that a tenant for life forfeited his interest if he removed slaves out of the state without the consent of the remainder men.[398] Apart from these, there was only a private act regulating the relations between a guardian and his minor wards [399] during the entire decade.   With only two exceptions [400] all the Alabama cases between slaveowners during this period concern the price. [401]

From 1820 to 1830, Missouri had one statute regulating the hiring out of slaves by executors and administrators. [402]   One case recorded a price as low as $200. [403]   Missouri shared the pioneering spirit of migrating with slaves to escape creditors. [404]

TAXES

Virginia taxed slaves over 12 years old at about 50 cents a head. [405]   In 1829, this was reduced to 35 cents. [406]   New Jersey at first taxed male slaves between the ages of 15 and 60 and able to work up, to 25 cents, and later up to 75 cents. [407]   South Carolina continued her tax of 75 cents a head on slaves [408] until 1829, when the tax was reduced to 60 cents. [409]   Georgia, a frontier community, also had low taxes. Slaves under 60 were taxed only 31-1/4 cents each. [410]

COMPENSATION

There were a few special laws granting compensation for slaves executed, or those who escaped awaiting execution. [411]   With Virginia becoming a slave breeding and exporting state, the problem did not often arise.   Miscreant slaves could always be sold south, where the demand was so great that even felons were snapped up.   This was usually the outcome even where the slave at first seemed headed for the death penalty. [412]   The enactment of a general statute to cover slaves escaping while under death sentence [413] makes one wonder whether the connivance of the authorities helped this happen.

Maryland, New York, New Jersey, Connecticut, Rhode Island, New Hampshire, Pennsylvania and Tennessee had neither additional statutes nor judicial decisions on compensation for executed slaves.   North Carolina had no new statutes nor cases directly bearing on the master's compensation for an executed slave, though there were several cases involving executed slaves. [414]

South Carolina likewise had no new general statutes on compensation for executed slaves, but there were a great many private acts granting compensation. [415]   In contrast to North Carolina, only one case even grazed the subject, and that one follows a slave insurrection. [415a]   Despite a moribund slave system, Delaware in 1827 enacted a new law granting compensation for executed slaves. [416]   There were however, no cases.   The compensation act which Georgia wiped off the books in 1793 [417] had not been restored by 1830.

Although Louisiana extended compensation by general law in 1823, to owners of slaves first sentenced to death but then commuted to life imprisonment,[418] we still find a special act for that purpose in 1825.[419] Both acts limit the compensation to $300 per slave. In 1827 compensation was granted by special act for two slaves sentenced to life imprisonment.[420]

PROTECTION OF SLAVE PROPERTY VS. PUNISHMENT OF SLAVES

A classic illustration of the continuous tension between slaveowners who wanted to save their slave-property, and the non-slaveholding community which wanted slaves punished for what it considered crimes, occurred in the North Carolina case of STATE v. JIM.[421] It is characteristic that the problem should have received its most pointed exposition in North Carolina, where the non-slaveholding population was the most assertive, but the slaveholders were nevertheless strong enough and sufficiently anti-industrial to swing the state to secession in 1861.

Earlier events had followed the same pattern. The slave was indicted for assault with intent to rape. The trial judge first overruled challenges for cause to prospective jurors who were not slaveowners, but afterwards arrested judgment because of nit-picking objections to the language of the indictment. The Attorney-General took the case on appeal for the prosecution, but then declined to argue it before the Supreme Court. The Supreme Court affirmed the arrest of judgment (leaving the slave unscathed) mainly because of the exclusion of slaveowners from the jury. It observed:

> The charge was no more than a misdemeanor at common law as it still continues in relation to all but the colored population. The late act of the assembly having elevated the offense to a capital felony, affords an additional reason for adhering to established forms. It appears to us that the act of 1793, extending trial by jury to slaves, and directing the jury to be composed of owners of slaves, is not repealed by any subsequent law.

> That the master would have assurance of an equitable trial by persons who had property constantly exposed to similar accusations, and who would not wantonly sacrifice the life of a slave, but yield it only to a sense of justice, daily experience is sufficient to convince us. [422]

Dissected, and with conclusions drawn from each part, this short passage gives a picture of the attitude of the North Carolina population towards its own slaves. It applies also, but less pointedly, to the other slave states.   First the legislature, drawn from a lower stratum of society than the judiciary, had succeeded in raising the attempted rape of a white woman by a slave from a misdemeanor to a capital felony. This encompassed both the jealousy and the resentment of a still lower caste, and the possessiveness resulting from the shortage of women in colonial and pioneer societies.

Secondly the judiciary, a stratum very near the top and certainly composed of slaveholders,[421a] responded by seeing in this "an additional reason for adhering to established forms." It observed that slaves were "constantly exposed to similar accusations." Very interesting. The non-slaveholding population uttered a continuous stream of accusations that slaves were trying to rape their women. The slaveholders, including the slaveholding judiciary, pooh-poohed such charges. So it concluded that a jury of non-slaveholders "would wantonly sacrifice the life of a slave" while slaveowners, having "property constantly exposed to similar accusations," could be expected to "yield the slave's life only to a sense of justice."

In Virginia, the jury was authorized to fix the punishment by stripes when a free Negro assaulted a white person with intent to kill, but the court did so when a slave made the assault.[423]   The restraint of the judiciary in one court, was however, thought sufficient to safeguard the slaveowners' property. If the court of Oyer and Terminer condemned a slave to death, there was no appeal.[424] The courts felt no call to relax the limitations imposed by the legislature. There were no other cases. The paucity both of litigation and legislation tallies with Virginia's transition to a slave breeding and exporting state.

In Maryland, justices of the peace could sentence a slave to 39 lashes.[425] Slavery, as distinct from emancipation, no longer posed much of a problem. New York, Massachusetts, Connecticut, Rhode Island, New Hampshire, Pennsylvania, Vermont, Ohio, Indiana, Illinois and Maine had no new statutes or cases on criminal trials of slaves.

In 1828 New Jersey sentenced to death and executed a 12-year old boy-servant after trial by jury.[426] This case is an extreme example of de Tocqueville's assertion that "race prejudice seems to be stronger in the states which have abolished slavery than in those where it still exists.[427]   The states where slavery has been abolished generally do their best to make free Negroes' residence within their borders unpleasant," he wrote. "And since there is a sort of competition among states on this matter, the unhappy Negroes have only a choice of evils."[428]

These two cases show how the system of trying slaves by juries of slaveholders, though a facet of caste, was more favorable to the defendant slaves than trial by a jury of their "peers." New Jersey had not yet abolished slavery, but she was on her way.

In 1820, North Carolina made the costs of prosecuting a slave who was later executed, payable by the county.[429] The following year that act was repealed.[430] One can only surmise that the costs of prosecution were then payable by the state, along with compensation for the slave. In 1825, the North Carolina legislature enacted a law stipulating that trials of slaves were to be conducted the same as trials of whites.[431] As already noted, in the following year the North Carolina Supreme Court balked at holding this sufficient to dispense with a trial by a jury of slaveholders, saying that that requirement was "not repealed by any subsequent law."[432]

In 1821, a divided Supreme Court held, after giving some reasons to the contrary, that a slave could be convicted of a capital crime on the uncorroborated testimony of another slave.[433] This conclusion was reached largely on the grounds that a statute had provided that slaves should be tried in the same manner as freemen. But later in the same year, the court reversed a judgment of death on the strict application of rules of evidence, and holding that even the slave's owner could not waive jurisdiction of the proper court.[434] Evidently, the slave-holding community felt that its collective interests outweighed even the choice of an individual slaveowner.

This case represents the general run of North Carolina decisions during the decade. There were not only quite a few prosecutions, but quite a few convictions in the lower courts. The Supreme Court however, representing slaveholding interests more exclusively than either juries or trials courts, reversed most of these convictions on technical grounds, avoiding the death penalty and sometimes any punishment at all.[435] In 1828, costs of prosecution were levied on the master even where the slave was discharged,[436] one of the burdens of the upper caste.

As would be expected, South Carolina tried slaves before magistrates or judges, and freeholders.[437] The common man was not allowed to touch the slaveowner's property. The requirement of a freeholder's court was strictly enforced. The seriousness of an offense charged did not shake the Supreme Court in the application of rules ultimately designed to protect the slaveholder.[438] Once in a while, a freeholder jury did sentence slaves to death.[439]

Beginning in 1826, Delaware prosecuted slaves charged with capital offenses before the same courts, and in the same manner as freepersons.[440] The overriding interest of slaveholders to protect their property against the non-slaveholding populace had disappeared.

Nominally, slaves were treated like freemen. We have already seen that the practical effect was to open the dikes to the occasional fury of non-slaveholding white juries. If the slave was convicted of joining a riot, the master had to pay the costs of prosecution.[441]

Georgia tried slaves before three justices of the peace and 5-7 freeholders.[442] There are no cases. The sparsity of litigation reflects the frontier nature of the state at the time.

Louisiana used the system of the older, patrician slave states. For capital crimes, slaves were tried by a jury of six freeholders convened by the judge or justice of the peace.[443] In 1827, the requirement of a slaveholder's jury for non-capital offenses was spelled out for the city of New Orleans.[444] In a city as large as New Orleans, a "freeholder" was not always a slaveholder. As Louisiana was both settled and full of litigation at this time, the absence of judicial decisions indicates that the procedure of trying slaves was accepted and raised no legal problems. It also indicates that slaves were not often charged with crimes.

Kentucky made no change from her existing laws of trying slaves, even in capital cases, in the same way as white defendants.[445] It has already been seen that this "equality" was of questionable benefit to the slaves. There are no cases.[445a] In Kentucky this was probably the result of the combined factors of a frontier society, relatively loose control over slaves by a state which was new, and which was not a cotton, but rather a tobacco growing area largely settled from Virginia.

Tennessee required jurors to be slaveholders.[446] In BOB v. STATE,[447] the opinion of Justice Peck reiterated the underlying thinking and policy.

> The court, whose judgment we are examining, is not only one of serious consequence to the class of persons subject to its jurisdiction, but is of utmost importance to those who may be the owners of slave property in this country. This judgment reaches the life of the person charged. It takes the property of a citizen to satisfy this judgment.[448]

The District of Columbia had no cases during the 1820s directly indicating the type of tribunal before which slaves had to be tried, perhaps because there was a noticeable leniency in the punishments imposed.[449]

In an evident confusion of values characteristic of the new slave states, Mississippi guaranteed to slaves (rather than to their masters) "an impartial trial by a petit jury" in capital cases.[450] This was the ambivalence in the communities which were both frontier and slave that showed itself in specific legislation. Under the Revised Code of 1824, slaveholders had to constitute half the panel for trials of slaves in capital cases.[451]   In expressly dispensing with indictment or information, even in capital cases,[452] the preemptory, pioneer nature of the Mississippi community came to the surface.

However there appeared to be a desire to preserve slave property. While assault on a white person with intent to kill was punishable by death,[452a] an 1829 law said malice aforethought had to be expressed where no actual killing took place.[452b] There were no cases. Mississippi was probably still too close to the frontier.

Alabama continued jury trials for slaves.[453]   Here the new trend was clearest. Even a Gulf state had discarded the old precaution of trying slaves before juries of slaveowners. Alabama had a substantial amount of slave-litigation during the 1820s, showing that the state had to some extent, become a settled society.   The interests of the slaveholders show themselves in iron application of the rules of procedure, even where they lead to the discharge of a slave accused and convicted of raping a white woman.[454]

Missouri guaranteed the "right" of trial by jury to slaves without any requirement that the jury consist of slaveowners.[455]   Obviously, Missouri was a new slave state. Such cases as there were during this time however, show the solicitude of judges, probably slaveowners themselves, to safeguard slave property. In HECTOR v. STATE,[456] a conviction for burglary was reversed because of an extorted confession. Missouri incidentally, did not adopt Mississippi's shortcut of dispensing with indictment and information.[457] The region was not quite the wild, impatient frontier which Mississippi was.

In STATE v. HENRY,[458] a prosecution for stealing from a colored barber, the defense offered the barber as a witness, but the appeals court ruled that his competence as a free witness should have been submitted to the jury. This peremptory exclusion required a reversal of the conviction. The style of criminal proceedings against slaves is one of the best barometers of the position of slavery vis a vis the Industrial Revolution in different parts of the United States.   The Industrial Revolution was at work from three directions.

First, westward expansion itself was a child of the Industrial Revolution.   Second, when the Industrial Revolution anomalously extended slavery, it presented the new slave system with the problem of competing with the new and more efficient wage system. Third, the Industrial Revolution brought the demand for, and belief in, "equality" and democracy.[459]

Where slavery was newly established on an unrelieved frontier, there was a tug-of-war between the demand that slaves be tried by slaveowners to protect slave property, the "democratic" demand that they be tried like everyone else, and the frontier's aversion to any kind of trial at all. At the same time, the necessity of competing with an industrial economy brought a harshness felt to be the only means of competing, and the desire to comply with the demands for "equality." This equality was often less favorable to the slave defendant, than the old aristocratic system of allowing only slaveowners to try slaves.

PENALTIES ON MASTERS FOR SECRETING OR ELOIGNING SLAVES

Hiding slaves to avoid punishment almost disappeared from the jurisprudence of slavery during the 1820s. By this time, the balance between the community's and the slaveholder's interests had probably been worked out sufficiently. The settlement of the country made it harder to place slaves out of reach of the authorities, and the Industrial Revolution made other problems more pressing. In fact, this last consideration dove-tailed with the more advanced settlement of the country. Taking slaves too far away could bring them too near the "free" states where they would be snapped up as cheap wage laborers.

North Carolina presented a single case, reminiscent of the old device of secreting slaves to avoid legal process. Here the process is not criminal but civil. In WILSON v. TWITTY,[460] the Supreme Court of the state said, "The sheriff was not to blame for not selling the personal property first. The Negroes were kept back by the defendant himself."

South Carolina also has one such case during this decade, STATE v. WESTFIELD,[460a] in which the defendant was convicted of concealing and carrying away a slave charged with murder. Alabama imposed a fine of $500.00 on anyone having charge of a slave who concealed or carried him away to avoid prosecution for a capital offense.[460b] There was also one case from the District of Columbia where the owner attempted to carry away slaves who had filed a petition for freedom.[461] The disappearance of prosecutions against masters for secreting slaves to put them beyond reach of the law was one of the most arresting signs of the new era. Masters now had other enemies to fear than their own governments.

SLAVES TRADING FOR THEMSELVES

In the decade 1820 to 1830, Virginia had neither statutes nor cases on slaves trading for themselves. In Virginia, slaves were steadily being sold south. The problem substantially did not arise there. In Maryland however, the problem of slaves hiring themselves out gives occasion for another display of schizophrenia. A new, stricter law was enacted, which allowed slaves to hire themselves out as pilots and removed all restrictions for twenty days at harvest time.[461a] A year later (1822), a penalty was added, to be imposed on constables who failed to carry out the act. [461b]Slavery had a precarious foothold in Maryland.

North Carolina enacted a new law in 1826 to prohibit trading with slaves. [462] The act of 1819[463] was extended by adding sections against free Negroes trading with slaves, and against slaves found in a storehouse, warehouse or shop. In 1828, still another specific prohibition was promulgated against selling, harboring or otherwise delivering any firearms to a slave, by either a white man, a Negro or Mulatto,[464] as was a sweeping enactment against granting badges permitting slaves to work as laborers.[465] The prohibition against gambling with slaves was extended to whites.[465a] North Carolina's rickety slave system was causing more headaches than ever.

The decade of the 1820s saw no new South Carolina statutes on trading with slaves, but there are two cases.[466] The state was becoming static, but as RHODES v. BUNCH[467] shows, there is a loosening of civilized legal processes, and a tendency to substitute much violence. Georgia, having started without slavery, did not have a fully developed slave system at first. As a result, some trading with slaves, and independent trading by slaves had been countenanced. This was gradually reduced as the 1820s wore on.[468]

There were no new Kentucky statutes on the subject, but one case showed the independence which slaves in Kentucky exercised, if not enjoyed. In MITCHELL v. WARDEN,[469] the court related that while one of the parties:

> had a runaway Negro in his custody as jailer, the Negro gave an order to his former master for a horse which the Negro claimed, and then in possession of Mitchell, requesting the witness to get the horse and deliver him to the Negro's wife.

> Smith, the former proprietor of the Negro, deposed that the Negro had been in the habit of riding his horse at night, to prevent which he had given the Negro a pony. The Negro had swapt several times until he got a very good horse.

At almost the very same time, the Court of Appeals strongly expressed its disapproval of any agreement by which a master allowed a slave to trade for himself.[469a] This vehemence was a luxury in a suit between the master and another who had treated the slave as a fugitive. The master could get no legal redress, but here as well as in

MITCHELL v. WARDEN, we are left to speculate how general the practice was.

Tennessee went out of her way to forbid slaves from selling liquor to other Negroes without their owner's permission.[470] This was the only new legislation, and there were no cases. Mississippi fined the slave's owner if the slave hired himself out.[471] No cases arose between 1820 and 1830.

Mississippi was probably still too sparsely settled, and too close to the frontier in spirit for extensive integration, but the form of the law was significant. The master was punished if he allowed the slave to hire himself out, but nothing was said except by references, about any person who dealt with the slave. The Mississippi slave system was evidently quite strict. The master was expected to exercise iron control over the slave. The state tolerated no nonsense in this regard.

Missouri on the other hand, punished those dealing with slaves by a heavy fine.[472] The onus of the prohibition bespeaks a looser slave system than that of Mississippi. The other states had neither cases nor new statutes on trading with slaves. The picture was constantly changing. As with the secreting or eloigning of slaves, trading was a problem which antedated the Industrial Revolution. Since 1793, and even more distinctly since 1820, slave owners were more worried about other threats.

SLAVE REVOLTS

After the Missouri Compromise, the era of continental North American slave revolts began. Few episodes have been more misconstrued by historians. As was shown previously, slave revolts were primarily a phenomenon of the small islands of the West Indies, where there was no region into which to escape. The earlier problem of "outlying" or "marooning" slaves, was the counterpart to the relative absence of slave revolts on the North American continent during the 18th century.

While some parts of the continent became settled by the beginning of the 19th century, this was not at all true of other areas like Alabama and Mississippi. And even an old state like Virginia still had laws against outlying slaves in the 1840s.[472a] Yet the legislation of all the slaveholding states, without apparent distinction, manifested a new nervousness about impending slave revolts.

On the other side of the coin, after 1820 slave revolts in northern America appeared for the first time on a large scale. Why? And where did they come from? They then began to be celebrated by pamphleteers and would-be historians.

The fashionable explanation was that a wave of "freedom" was sweeping the western world and slave revolts were part of it. Virtually nothing was said about what went before, nor about the connection of these new slave revolts with the past. Reading 19th century history, one would surmise that an era of slave revolts sprang up as a finished product, like Adam, or Eve from Adam's rib, or Athena full-blown from the head of Zeus. But "historic continuity with the past is not a duty, it is only a necessity." [473] The "wave" of "slave revolts" which followed soon after the Missouri Compromise was no more a bloom of "freedom" out of nowhere, than the new demand for general literacy was a product "of the enlightened will of 19th century politicians."[474]

Obviously, the more "slave revolts," the deeper the well of cheap wage labor for northern industries. It must be remembered, that unlike the southern and western states, New England, New York, New Jersey and Pennsylvania did not prohibit the entry of free Negroes. So the 1820-1830 decade had the first "name" slave revolt on the North American continent, Denmark Vesey's rebellion in South Carolina in 1822.

During the decade, Virginia seemed untouched by the "freedom" propaganda spread by northern industrialists hunting for underpaid wage labor. Nat Turner's rebellion (1831) lay just beyond. In the meantime, Virginia was busily selling her slaves south. It is more likely that slave rebellions would break out elsewhere. Through 1830 neither statutes nor cases suggest slave revolts in Virginia.

Maryland, New Jersey, Massachusetts (without slavery), Connecticut, Rhode Island, New Hampshire (without slaves),[474a] Pennsylvania, Vermont (without slaves), the District of Columbia, Ohio and Maine (without slavery) had no statutes nor cases on slave rebellion. The only suggestion of a slave revolt in New York was U.S. v. JONES, [475] in which there was a mutiny on a vessel, partly at Curacao and partly on the high seas.

In 1830, North Carolina, passed "an act to prevent the circulation of seditious publications, and for other purposes."[476] The accompanying statute, which forbade teaching slaves to read and write was likewise aimed at anticipated rebellions.[477] At the same time slaves and free colored persons were forbidden to preach, even at church services.[478]

These statutes were passed just before Nat Turner's rebellion in Virginia. Ten years after the Missouri Compromise, slave rebellion was in the air. It had not been so before. And it was felt that the impetus for such rebellion came from outside the state. All this dove-tailed with the demands of rising industries in the north for cheap labor.

The second statute, forbidding slaves to be taught reading and writing, but allowing the teaching of arithmetic, encapsulates the dilemma in which the slave states found themselves. North Carolina, never having anything but a loose slave system, expressed this dilemma. The Industrial Revolution demanded literate employees because of its higher technological development.[479] North Carolina tried to meet this situation by limiting slave education to arithmetic. It was evidently hoped that slaves could acquire technical competence, but remain beyond the reach of propaganda.[479a]

South Carolina experienced Denmark Vesey's Rebellion in 1822. It has already been suggested[481] that the combination of looseness and strictness in the treatment of her slaves was an Achille's heel in the state's slave system. The rebellion was reflected in an act passed the very same year "for the remuneration of Peter, of George and of Scott."[482] The preamble states:

> It is expedient to liberally reward such persons as have given important information tending to the discovery and suppression of a very dangerous plot, in which many slaves have been lately engaged, against the peace and security of this state.

By special act, compensation of $122.44 was also granted to the owners of slaves executed for having taken part in that rebellion.[483] In the same year the death penalty was enacted for counseling or hiring a slave to raise a rebellion, even if no actual rebellion took place.[484]

Denmark Vesey's rebellion did not give rise to any cases which reached the appellate courts. Apparently all private claims were adjusted before the legislature. But South Carolina had another slave rebellion in 1830. One owner's slave was sentenced to transportation out of the country. The owner tried to have the judgment arrested because the slave had not been tried within three days, as required by the act of 1740. However, the justices of the South Carolina Supreme Court seemed to be thoroughly frightened. While conceding that the statute had not been followed, they nevertheless decided to let the judgment be carried out.[485] The court's language gives an idea of the atmosphere, then prevailed.

> Besides, it was discovered that so many were concerned in the plot that the public safety required this delay in order to find out the ramifications. Counsel was refused permission to see Quico while in confinement, and all other persons, for fear of tampering with him.

> It is true that the act of 1740 did require that slaves accused of offenses should be tried within three days after their apprehension; and the act of 1754 limited the

time to six days. Nothing however, in this act says that magistrates and freeholders shall not proceed to trial after the time limited. It is a matter entirely within their discretion if they think it proper to prevent persons of any description whatever, from visiting or tampering or advising with persons of that description. Their consciences are made the rule of action. Their judgments are final.

When the dreadful consequences of the insurrection of slaves in South Carolina, are taken into consideration . . . the judges of the Superior Courts ought to be extremely cautious in interferring with the magistrates and freeholders. And they ought not to be eagle eyed in viewing the proceedings, and in finding out and supporting every error and neglect, where the real merits have been duly and fairly attended to, and determined according to justice.

Fear tipped the balance. While in the past, the garrison state had existed side by side with easy familiarity between master and slave, the garrison state now became predominant. This shift coincides with the rise of northern industrialism.

Delaware had no cases, and no statutes beyond the general one forbidding slaves to "join or be willingly present at any riot, rout or unlawful assembly."[486] The fact that the law went this far but no further shows that there were no slave revolts. Delaware had few slaves, and freedmen who could not generally be removed from the state, must have been employed locally.

In 1821, and again in 1829, Georgia made insurrection or an attempt to excite it, a capital offense when committed by a slave or free person of color.[487] A white overseer capable of bearing arms was now required on plantations that had as few as ten slaves, instead of twenty-five, as under the law of 1770.[488] The fact that the statues went no further, and that there were no judicial decisions at all, suggests that as yet, Georgia knew about slave revolts only through hearsay from her neighbors to the north.

Interestingly enough, Louisiana had no statutes, and despite a volume of litigation, only one case, which basically was a family quarrel.[489] Apparently, the state was still far enough away from the new industrialism that she did not yet feel its impact.

Kentucky while complaining about the fugitive slave industry,[490] had neither statutes nor cases on slave revolts. In a state both on the frontier and on the northern boundary of slavery, the same factors were at work which induced "outlying" and "marooning" slaves. Escape was much less dangerous than rebellion. Besides, as Kentucky was also a slave-breeding state, intractable slaves were sold south.

Tennessee had nothing on slave revolts. Perhaps she was like Kentucky, too close to the border to make revolts worthwhile. The western part of the state was the cotton-growing region. North of this, Kentucky has the smallest north-south extent. Besides, western Tennessee may have been out of the way of northern recruiters of free Negroes.

Mississippi forbade seditious speeches, but punished them only by stripes.[491] They were bracketed with riots, routs, unlawful assemblies, and private brawls. White persons present at any unlawful assembly with slaves, free Negroes or Mulattoes were penalized separately, but only up to a $20 fine and 20 lashes.[492] Slave insurrection itself was punished by death,[493] as was incitement of slave rebellion by a white person.[494] Mississippi as a frontier community, shrugged her shoulders at a good deal of violence, but she was also sensitive to the campaign for "freedom" coming from the north.

The dread of Abolitionists coupled with an inability to take violence seriously was reflected in the act of 1830.[495] White persons circulating books or pamphlets calculated to produce slave disaffection or rebellion were punished specifically, and separately, by imprisonment of 3 to 12 months, and fine of $100 to $1,000. But slaves or free persons of color doing so faced the death penalty.[496] There were neither cases nor private acts mentioning any rebellion. In Mississippi as in Georgia, slave revolts were mostly hearsay.

Indiana and Illinois, while enacting no new legislation, retained their statutes against "riots, routs, unlawful assemblies or seditious speeches by servants or slaves."[497] There were no cases. Alabama refused compensation to the owner where slaves were executed because of rebellion.[498] But there were no new statutes, either public or private, on slave rebellions nor any judicial decisions. Alabama was still too far away from northern industry. Missouri retained her law against slave rebellions,[499] but had neither new legislation nor cases in court.

Slave revolts increased somewhat, and southern nervousness about them increased a great deal in the ten years following the Missouri Compromise. However, such revolts may have been glamorized, since they accompanied the rise of industry in the northern states, rather than any desire for freedom on the part of the slaves. The latter had always existed, but in a large, unsettled country like the United States, the more likely outlet was escape, not rebellion. But rising industry had an almost insatiable hunger for wage laborers, the worse paid, the better. Inducing slaves to rebel in the name of liberty, and then employing them at coolie wages, killed two birds with one stone.

FREE NEGROES AND MULATTOES

The plight of free Negroes during the years which followed the Missouri Compromise can be inferred from what has already been said. In the slave states they sank closer and closer to the status of slaves (and were sometimes treated worse than slaves). In the non-slave states they were made an inferior caste in the wage economy.

In Virginia, free Negroes were bracketed with slaves with respect to rape,[500] and shortly afterwards this benefit was abolished. They were also bracketed with slaves with respect to assault with fatal consequences,[502] and attempted rape.[503]   Imprisonment however, replaced the penalty of stripes, as well as the punishment of being sold into slavery.[504]

Apparently, free Negroes were here equated with whites. This change coincides with the rise in "emancipation" activities in the northern states. Corporal punishment had originally been retained for slaves because of a labor shortage. That became a thing of the past. On the other hand, imprisoning a free colored man put him out of the way for awhile. This was deemed safer than selling him back into slavery, where he might be the source of undesired propaganda among slaves. Ordinarily emancipated slaves had to leave the state. Sometimes private acts allowed them to remain either permanently,[505] or for limited periods.[506]

The courts in general, held Negroes to be free in cases of doubt. Whatever restrictions Virginia might otherwise place upon free Negroes, the maxim "In obscura voluntate manumittentis, favendum est libertati"[507] was pretty faithfully followed.   Perhaps the most interesting is COMMONWEALTH v. TYREE,[508] in which freedom was held res judicata, after an erroneous decision. The defendant was charged with rape, as a free Negro. The master then came in to show that the defendant was actually his slave impersonating a free Negro. The court held such evidence inadmissible, as the defendant did not object to the court's jurisdiction, which existed only over free Negroes. The legislature later compensated the master for loss of the slave.[509]

The same attitude was taken with regard to the emancipation laws of other states. If a person was free under the laws of another state, he was treated as free in Virginia.[510] So attempts to reserve obligation of service, or attempted revocations of emancipation were held repugnant to the grant.[511]   And the Commonwealth Court of Appeals was willing to discharge a free Negro entirely from an indictment because of inadvertent gaps in the law.[512]   Even the statutes against cohabitation between whites and free Negroes were narrowly applied.[513]   Virginia wanted as few free Negroes as possible but she accorded mild treatment to those within her borders.[514]

Maryland on the whole enacted sterner general laws against free Negroes, but continually created exceptions by special acts. Oddly, the penalty of selling free Negroes back into slavery was extended.[515] This sanction was aimed at vagrants. Maryland apparently felt these persons did not fit into a wage economy, and if restored to slavery, could be sold south. It is not clear however, why Maryland and Virginia should have gone in opposite directions in this respect.

A more general law made free Negroes and Mulattoes subject to the same sentences of confinement as other free defendants.[516] But no length of residence was allowed to give immunity against penalties and deportation for illegal entry.[517]   New restrictions were imposed on the selling of corn, wheat, or fabrics by free Negroes.[518] All Negroes were forbidden to sell liquor within a mile of camp meetings.[519]

In the fifth election district of Prince Georges County, free persons of color were forbidden to have any early morning or evening meetings except religious meetings attended by whites.[520]   In the course of tightening the laws on free Negroes, the legislature apparently discovered that they had not been required to work on the roads, and had frequently not been taxed. These defects were remedied.[521]

Most of the private acts validate doubtful manumissions.[522] Others authorized an East Indian to hold real property,[523] the state to release its claim to an inheritance from a free woman of color,[524] and another free woman of color was tardily released from jail by special act.[525] None of this gave rise to litigation, and there are no cases on free Negroes[526] in Maryland (as distinguished from cases on emancipation) during the decade.

By the 1820 census, New York had the fourth largest population of free Negroes. [527] Unlike many others, the state was in the process of making citizens out of them. The right to vote was granted,[528] and there was also an element of over-protection in partial relief from taxation.[529] This guardianship reflected their still being a depressed caste, excluded from the militia.[530]

New York continued her parade of cases where towns squabbled over which one was liable for the support of a "free" colored pauper.[531] Hardly any other disputes involving free Negroes reached the appellate courts. There was only CARRANEE v. McQUEEN[532] which held that a slave illegally imported from Jamaica to Georgia, and therefore free, who nevertheless agreed to buy his freedom, could recover money paid under the agreement, but not wages for the time he illegally worked as a slave.

Though the number of free Negroes in New York reached 18,307 by the 1830 census, no legislation touched them except an amendment to the incorporation of "the society for the education of free colored children and youth in the United States."[533] In two cases, towns contested with private persons over the duty to support a colored pauper.[534]

Perhaps it was because Masschusetts was industrializing so rapidly that her citizens could employ almost anybody at something, because there were no cases during the 1820s, of contests over the support of colored paupers.[535] There were however, a few statutory appropriations for support.[536]

By the 1820 census, Connecticut had only 97 slaves, but 7870 free colored. The editor's note to the statutory Revision of 1821,[537] says: "The number of Negroes however, is increasing, rather than diminishing like the Indians."

In 1830 Connecticut enacted her only new statute on free Negroes, fixing a term of 2 to 5 years imprisonment for kidnapping a person out of the state with the intent to sell them into slavery.[538] There was a clause saving the right to retrieve fugitive slaves. Presumably, the idea was that free Negroes might be kidnapped under the pretense of recovering a fugitive slave. But even so, the law must have been passed more as an expression of feeling and policy, than to meet a concrete problem. Connecticut was pretty far from the cotton states. As Webster pointed out later, there were not many fugitive slaves in Connecticut.[539] Through 1830 there were no cases directly involving free Negroes.[540]

Rhode Island excluded Negroes from the militia,[541] stamping them as an inferior caste. Otherwise there were no statutes and no cases. New Hampshire had only 786 free Negroes by the census of 1820. Consequently there was neither legislation nor litigation. In at least one county, Pennsylvania registered all Negroes.[542] In a burst of self-adulatory philanthropy, the state proposed in 1828 to transport all free Negroes to Africa.[543]

Pennsylvania strengthened her laws against the kidnapping of free persons as slaves,[544] which merely reflected competition for labor between the wage and slave economies. There was one private act for the benefit of free Negroes,[545] and during the decade there was only one contest between towns over the duty to support a destitute free

Negro.[546] Where it was a question between slavery and "freedom,"[547] fine points of law were resolved in favor of freedom, again reflecting the demand for wage labor.

As loose as North Carolina was, she did not want free Negroes. This first expressed itself in an exclusion act.[548] By the end of the decade there was great nervousness about communication between incoming free Negroes and North Carolina slaves.[549] The state evidently feared that free colored persons from other states would be missionaries of insurrection, a belief certainly borne out by occurrences such as those described in the Massachusetts case of COMMONWEALTH v. ROBINSON.[550]

Where immigrant free Negroes did not depart as ordered, they were enslaved, the state evidently feeling that it could exercise more control that way. The growing sense of insecurity was reflected in the imposition of the death penalty for assault on a white woman with intent to commit rape.[551] Peddling was restricted,[552] narrowing the circle of occupations available to free colored persons.

The anomaly of slavery in North Carolina appeared once more in a statute requiring a free Negro's landlord to pay taxes if the tenant himself failed to pay.[553] The landlord was authorized to sue the tenant for taxes thus paid,[554] an empty right, since the statute springs from "the small value of their chattels." Free Negroes were treated like slaves, but benefited from the arrangement.

North Carolina cases touching free Negroes were few and for the most part, indirect. RED v. RED,[555] tells how the decedent, who "was never a bright man and drank very hard" sometimes went to Negro doctors. In WEAVER v. CRYER,[556] it was shown that a white man and a Mulatto woman were living together and reputedly married. But a jury granted substantial damages where a free Negro was held in slavery; and this verdict was affirmed on appeal.[557] A free Negro could not be sold into slavery because he or she was unable to pay a fine adjudged on a conviction for assault and battery.[558] After 1820, North Carolina, with an uncertain slave system to begin with, presented a disorderly melange of parts of the old slave sytem and parts of the new wage economy.

Two main lines of legislation appeared in South Carolina during the 1820's. There were increasingly severe laws excluding free Negroes, but also a greater paternalism towards those already there. The first appeared in the statutes of 1822,[559] 1823[560] and 1825.[561] The act of 1825 made specific reference to colored persons coming by sea from northern states. In requiring vessels which carried them to stay 150 yards from the wharf, and to be loaded and unloaded by lighters, the slave economy again added to its handicap in competing with the wage

economy, as docking became more expensive.   This might fall on the
South Carolina port, or send such ships elsewhere.   The fact that during
the ten years from 1820 to 1830, there was only one private act permitting a free Negro to remain in the state[562] illustrates this policy.

The severe $2 poll tax was also retained, with only a small modifi-
cation in 1829.[563]   A special statute was devoted to punishing free Negroes for harboring slaves.[564]   Evidently, there again was fear of con-
tamination by "freedom" propaganda.   A statute making free Negro defendants pay the costs of criminal prosecutions in two parishes, but excusing them if unable to pay, stands at the borderline.[565]   There was
both harshness and leniency.

The same was undoubtedly true for the new requirement that in
those two parishes, free Negroes must be tried before a jury of
slaveholders,[566] and that free Negroes had to have a guardian.[567] Both
of these laws enabled slaveholders to keep a closer watch over free
Negroes' activities.   But a jury of slaveholders was still expected to be
tinctured with its old noblesse oblige, and the statute expressly refers to
the guardianship of free Negroes as a "trust." Completely on the side of
paternalism, was the refund of taxes.[568]

However a case at the beginning of the decade suddenly illuminates
the hardening of South Carolina's attitude toward free Negroes.   They
were held incompetent as witnesses,[569] with the statement:

> There is no instance in which a Negro has been permitted
> to give evidence, except in cases of absolute and indis-
> pensable necessity, nor indeed has this court ever recog-
> nised the propriety of admitting them where the rights of
> white persons were concerned. When we consider the de-
> graded state in which they are placed by the laws of the
> state, and the ignorance in which most of them are
> reared, it would be unreasonable, as well as unpolitic to
> lay it down as a general rule that they are competent
> witnesses.

The only way to reconcile this decision, and the court's language,
with STATE v. McDOWELL,[570] decided in 1807, was that in 1820 the
witness is a Negro, while in STATE v. McDOWELL he was a Mulatto (by
a white mother). But court does not seem interested in any such distinction,[570a] and does not refer to its decision in the McDOWELL case.
Reading the two opinions together shows a transformation of attitude.

Yet the movement was not uniform.   Historical changes, absent a
war or a revolution, are like water washing up on a beach.   A finger of

water comes here; another there.   Only later is the whole stretch
flooded. At first the water does not rise in an unbroken line.

In 1823 the Federal District Court at Charleston held unconstitutional the third section of the Act of 1822,[571] forbidding any vessel
from landing free Negroes under penalty of a $1000 fine.[572] The opinion
itself sums up the violent pros and cons which had already developed in
South Carolina.

> The law is in effect a repeal of the laws of the United
> States pro tanto, converting a right into a crime.

> One gentleman likened the importation of such free per-
> sons of color to that of clothes infected with the plague,
> or of wild beasts from Africa. The other to that of fire-
> brands set to our own houses only to escape by the light.
> I am decidedly of the opinion that the third section of the
> state act is unconstitutional and void. This act operates
> only as to freemen—free persons of color—and not as to
> slaves, so that a whole crew of slaves entering this port
> would be free of its provisions.

Several other cases were careful to give free Negroes full legal
rights.[573]   It was even conceded collaterally that they could hold
slaves. [574] The same was true where the rights of a white person depended indirectly on the position of a free Negro. The prohibition
against bringing in free Negroes was narrowly and technically
applied. [575]

These cases may be contrasted with the loosening of technical rules
brought on by the fright of slave insurrections. Slave insurrections had
occurred in the 18th century,[576] but they did not unhinge the ruling
class of South Carolina the way they did in the 19th. Both the dread of
insurrection and the gradual stiffening in attitudes toward free Negroes
coincided with the growth of industrialism and the concomitant campaigns for "freedom" in the north.

That Delaware was at a loss as how to classify free Negroes can be
seen from several statutes authorizing various persons to remove "manumitted" slaves into the state.[577]   And this uncertainty led to laws
pointing in both directions. Protection came twice during the decade
when the state enacted laws against kidnapping free Negroes. [578] This
was undoubtedly a genuine measure to shield them rather than to preserve them for local business. Delaware had a substantial number of
free Negroes, [579] but she was not developing industry.

In the middle of the decade, a niggardly charter was granted to the African School Society of Wilmington.[580] Hostility appeared when pauper relief laws for destitute "free" Negroes were shaped for selling the "beneficiary" as a servant wherever possible.[581] Intermarriage between whites and free Negroes was forbidden.[582] Larceny by a free Negro was made a distinct offense.[583] On the other hand, the only case during this period held a free Negro to be a competent witness.[584] Delaware was among the most advanced states in granting free Negroes legal rights.

Insurrection was first on a list of capital crimes enumerated by the Georgia statutes in 1821.[585] As in many other instances, Georgia modelled her quarantine laws on those of South Carolina. There was the same frightened concern about preventing communication between Georgia slaves and free Negroes from other states.[586] At first an exception was made for seamen coming from South Carolina,[587] but even that was soon discontinued.[588] A special section prohibited free Negroes from circulating written or printed matter "for the purpose of exciting insurrection."[589] As a matter of course, free Negroes could not be taught to read and write, nor teach others to do so,[590] nor could they be employed in typesetting establishments.[591] At this juncture, the death penalty for burning houses,[592] though harking back to an earlier era, was undoubtedly linked to the fear of slave insurrections.

Georgia began to feel the impact of industrial slave-raiding under claims of "freedom." New restraints were placed on issuing certificates of freedom,[593] and vessels were prohibited from inveighing or carrying off "any free person of colour or any other person of colour, claiming, or pretending to claim to be free."[594] As a precaution against abductions under false claims of freedom, Georgia interned Negroes who were actually free. Laws also narrowed their means of gaining a livelihood.[595]

Two moves however, seem to have been really designed to improve the lot of free Negroes. Guardians were authorized, especially in litigation,[596] and the penalty of selling into slavery was abolished.[597]

Louisiana passed only one private act concerning free Negroes in the 1820's.[598] The right of third parties to aid them in maintaining their status has already been noticed in connection with emancipation.[599] Likewise, COPELLY v. DWERGES,[600] a liaison between a white man and a free colored woman, has already been considered under sexual relations. Descendants of Indian women were free.[601]

The general Louisiana attitude toward free colored persons was summed up in BARE v. BUSH,[602] where a free Negro sued a justice of the peace and his constable for false imprisonment. Reversing a nonsuit, the State Supreme Court said:

> Free persons of color are bound to treat citizens with respect. If they do not, they are subject to fine and imprisonment. But they are entitled to a trial by jury. Justices of the peace have no right to summon juries. It is a necessary consequence that the defendant was without power to try.

In Louisiana, free Negroes sometimes held slaves,[603] and they could and did take other kinds of property inter vivos, or by inheritance.[604] Louisiana law governing slaves and free Negroes was largely Roman law. The status of free Negroes was shown by the way in which the colored mistresses of the Spanish governors formed an intermediate aristocracy. Their status would improve in the future.

Kentucky forbade ships to remove free colored persons without affirmative evidence of freedom.[606] In other words, Kentucky without a seacoast, did not go as far as Georgia, but followed the same idea. Persons actually free had to be kept in the state to guard against the abduction of alleged slaves. Kentucky required that free colored children who were bound out, be taught to "spell and read."[607] Considering the number of slaves in Kentucky, [608]this seems astonishing. It foreshadows the state's siding with the Union in the Civil War. Otherwise, Kentucky legislators realized that free Negroes could be drafted for highway work [609] just as well as whites, and one free Mulatto immigrant was granted permanent residence.[610]

While a slave marriage was legally ineffective, it did take effect at the moment of emancipation.[611] Usually, purported contracts executed during slavery did not bind a colored person after emancipation.[612] If a slave was emancipated by will, no restraints could be imposed on a legacy bequeathed to him as a free [613] Negro.

Tennessee acts on free Negroes during the 1820s were mostly private.[614] Also, the state realized that free Negroes were capable of road building.[615] The only case indicates that Tennessee was one of the states in which there was a movement to give free Negroes civil rights, rather than to merely use them as labor. Undoubtedly, this is one result of attempted collaboration between widely differing eastern and western Tennessee. In VAUGHAN v. PHEBE,[616] the Supreme Court set forth its point of view. What is arresting about this case, is that the attitude it expresses is quite different from that of some Tennessee statutes.

One can only guess that the legislature and the Supreme Court judges either came from different strata of society, different parts of the state, or both. In this clash, events again cast their shadow. Tennessee was the last state to secede. She furnished Lincoln's second Vice-President, and was excepted from the Emancipation Proclamation.

In the District of Columbia, free Negroes could be witnesses when the government needed them in criminal prosecutions,[617] but otherwise not.[618] Free Negroes were still subject to stripes, but the courts did not hesitate to withhold punishment if there seemed to be legal objections.[619]   Likewise, they were protected against retroactive legislation. The new Washington City Charter was applied only to those who came to reside after its enactment.[620] They were held liable on contracts made directly after emancipation.[621]   Contrary to the law in some states, children of a state libera were free. [622] Obviously, the city was the capitol of a nation, one part of which was trying to hold on to slavery, the other trying to abolish it.

Ohio, the haven of slaves seeking freedom from the south, segregated her schools,[623] and would not allow incoming free Negroes to become residents.[624]

Mississippi embodied her hostility towards free Negroes in excessive taxation. While the poll tax on free whites was seventy-five cents, that on free colored persons was three dollars.[625] In fights between slaves and free Negroes, the law was intent on punishing the latter.[626] The death penalty for selling free persons as slaves was continued.[627] (Here Mississippi borrowed from, and went beyond the industrial states.) But otherwise, free Negroes were treated legally much the same as slaves.[628]

In addition, free Negroes could not carry weapons without special permits,[629] there were elaborate provisions for certificates of freedom,[630] and severe penalties were imposed for transfering such certificates to slaves. Nor were free Negroes allowed to enter the state.[631] A few private acts authorized some to remain as residents.[632]

In Illinois, the militia was limited to whites.[633] Free Negroes were considered an inferior caste, excluded from the military. In the same way, they were disqualified as witnesses against a white person.[634] And like other western free states, Illinois kept free Negroes out of the state in practice, if not wholly in theory.[635] At first intermarriage seems to have been allowed,[636] but in 1829 that too was made illegal.[637] Perhaps as a gesture of magnanimity, there was no restriction on making wills.[638]

Two cases during this period both refused to enforce indentures which attempted to bind individuals to service.[639] Only the second of these is interesting.[640] The court first held that the state upon admission, became free of the restrictions of the Northwest Territory

Ordinances, so that even indentures which had been void before were given validity. But it then decided that the indentured servant did not pass to the master's estate after his death, and was therefore beyond the control of either the administrator or the heirs. This was a perfect example of the schizophrenic thinking in states which first wanted slavery, and then turned away from it.

At the beginning of the decade, Alabama diverged from Mississippi by repealing the discriminatory tax against free Negroes, and subjecting them to the same poll tax as whites. It even refunded past payments,[641] but it is not clear what induced this softening. However, free Negroes were bracketed with slaves in prosecutions for serious offenses,[642] and they were not allowed to sell spiritous liquor.[643] A private act authorizing a free Negress to emancipate her daughter [644] shows that free Negroes could hold slaves, at least within their own families. During the 1820s there were no Alabama cases on free Negroes.

In 1826, Missouri abolished the pillory and stripes.[645] That was the only law even remotely touching free Negroes. They could sue in forma pauperis to establish their freedom.[646] Indians or their descendants were free.[647] There were no other cases.

The situation of free Negroes during the 1820s, has already been outlined. The closing of the slave trade and the expansion of northern industry put them in a nutcracker. Endless demands for cheap wage labor led to "liberation" raids, and to northern legislation making free colored persons a new inferior caste in the wage economy. The closing of the slave trade led to the kidnapping of free persons of color in the slave states, and selling them as slaves. At the same time, many slave states refused to allow free persons of color to cross their borders. Some states which were neither totally slave nor totally operating on a wage economy, also excluded free Negroes.

PROHIBITION OF THE SLAVE TRADE AND FIRST ABOLITION

Closing the legal slave trade triggered a string of violations of the new rule.[647a] Such cases were necessarily federal and from districts on the coast. Most of the states did not enact statutes. Only Alabama had a single special act arising out of the now prohibited traffic.[648]

Ironically, the first federal law after prohibition of the slave trade was not to strengthen the barrier, but to create an exception. The President was given discretion to admit the slaves of refugees from Cuba (the context suggests that they were originally from Haiti).[649] Strengthening acts were passed in 1818,[650] 1819, 1820, 1828 and 1830.[654]

While the majority of the slave trade violations came out of the deep South, from South Carolina to Louisiana, there were also cases from Maryland, New York and Massachusetts. Business is business. The same urge for financial gain which had sparked the development of industry, also brought forgetfulness of the noble sentiments for ending the slave trade, and led mercantile entrepreneurs to try for an illegal profit if they could get it.

Local courts in South Carolina were still reluctant to condemn the slave trade,[655] but the United States Supreme Court brooked no nonsense. [656] Led by Chief Justice John Marshall, it dismissed ostensible innocence as a sham and condemned in case of doubt.

There were no new abolition laws in the 1820s. Older states, like New York and Pennsylvania let their slave populations die off under laws providing that all born after a certain date were free. The new states carved out of the Northwest Territory, were admitted under constitutions providing that there should be no slavery or involuntary servitude except as punishment for crime. The rest retained slavery until the XIIIth Amendment.

The Missouri controversy focused the interests of the anti-slavery forces. Most attention was concentrated on the new territorial expansion leaving little room for anything but a few great-hearted resolutions looking towards the eventual abolition of slavery. These were usually coupled with a plan to ship freedmen out of the country. [657] However, Pennsylvania did propose a resolution to abolish slavery in the District of Columbia.[658]

FOOT'S RESOLUTION

The decade closed with Foot's Resolution. This was rising industrial capitalism's last spasm of uncertainty in the United States. Thereafter, the juggernaut rolled on to crush the slave economy, by now a relic of bygone days. After 1830, the chips were down and the game was about to be played out. On December 29, 1829, Senator Foot of Connecticut, proposed the following resolution to Congress:

> Resolved, that the Committee on Public Lands be instructed to inquire into the expediency of limiting for a certain period, the sales of public lands to such lands only as have heretofore been offered for sale, and are subject to entry at the minimum price. And also whether the office of Surveyor General may not be abolished without detriment to the public interest.[659]

The first thing to notice is that this resolution came from Connecticut. New England was then the most advanced industrial section of the country, the section where a wage economy was in full swing. The essence of the wage economy is a labor surplus, so that the threat of firing—which costs the employer nothing—can be used as an instrument of discipline and control.

Sen. Thomas Hart Benton of Missouri, saw that the effect of this resolution, if adopted, would be to limit migration to the west. He said in Thirty Years' View:

> At the commencement of the session 1829-30, Mr. Foot of Connecticut submitted in the Senate a resolution of inquiry which excited much feeling among the western members of that body. It was a proposition to inquire into the expediency of limiting the sales of the public lands to those then in the market . . . to suspend the surveys of the public lands . . . and to abolish the office of Surveyor General. The effect of such a resolution, if sanctioned upon inquiry and carried into legislative effect, would have been to check emigration to the new states to the west . . . to check the growth and settlements of these states and territories.[660]

Not only was Senator Foot from New England, but in the words of a modern historian, he ws the "spokesman for northeastern industrialists."[661] If Senator Foot was their spokesman, what were "northeastern industrialists" actually saying in the resolution? As Senator Benton points out, the resolution would check emigration to the west. Checking westward migration would tend to keep people in the eastern states, and furthermore, would keep new immigrants from Europe there too.

The thought behind the resolution evidently was that westward migration would drain off the labor surplus which the New England industrialists considered essential to their economic system. Checking this migration would not only retain the existing labor surplus, but would see it increased by immigration from Europe. In short, Foot's Resolution was a northern counterpart to the Fugitive Slave Law.

Foot's Resolution was rejected, but the industrial advance of New England kept on nevertheless. Emigration to the west might continue, but immigration from Europe was so heavy that the northeastern industrialists had all the labor surplus they needed. Foot's Resolution failed because it was unnecessary even to the New Englanders.

And what was true in 1830, became more emphatically true as time went on. The swell of European immigration went to the non-slave states.[663] A society based on a wage economy not only had plenty of human material with which to operate, but also gained an increasing numerical advantage over its slaveholding rivals. More than ever, the rest was now only a matter of technique.

From Foots' Resolution (1830) to the Compromise of 1850

The question is, shall we perish in the dark, slain by our
own hand, or in the light, killed by our enemies.

– Lord Selbourne – British House of Lords, 1911[1]

The period 1793-1820 saw the American economy slowly swing from
one that was predominantly agricultural and employed slave labor, to
one that was predominantly industrial and employed wage labor. This
change came about despite the added life which invention of the cotton
gin gave to the slave system. The change came almost silently. The
only outstanding event during this period was the closing of the slave
trade.

Ironically, the shutdown of the slave trade, and the upsurge of
slavery generated by the cotton gin came at the same time. The upsurge
created a class of slaveholders who were strong enough to believe
themselves able to resist the advance of the Industrial Revolution. But
the fact that the Industrial Revolution succeeded in illegalizing the slave
trade at this juncture foretold who would prevail in the end. The
Missouri Compromise was the next step.

Present day writing on American slavery has generally focused on
the years after 1830. This is a little like the Iliad—twenty-four books
devoted to the last year of a ten-year war. While most of the fireworks
of the controversy over slavery ran from Nat Turner's Rebellion in 1831,
to the end of the Civil War, they constituted only the last act.
Dramatically, this period may be the most interesting, but as a matter
of economic history it is merely the final act of the drama. After 1830,
the question was no longer "whether", but "how?"

Brooks Adams summed up the "how?" when he wrote in 1913:

> Only a generation ago the aristocracy of the South
> deliberately chose a civil war rather than admit the
> principle that at some future day they might have to
> accept compensation for their slaves. [2]

243

The arc from Nat Turner's Rebellion to the Compromise of 1850 extends from the most celebrated slave revolt to the moment when non-slave states achieved a majority in the U.S. Senate. They had gained a majority in the House at the time of the Missouri Compromise of 1820.

Nat Turner's Rebellion, (1831) and South Carolina Nullification[3] the following year, foreshadow the violent course lying ahead. Newell Dwight Hillis has called the 1830-1850 era "the epoch of agitation." Turner's Rebellion is distinguished not only because it happened, but because it is celebrated. It dovetailed with the campaign to acquire as much low paid wage labor as possible—if in fact it did not actually spring from that campaign. South Carolina Nullification gave a first taste of the violence that would be used by an aristocracy in full decline.

The twenty years after 1830 saw seven new states admitted to the Union. Just as the admission of Missouri was the climax of the 1873-1820 period, so the admission of California (1850) highlighted the years between 1830 and 1850. Until that time, a slave and non-slave state had always been admitted in pairs. California joined the Union as an unpaired free state, and gave the non-slave group a majority in the Senate. The seven new states were Arkansas, and Michigan; Florida and Iowa; Texas and Wisconsin, and California.[10]

Soon after 1830, it became clear that the slaveholders were determined to "perish . . . in the light, killed by our enemies." But since they were still strong,[11] this urge generated some original economic thinking.

In his Senate speeches, John C. Calhoun, evolved the view that in every civilized and wealthy society, wealth is produced by labor. The laborer gets only a small fraction of what he creates. In all such societies part of the population lives off the labor of others. In a wage economy, this leads to never-ending conflicts between capital and labor. A slave economy avoids such conflicts.[12]

The labor theory of value stems from Ricardo,[12a] but the idea of surplus value—that only a small part of the value produced goes back to the laborer, while others live off the rest of the laborer's product—is a preview of Marx's Kapital.[13]

Nat Turner's Rebellion took place in Southampton County, Virginia in August, 1831. It was the most famous, and the last, of the few slave revolts on the North American continent. Garrison's Liberator began publication in January 1831, and Nat Turner's Rebellion broke out seven months later.[13b]

Almost thirty years later, President Buchanan, glancing backwards, was convinced that the propaganda of the Abolitionist societies had reached the slaves. His last message to Congress, on Dec. 3, 1860, observes:

> The immediate peril arises not so much from these causes as from the fact that the incessant and violent agitation of the slavery question throughout the North for the last quarter of a century has at length produced its malign influence on the slaves and inspired them with vague notions of freedom.[13C]

His speech had its legislative repercussions in Virginia, but produced no cases in the upper courts. For the most part, the same was true in the other states.

As has happened so often, when Turner's rebellion broke out, it caught everyone unawares, though the signs had been there for all to see. T. R. Gray's report on Nov. 5, 1831,[14] says:

> It will thus appear that whilst everything upon the surface of society wore a calm and peaceful aspect; whilst not one note of preparation was heard to warn the devoted inhabitants of war and death, a gloomy fanatic was revolving in the recesses of his own dark, bewildered and overwrought mind, schemes of indiscriminate massacre to the whites.

Not only did not "everything upon the surface of society wear a calm and peaceful aspect", but the slaveholders of Virginia knew it! Only four months before they had enacted a stiffer law against meetings of Negroes, free or slave.[15] Once the revolt took place, severer laws followed almost as a matter of course. Gray's report had recommended only strict enforcement of those laws already in existence.[16] It would have been astonishing however, if the reaction had stopped there.

On March 15, 1832, the Virginia legislature prohibited all preaching by slaves, free Negroes and Mulattoes. Citizen's arrests could be made without warrant.[17] Free Negroes were now expressly forbidden to keep weapons.[18] Special sections were directed at slaves, free Negroes or Mulattoes circulating books or pamphlets counselling rebellion.[19] The 1819 law against riots, routs and unlawful assemblies was retained, and assaults with intent to kill by Negroes on white persons were made punishable by death,[20a] or in case of free Negroes, by death or imprisonment.

Before this, free Negroes had been ordered removed from neighboring Northhampton County for their "safety".[21] Private acts of the time suggest rewards to "loyal" slaves who betrayed the rebellion,[22] and special payment to one slave who apprehended a member of Nat Turner's band.[22a] Legislation against anyone advising about insurrection was enacted.[23] Soon after, we see acts "to suppress the circulation of incendiary publications,"[24] which point the finger at Abolitionist societies. The authority of patrols to search for firearms was enlarged.[25]

In addition, the death penalty was expanded. Slaves could be executed for crimes for which free persons received not less than three years in prison.[26] As a departure from the ordinary practice, compensation was paid for slaves executed for rebellion.[27]

Preventive legislation bloomed in the form of new prohibitions against the immigration of free Negroes.[28] Yet only one case on inciting disaffection among slaves reached the Virginia Supreme Court during the 1830-1850, period and there the court was remarkably strict against the Commonwealth in view of the recent rebellion.

> It is incumbent upon the Commonwealth to show, in the alleged speaking, that the defendant denied the right of owners to property in their slaves. The defendant's language must plainly express that denial, or in its plain meaning, necessarily imply it. To dissuade a member of a Christian flock from merchandizing its slaves, or keeping human beings in slavery, may be done by a pastor without any denial of owners to property in their slaves[28a]

the Virginia Supreme Court said.

Virginia's old objections to the slave trade apparently overrode her fear of slave revolts, although two years earlier, the Supreme Court had still been adverse to congregations of slaves.[29]

Shock waves from Turner's rebellion went beyond Virginia. The 1831-32 session of the Maryland legislature forbade all religious assemblies of slaves not conducted by a white man, or in Baltimore and Annapolis, upon written permission of a white ordained preacher.[30] Free Negroes were made subject to the same punishment as slaves if present at any such unlawful meeting, or if committing any offenses with a slave or slaves, either as principal or accessory.[31]

The same legislature (1831-2) passed a resolution for the more ready removal of free persons of color because "recent occurrences in this state, as well as in other states of our union, have impressed more deeply upon our minds, the necessity of devising some means by which we may facilitate the removal of free persons of color from our state and from the United States."[32]

There is an apparent inconsistency here with the other argument of slaveowners, that free persons of color were worse off than slaves. But the inconsistency is only apparent.   We have seen how white Abolitionists used free Negroes as their agents.[33]   Arms had been denied to free Negroes soon after the rebellion.[34]   Further immigration of free Negroes into Maryland from other states was prohibited in 1839,[35] and immigration from the District of Columbia was stopped in 1845.[36]

As in Virginia, new and stronger laws were enacted against circulation of Abolitionist pamphlets or pictures.   The second of these laws was specially directed at free Negroes.[37]   For second offenses, free Negroes who had previously been sentenced to the penitentiary could be sold out of the state after 1835.[38]   But no cases reached the appellate courts.

In North Carolina, coming events cast their shadows before them. Two statutes against distribution of seditious pamphlets,[39] and anti-slavery preaching and teaching[40] were enacted a few months ahead of Nat Turner's rebellion in Virginia.   Insurrection was in the air in 1831, the same year in which Foot's resolution was killed.   Immediately after Turner's rebellion, the Governor of North Carolina was given authority to convene courts to try cases of insurrection.   The same statute also conferred the right to trial by juries of slaveowners.[41]   In this particular situation, a jury of slaveowners was probably of minimum advantage to the defendant slave.

The power to license slaves to carry guns was withdrawn from the county courts.[41a]   A resolution of 1833[41b] sums up the fright which followed the uprising in Virginia:

> Whereas during the late Negro excitement or threatened insurrection, the arsenal in the City of Raleigh was entered, and many of the public arms taken therefrom in an illegal manner and without the consent of the Governor or Adjutant General, which are now scattered about and becoming injured for want of care. For remedy whereof the Adjutant General is authorized to collect arms and draw on the Treasurer for expenses.

In 1835, a resolution was sent to Congress against Abolitionist propaganda activities among slaves.[42]   In 1840, free Negroes who had been punished by a fine were excluded from the insolvent debtors act,[43] and were forbidden to carry firearms.[44]   In 1846, another law against the furnishing of firearms to slaves was passed.[45]   As with the other states, there were no cases.   This dearth of court proceedings indicates how isolated an event Nat Turner's Rebellion was.

By 1831, South Carolina was the focus of almost all the mutually antagonistic forces at work prior to the passage of the XIIIth Amendment.   Apart from Nullification, there were the relics of the combined looseness and strictness which had led to slave revolts in the 18th century.   Economic decline gnawed at the aristocratic tradition, yet the sense of impending catastrophe was spasmodic and was interrupted by stretches of euphoria, during which the aristocrats could feel that things were as good as they ever had been.

At the outset, a cascade of new legislation contrasted sharply with the somnolence of the 1820's.   Denmark Vesey's rebellion had evidently been thought no different from the uprisings of the 1740's.   After 1831 though, Nat Turner's rebellion and the Abolition agitation jarred the state into the belief that something new was indeed taking place.

Response at first was slow.   Not until 1834 did South Carolina do anything.   Then she joined the states which forbade teaching slaves to read and write.[46]   A harsher law was enacted against free Negroes entering the state.   Where sale into slavery for five years had been the previous maximum penalty, it was changed to sale for life,[47] and new penalties were inflicted on outsiders entering the state to agitate for abolition.[48]

There would be no more leniency as in BELL v. GRAHAM,[49] where the patrol was held to have exceeded its power, although it had been impossible to tell whether the majority of the congregation was black or white.[50] The requirement that patrols have a warrant to enter religious meetings after 9:00 P.M. was repealed.[51]   And, as a reflection of the pressing need now felt, slaves to be executed for insurrection were looked upon as no different from those for whose execution the master was entitled to compensation.[52]

Strangely enough, the cases present a different picture.   It is as if the legislation mirrored the dreadful forebodings raised by Nat Turner's rebellion, while the cases in court represented people's day-to-day existence which Turner's insurrection never touched.   The earliest is STATE v. GREEN, decided in 1836.[53] Here the memory of slave revolt must still have been recent enough that the defendant, bent on shooting her husband, thought she could trade on a threatened revolt.   When her husband was shot, "She instantly cried out, 'Henry is killed . . . the Negroes have risen . . . we shall all be killed.'"[54]

But the court calmly says, "There did not appear to have been any apprehension of a rising among the Negroes."[55]   The jury's attitude was the same.   Since the defendant (the wife) said that a slave had done the actual shooting, and this slave was a co-defendant, the jury necessarily consisted of slaveholders. The jury acquitted the slave and found the wife guilty as an accessory before the fact.[56]

Eleven years elapse before the next case. A slave has been arrested for "insolent language towards Mrs. Crook."[57] A motion for a writ of prohibition to stop the trial was dismissed. The Supreme Court affirmed the dismissal, but over an interesting dissent. The majority merely says:

> In the very nature of things, he is subject to despotism . . . trials of slaves for insolence have been, since 1796 (and without doubt they were before) frequent and unquestioned."[58]

Forgetting the cautionary language of 1813 in STATE v. PORTER,[59] all that the court actually held is that they would not stop the trial before it took place (and in which the defendant could still be acquitted). The dissenting opinion echoed the enormous self-confidence of the state's ruling class, looking down its nose at the flightiness of the inferior orders, and thinking of impertinence as pinpricks. Judge Neall said:

> The Legislature have not thought proper to declare it to be a crime. Some of the most faithful and devoted slaves have been remarkable for their liberty of speech, and who has ever dreamed that an openmouthed, saucy Negro, is the deep intriguer calculated to raise an insurrection? It is said that it is the practice of the whole state to try slaves for insolence before a magistrate and free-holders. I have been tolerably familiar with the administration of justice for the last thirty-three years, and this is the first case which I have ever met with. Yet this Court, in STATE v. FISHER, with the assent of every member (except myself) declared that insolence on the part of a free Negro, would not justify a white man in striking him! No jurisdiction ever did exist which is liable to more abuse than that exercised by magistrates over slaves. Clothe them with the power to try slaves for insolence, and the result will be that passion, prejudice and ignorance will crowd abuses on this inferior jurisdiction to an extent not to be tolerated by slaveowners. [60]

By 1850, it was as if Denmark Vesey's and Nat Turner's rebellions had never happened. The rebellion of 1740 was remembered, but the resulting legislation dismissed as the product of passing fright. "They have learned nothing and forgotten nothing,"[61] has its positive side. STATE v. BOOZER[62] not only re-established much of BELL v. GRAHAM,[63] but is even more emphatic in its result. The jury convicted members of a patrol for unlawfully whipping slaves at a quilting party, and the South Carolina Supreme Court affirmed the conviction, saying:

> The defendants comprising a patrol were indicted under the Act of 1841, for unlawfully whipping the slaves of Fikart. Hunter retired to bed about ten o'clock. He had been about, and the meeting was orderly. About midnight one of his Negroes informed him that the patrol was there. The defendants in turn whipped all of the Negroes present except Hunter's. The jury returned a verdict of guilty.

> How many of us have permitted to our slaves the enjoyment of a wedding party and ceremony in imitation of the custom of the higher class, and even contributed liberally to the good cheer of the occasion? Our fundamental code is that of 1740. It was enacted soon after a violent, barbarous and somewhat bloody servile outbreak at Stacco. Not a few of its provisions took their hue from the exigency of the occasion. It would seem simply ridiculous to suppose that the safety of the state or inhabitants was implicated by such an assemblage.

Even KINLOCK v. HARVEY[64] had faded away.

In 1835, Delaware prohibited the use of firearms by free Negroes,[65] as well as assemblages of more than a dozen after 10:00 P.M., "unless under the direction of three respectable white men,"[66] and "non-resident blacks" were forbidden to preach without a license.[67] Despite the reaction to Nat Turner's Rebellion, slavery in Delaware was too moribund for insurrection to bring cases into the appellate courts.

Georgia continued and codified her previous laws against insurrection and abolitionist propaganda,[68] but did not produce anything substantially new, except the unlimited penalty on an owner bringing a slave back to the state after having had been in a non-slaveholding state.[69]Georgia was the state furthest removed from Virginia, where Nat Turner's rebellion took place, the furthest removed from the northern wage states, and still very near the frontier. By 1849, Nat Turner's Rebellion was so remote that fear of one's own slaves was considered a sign of derangement.[69a]

Louisiana was not so much concerned with a slave revolt in faraway Virginia, but with two small revolts of her own. The first of these occurred in 1837, and the legislative evidence gives no clue as to whether it was an echo of Turner's rebellion. The repercussions were both compensation to the owners of slaves taking part in the rebellion,[70] and compensation to the owner of a slave freed for betraying it.[71]

Another act, in 1838, granted compensation for four slaves executed in St. James Parish,[71a] raising the suspicion of an insurrection, but the grouping of the slaves is the only thing which lends support to this view. The second insurrection broke out soon after, in the summer of 1840.[72] In 1843, the death penalty was imposed for insurrection, but without apparent reference to any new uprising.[73]

The only case, decided in 1844, holds that there was no justification for whipping a man because he supposedly tried to incite insurrection among the defendant's slaves.[73a] The slaveowner's interest in protecting his property was indicated not by proceedings in court, but through statutory compensation. The limit of $300[74] was evidently accepted without murmur, however sharply it contrasted with the $1,500 paid for the slave who betrayed the rebellion of 1837.[75]

The states which were building a wage economy upheld their abolitionist propaganda as freedom of expression. So the southern efforts to suppress such propaganda were countered by a Vermont resolution of 1836 which stated that:

> Neither Congress nor the State Governments have any constitutional right to abridge the free expression of opinion, or the transmission of them through the public mail.[76]

The year 1835 began a war of words, foreshadowing the war of arms. While things were still political and vocal, Kentucky sided with her slaveholding sister states, and resolved:

> Their (abolition societies) object is to produce an entire abolition of slavery in the United States by printing and circulating through post-offices and other modes of communication, tracts, pamphlets, alamanacks and pictorial representations, the manifest tendency of which is to produce a spirit of discontent, insubordination and perhaps insurrection, with the slave population of the country.

> Enough has transpired to convince them (the reporting committee) that under the miserably perverted name of

free discussion, these incendiaries will be permitted to scatter their fire-brands throughout the country with no check, but that which may be imposed by the feeble operation of public opinion. Your committee is as deeply impressed with the value of the high privilege which is secured to the citizens by the constitution of the country—the right to full and free discussion—as can be those who are prostituting it to such unlawful purposes.

But the freedom of the press is one thing, its licentiousness another. Whilst the one is justly dear to every freeman, the other is the object of deep reprobation. It cannot be that the right of discussion at the north carries with it a right to excite a portion of the population of a sister state to rapine and murder.[77]

However there was no legislation until almost the end of the period (1845).[77a] The slaveholders of Kentucky, a border state, were plagued by fugitive slaves, but not by slave revolts. That slavery in Kentucky was perhaps the least oppressive, undoubtedly contributed to the result.[78]

Legislation, when it came, was part of a general overhauling of the state statutes. An attempt to incite a slave insurrection was made punishable by 5-20 years imprisonment.[79] Death was imposed on slaves and free Negroes either for insurrection,[80] or for blowing up the locks of the Louisville and Portland Canal.[81] Assemblies without license were forbidden. Preachers, and teachers of colored persons were narrowly restricted.[81a] Being part of a general revision, these statutes had no connection with any specific incidents. There are likewise no cases.

In 1831, Tennessee prohibited the immigration of free Negroes[82] and passed extensive amendments to her slave laws. These are the last two acts of the year touching slaves, and so may be taken as a sequel to the Turner rebellion. The second act declared all assemblages "not expressly authorized by the owners to be unlawful if held in 'unusual numbers' or at suspicious times and places".[83] Persons permitting such assemblies were subject to an unlimited discretionary fine.[84]

Conspiracy to rebel could draw death, stripes, pillory or jail "according to the extent of the plot and the participation of the accused therein."[85] No appeal was permitted in case of insurrection.[86] Owners permitting their slaves "to go about the country under the pretext of practising medicine or healing the sick" were subjected to discretionary fines, and the slaves to a maximum of 25 lashes.[87] Four years later, in 1835, the state prohibited the distribution of seditious pamphlets "calculated to excite discontent, insurrections or rebellion amongst the slaves or free persons of color,"[88] and forbade giving arms to slaves without the owner's consent.[88a]

MACON v. STATE[89] says that in the section against practicing medicine "the legislature was guarding against insurrectionary movements on the part of the slaves. A slave under pretext of practicing medicine, might convey intelligence from one plantation to another of contemplated insurrectionary movement, and thus enable the slaves to act in concert to a considerable extent, and perpetrate the most shocking massacres. It was thought most safe to prohibit slaves from practising medicine altogether." Tennessee was close enough to Southampton County, Va., that she had been badly scared by Nat Turner.

There is only one case in the District of Columbia, and it gives the jury's viewpoint, rather than that of the judiciary. In 1836 a member of an anti-slavery society was acquitted on a charge of "publishing libels tending to excite seditions among the slaves and free colored persons in this district."[90] This verdict showed which way attitudes were drifting.

Mississippi tried to avoid an aftermath of Nat Turner's rebellion by forbidding the importation of slaves.[90a] Simultaneously, slaves and free Negroes were forbidden to act as ministers of the gospel.[90b] Abolitionist activities began seriously in 1835.[91] In 1836, the legislature passed a resolution, mild and polite-enough in its language, urging the non-slaveholding states to restrain their citizens:

> from associating, plotting or conspiring to undermine, disturb or abolish our institution of domestic slavery in any manner or by any means and under any pretext whatever, and that their citizens and other person among them be interdicted also, under suitable and sufficient penalties from writing, speaking, printing or publishing, sentiments and opinions, expressive of advice of suggestion to the public or others calculated in temper and spirit to induce disaffection among our slaves or to enlist others in the commission of acts tending on this subject to endanger our rights of property or domestic repose.[92]

In practice, forbidding slaves to learn reading and writing was no more effective than forbidding sexual intercourse between whites and Negroes.[93] In 1839, the only statute was passed as part of a general revision of the criminal code. It was aimed at "Exciting Insurrections," by "compositions, manuscripts"—or otherwise.[94] It betrays confusion on the part of the new Gulf Coast slaveholders about what to do next. Some penalties were made more lenient,[95] but those for circulating seditious pamphlets became more severe.[96]

This dual approach recurred from the 1830's until the outbreak of the Civil War. Before they finally seceded, the slave states tried both severity and conciliation. There were no cases. Mississippi was not actually touched by Nat Turner's rebellion. But as late as 1845, Illinois inflicted up to 39 stripes for seditious speeches by slaves.[97]

In 1843, Alabama imposed the death penalty for conspiring or being involved in an insurrection against whites, as well as for similar activities thought to point in the same direction.[98] But Alabama was not consistent. Laws passed in 1832 enslaving free Negroes who had entered the state after that year were repealed in 1831-9.[99] Of course, it may have occurred to some of the gentlemen that if they wanted to forestall a Nat Turner rebellion in Alabama, keeping out-of-state Negroes among their slaves was not the best way to do it.

The codification of 1852 contains laws prohibiting more than five slaves to gather at a house other than that of their common owner,[100] and forbids slaves to carry guns,[101] participate in riots, routs and unlawful assemblies or make seditious speeches.[102] Free colored crews of ships in port were not allowed to leave the ship or communicate with Alabama slaves.[103] There was however, some real casualness about the possibilty of rebellion.

In 1837, only six years after Nat Turner's rebellion in Virginia, the Alabama Supreme Court limited the statutory words "assisting any such insurrection" to "an actual or meditated rebellion." Merely talking insurrection to a slave was not enough.[104] Superficially, the case looked serious. "The defendant said that the Negroes ought to rise, that they had hard masters. That they must raise five hundred men, but he would start with three hundred." Frank was to furnish a horse. The defendant promised to give the rifle he had with him to Moses, the decoy slave, when they started. They would go to Mobile, and if they did not like that, to Pensecuth, a weaker place, get arms and ammunition there, press a ship with which they could go to Texas, a free place where they would be joined by other slaves on their way.

The defendant then told the slave that he must get him a thousand men, but he would start with five hundred. They could get guns from their masters, along with ammunition and horses. The defendant said there were no white men engaged. ("This would indicate that the person was colored"—Catteral). He would head them, Frank would be second in command, and Moses third. The witnesses all stated that there was no disturbance in the county among the slaves, no evidence of any illegal conduct further than these conversations. The jury convicted, but the Supreme Court of Alabama reversed the conviction saying:

> The indictment intended to embrace the first class of offenses, declared by the second branch of the act for advising, plotting or consulting with a slave, for the purpose of assisting any such insurrection—the words mean an actual or meditated rebellion. The witnesses all state that there was no insurrection. The conviction of the prisoner was unauthorized.

What would later become Justice Holmes' "clear and present danger" rule was here applied to acquit. As we have already noted,[105] a caste society which feels secure, may be more generous to all concerned than a "free" society which is on edge.

Missouri for the most part, remained with her original Law of 1804.[106] A new statute against unlawful assemblies was enacted in 1833,[107] perhaps as an academic reaction to Nat Turner's rebellion. In 1850 the Town of Hartsville was incorporated and authorized to prevent or restrain meetings of slaves.[107a] In 1837 the state forbade anyone to:

> publish, circulate, either by writing, speaking or printing, any facts, arguments, reasoning, or opinions tending directly to excite any slave or slaves or other persons of color in this state, to rebellion, sedition, meeting or insurrection, or murder with intent to excite such slave or slaves, or other persons of color to rebellion, sedition or insurrection.

This expanded the Law of 1804[108] to include writing as well as speech. Two things should be noted. First, it was probably more of a reaction to the abolitionist agitation which was at full throttle in 1835, than to Nat Turner's rebellion. Second, it showed the futility of forbidding slaves to learn to read and write. The Industrial Revolution required a literate proletariat. Here as elsewhere, it clothed its practical demands in idealistic formulae. The Nineteenth century surge toward general literacy was too strong to be stopped by laws. Nevertheless in 1845, Missouri went out of her way to specifically make it unlawful to teach slaves to read and write.[109]

Two resolutions were also passed by the state legislature, but considering that there are no cases whatever, these too, must be put down as academic. One, Article 12, passed in 1839, declaimed against interference with the slave states' domestic institution of slavery by persons from non-slave states.[110] The second, passed in 1814, joined the other slave states in inveighing against the distribution of abolitionist literature in the mails, with the xenophobic spice of blaming everything on British capitalism.[111]

Arkansas was not admitted as a state until 1836, but since territorial laws existed before then, her treatment of slave rebellions (and other phases of slavery) will be recounted from the beginning. The Arkansas Territorial Act of 1818,[112] apparently included the Missouri provisions against unlawful assemblies and seditious speeches.[113] The legislation of 1835 reenacted these provisions.[114] Laws against attending unlawful meetings and conspiracy to rebel were likewise continued.[115]

These provisions were re-adopted in 1837[116] and 1848.[117] In between, in 1844, the state adopted a resolution seconding South Carolina's actions "in expelling the emissary sent by the State of Massachusetts to reside within her territorial limits for the purposes and intentions avowed by said emissary."[118] The resolution embraced the following clauses:

> Resolved that the right to exclude from its territory, by legislation, or any other means which the exigency of the case may demand, seditious persons or any other class of persons whose presence may be dangerous to its peace, is essential to every State, and may be effectually exercised.

With regard to Massachusetts it was resolved specifically,

> Resolved, that we view the conduct of the Massachusetts legislature in their attempting to interfere in the domestic institution of the southern states, as acting with the Abolitionists and tending to destroy the peace and quiet of our citizens, and should be promptly met and rebuked by all lovers of good order, and more particularly, by the slave holding states.

Envisaging the possibility of a similar envoy being sent to Arkansas, the resolution continued.

> Resolved, his Excellency, the Governor of this State is hereby authorized and required to take the most efficient means of freeing this State from so dangerous and unworthy an agent.

This resolution itself embodies history. In the first place, it was triggered by the sending of a delegate from one state to another, from

Massachusetts to South Carolina. They are not close together geographically, but in 1844-5 they were the leaders of their respective regions. The antagonism between regions which formed relatively solid blocks, is in line with Gorer's theory that this situation was what brought on the American Civil War.[119]

In the second place, it reveals the active proselytizing which the non-slave states encouraged in the slave states. There had been no such movement before the Industrial Revolution. Here an emissary had been sent from Massachusetts, the most industrialized state, to South Carolina, considered the leader of the slave states. What would such emissary accomplish? The freeing of the slaves for what? For human liberty and equality, of course. Then as a by-product, there would be dirt-cheap and docile labor in Massachusett's rising industries.

There were no cases. Until 1850, Arkansas was both sparsely populated and still on the frontier. How far the inhabitants were inclined to coerce their slaves extra-legally will become clear later.

With Florida, we have the same situation as Arkansas. She was not admitted as a state until 1845, but had been a slave territory before then. Narration of Florida's legal history therefore begins before its admission date. Florida, Spanish until 1819, situated below the cotton belt and furthest from the industrializing North, seems to have been uncertain about how to behave towards slavery when she became an American territory.

This uncertainty appeared in its attitude towards slave rebellions. Sometimes Florida reflected the harshness of the frightened states. At other times, slave rebellions seem like a fairy tale or something far away, which cannot be taken seriously. Soon after becoming part of the United States, the territory made rebellion, or conspiracy to rebel, punishable by death,[120] and killing a slave in revolt was made justifiable homicide.[121] In the same year (1824) however, seditious speeches by slaves were punished only with the common 39 stripes,[122] and three years later the same penalty was enacted for free Negroes.[123]

In the meantime, the death penalty was re-enacted for conspiracy to rebel.[124] Yet in 1828, the state went back to 39 stripes for inciting insurrection.[125] Since this section refers to "any person" it is evidently aimed at northern proselytizers, of whom the neighboring slave states were soon to become so afraid. This suggests that Florida was trying to copy pre-existing slave codes, but did not have her heart in it.

But Nat Turner's rebellion had created a dreadful legend which somehow did not seem quite real. In 1832, free Negroes were forbidden to assemble even for worship, unless a white person was present.[126] The penalty was 39 stripes, the same penalty which had been imposed for

inciting insurrection.   An act enslaving any Negro found with the
Seminole Indians, and inflicting the death penalty on any armed Negro
was passed in 1836,[127] but repealed the next year.[128]

By 1839, Florida had swung over to panic legislation,[129] but nothing
concrete had happened. Yet the state's continuing uncertainty is clear
from the retention of the 39 stripe maximum penalty for seditious
speeches by free Negroes,[130] supposedly the most dangerous group.
White persons attending an unlawful meeting with slaves or free Negroes
were punished by a fine of not more than $100, a maximum of 39 lashes
or two months in jail. There are no cases, or any further legislation
through 1850.

The Republic of Texas, before its adherence to the Union, made
insurrection by a slave or free person of color a capital offense.[131]
There are no cases of further legislation. Giving full weight to Texas'
frontier conditions, the reason for the absence of both legislation and
litigation was probably because the entire subject was academic.

In general, the slave states were scared by Nat Turner's rebellion,
but also tended to view it as an isolated occurrence, which it was. Slave
revolts were pleasures of the imagination for the idealists in the
Abolition movement, and occasionally produced martyrs. The real issue
was not liberty from the standpoint of the slaves. The real issue was
how (no longer whether) slaves should be transferred from slave labor to
coolie-level wage labor.

SOUTH CAROLINA NULLIFICATION

South Carolina attempted in 1832 to nullify the Federal Tariff Act
of 1828. This was significant first in spotlighting the economic relations
between the different sections of the United States, and second as the
first ominous violence of an aristocracy[132] that sensed it would soon be
a ruling class no more. To put South Carolina's nullification attempt in
perspective, it must first be remembered that the "Virginia Dynasty" had
lasted until 1824,[133] only eight years earlier.

The antagonism between Virginia and South Carolina which existed
at the Constitutional Convention, had disappeared with the closing of
the legal slave trade.[134]   South Carolina's demand for slaves and
Virginia's surplus no longer clashed.   Virginia simply became the
supplier.[134a] The commanding figure of John C. Calhoun had
overshadowed South Carolina's decline since 1820, and leadership had
actually passed from Virginia to South Carolina, but that was all.

President Jackson on the other hand, was from Tennessee, then the
West, and the West joined with New England to pass the Force Bill[135]
which was designed to crush Nullification. The country's destiny was

slipping out of South Carolina's hands.[136] The legislatures of New Jersey[137] and Indiana[138] passed resolutions against Nullification. Daniel Webster characterized Nullification in much the same language that was used regarding the slavery question in the Great Debate of 1850. "These words of separation, it appears to me, are now industriously sown; their growth ought to be prevented."[139] Clay, perspicacious as ever, foresaw the possibility of civil war should there be secession over the tariff.[140]

Slavery was the main issue. In nullification over the tariff, storm warnings were temporarily raised from another quarter. As Mommsen was to say later, "but every political alliance is inwardly broken up where the relative preparations of the power of the parties are materially altered."[141]

The period after 1830, the beginning of the end of the drama, saw the slave and non-slave states forming two solid opposing blocks.[141a] These blocks would continue solid until secession, except for the five border slave states which stayed with the Union.

After 1830, the slave states, with power slipping out of their hands, sought new areas to be organized along pro-slavery lines[142]—new states to which they could bring their slaves. The non-slave states made organized efforts to help slaves escape via the "underground railway," and to extend the non-slave economy into new territory. Thus these two activities became counterparts, one aimed at increasing the area controlled by slavery, the other to turn slaves into underpaid wage hands and increase the area of the wage economy. The question of enlarging or limiting the slave area, which had been the major point of contention during the Missouri controversy, broke out again upon the annexation of Texas.

As might be expected, there was a whole new raft of legislation in Virginia after 1830 on every aspect of fugitive slaves and slave stealing, from enticing slaves to abscond,[143] to the sale of runaways,[144] pilots and ferrymen,[145] slave-stealing itself,[146] and the issuance of false passes to slaves.[146a] There were even statutes authorizing the organization of a company to write insurance against absconding slaves,[147] and such a company was set up.[148] Resolutions,[149] and later a statute, were aimed specifically at the slave-stealing activities of New York citizens.[150]

On the eve of enactment of the Federal Fugitive Slave Act of 1850, there was a state resolution and statute on recovery of fugitive slaves.[151] Virginia passed a resolution against the Wilmot Proviso (prohibiting slavery in newly acquired territory),[152] which was soon followed by others.[152a] The first resolution spelled out the Wilmot

Proviso and protested that the way in which Texas was annexed was contrary to the Constitution and the terms of the Missouri Compromise. It said,

> Whereas a bill appropriating money to prosecute war or negotiate peace with the Republic of Mexico has passed the House of Representatives, with the following proviso attached thereto: 'Provided, that as an express and fundamental condition to the acquisition of any territory from the Republic of Mexico by the United States by virtue of any treaty which may be negotiated between them, and to the use by the executive of moneys herein appropriated, neither slavery nor involuntary servitude shall ever exist in any part of said territory, except for a crime whereof the party shall be first duly convicted.' And this general assembly deeming this proviso to be destructive of the compromise of the Constitution of the United States, and an attack on the dearest rights of the South, as well as a dangerous and alarming usurpation by the federal government, it is therefore resolved:

> That if in disregard alike of the spirit and principles of the act of Congress on the admission of the State of Missouri into the Union, generally known as the Missouri Compromise, and of every consideration of justice, of constitutional right and of fraternal feeling, the fearful issue shall be forced upon the country which must result from the adoption and attempted enforcement of the proviso aforesaid as an act of the general government, the people of Virginia can have no difficulty in choosing between the only alternatives that will the remain of abject submission to aggression and outrage on the one hand, and determined resistance on the other, at all hazards and to the last extremity.

Here was not only a call for disunity but the tocsin of Civil War. Once more the slave states were caught in the paradox that in North America, the Industrial Revolution had fostered an anti-capitalist society. Carlyle has said that all wars are the result of a misjudgment of forces. "But, alas, what man does know and measure himself, and the things that are around him. Else where were the need of physical fighting at all?"[153]

The contest between the slave and the wage states, however, was not the ordinary contest between capitalism and feudalism. The slave economy of the 19th century while anti-capitalist, had been set in motion by the Industrial Revolution, had received some of its benefits and had been strengthened by them.[154] The sides were much more nearly equal than in Cromwell's Revolution, the Scottish Civil Wars of the first half of the 18th century, or the French Revolution. Under such circumstances, even measuring is not a sure guide. A little wishful thinking is all it takes to get the wrong result.

At the beginning of the period, the cases which arose were still from an earlier era—slave stealing between slaveowners or would-be slaveowners.[155] In 1837 came the first conviction for aiding and abetting a slave to escape from the possession of his owner.[156] From then on, Virginia felt the impact of the Abolition movement, but was very circumspect about prosecutions arising from it.

Advocating abolition of both the slave trade and slavery itself was crucial only if "the person accused was a member of an Abolition or anti-slavery society."[157] Furthermore, the offense could not be prosecuted by information. Where all acts of slavestealing across the Ohio River were done in Ohio, the court was perfectly willing to find a lack of jurisdiction in Virginia.[158] By 1850 however, there were repeated convictions for operating the "underground railway"—systematically aiding slaves to escape into wage areas.[159]

Virginia had opposed the slave trade at the Constitutional Convention. After 1808 the problem became primarily federal. Yet as late as the 1830's and 1840's, Virginia continued to enact state laws against the slave trade.[160] In this respect, the old conflict with South Carolina survived. There were however, no slave trade cases, either state or federal, coming from Virginia. With a surplus of slaves, the state had no incentive for importing Negroes from Africa.

DISCIPLINE

Many phases of slave discipline remained unchanged in Virginia from 1830-1850.[161] Some penalties became more severe.[162] Virginia was an example of what occurs over and over again. Where a society is faced with the prospect of a basic and unpalatable change, it imagines it can stave off the inevitable by terror. Perhaps as a reaction against their own harshness, and the inconvenience it caused to slaveowners, the Legislature also passed a special law making slaves bailable during criminal prosecutions.[163] To resolve the dilemma posed by EX PARTE BELL,[164] a specific procedure was formulated to deal with Negroes prosecuted as freemen and then claimed as slaves.[165]

Virginia passed a new law between 1830 and 1850, authorizing patrols to break into the houses of slaves or free Negroes in search of arms.[166] This was clearly in response to Nat Turner's Rebellion. There were no cases on patrols, something to be expected in a state which was selling her slaves south.[166a] As in the past, Virginia had no statute limiting slaves' hours of labor. It was hardly needed in a state which had no labor shortage, but was selling slaves beyond her borders.

The concern about furnishing slaves with adequate food and clothing virtually disappeared. As a border state particularly exposed to abolition propaganda and with surplus slaves,[167] Virginia had other problems. There were no new general statutes for providing slaves with adequate support, food and clothing.[168] There was only one case, but it shows the trend of the times. RANDOLPH v. HILL[169] arose not from a plantation but from a mine. The owner recovered damages from the hirer for the death of a slave sent to work in a badly ventilated shaft. There is only one further statute on the care of aged or infirm slaves,[170] and restrictions on their emancipation. There are but two cases,[170a] as Virginia now focused her attention elsewhere.

Cruelty to slaves had all but disappeared from Virginia jurisprudence. There were no further statues, nor further prosecutions against masters, hirers or overseers. Charges like this are a barometer of altered and changing economic and political conditions.

SEXUAL RELATIONS

As in the past, Virginia took Mulattoes for granted,[171] but forbade intermarriage.[172] This was clear implementation of the caste system. Marriage makes the parties social equals. In 1837, Harriet Martineau[172a] gave a picture of sexual relations between whites and Negroes, with special reference to Virginia.

> Every man who resides on his plantation may have his harem, and has every inducement of custom and of pecuniary gain to tempt him to the common practice.

> There is no occasion to explain the management of the female slaves on estates where the object is to rear as many as possible, like stock, for the southern market, nor to point out the boundless licentiousness caused by the practice, a practice which wrung from the wife of a planter in the bitterness of her heart, the declaration that 'a planter's wife was only the chief slave of the harem.' Mr. Madison avowed that the licentiousness of Virginia plantations stopped just short of destruction, and that it was understood that the female slaves were to become mothers at fifteen.

The caste system likewise shows through in the case of COMMONWEALTH v. JAMES[173] where the white defendant was prosecuted for keeping and cohabiting with a female slave. He alone could be punished. She as a slave could not. Considering the number and general acceptance of Mulattoes, the violation in this particular case must have been more notorious than the community found palatable. The court said tersely, "this Court perceives no reason why, because one of the offending parties is exempt from the operation of the statute by reason of being a slave, the other, who is not a slave, should also be exempt." Noblesse oblige. The ruling class must observe its own rules. What happens to the lower orders didn't count.

Aside from this, the Virginia courts were remarkably lenient towards sexual relations between free Negroes and whites,[174] as free Negroes were not anyone's property. Several cases mention Mulattoes incidentally, and as a matter of course, either in the judges' opinions or in the statute on which the case is based.[175] One private act countenances "passing," observing, "Where it appears that (names) are not Negroes or Mulattoes, but white persons, although remotely descended from a colored woman."[176] The Mulatto child of a white couple was an exception to the rule that the child of a wife cohabiting with her husband is conclusively presumed to be legitimate.[176a]

EMANCIPATION

Just as Virginia was selling her slaves to other states, she was undergoing a wave of emancipation. (Again inconsistent with the concern over seduction of slaves by northern agitators.) In 1837, the courts were given power to grant leave to emancipated slaves to stay within the commonwealth because of the mass of petitions which had previously been presented to the legislature.[177] Both before and after this time there was a stream of emancipations, and before and after 1837 there was a string of special acts allowing emancipated slaves to remain[178] in Virginia either permanently or for a limited time.

There was likewise a large volume of litigation arising from emancipation. The earlier cases were still unfavorable,[179] but the judiciary was becoming more and more inclined to effectuate emancipation as time went on.[180] So relations between masters and slaves in Virginia between 1830-50 reflected both the actions of the northern Abolitionists and the increasing unprofitability of slave labor in Virginia. As the Virginia Court of Appeals noted in 1848, "the scantiness of net profit from slave labor has become proverbial."[181] The slave states, caught in the original paradox of an anti-capitalist economy brought into being by capitalism, now proceeded to the next paradox of fighting for an institution which they knew had become unprofitable, an example of the "intractability of institution."[181a]

Apart from an act regulating the hire of slaves awaiting appeals,[182] and one authorizing jailers to receive slaves taken under attachment,[183] legislation on relations between slaveowners dwindled down to a few private acts authorizing sales,[184] or permission to take slaves out of the state.[185]   However, there was plenty of lively litigation between slaveowners. The only mark of changed conditions was the frequency of provisions against allowing slaves to be sold.[186]   Prices for slaves ran from almost $200 down to twenty-five cents.[188]   Otherwise, there was every variety of contests arising from personal property.[189]

Virginia law regulating the relations of masters and the community at large shifted between 1830 and 1850. As the slaveowners of Virginia felt more and more on the defensive against the Abolitionist movement, they increased the surveillance which the community exercised over individuals.

Taxes ranged from 25 cents[190] to 40 cents[191] a slave. Special acts for state care of insane slaves made their first appearance during this period.[192]   This may well have reflected "the scantiness of net profit from slave labor which had become proverbial."[193] The state no longer expected the owner to assume the entire burden of caring for an insane slave.

Virginia continued the system of compensating owners for slaves executed or transported for crime,[194] more so after Nat Turner's Rebellion. Compensation for imprisonment of a slave or apprehension of a slave stealer was also granted in some circumstances.[195]

Slaves still had to be tried by justices,[196] but the number of statutory death penalties increased[197] after Nat Turner's Rebellion. The slave owners were frightened enough to tip the scales in favor of punishment of slaves, and to protect their property interests by compensation. But there were no capital cases against slaves during the period. After Nat Turner's Rebellion, Virginia reinforced her laws to control slaves, but found herself punching air.

Penalties, light enough, were renewed for secreting or eloigning a slave to prevent prosecution. In 1841 it was still only a $5-$20 fine.[198] There were no cases. Masters hiding their slaves to avoid prosecution was no longer a problem in Virginia.

The prohibitions against slaves trading for themselves were retained without substantial change.[199]   The laws were expressly extended to cover free Negroes.[199a] One case, set in motion by an informer, reached the Court of Appeals.[200]   The state regulated slave owners in a number of other ways, outstanding among them was the prohibition against allowing liquor to be sold to slaves with the intent that it be bartered for their own use.[201]

FREE NEGROES AND MULATTOES

The attitude of the ruling class, the slaveowners, towards such free Negroes as were permitted in Virginia, was pretty much as before, that of tolerant paternalism. But there were signs that the slaveowners had lost control of the population at large, with the result that outbursts of popular violence began to override the decisions of the courts.

The bell-whether case is GRAYSON v. COMMONWEALTH,[204] where in 1849 and 1850 a free Negro was twice convicted of murder. The Court of Appeals held the evidence insufficient both times. On the second appeal, the appellate court said:

> We are again unanimously of the opinion that it (the evidence) is wholly insufficient to sustain the verdict and judgment. Declarations of persons accused are not much to be relied on. But in this case the truth of the declarations was persisted in under peculiar circumstances, severe torture, which we are sorry to say the bystanders, under great excitement of the moment, forgetful of the mild spirit of our law, thought themselves at liberty to inflict. The testimony is hardly sufficient to raise a suspicion against him.

There follows this note by the reporter.

> After the decision of the court granting to the prisoner another trial, an armed mob in the daytime, took him from the jail and hung him; and thus to punish a man suspected of murder, they committed murder themselves.

By the census of 1820, Virginia had more free Negroes than any other state except Maryland.[205] The border states could no longer use their slaves. Along with selling slaves south, Virginia was allowing them to become emancipated in spite of all the excitement about the activities of northern Abolitionists.[206] There is a longer list of public and private acts on free Negroes during this period than on any other subject.[207] The Virginia statutes show that free Negroes could hold slaves, at least when the slaves were their wives or children.[208] But the policy of refusing entry to free Negroes remained unchanged,[209] and was extended to those returning after having left the state to be educated.[210]

This was an enlargement of the suicidal policy of not permitting slaves to learn reading and writing. The Industrial Revolution required a literate proletariat but the slave states went out of their way to create a stratum of illiterates, thus insuring their own backwardness. Hand in hand with the policy of excluding free Negroes came various projects for deporting them, either to Liberia or elsewhere.[211]

There was considerable restriction on the opportunities of free Negroes to earn a living,[212] and Virginia took a page from the book of her northern neighbors, and brought free Negroes under the general vagrancy laws.[213] A series of taxing acts,[214] criminal statutes[215] and miscellaneous provisions[216] are given in the footnotes. One of the criminal laws shows a startling movement away from slavery. The procedure applicable to free Negroes was also applied to all plaintiffs in suits to establish their free status. Where the right to residence was admitted, a person claiming "freedom" from slavery, was given the benefit of the doubt before the issue was resolved.[217]

The courts exercised strict legality to protect the rights of free Negroes.[218] This was patrician noblesse oblige. We have already noted that in GRAYSON v. COMMONWEALTH,[219] the fabric began to come apart at the seams. A problem never resolved was what to do with children of a slave mother who had the right to emancipation at a future date. In 1824, the Virginia Court of Appeals held such children to be slaves.[220] The courts followed this decision though they thought it wrong,[221] but made as many exceptions to it as possible.[222]

Virginia adhered to the rule that persons adjudged free were not entitled to wages for the time they were wrongfully held in slavery,[223] and at long last gave a reason.[224] Slave labor was too unprofitable. In any event, the person declared free had received at least part of his wages in the form of board and housing. Since this was a late ruling (1848), one suspects that the logical reasons may have dawned on the court because of the increasingly stark economic picture. A few other miscellaneous holdings regarding free Negroes are given in the footnotes.[225]

Virginia retained[226] and re-enacted[227] her existing laws against importation of slaves from foreign countries. Virginia's reaction to the abolition activities from the northern states has already been described.[228] The dogged opposition to such activities, despite the declining profit from slave labor, presages Virginia's secession in 1861.

Maryland was still a slave state and continued so until November 1, 1864,[228a] but the laws enacted between 1830-50 made it quite clear that she was not going to secede. Slavery was a dying institution. There were a few statutes passed against fugitive slaves,[229] and the related activities of free Negroes,[230] showing that the Abolitionists viewed Maryland as a poaching ground. There were a few vacillating resolutions declaring Maryland to be a slave state, but it was like whistling past a graveyard. Otherwise there were only exceptions to the rule against importing slaves,[232] and a stream of little private acts[233] which were later summed up in the repeal of all laws against bringing in slaves from other states.[234] In Maryland, slavery was no longer an active force, but litigation went merrily on. It is interesting how far private disputes lagged behind events.

In these private actions, Maryland indicates an illegal (in Maryland) participation in Virginia's business of selling slaves south.[235] At the end of the period, we meet one of the first cases under the Fugitive Slave Act of 1850,[236] although Maryland prided herself on the humane treatment of her slaves.[237] There were nevertheless, a substantial number of fugitive slave cases,[238] showing both Maryland's vulnerability as a border state, and the revolutionary spirit which had begun to enter the Abolition movement.[239] Two Maryland cases reveal the continuing temptations of the slave trade,[240] even though slavery was on its way out in the state itself.

Patrols no longer existed in Maryland after 1830. Of the few disciplinary cases, some imposed a jail sentence,[241] showing again that there was no labor shortage in the state. One case complained that a slave had been made valueless by constant beatings.[242] With slavery a dying institution, cases on the obligation of the master toward his slaves all but disappeared. The good relations of which the slaveowners boasted have already been noticed.[243] It was almost axiomatic in Maryland, not to separate members of the same slave family,[244] or even to break the personal relations between the slaves and the master.[245]

The same was true for furnishing food and clothing.[246] Needless to say, there were no cases directly involving cruelty to slaves.[247] The rule that emancipated slaves must be able to earn their living was still enforced. In one case, an attempted emancipation was held void because the intended freedmen were too young.[250]

The pattern of sexual relations between masters and slaves in Maryland during the 1830's and 1840's was no different from any other place or time. The objection to marriage between whites and free Negroes was a rule of caste. But sexual relations existed where they could be fitted into the caste structure.[251]

With slavery a dying institution in Maryland, there were a number of testamentary manumissions, which were usually enforced.[252]   There were also a few deeds of manumission <u>inter vivos,</u> which were like wise upheld. [253] On the other hand, the Maryland courts were reluctant to find involuntary manumissions where a slave had been taken to another state. [254]

North Carolina did not operate on a sufficiently large scale for any one to be tempted to engage in illegal and foreign slave trade. There were neither statutes nor cases. There were no new statutes on disciplinary measures against slaves, but quite a few criminal prosecutions. [273] North Carolina's slave system was as unstable as ever, but that merely continued what went before. These cases will be considered again as part of the never-ending dilemma of a slave society to reconcile the need of punishing offenses with the master's desire to preserve their own property.

Patrols continued pretty much unchanged as a regular part of the North Carolina slave machinery. [274] This too, indicates that slavery was vigorous enough and of sufficient scope to induce the state to secede in 1861. There was however, only one case on patrols during the entire twenty-year period. It held that patrols could act only by a majority.[275] We have seen signs that North Carolina would secede in 1861. Here were the forebodings that when she did secede, it would be reluctantly, and late.

No further legislation appeared on the obligations of masters towards their slaves, again disclosing the negative side of North Carolina slavery. As in Virginia, care was taken not to separate families if it could be avoided. [276] Likewise, it was virtually taken for granted that a master would treat his slaves well, [277] and would care for over-aged slaves. [278] North Carolina went much further than most of the English states in allowing <u>peculium</u> to slaves;[279] and in a limited way recognizing slave "marriages."[279a]

Casualness toward voluntary sexual relations between whites and Negroes[280] was continued during the first part of the 1830-1850 period, that is to say, until 1838.[281] From then on, the ruling class became conscious both of its caste system, and its insecurity. Here too, the lines were suddenly tightened, presaging the state's ultimate secession. So we see the judicial decisions remarkably tolerant until 1838,[282] but after that they began to become almost violent, punishing as "adultery" continued cohabitation on the strength of a marriage celebrated before that year.[283]

In emancipations perhaps as much as anything, one sees the state at loggerheads with itself, and the instability of her slave system. Official policy in North Carolina swung from opposing emancipation to favoring it on condition that emancipated slaves leave the state. The colony had objected to emancipation. "Emancipation was not favored in the province," Catterall noted. But by 1845, the state was glad to get rid of her slaves, provided emancipated Negroes removed themselves.

In COX v. WILLIAMS (1845), the court said:

> by a modern statute, the policy is avowed of encouraging the emancipation, upon the sole condition, that the people freed should not disturb or be chargeable to us, but keep out of our borders.

At the time of its enactment, the law of 1830 seemed like a restriction.[284] In retrospect, the courts thought of it as an enlargement, but it was not enough to satisfy the growing desire to do away with slavery. A whole series of private emancipation acts followed,[285] in all of which the freemen were authorized to remain in the state upon posting bond for good behavior.

The courts generally gave effect to emancipation,[286] except where it was clearly intended to keep the freeman in the state.[287] So bequests of North Carolina realty to slaves freed by will were held void, as contrary to the policy of making manumitted slaves leave the state.[288]

In North Carolina, the slave system was weak, but strong enough to insure the state's ultimate secession.

A single act on the measure of damages for slaves[289] represents the totality of legislation on relations between slaveowners. The preoccupation with techniques which marked the preceding decade,[290] had disappeared. North Carolina, like Virginia, was interested in other things. The measure of damages for taking a slave was merely the civil side of slave-stealing.

On the other hand, there was an unprecedented volume of private litigation. There is a veritable torrent of sales and purchases. To some extent, North Carolina was catching up with Virginia and, like her neighbor, was selling her slaves south and west.[291] But there was also an immense amount of business between North Carolinans. The price of slaves was going up,[292] yet at the same time there seemed to be doubts about the future of slavery. North Carolina's new role as slave-supplier, coupled with the high prices of slaves,[293] were unquestionably factors which later tipped the balance in favor of secession. There was comparatively little new legislation on relations between slaveowners and the state. Here, too, other problems were more pressing.

One law, seemingly designed to kill two birds with one stone, taxed free Negroes in three counties to compensate patrols.[295] In one county, women slaves were taxed specially. A tax was also enacted on the domestic slave trade,[296] the logical sequel to the great increase in that business.

There were no new statutes or any cases whatever on compensation to owners for executed slaves.[297] The only thing remotely touching the subject was a resolution of protest against the British for freeing slaves on a ship forced by bad weather to find port in the British West Indies.[298]

The absence of slaves executed for serious crimes again shows the isolated character of Nat Turner's Rebellion. It also shows a decline of slavery in North Carolina. Never very strong or stable, the institution was further weakened as the state followed Virginia as a slave supplier to the South and West. This was a circular process. Because slavery was ill-suited to the state's agriculture, slaveowners tended to sell, rather than employ their slaves. But the stream of sales was also a safety valve. Potential sources of tension were merely dispersed or shunted away. At the same time, this disintegration lined North Carolina up with the future Confederacy. The role of slave supplier bound her, like Virginia, to the other seceding states.

The tug of war continued between slaveowners who wanted to preserve their property, and non-slaveholding whites who wanted to see slaves punished like other people, or more so. The only new statute was a reaction to Nat Turner's Rebellion.[299] The cases show a strong inclination to protect the slaveowner. Nowhere was this clearer than in STATE v. LEIGH.[300] There a defendant's slave was alleged to have murdered another slave. The defendant, a justice of the peace, was prosecuted for not issuing a warrant against his own slave.

First, it should be noted that the grand jury issued such a presentment. This in itself embodies a point of view directly opposed to that of the North Carolina Supreme Court in deciding the case. The trial judge quashed the presentment. The Supreme Court affirmed the judgment with the following comment:

> A master is not bound, if the slave is at liberty, to be officially active against him at any stage of the prosecution. Their relation imposes on him the obligation of the slave's defence.[301]

Secondly, the same sort of opposition between the Supreme Court and petit juries may be seen in the high percentage of reversed convictions.[302]

No further statutes were aimed at masters who spirited away slaves to avoid punishment by the authorities. But a single case still suggests

this tactic.[303] North Carolina showed signs of a backward region beginning to move forward. Practices of the industrializing North exist side
by side with the most antiquated features of the old regime.[304]

North Carolina's loose slave structure continued to have problems
with slaves trading for themselves.[305] But after one last try at repression,[306] the state began to reverse her policy and make a virtue out of
necessity. During the 1820's the master's right to grant licenses was
abolished. [307] In 1835 this right was restored <u>ex industria</u> for the town
of Wilmington. [308]

But when it came to specific applications, there was still a policy
against slaves trading for themselves. In 1832, the Supreme Court held
that the master could not be punished for allowing a slave to trade for
himself. It added the dictum "the remedy being against the slave
alone."[309] After that however, persons trading with slaves were subjected to both criminal[310] and civil[311] liability. In 1846, the rules of
pleading an indictment were simplified by statute. [311a] This see-sawing
was typical of a society, unstable in the first place, and in the early
stages of a fundamental change.

North Carolina prohibited whites from gambling with slaves. This
was thought to be corrupting to the slave population.[312] An interesting
picture emerges from these laws. Among some sections of the white
population, the caste lines had almost disappeared, and one form of
amusement was to play with slaves as equals. The fear that this would
"corrupt" the slave population was palpable enough. If slaves were
treated as equals in matters of recreation, the whole caste structure
could crumble. If however, the association with whites, though for pleasure, was with the master's benign condescension, it was allowed and approved.

Here too, there was a difference in attitude between the slaveowners, who were also Supreme Court justices, and the lower strata of
the white community. STATE v. BOYCE [313] was a uniquely apt illustration of the leeway permitted by the rulers of the slave society, in contrast to the restraints which the lower orders wanted to impose.

The defendant-slaveowner had been convicted of keeping a disorderly house. The conviction itself revealed the views of the jurors:

> A witness stated, that at Christmas, 1845, he went to a
> Negro quarter on the defendant's plantation, about 200
> yards from his dwelling house, and found a quilting going
> on and dancing by Negroes. A daughter of the defendant
> was there, and some of the Negroes did not belong there.
>
> Roberts deposed that on Christmas night 1846, he and

other patrollers went to the defendant's plantation between 8 and 9 o'clock. There was much noise. They went to the Negro quarter first and found several Negroes dancing. They then went to the house in which Boyce lived and found therein twelve or fifteen Negroes, of whom one was fiddling, and the others dancing and talking loud. Some acted as if they were drunk, and he smelt spirits.

The Court instructed the jury, that if they found that the defendant had upon two or three occasions suffered white persons and Negroes of both sexes to meet together at his house and fiddle and dance together, and drink and make a noise so as to disturb the public, they should find the defendant guilty. The jury accordingly found the defendant guilty, and after sentence he appealed.

The Supreme Court reversed the conviction with the following paternalistic observations, diverging from the attitudes both of the jury and the trial judge.

It would really be a source of regret, if contrary to common custom it were denied to slaves in the intervals between their toils, to indulge in mirthful pastimes. But it is clearly not so. We may let them make the most of their idle hours, and may well make allowances for the noisy outpourings of glad hearts, which providence bestows as a blessing on corporal vigor united to a vacant mind.

There was nothing contrary to words or law in all that unless it is that one feel aggrieved that these poor people should for a short space be happy at finding the authority of the master give place to his benignity, and at being freed from care. Then, as to the ingredient that some of the white people also joined in their dance, there is much question as to the truth. But supposing it to be so, though it be not according to the custom of this part of the country, there is nothing in it forbidden by law. And it is very possible that the children of the family might, in Christmas times, without the least impropriety, countenance the festivities of the old servants of the family by witnessing, and even mingling in them.

Selling liquor to slaves came under a double prohibition. There was the general objection to trading. There was also the concern over having them become drunk or obstreperous without authority from the master. A new statute forbidding free Negroes from selling any liquor whatever (except of their own make)[314] was undoubtedly aimed at preventing sales to slaves. There were only a few cases, and as far as they went, indicated increasing severity.[315]

At the end of the preceding decade, North Carolina was coming abreast of the more developed slave states as two of its counties required a white overseer to be kept on all plantations having fifteen or more slaves.[316] Yet, as assimilation to the large plantation economy and to the new industrial economy went almost together, slaves might be sent to do the road work demanded of most citizens.[316a]

The initial handicap of free Negroes and Mulattoes was epitomized in a case just cited,[317] in which a black person was presumed to be a slave. Such rights as were accorded to them went only to those able to prove their "freedom."

The 1830's however, brought a striking new development. For the first time, colored apprentices in North Carolina were ruled to be covered by the law of 1762 that said apprentices must be taught to read and write.[318] Putting this provision into practice for free Negroes went much further than the previous statutory exception which authorized teaching slaves arithmetic.[319]

Here again, there were faint signs of "overstepping." As late as 1850, North Carolina still had the third largest number of native-born illiterates in the nation.[320] At the same time, she had the second highest number of pupils among the slave states.[321] Insisting that colored apprentices be taught to read and write was a complete reversal of the policy by which other slave states were bent on creating an illiterate (and therefore incompetent) caste.[321a] The remarks of the State Supreme Court in DOWD v. DAVIS[322] show that this new enlightened attitude was something which had just begun to appear at the beginning of the 1830s. Otherwise the legislation on free Negroes was restrictive, reflecting the general hostility of the slave states.[323]

The judicial decisions swing like a pendulum. Every second or third adjudication for or against a free Negro was accompanied by a philosophical enunciation of society's attitude toward such persons. In 1833, the North Carolina Supreme Court made a ringing declaration on the property rights of free Negroes, and then declined to honor them in the case before it.[324] The laws against selling free Negroes as slaves were rigorously enforced. Violation was punished by death.[325] Until free Negroes were flatly excluded form the poor debtors act,[326] the courts seemed anxious to find excuses for giving them its benefits.[327]

More interesting than specific holdings were the fluctuating views of the status of free Negroes in North Carolina. First came an altogether favorable view, recalling that before the Revolutionary War their status had even been higher than it was in the 1830's. STATE v. MANUEL (1838) noted:[328]

> Upon the Revolution slaves remained slaves. Slaves man-umitted were become freemen, and therefore, if born within North Carolina, are citizens of the State. Our constitution extended the elective franchise to every freeman who had arrived at the age of 21, and paid a public tax. And it is a matter of universal notoriety that under it, free persons, without regard to color, exercised the franchise until it was taken from freemen of color a few years since by our amended constitution. But the possession of political power is not essential to constitute a citizen.

Only six years afterwards the climate changed. STATE v. NEWSOM, (1844), stated:

> Free people of color cannot be considered as citizens in the largest sense of the term, or if they are, they occupy such a position in society, as justifies the legislature in adopting a course of policy in its acts peculiar to them, so that they do not violate those great principles of justice, which ought to be at the foundation of all laws. There was error in rendering judgment against the State on charge of carrying a gun without a license .

Four years later the pendulum swung back and an acquittal on a charge of carrying a pistol without a license was affirmed on reasoning almost opposite to that of 1844. STATE v. LAW (1848) reasoned:

> Degraded as are these individuals as a class, by their social positions, it is certain that among them are many worthy of all confidence, and into whose hands these weapons can be safely trusted. He was complying with a contract, he had a right to make.

By 1850 however, the North Carolina Supreme Court was saying that white people were entitled to treat free Negroes like slaves. STATE v. POWERS (1850) arose from a minor dispute.

The defendant, a white man, was indicted for an affray

with Bob Douglass, a free black man. The defendant and Bob got into a quarrel when the defendant asked Bob why he had reported that he, the defendant, had told a lie, to which Bob replied, because he had told one. Upon this the defendant struck Bob, and a fight ensued, in the course of which Bob struck the defendant with the butt of a wagon whip, and the latter knocked him down with the broken limb of a tree.

The presiding judge charged that though the Courts may have held that insulting language used by a slave may justify a white man in striking him, yet this principle did not apply to the case of a free Negro stricken under similar circumstances by a white man. The defendant was convicted, and judgment being pronounced against him, appealed.

The North Carolina Supreme Court ruled however that,

A free Negro has no master to correct him, and unless a white man to whom insolence is given has a right to put a stop to it in an extra-judicial way, there is no remedy for it. This would be insufferable. Hence, we infer from the principles of common law, that this extra-judicial remedy is excusable, provided the words or acts of a free Negro be in law insolent.

The notable feature of this case was that the jury and trial judge, all commoners, were more favorable to the free Negro than the State Supreme Court. Lines were already being drawn for a hundred years to come. The ruling stratum was strong enough to take the state into secession, but signs were appearing that North Carolina would, of all the seceded states, most readily adapt to the conquering industrial economy.

There were no attempts out of North Carolina to continue the African slave trade. But impending abolition was forecast, both in resolutions and counter-resolutions between the slave and non-slave states, and in statutes by which the later sought to nullify the Fugitive Slave Act of 1850. [329]

The North Carolina resolutions of 1835 and 1848 regarding abolition activities and slavery in the territories, have already been mentioned. [330] In 1850, the legislature passed another "Resolution in relation to Vermont," [331] acidly objecting to advice from Vermont on how to keep the peace, and decrying Vermont's supposed nullification of the Fugitive Slave Act. Before the courts, impending abolition manifested itself only indirectly in the activities of the Quakers[332] and the dream of shipping ex-slaves to Liberia.[333]

In South Carolina, the mobility of slaves was taken for granted, and newly recognized by forbidding slaves to be brought back who had been taken to other states.[334] It was reaffirmed in 1847 and 1848 by permitting slaves to be brought back from Cuba,[335] and from the Maryland ports on Chesapeake Bay, especially Baltimore.[336] There were no further statutes on fugitive slaves.

In court cases it appeared often enough that slaves were not tied to the soil, especially with the trend to leave South Carolina for the South and West.[337] South Carolina seems to have felt almost no pressure from Abolitionists spiriting slaves to the industrial regions of the north. The cases took a peculiar course.

Until 1839, fugitive slaves appeared several times, but they were almost all fugitives within South Carolina (or other slave states). Slave owners looked at this sort of running away as one of the facts of life, and shrugged their shoulders at it.[338] When the movement west and south was under way, escaping sometimes took a reverse form. The slave would refuse to leave South Carolina with the master.[339] This, too was tolerated almost as a matter of course. In one case, slaves even returned to South Carolina after having been declared free in the Bahamas.[340] Beginning with the 1840's, with Abolitionist activity mounting, fugitive slave cases almost disappeared.[341]

In 1837, the South Carolina Legislature imposed fine and imprisonment for the abduction of free colored persons living in the state.[342] This indirect reaction was the only new statutory consequence of the illegalization of the foreign slave trade. Though the prices of slaves were steadily going up,[343] there were no cases of foreign slave trade. There was just one tangible effect—privileged treatment for breeding women.[343a]

In 1833, South Carolina discarded relics of more barbarous punishments (like cutting off ears or castration), leaving only whipping and confinement in stocks or on a treadmill.[344] In 1834, the state introduced imprisonment for slaves.[345] There was no longer a labor shortage, and South Carolina's economy had become static. Only one case mentioned punishment of slaves by masters. South Carolina was making a small effort to get something more efficient than physical penalties.[346] Separating slaves from their families was now used as a sanction.[347]

In 1839, the state made all free whites, citizens or aliens, subject to patrol duty if they resided within the state for six months.[347a] Patrols

were authorized to whip slaves found off their master's plantation
without a pass, but were fined fifty dollars for whipping a slave on his
proper plantation or in possession of a pass.[347b] Fines were also imposed
on the patrol for disorderly conduct.[347c] In 1845 the Commissioners of
Cross Roads on Charleston Neck were authorized to build a guard house
in which to lodge slaves seized by patrols, again showing that labor
shortage in South Carolina was a thing of the past.[347d]

The scare caused by Denmark Vesey's rebellion [348] was subsiding,
and Nat Turner's in Virginia seemed to have little impact. After the
middle 1830's, South Carolina resumed her tight reins on patrols. They
were governed by regulations almost as severe as those on the slaves
themselves. In TENANT v. DANDY,[349] the Supreme Court affirmed a
judgment for damages against the captain of a patrol for whipping a
slave before 9 PM (when the patrol's authority commenced). The court's
remarks are significant.

> Slaves are our most valuable property. Too many guards
> cannot be interposed between it and violent unprincipled
> men. The slave ought to be fully aware that his master is
> to him a perfect security from injury. When this is the
> case, the relation of master and servant becomes little
> short of that of parent and child, and hence result in
> those striking instances of devotion, which, at least on
> one occasion in this state, induced a slave to peril his life
> to save that of his master, and failing in that attempt,
> nobly to perish with him.[350]

The important thing in this case was that the patrol was punished
criminally for unlawfully whipping slaves who were holding a quilting
party by permission. The attitude toward such diversions[352] was substantially the same as that expressed in the North Carolina decision of
STATE v. BOYCE.[353]   But the South Carolina court went much
further. While STATE v. BOYCE merely relieved the master from the
charge of keeping a disorderly house, STATE v. BOOZER penalized the
patrol.

The statute books retained the requirement that there be a white
man capable of patrol duty, but in the entire twenty years, 1830–1850,
only one such case reached the appellate courts.[353a] Thus, for good or
evil, South Carolina approached the Great Debate of 1850 with one foot
still in the 18th century. South Carolina slaveowners felt a virtually
feudal relationship to their slaves. This attitude ran like a thread
through statutes and judicial decisions. The only statute during the two

decades raised unlawful whipping or beating of a slave to an indictable offense.[355]   While this act refers to persons not having charge of slaves, it expresses the attitude of the time.

Yet after 1830, all was not well. Behavior towards slaves began to polarize side by side with the old noblesse oblige, resulting in an increasing violence towards them.   Quite apart from Abolitionist propaganda, South Carolina society appeared to be breaking up.   The most noticeable sign of survival of the old order was that many slaves were still in command of ships.[356]   Unlike the rule on large plantations,[357] the master was liable by respondent superior for acts of his slaves[358] which took place on board ship.

Delcarations of the close affinity between master and slave abound.   They were even more striking for their affirmation of the intimacy, than for the mere demand that slaves be treated well.[359] Kind treatment was put forth as the best way to combat Abolitionist activities,[360] but there was also a noticeable increase in the number of slaves murdered,[361] or subject to mistreatment coming close to murder.[362]

No new legislation directly touched sexual relations between whites and Negroes, but there were numerous statutes dealing with "free colored."[363]   The cases likewise took sexual relations as a matter of course.[364] The resulting caste or status of children follows no iron-clad rule, but depends upon the circumstances of each case.[365]

After 1830, South Carolina virtually ruled out emancipation. The law of 1841 even made void emancipation with the intention of removing the freedman out of the state.[366]   After that date, judicial decisions effectively eliminated direct emancipation.[367]   For a long time, South Carolina recognized what other states generally denied,[368] emancipation by prescription.   Twenty years acting as a freeman (and sometimes less) made a person free in law.[369]   But towards the end of the 1840's a divided South Carolina Supreme Court turned its back even on that rule.[370]

There was no new legislation on the relations between slaveowners. In this area, South Carolina became even more static than Virginia and North Carolina. But as in these states, there was plenty of private litigation. As elsewhere, the closing of the legal slave trade led to a steady increase in the price of slaves.[371]   Prices or valuation, account for about three quarters of the private litigation between 1830 and 1850. "In this State, slaves are a more valuable part of our property, than even land,"[372] said one prominent South Carolinian.

Prices for slaves in good health ranged from $210[373] to $1,500.[374] If the slaves were diseased, the prices were lower, but still high enough.[375]   Other litigation between slaveowners, with accompanying subordinate rules, are listed in the footnote.[376]   Slaves were taxed 60¢ a head until 1842.[377]   The tax was then reduced to 55¢[378] and to 52¢ in 1847,[379] but raised again to 56¢ in 1849.[380]

Lunatic asylums were not made available to colored persons until 1848.[381]   This was undoubtedly one of the several relics of feudalism in South Carolina.   Until the middle of the 19th century (and less than 20 years before Abolition), the owners of slaves, or the guardians of free colored, were expected to care for them if they became insane,[381a] rather than the state.   After the rash of private acts during the 1820's granting compensation for executed slaves,[382] the legislature passed a general compensation law in 1843, with a $200 maximum.[383]

As the 19th century wore on, South Carolina's ruling class made the trial of slaves more and more its exclusive province.[384]   In 1843 however, there was a concession to what was probably popular clamor, and assault with intent to rape was made a capital offense.[385]   The courts stayed pretty strictly with the principle of protecting slave property rather than punishing the slave, wherever the two clashed.[386] They also allowed retrials after a hung jury,[387] rejecting the extreme position of North Carolina.[388]   Only a few courts reported cases that enforced severe penalties.[389]   But if there was anything that marked South Carolina as still living in the 18th century, it was a new statute imposing criminal penalties for concealing or conveying away slaves accused of capital crimes.[390]

South Carolina strictly enforced the laws against slaves trading for themselves.   Doubts and presumptions were resolved against the defendant, and statutes were added in 1834, 1836 and 1849 designed to make the prohibition more effective.[391]   There were likewise a considerable number of cases on trading with slaves, or allowing them to trade for themselves. Most of these resulted in convictions.[392]

Like North Carolina, South Carolina sought to prevent gaming between free persons and slaves.[392a] Violators were occasionally brought to court[393] where the laws were applied very strictly, but the fact that there were fewer cases than in North Carolina, indicates that the caste lines were more firmly drawn.

There were only a few cases of selling liquor to slaves.[394]   With a firmer caste society, South Carolina did not seem to have had as much trouble with this activity as her neighbor to the north.   A series of isolated instances (statutes and cases) of relations between the state and slaveowners are given in the footnote.[395]

South Carolina continued the same schizophrenic policy toward free Negroes which it began in the 1820's.   Since 1822 they had to have a guardian,[396] but that done, they were treated more like slaves. They were object of a good deal of paternalistic generosity,[397] but were subjected to heavier penalties than before and excluded from some types of work.[398]　Domestic free Negroes could own slaves.[399]　Those from outside the state continued to be excluded.[400]　Passing from free colored to free white was considered a political, rather than a legal question, left to the reactions of whatever jury tried the case.[401]

There were no statutes and no cases during the 1830's and 1840's dealing directly either with Abolition or the slave trade. Impending Abolition hung over the state, stifling the atmosphere. For the present, its practical impact comes through the British West Indies, where Abolition had already been accomplished.[402]　Expressions of opinion against Abolition and in favor of southern institutions were welcomed with a suggestion of desperation.[403]

By 1850, the world had moved away from South Carolina, and South Carolina was not taking it well. In the 18th century, a ruling class accepting its position as a matter of course displayed a supercilious generosity. With its position no longer secure, it tried to stiffen against the oncoming tide. The result was disastrous. Only a few years later, Hinton Rowan Helper would write:

> Poor South Carolina. Folly is her nightcap. Fanaticism is her day-dream. Fire-eating is her pastime. She has lost her better judgment; the dictates of reason and philosophy have no influence upon her actions.[404]

Slavery was dying out in Delaware between 1830 and 1850, so much so that the Legislature passed resolutions against the extension of slavery and against the annexation of Texas.[405]　Even marriages of slaves received limited recognition.[406]　There was some legislation on legal[407] and illegal[408] exportation and importation of slaves, and a few private acts.[409]　All other statutes concerned free Negroes.[410]

However the judicial decisions show how medieval the state remained, despite her moribund slave system. Unlike North Carolina,[411] free colored apprentices were not taught to read and write.[412]　On the other hand, there was no presumption of slavery from color,[413] for the simple, practical reason that the number of free colored was far greater than the number of slaves in the state. And, as a corollary, free colored were almost always qualified as witnesses.[414]

Otherwise there was only a handful of cases on slaves during the twenty-year period.[415]　The great majority of disputes reaching the courts concerned free Negroes.[416]　An amusing illustration of people's fear of the unknown were the dire forebodings expressed by the Delaware Supreme Court if free Negroes were allowed to hold slaves.[417] It also shows how far the states were isolated from each other. It was not necessary to go further than South Carolina for a contrary precedent.[418]

The migration of slaveowners continued in Georgia as in the other Eastern states.[418a] After 1830, most of the movement was away from Georgia,[419] although there remained a remnant of the earlier migration to the state.[420] In the 1840's, Georgia tightened her fugitive slave laws,[421] showing that northern industrial Abolitionist activities had gone that far south. During the 1830-1850 decades, Georgia was entirely outside the temptations of the illegal slave trade. There were neither statutes[422] nor cases.

Georgia, as a new slave state, retained corporal punishment without substantial alteration.[423] No cases reached the appellate courts. Patrol-riding showed Georgia was a frontier society adopting the ways of an industrial community. The Code of 1845 expressly exempted women from patrol duty,[424] indicating that it had been required of them before. In this respect, Georgia was a frontier state. On the other hand, Georgia was almost at the opposite pole from 18th century South Carolina, where patrol riding was a diversion for gentlemen.[425]

From the beginning of the 1830's, the statutes show a concern with defaulters from patrol duty.[426] Ten years later, a poll tax was imposed in Columbus to allow commutation from patrol service.[427] From a gentleman's pastime, patrolling had become an unpleasant burden. Those who could, simply bought their way out. The pendulum had swung from the feudal to the industrial age.

Georgia had enacted a sixteen-hour law in 1755.[428] In 1833, a general law made it criminal to "require greater labor from such slave or slaves than he, she, or they are able to perform."[429] Georgia continued to follow the basic rule of a slave economy, that the master had to furnish the slaves with adequate food, clothing and medical attention.[430]   Like North Carolina,[431] Georgia allowed a certain amount of peculium (private property) to slaves.[432] The few cases reported on the general subject of good treatment are given in the footnote.[433]

If owners did not take sufficient care of infirm slaves, the state assumed care, and charged the expenses to the owner.[434] Here we see a stage midway between landed aristocracy, and industrial society as described by de Tocqueville.[435]

Restrictions on the emancipation of incapable slaves were

swallowed up by the denial of any but special legislative emancipations. Prohibition of cruelty to slaves was part of the same statutes which limited hours of labor and required sufficient food and clothing.[436] In her legislation on duties of masters towards slaves, Georgia presented the picture of a classical slave state. Only the sparsity of litigation echoed the frontier.

Georgia used the same expression as other slave states—"free person of color"—implying that Mulattoes, or other proportions of mixed blood were taken for granted. Sometimes Mulattoes were expressly distinguished from Negroes.[437] Two verdicts of freedom show that juries were willing to apply legal rules in practice. Freedom was claimed by descent from a white woman in South Carolina[438] and granted by a jury, but very few such cases reached the courts.

Georgia continued to operate under the law of 1818[439] that halted virtually all emancipations, except those granted by the legislature. The courts generally enforced this rule.[441] Manumissions which sent freedmen out of the state were encouraged.[443] Georgia still had traces of her original policy of excluding slaves altogether.

In 1842, Georgia refused to apply the fellow-servant rule to slaves.[444] The decision was based upon both "interest to the owner, and humanity to the slave." Of course, "interest to the owner" was paramount. However hypocritical some considerations of humanity might be, there was also genuine humanity. The fellow servant rule, like assumption of risk, was designed to free budding industry from the costs of "human overhead".[445] The slave system could not afford the bloody efficiency of rising industrialism, climbing to the top on the corpses and mangled bodies of its workers. As a result, it was both more humane and less efficient.[446]

Nearly all litigation between slaveowners came over prices. On the whole, they were somewhat lower than in the Carolinas or Louisiana, generally around $500.[447] In a few instances however, they went as high as $1,700.[448]   Besides these controversies, there were some miscellaneous contests between slaveholders.[449]

Taxing acts were not included in the Georgia statutes after 1830. There were neither statutes nor cases on the care of lunatic slaves. The state was perhaps too close to the frontier to bother with this problem. Compensation for executed slaves was like the proverbial chapter on "snakes in Ireland." Allegedly, "there are no snakes in Ireland." Georgia expressly refused to compensate the master for any slave executed by legal process.[450] Georgia's character as a frontier community came to the fore in yielding to the popular clamor for punishment of slaves at the expense of slaveowners' property.[451]   Any such tendency was of course, much aggravated in a state which granted no compensation for executed slaves.

Another indication of the same social balance (or imbalance) was the exceptional rule that in one county freeholders trying slaves need not be slaveholders. [452]   The anxiety of slaveowners to protect their slave property was not wholly absent however, and on some occasions, got the upper hand. [453]   In non-capital cases, the master had to pay the expenses of prosecution. In capital cases, the state paid them.[453a]

Traces of Georgia's original prohibition of slavery continued well into the 19th century. The state could not make up her mind whether or not to allow slaves to be brought in from other states. Prohibition alternated with repealers, and repealers of repealers, throughout the 1830's and 1840's. [454] Concealing slaves was considered a phase of slave-stealing, not of escaping the law. If the person concealing the slave had a well-founded claim of ownership,[455] it was thought to be a good defense to a charge of concealment.

Georgia statutes showed great concern about slaves trading for themselves, [456] which indicates a certain looseness in the slave society. This undoubtedly reaches back to the time when Georgia had no slaves. When slaves were introduced, a hybrid system evolved. Other aspects of the relationship between the state and slaveowners ranged all the way from a law against selling drugs to slaves, to payment for services of slaves at the state arsenal.[457]   There was also the eternal problem of gambling between slaves and whites.[458]

Georgia's position with regard to free Negroes was summarized by the State Supreme Court in COOPER & WORSHAM, etc. v. MAYOR AND ALDERMAN:[459]

> Free Negroes and person of color have never been recognized here as citizens.   They have always been regarded as our wards, and we should be extremely careful to guard the right secured to them by our municipal regulations. They have no political rights, but they have personal rights, one of which is personal liberty. When we take into consideration the object of the ordinance, our minds are irresistably forced to the conclusion that the section which imposed the payment of one hundred dollars is nothing but a tax, and being a tax, its collection cannot be enforced by the imprisonment of the petitioners. The mode for collecting is pointed out by the act of 1815, which provides the petitioners shall be

hired out, and that portion of the ordinance which
declares that prisoners shall be imprisoned for the non-
payment is repugnant to the laws of the State and
void.[460]

Thus, for non-payment of taxes free Negroes could be hired out, but
not imprisoned. That delineates their "personal rights." Repeal of the
right to sell, (as distinguished from hiring out) free Negroes into slavery
was reaffirmed in 1846.[461] Masters of indentured free Negroes had to
furnish them with sufficient food and clothing. The servant was transferred to another master if a complaint was made and sustained.[462] If
convicted of being unregistered, free Negroes were not compelled to
leave the state.[462a] Persons held as slaves but claiming freedom were
treated as free, pending litigation.[462b]

Otherwise the laws imposed restrictions. They did not grant
rights. Free Negroes were more heavily penalized for harboring
slaves.[463] The long list of disabilities in the Code of 1845 forbids them
from holding slaves,[464] from making conveyances,[465] and from getting
credit of any kind except on a written order of their guardian.[466] If insolvent, they could be bound out to service.[467] If any one claimed a
free Negro defendant as a slave, he could make an oath and withdraw
the defendant from the prosecution. Otherwise the penalties on free
Negroes were imposed.[468]

Free Negroes were heavily poll-taxed, while whites over 60 were
exempted in 1842.[469] They were still subject to road duty[470] however,
as they were in other states.[471] Finally, any one could file a complaint
against anyone else, alleging that he was wrongfully claiming to be a
free white and was in reality only a free Negro.[472] On the frontier,
with its many insecurities, "passing" was taken less casually than in settled, patrician and self-satisfied South Carolina.[473] The illegal slave
trade did not raise its head in Georgia during the 1830's and 1840's, nor
were there any reactions to the Abolition movement beyond the indirect
ones which have already been mentioned.

In a diluted form, Georgia continued the anomalies of her history.
The last, and southern-most of the original thirteen colonies, and the only colony originally without slavery, she was partially a frontier state
well into the 19th century. Geographically she was removed from northern Abolitionist activities, but retained hesitancies which can be read
most simply as remnants of the policy of excluding slavery. Yet the
state was a major cotton producer and would join the secession without
question.

From 1830 to 1850, Louisiana seemed to be an old-style slave state which was still prosperous. She was not on the frontier like Georgia, nor was she a savage new slave state like Mississippi. Nor did lost glories deprive her of judgment, like South Carolina. She was prosperous[473a] enough, so that unlike Virginia,[474] free persons of color could recover damages for the time they were unlawfully held in slavery.[475]

Westward expansion however, did not leave her untouched. As a result, Louisiana was similar to Georgia in one respect. Slaves not tied to the soil were moved in [476] and out of the state. [477] As long as Texas was Mexican, and did not allow slavery, the fugitive slave problem was very real. [478] But Louisiana slavery too, was approaching its end. The days of labor shortages were past. Imprisonment was now used to punish slaves. [479] The slave system could not long survive.

There was a single case on the foreign slave trade, one with South America.[480] The court dodged the necessity of condemning the vessel by presuming the transported Negro to be a freeman. However, litigation still flowed from the condemnation of the ship the Josefa Segunda.[480a]

In general, Louisiana continued the classical pattern of corporal punishment for slaves. New statutes appeared[481] because the industrial revolution brought new situations and new problems.[482] As already noted, imprisonment for slaves was one of the first signs of a labor surplus.[483] There were neither new statutes nor cases on patrols in Louisiana during the 1830-1850 decades. This indicates that things were running smoothly—in sharp contrast to the bumpy road of the patrol system in declining South Carolina.[484]. Only ARNANDEZ v. LAWES[485] deals with the kind of activity which would be performed by patrols. While giving patrols lip service, the court awarded damages for their abuses. The same is true in the field of maximum hours. "No news is good news", and the fact that the question was nowhere the subject of legal attention indicates that no problems arose on this score.[485a]

It wasn't difficult for a state as rich, and as much at home in the old slave system as Louisiana, to continue her laws for the adequate care of slaves.[486] It also required support for aged and infirm slaves[487] and prohibited cruel treatment.[488] A picture perhaps overdrawn, but yet important, was the New Orleans household in Uncle Tom's Cabin.

During the 1830's and 1840's, Louisiana statutes continued to take white-Negro mixtures for granted. Free persons were always referred to as "free persons of color."[489] The courts did likewise. The issue of mixed unions were seen as part of the everyday world.[490] There were also a large number of cases[491] dealing specifically with sexual relations between blacks and whites. Perhaps the best commentary on the community's attitude toward such liaisons was the extraordinarily high position of the free colored in Louisiana society, which is set forth below.

After 1831, [491a] Louisiana's general policy was against emancipation. In 1846, an act was passed specifically providing that freedom did not follow being on free soil. [492] There were a few private emancipation acts. [493] At first the majority of cases denied manumission when the question came up in court. [494] By the 1840's though, there was a shift towards upholding emancipation. [495]

From 1830 to 1850, there were two private acts which indirectly involved dealings between slaveowners. [496] The cases in court present the usual run-of-the-mill series of private disagreements. [497] Prices were very high-ranging up to about $2,000 for a single slave. [498] This undoubtedly reflected the prosperity of Louisiana. Such prices were asked and paid because they could be obtained, in sharp contrast to the modest rates in Georgia. [499] Masters were consistently held liable in respondent superior for a slave's acts. [500] The South Carolina exemption for large plantations [501] was never mentioned. As in the past, Louisiana was plagued by the problem of slaves who drank to excess. Characteristically, this was not held to be any reason for rescinding a sale. [502]

Louisiana statutes did not list individual taxes for each year. [503] The main innovation was a special tax on "Negro traders." [504] There were also a few private acts. [505] There were no cases, or were there as in some other states, legal problems arising from insane slaves. New statutes generally continued the schedule of compensation payments for executed slaves that were previously in force. [506] As in the previous decade, there was a string of private compensation acts [507] in addition to the general statutes.

Consistent with her condition as an old-line slave state which was still prosperous, Louisiana continued the system of trying slaves before a jury of slaveholders. [508] But signs of tension began to appear. There were many more prosecutions of slaves for violent crimes than during the preceding decade. [509] Even here however, a large percentage of the convictions were reversed. Penalties for secreting or hiding away slaves charged with crimes disappeared from Louisiana jurisprudence. Of all the states, Louisiana was the one in which the slave system was then functioning most smoothly.

Apart from selling liquor to slaves, Louisiana had only one case after 1804 concerned with slaves trading for themselves. [510] This was another instance where the state's prosperous economy caused fewer difficulties than the system did in many other states. Louisiana, like other states, did not allow liquor to be sold to, or by slaves.[514] Curiously, the state seemed to promote its special difficulty of drunken slaves by forbidding only the selling, but permitting liquor to be given to slaves.[515]

The status of free Negroes and Mulattoes in Louisiana was far removed from the lowly position which they occupied in North[516] and South Carolina,[517] and Kentucky.[517a] Foremost among court decisions was MACARTY v. MANDEVILLE[518] which describes the family of the decedent's colored concubine as "one of the most distinguished in Louisiana." The estate which was awarded to her (rather than to the decedent's collateral heirs) as being the product of her own labor, was appraised at $155,000.[519] STATE v. LEVY & DREYFUS[520] decided in 1850, gives a bird's-eye view of the condition of free persons of color in Louisiana, pointing out how far it differed from that of the same persons in the other slave states.

> Our legislation and jurisprudence upon this subject differ materially from those of the slave states generally. This difference had no doubt arisen from different condition of that class. At the date of our earliest legislation, as well as at the present day, free persons of color constituted a numerous class. In some districts they are respectable for their intelligence, industry and habits of good order. Many are enlightened by education, and the instances are by no means rare in which they are large property holders. Such persons as courts and juries would not hesitate to believe them under oath.

In the light of subsequent history, it is an indication that in 1839, the Supreme Court of Louisiana referred to a free man of color as "Mr. Jones".[521] Persons of color were presumed to be free[522]—exactly opposite from the rule in North Carolina.[523] Nor was the $155,000 estate in McCARTY v. MANDEVILLE a lone exception. Recorded estates of free colored in Louisiana ran from $2925[524] to $184,640.[525] There was also a series of pension acts to colored veterans, first granting, then increasing the pensions.[526] This was a logical continuation of the policy of having enlisted colored soldiers in the war of 1812.[527]

Most significantly, Louisiana allowed free Negroes wrongfully held in slavery to recover damages or compensation. Earlier in the century, the Louisiana Supreme Court had avoided deciding this question.[528] But after 1830, compensation or damages were regularly granted,[529] showing how much the economic condition of Louisiana had improved, while Virginia's deteriorated.[530] Actions for wages were sustained in the ordinary way,[531] and as in the past, [532] free persons of color could hold slaves.[533]   They were seen as competent witnesses against whites, [534] and there was a whole string of laws for the protection of their civil and property rights,[535] as well as the rights of state liberi.[536]

There were a remarkably few cases restricting the rights of free persons of color. [538] But a foretaste of the future came in a decision of 1838, that states that "freedom" destroys the right to support.[539]   All this however, applied to free persons of color within Louisiana. Those seeking to enter from other states were excluded from Louisiana,[540] as was the custom elsewhere in the slave regions. There were no further consequences of the abolition of the slave trade beyond the few mentioned above.[541]   In view of her geographical location, Louisiana felt little impact from the Abolition movement.[542]

Kentucky was unique. She was the only state where slavery came to a full, active bloom, but which nevertheless remained with the Union in 1861. Several characteristics distinguished the state. The immigration into it was largely by slaveowners with the experience and tradition of a settled society and the noblesse oblige of a superior caste. By the 1850 census, Kentucky had 210,981 slaves. [543] Secondly, Kentucky was a new tobacco state, just beginning the cycle of overproduction[544] which Virginia had entered more than a century and a half before.[545]   Thirdly, Kentucky was a border state.   Immediately to the north lay Ohio, Michigan, and then Canada. Finally, the combination of these factors produced the seemingly contradictory rule that immigrants could import slaves, but persons residing in Kentucky could not.

The fact that slaves could move with their masters, along with a considerable concern over fugitive slaves, were necessary consequences of Kentucky's history and geographical location. Kentucky attracted slaveowners who brought along their slaves. Her whole development was based on slaves not being tied to the soil. [546] Yet as a border slave state, and close to Canada, she had endless difficulties with fugitive slaves. [547] And because of her inland position, Kentucky felt no legal repercussions from the prohibition of the foreign slave trade.[548]

Corporal punishment for slaves fit naturally into Kentucky's position. [549] A new slave state blooming in full flower, she had the usual motives for methods of discipline which did not remove slaves from their work. But there were few statutes or cases. The Louisiana Supreme Court's description of the mild treatment of slaves in Kentucky[550] was evidently accurate.

As Kentucky became populated, she also became more interested in patrols.[551-2] However gently she may have treated her slaves, she established a full-fledged patrol system in the best tradition of the older slave states.[553]   The one innovation probably came as the result of lessons learned from the sad experiences of other states. [554] Patrols could be required to put up a bond to indemnify anyone they may have injured. [555]   There was only one case on patrols during the two decades,[556] indicating that while Kentucky had the classical machinery, she did not often use force on her slaves.

As in the past, Kentucky had no maximum labor laws. But here again, NOTT v. BETTS[557] suggests that she did not need any. The 1850 Revision continued the former policy[558] of requiring the master to furnish adequate food and clothing,[559] as well as to care for overaged, insane, or otherwise infirm slaves.[560]

In both instances, Kentucky showed herself not to be a classical slave state, but rather a hybrid between the slave states and the industrial "free" states. Slaves, if mistreated, were sold for the benefit of the owner—approximately the same remedy used for indentured servants. The city, county or state contemplated taking over the care of infirm slaves, and charging the owner with the costs. The few judicial decisions touching the subject[561] evoked the same policy. That there were but two cases, shows that as a practical matter, such questions did not arise in Kentucky.

Like other states, Kentucky used the term "free persons of color,"— implying that at least some were not full-blooded Negroes. Other statutes specifically say "Mulattoes."[562] There were any number of cases on sexual relations between blacks and whites,[563] but marriages were prohibited "as inconsistent with decorum, social order, public policy and national sentiment." [564] A marriage implies equality between the parties, and therefore would violate the caste-structure. Kentucky approved voluntary emancipation until 1841.[565] Then the legislature began to raise barriers against it.[566] The courts however, continued to be favorable towards it throughout. [567]

The state adopted a general policy against allowing sales of slaves. But slaveowners did not feel altogether comfortable with this arrangement, and there was a whole series of private acts authorizing individual sales or purchases.[568]   The few public acts during these decades either regulated the relative rights of owners claiming an interest in the same slave or slaves, or made general authorizations for sales.[569]

The price of slaves was not as high in Kentucky, as in Louisiana. A single case fixed the value at $1500.[570] However, the maximum was generally around $1000,[571] with other prices ranging down to $90.[572] A substantial amount of litigation arising out of the hire[573] of slaves reflected the character of the immigration. Some brought slaves with them. Others did not. But all expected to work slave labor.

Slaves and land were kept together where possible.[574]   Otherwise there was the usual run of disputes between property owners,[575] with perhaps only one decision especially characteristic of Kentucky. A slave could be an agent for his owner,[576] again bearing out the view of the Louisiana Supreme Court that in Kentucky, slaves "are treated almost on equality with their master."[577]   After 1830, the practice of working hired slave labor was revealed in the taxing acts.   Kentucky was unusually explicit in her provisions about hired slaves.[578]

The general picture of Kentucky slavery leads readily to the conclusion that slaves were executed infrequently, or not at all. Though the possibilty was recognized by the statutes,[580] there was no recorded instance of it actually happening.

The same tug-of-war between slaveowners and the non-slave-holding population, which existed in a state like North Carolina also characterized Kentucky. A great many immigrants brought slaves, but many others did not. The latter were sometimes excited to mob fury against slaves. This showed up in two conflicting lines of legislation. On the one hand, slaves were subject to the death penalty for certain crimes, including rape.[581] On the other, a series of private acts granted changes of venue to slaves, sometimes noting that the slave could not get a fair trial in the county where the crime was alleged to have been committed.[583]

The crimes which carried a mandatory death penalty comprised two different classes. Capital punishment for insurrection clearly came at the behest of the slaveowners. On the other hand, rape laws were a response to mob demands,[583a] particularly on a frontier where there was a shortage of women. In some areas, the slaveowners' policy held the upper hand, and revealed a certain amount of noblesse oblige. Robbery was made a felony for white persons, but only a misdemeanor for slaves.[583b] The revision of 1850 explicitly gave masters the right to defend their slaves,[584] and continued the law according slaves the same right to trial in capital cases as free persons, a doubtful advantage.[585]

Secreting slaves to avoid prosecution drew no legal notice in Kentucky. The Revision of 1850 did not refer to it.[586] This could be inferred from the relations between slaveowners and slaves. The treatment was generally so mild that crimes were too infrequent to require legislation.

It was logical that Kentucky should have the problem of slaves trading for themselves. Yet statutes on the subject appeared relatively late,[587] which suggests that problems began when the state became settled and population increased. The device used in Louisiana since 1804[588] was adopted in Kentucky. Slaves were sent to the workhouse, not merely as a provisional remedy, but as a final judgment.[589] Presumably, the thinking went, if the master allowed the slave to trade for himself, if he held the slave with such a loose rein, then the master didn't need the slave's services very badly. In some areas of Kentucky, there evidently was no labor shortage. Likewise, litigation on the subject does not begin until 1837,[590] and then it very gradually picks up in volume.[591]

The remaining Kentucky statutes and cases are a mixed bag. Druggists could not sell poisons to slaves.[593] Prisoners in the penitentiary were segregated.[594] A railroad corporation was given power to hold slaves.[595] A jail was reimbursed for money paid out to bring back an escaped slave. On one occasion, authority was given to invest the proceeds of real estate for the benefit of a slave.[597] When a slave jumped bail, the owner was liable for the forfeited bail.[598] However, no bond was required of devisees to support two old slaves belonging to the estate, where the will provided for emancipation at age 30, and the two were over that age when the will was made.[599]

Citizens of Kentucky, as in most of the slave states, were under constant temptation to sell liquor to slaves, and sometimes to buy from them. Hence, there were the usual line of statutes and judicial decisions to impose and enforce the prohibition of this practice.[601]

Most of the statutes on free Negroes during the period 1830–1850 were private acts. These usually granted an individual exception to some general prohibition. Otherwise they made appropriations to pay government wages.[602] The general laws showed a progressive whittling away of the rights and scope of activity of free Negroes.[602a] A bond to guarantee that a freedman would not become a public charge, had to be given before a certificate of emancipation was granted.[603] Gaming with Negroes was forbidden,[603a] and after 1845 they could not manufacture or sell liquor.[604] Free Negroes were expressly disqualified from holding slaves other than members of their own family,[605] and immigration was prohibited under heavy penalties after 1850.[606]

If found guilty of a misdemeanor, free Negroes were hired out for up to six months.[608] The Code of 1850 imposed the death penalty in the same way it did on slaves, but in general, provided for imprisonment instead of corporal punishment.[609] On the other hand, free Negroes had been accorded jury trials since 1837. This was perhaps a dubious benefit, but it was the best that could be had where the master-slave relation did not exist.[609a]

Kentucky gave partial compensation for time worked by a free Negro unlawfully held in slavery, a measure of the state's prosperity.[610] In general, the courts were ready to decide in favor of an individual's freedom,[611] and they were usually willing to protect a free Negro's rights.[612] As in Louisiana,[612e] masters benefited by the slaves' freedom, as they were relieved of the duty of supporting them.[613] As an inland state, Kentucky was not concerned with the foreign slave trade, but as a border state she was much concerned with the Abolition activities of the industrializing North.[614]

Tennessee had always been like North Carolina—a state where slavery became only partially embedded. Yet the institution was more at home there. Between 1830 and 1850 there was little new legislation, but a great volume of lawsuits. Divided as the state may have been, where slavery was profitable at all, it was a brisk business. Some of the cases reveal the noblesse oblige attitudes of a superior caste which marked South Carolina.

Tennessee had her share of migration, both departures for the South and West,[615] and arrivals from the North and East.[616] Likewise, she had her share of slave stealing or enticement, again in both directions. Slaves were stolen or enticed into the industrializing North,[617] and also into the new cotton states.[618] Tennessee, being an inland state, did not have any illegal foreign slave trade.

There were no new statutes and only one case on the right of the master to discipline his slaves. But one case denied all restraints and barriers, except "life or limb". Otherwise, the master's power was absolute.[619] In 1831, patrol duty was declared an unavoidable burden which exempted the patroller from certain other duties.[619a]

In 1837, the power to appoint patrols was transferred from patrol captains to justices of the peace.[620] Presumably the patrol system was shifting from military to civilian administration. This indicates first, that slavery was functioning relatively smoothly in Tennessee, but that the organization which was taking shape was more along the lines of 19th century industrialism, than of 18th century quasi-feudalism, forewarning that Tennessee would never feel quite at home in secession. There was only one case on patrols during the 1830-1850 years, and that one restricted the patrol's scope of action.[621] Patrols were evidently falling into disuse in Tennessee—a trend directly contrary to the increasing disorders in South Carolina.[622] True to form, in 1860-61, South Carolina seceded first, Tennessee last.

Originally, slavery was too uncertain in Tennessee for the state to bother with maximum hour laws. But as the institution became stabilized, the state moved in the direction of 19th century industrialism. Maximum hour laws were out of the question. In the paternalistic care of slaves, Tennessee acted like one of the old, developed slave states. This continued into the 19th century. Not only was there the direct requirement of feeding and humane treatment,[623] but in practice the same policy extended to collateral matters, such as not separating families [624] and avoiding ownership by unsympathetic masters. [625] Legal contests simply did not arise over the support of aged or infirm slaves,[626] or cruel treatment. Tennessee developed the paternalistic side of the master–slave relation far enough so it appeared to have caused no problems.

After 1830, Tennessee had the usual run of statutes and cases referring to "free persons of color", or Mulattoes. [627] That Tennessee was an old–style, patrician slave state was shown by the fact that only the white partner was punished for cohabitation between blacks and whites.[628] However, the constitution of 1834 echoed the Abolitionist campaigns from the North. It was a constitutional rule that slaves could not be emancipated without their master's consent.[629] The statutes, however, showed a cautious broadening of the concept of emancipation,[630] and the judicial decisions were overwhelmingly favorable.[631]

There is perhaps, an explanation for the state's later history. To an extent probably unequalled anywhere else, Tennessee contained the classical features of a fully developed 18th century slave society, but at the same time had a strong tendency to walk in the footsteps of the industrializing North.

Only one new statute appeared in Tennessee between 1830 and 1850 on the relations between slaveowners,[632] but litigation was plentiful. Among other things, we are informed of the elements which determined the value of a slave:

> The value of a slave depends upon his physical strength, upon intellectual capacity, upon mental culture, upon moral worth, as fidelity, honesty, obedience, etc., and upon handicraft skill. In short, upon a thousand things. It is only in the wretched market of the slavetrader, that his value can be rated by the pound. [633]

Prices were generally moderate—in the middle hundreds,[634] with men slaves commanding consistently higher prices than women.[635]

Once in a while, prices for both men and women rose substantially over $1,000.00.[636] Hires were $100 a year, sometimes a little more for men and somewhat less for women.[637]

The concentration of slaves varied remarkably from plantation to plantation. There might be only eight on 2,000 acres,[638] 39 on 500 acres,[639] or 15 to 20 slaves on 160 acres.[640] This indicates that some parts of the state were suited to slave agriculture, but other parts less so, or not at all. It also explains Tennessee's hesitation towards secession, and its ambivalence during the Civil Was itself. Tennesseans got another glimpse of the future when slaves were used in iron mines both during and after the Civil War.[641] Forces at odds with the state's agricultural economy first served as a hobble, and later speeded accommodation with industrialism. This was underscored by the fact that by 1836 slave agriculture was known to be more profitable in Mississippi.[642] Otherwise, there was the usual train of contests between property owners,[643] with respondent superior sometimes applied,[644] sometimes denied, against the master for acts of the slave.[645]

Tennessee was like North Carolina in the shaky underpinnings of her slave system. The slaveowners were strong enough to impose their will on the entire state, but the non-slaveholding population gave them continual trouble. This first appears in the favorite point of friction between whites and blacks—rape. [646]

The legislature, evidently representing lower economic interests, imposed the death penalty for assault with intent to rape in 1841.[647] But, in not a single such case which reached the Tennessee Supreme Court, was the conviction of a slave for rape upheld.[648] There was almost the same reluctance to sustain murder convictions.[649] Other legislation attempted to give slaveowners a firm hold on the trials of their slaves. [650]

The constitution of 1834 made all slaves between twelve and fifty years old taxable. [651] Tennessee had a general tax act,[652] and not annual legislative appropriations like other states. There were still neither statutes nor cases on compensation for executed slaves.[655] Initially, the state was too imperfectly developed to have that problem. Later, she could sell recalcitrant slaves south. The disinclination to impose the death penalty and consequent readiness to reverse convictions have already been noted.

In 1831, the Legislature repealed the punishment of nailing ears to the pillory and then cutting them off. [656] Apart from the milder forms of punishment which came in with the 19th century,[657] one may infer that since the closing of the slave trade, slaveowners felt they could no songer afford permanent mutilation. The legislature likewise repealed the right to kill the "ringleader" of any plot to kill a white man, if arrest was not practicable.[657a]

Contradictory tendencies may be seen in two other laws enacted during this period. A new statute went out of its way to prohibit slaves from acting as free persons.[658] On the other hand, entry was permitted to out-of-state slave women who had married free Tennessee Negroes.[659] In short, every effort was made to keep slaves working as slaves. There were no reported instances of masters hiding slaves to avoid prosecution. As noted previously, this problem largely belonged to the past. But there was one case in which the master was punished for the mismanagement of slaves.[660]

The general problem of slaves hiring their own time seems to have been no more important during the 1830's and 1840's[661] than it had been previously.[662] The special problem of dealing in liquor looms much larger. Drunkenness among slaves played no such part in any of the states settled by the English, as it did in Louisiana, but from the middle of the 1840's, slaves in Tennessee participated in liquor traffic to an extraordinary extent.[663]

One may surmise that even in the first half of the 19th century, "moonshining" was not unknown in Tennessee. In 1845, the legislature passed a resolution directing that no penalty be imposed for the offense of tippling under the act of 1837-8, except for selling liquor to slaves.[664] In practice, slaves were neither exempt nor excluded from these popular activities.

One of the first pieces of legislation on free Negroes during these two decades, was another expression of the dream of sending them all back to Africa.[665] This brainstorm followed on the heels of an act prohibiting immigration.[666] So while emancipation was widened,[667] (provided the emancipated slave left the state) the restrictions on free Negroes within the state were made more severe.[668] Tennessee's basic philosophy about free Negroes was the same as in most states outside of Louisiana. They were viewed as "a degraded race." The Supreme Court used just those words in STATE v. CLAIBORNE:[669]

> Free Negroes have always been a degraded race in the United States with whom public opinion has never permitted white people to associate on terms of equality, and in relation to whom, the laws have never allowed the immunities of the free white citizen. The citizens spoken of are those entitled to all the privileges of citizens. But free Negroes were never in any of the states, entitled to

all, and consequently were not intended to be included.
The word 'Freeman' as used in the Bill of Rights of Tennessee is of equally extensive signification with the the
word citizens as used in the Constitution of the United
States. Although the defendant by his emancipation obtained a qualified freedom, he did not become a 'freeman'
in the sense of <u>Magna Carta</u>, or of our Constitution.

This view led to much the same paternalistic treatment given
slaves.   The   Memphis   curfew   on   free   Negroes   was   held
unconstitutional,[670] ostensibly to protect their rights, but probably
because whites needed their services after dark. (The statute and the
Court's decision are a good example of the divergent viewpoints of the
city's legislative body and the Supreme Court.)

Both extremes came through in the cases. Fraud committed <u>on</u> a
free persons of color was paternalistically remedied.[671] Fraud <u>by</u> a free
persons of color was savagely punished.[672] The judicial authorities were
generally willing to allow "freedom" to establish[673] such rights as the
statutes allowed. The disqualification of colored witnesses was however,
enforced.[674] For a while free colored persons voted in Tennessee, which
was in turn used as a reason for restricting emancipation.[675] There was
no appeal from a refusal to allow a free Negro to remain in the state,[676]
but Tennessee was one of the states which granted damages for illegally
holding a free person in slavery.[677] Aside from this, when it became
necessary to make a choice, the rules of slavery were always applied to
slaves whose emancipation was as yet in doubt.[678]

One significant law showed control of the state shifting from
slaveowners to the non-slaveholding population, with the consequent
hardening of attitudes towards free Negroes. The statute passed in
1849, imposed death by hanging on free Negroes for rape, and for being
an accessory before the fact in first degree murder.[679] This law, passed
twelve years before the Civil War, presaged the uneven way in which the
state would approach secession, and the war itself.

As an inland state, Tennessee had no legal encounters with
prohibition of the foreign slave trade. More surprising was the fact that
she did not seem to feel the impact of northern abolition agitation.
During two decades there were neither statutes nor cases. Her
geographical position probably played a part in this. First, Tennessee
had other slave states on all her borders. Second, slave agriculture was
located primarily in the western part of the state, perhaps the area least
accessible to agents from the Northeast.

As the District of Columbia, which allowed slavery but was under federal jurisdiction, became the target of Abolitionist activity, it also become a center of litigation. Statutory law was largely that of Maryland and Virginia,[680] but the amount of litigation from 1830-1850 when compared with the various states, was far out of proportion to the population. In general, the District objected to the importation of slaves, but in a few instances permitted it,[681] thereby showing that it didn't consider slaves tied to the soil. But Congress had to wrestle with the problem of damage done by fugitive slaves who had joined the Indians.[681a] There were also some prosecutions for slave stealing.[681b]

The Federal Fugitive Slave Act closed the period in 1850.[681c] It was marked by three points. First, there was the reversal of roles. Pro-slavery interests until then had been insisting on "state's rights" and freedom from federal interference. With the Federal Fugitive Slave Act, they suddenly asked and got, the federal government to aid them.[681d]

Secondly, the very severity of the act foredoomed its failure. Anyone claimed as a fugitive slave was disqualified from testifying in his or her own defense.[681c] The commissioner was awarded a fee of $10 if he found that an alleged fugitive should be returned to slavery, but only $5 if he released him.[681f] The judge's certificate in the state from which the supposed fugitive is alleged to have escaped, containing "a general description of the person so escaping with such convenient certainty as may be"[681g] was made conclusive evidence in every other state.

Finally, and most importantly, the Fugitive Slave Act was an anachronism. When the continent was unpopulated, the forcible return of fugitive laborers (slaves) was a necessary component of large-scale operations. Now, with the continent filling up, such a cumbersome method of tying workers to their jobs was not only unnecessary, but inconvenient. Forcible return of fugitive workers, a keystone in the arch of an organized society on an empty continent, became a block in the path of progress on a populated continent.

As Brooks Adams said about the French Revolution, "The environment which had once made caste a necessity, had yielded to another which made caste an impossibility."[681h] So the environment which had once made the forcible return of fugitive workers a necessity to large-scale operations, had yielded to another which made such returns an encumbrance and a nuisance.

The District of Columbia was necessarily the source of the federal statutes against the slave trade. However only one such statute was added in 1841,[682] and there was one private act,[682a] but no cases were reported during the 1830-1850 period. Patrols were not a feature of the

District.   Problems of discipline rose infrequently, but when they did, the courts restated the classical power of the master over the slave. [683]   Discipline was unlimited, provided only that no cruelty was inflicted. For crimes, corporal punishment was still imposed. [684]

Since neither Virginia nor Maryland had maximum hour laws, the District of Columbia had none either. Also, no cases arose over the requirement that masters furnish adequate food, clothing and medical attention. Quite evidently, these problems arose on large plantations, but not in a city where everyone lived close to each other, and nearly all slave labor was in domestic service. The same was true for the support of the aged and infirm, and for governmental measures to prevent emancipation from being used as a device for escaping the obligation to support non-productive slaves.

The prohibition of cruelty to slaves appears through the prosecution of serious assaults. [685]   It is a little hard to see the reason why there were at once so few such cases, but that those few should be so extreme. Perhaps the answer is that in a city, (with most of the slaves household servants) the situation did not generally arise.   One particularly violent master had immigrated to the Capitol and was still behaving in his old way.

The cases from the District of Columbia contain plenty of evidence of sexual relations between blacks and whites. [686]   One feature appears, which was almost unique on the North American continent, although well known in the West Indies. [687]   This involved the gradations of mixed blood. Some cases gave precedence to children of a free colored man and a white woman over children of a free colored man and a free colored woman. [688]

The District, in the uncomfortable position of being the capitol of a country split into near-warring factions, but deriving its own local laws from two slave states, was very strict on the law of importation and emancipation for failure to comply. Emancipations as a consequence of illegal transportation occurred constantly. [689]   The law as to voluntary emancipations was also gradually broadened. [690]   The courts found that a restrictive Maryland statute, supposedly the governing law, was intended for conditions which had ceased to exist. [691]

Among the relatively few reported valuation transactions, the sum of $600 occurs a little more often than any other price. [692]   Valuation (though not sales) of a group runs as high as $2000. [693]   One sale of 49 slaves priced them at about $386 each. [694]   There were some cases charging fraud for selling a free Negro as a slave. All were prosecuted through the criminal courts, and all resulted in acquittals. [695]   Similarly, there was an attempted extortion by seizing the complaining witness' slaves which was also pursued through the criminal courts.[696] Cheating was still a favorite pastime,[697] and there was a scattering of the usual controversies between slaveowners.[698]

Where a colored person was jailed during the trial of his suit for freedom, the United States government paid the jail fees if he or she was ultimately declared free.[699] There were no cases of insane slaves. Perhaps all slaves showing the slightest symptoms of insanity had already been sold South.

The District of Columbia did not give any compensation for executed slaves, but there were a few instances of federal compensation to slaveowners. Prize money to troops fighting fugitive slaves and Indians has already been noted.[700] Otherwise compensation arose mostly out of indemnity for violation of international rights,[701] and special pay for services to the federal government.[702]

The reluctance of slaveowners to destroy or reduce the value of their own property appears strikingly in U.S. v. FRYE,[703] where burning in the hand and twenty-five stripes was the punishment for manslaughter. That Daniel Webster's slave was acquitted on a charge of violating the curfew[704] makes amusing reading from several standpoints. For one thing, there was a disinclination to remove slaves from their work. For another, even a Senator from Massachusetts was not averse to owning a slave where it could legally be done. Slaves were also punished by stripes for disorderly meetings, but an alternative of six months in jail was added, indicating that there was no labor shortage.[705] And there was one case in which a master tried to spirit a slave away—in this instance, to avoid emancipation.[706]

There were no District of Columbia cases on slaves trading for themselves. Household servants were not prone to activities outside the home. Moreover, there were so many free colored people in the District that business which might otherwise have been done by slaves, largely found its way into their hands. Washington had an unusual rule on the ever-present question of selling liquor to slaves. Such sales were forbidden only on Sundays.[707] Here we see the concurrent operation of three factors. First, there was the city, with slaves used as household servants. On the one hand the owners wanted to be able to send them out to buy liquor. On the other, the city did not have large groups of slaves like the plantations did.

Secondly, there was the national Capitol, the center of contending factions, trying to work out a compromise. Thirdly, the compromise took the form of Sunday laws—a regimen not unknown to the New

England states themselves. Relations between slaveowners and the government do not seem to have given rise to any other problems in the District of Columbia.

Washington, as the meeting point between North and South, had a great many free Negroes. For the same reason, the city was uncertain as to what should be done with them. Statutory emancipations were protected. [708] But the children of slave women, who had been set free at a future date, were rigidly held to be slaves. [709] The liberties of free colored persons were upheld where they were serviceable to the white population. [710] Where they were not, free colored people were treated much the same as slaves. [711] The punishment for selling free Negroes into slavery was relentless, and grew more severe as time went on. [712] This was part of the larger picture of "emancipation"; i.e., changing the Negro population from the status of slaves to that of underpaid wage laborers.

The District of Columbia, not having a port, had no cases peculiar to itself arising from violation of the slave trade laws. Such cases were federal, but they have been arranged according to the states where they arose. One statute anticipates future events. Hindsight tells us that the existence of Texas as an independent nation was but a transition between being part of Mexico and being part of the United States. So transitional legislation made an exception to the slave trade laws. In 1844, slaveowners who had been residents of Arkansas and Louisiana, but who found themselves in Texas after international adjustments, were authorized to bring their slaves into the United States. [713] Over all, the District of Columbia was in the uncomfortable position of being a single city at the center of a deadly contest between two sections of the country.

As Georgia had been "the place to go" in the 1780's, so Mississippi was "the place to go" in the 1830's and 1840's. But the streaming to Mississippi was much less healthy than the earlier migration to Georgia. Too many of the immigrants to Mississippi were fleeing their creditors, [714] taking their slaves as their most moveable property, and leaving everything else behind. Mississippi was destined to be a state full of slaves, but grindingly poor. And this state of affairs existed side by side with enormously high prices paid for slaves by those who could pay. [714a] The right of immigrants to bring their slaves with them into Mississippi was insured by the Constitution of 1832:

> They the legislature shall have no power to prevent
> emigrants to this state from bringing with them such

persons as are deemed slaves by the laws of any one of the United States, so long as any person of the same age and description shall be continued in slavery by the laws of their state; provided, that such person or slave be the bona fide property of such emigrants.[715]

The same constitution,[716] and the law of 1837[717] prohibited the introduction of slaves as merchandise or for sale, but even that prohibition was repealed in 1846.[717] This mobility was used to dodge creditors. Litigation shows that absconding debtors ran both to[718] and from[719] Mississippi. Violence in other forms was also practiced between creditor and debtor.[720]   Not surprisingly, Mississippi's currency collapsed while that of other states held up:

BANK v. DOUGLASS (1848) noted:

> In the spring following April 1840, when bank notes of Mississippi banks ceased to pass, and Louisiana money became the standard of money . . .

Besides transactions like these, there was much other movement of slaves, both into,[721] and out of,[722] Mississippi. The violence which characterized the wild south, crops up in slave stealing (not merely by Abolitionists)[723] and in the use of self help to enforce or resist private claims.[724]   By 1850, the state also set up new mechanics for the taking up of runaways.[724a] In the 1830's and 1840's Mississippi was not straining against the interdiction of the foreign slave trade, and there are neither statutes nor cases. Only a few statutory changes were made during the two decades, and these were procedural.[725]

Relatively few cases arose out of disciplinary measures against slaves, despite a fairly large volume of litigation. Those which did arise gave a wide latitude to the corporal punishment which the master or overseer could impose.[726]   Decisions which avoid imposing the death penalty are considered below.

The only new statute on patrols changes the mode of their pay. Its language indicates that the patrol system itself continued unaltered.[727]   But one statute enacted as late as 1850, shows a peculiar looking to the past and the future at the same time. When practicable, a majority of each patrol had to be slave owners.[728]   This harks back to 18th century South Carolina, when patrol riding was apparently a sport of gentlemen bred to the saddle.[729]   To this extent it was opposite to contemporary South Carolina which looked down at "petty patrollers".[730]

At the same time, the proviso "when practicable" was ambiguous. It made the old law both more strict and less strict. Under the former statute, the slaveowner could send a substitute.[731] Whether he did or not was at his sole pleasure. Now the hired patroller could be sent only when it was not "practicable" for the slaveowner himself to ride patrol. The new standard was at least theoretically objective, but there was also a general recognition that at times it may not be "practicable" for the owner to come himself.

With the trend of the New Industrialism towards unlimited hours of labor, the competing cotton states did not restrict the working hours of their slaves either. And Mississippi had no laws on the subject. There were no further statutes either, on the master's obligation to care for slaves. Perhaps they were unnecessary. Judicial decisions both enforced the specific requirements of care[732] and clearly showed it working in practice. In a society as wild as Mississippi's, one was surprised to find stable and officially recognized ties of affection between master and slave.[733]

General restrictions on emancipation in Mississippi were so rigorous that there is no trace of the special restriction against "emancipating" aged or unsound slaves.[734] There were no statutes or cases on the duty of care and support for the aged and infirm. This was probably true for mutually contradictory reasons. Mississippi was both out of her frontier era and still in it. The paternalism which had grown up made legislation unnecessary, and tended to prevent legal problems from arising. Still, where the "spirit of the pioneers" survived, people simply did not care.

By contrast, legal problems not infrequently arose from cruelty towards slaves. The savagery of frontier society clashed with the paternalism that was beginning to emerge from large slaveowners. The consequences of physical cruelty were immediate, concrete and demanded attention.[735]

Whites and Negroes could no more keep from getting into bed together in Mississippi than anywhere else. Sexual relations between blacks and whites were taken for granted,[736] even being tolerated to the extent that rape by a slave on a free white woman was not a crime.[737] Only where the caste-relation was touched did the attitude change.[738]

There was no change in the general law that slaves be emancipated only for acts of special merit.[739] But emancipation by will was abolished in 1842, even for removal to another state.[739a] There were few private statutes of manumission,[740] but removal to a different state did not manumit, no matter what might be the law elsewhere. Whatever the law of any other state, such emancipation was against the public policy of Mississippi, and that was that.[741]

As Mississippi became settled by slaveowners, she also attracted some who were not merely fleeing their creditors. Exhaustion of the soil in the eastern states played a part, and drove large slaveowners to continue their former enterprises in the newly opened cotton belt. They brought with them some of the patrician traditions which had characterized South Carolina in the 18th century. But where this element had been controlling in the eastern states, in Mississippi it existed side by side with debtors escaping from the law. Consequently the 1830's and 1840's saw a very uneasy, often violent coexistence between three elements which made up the population, the two streams of white immigrants and the large number of slaves which both had brought with them.

The settlement of Mississippi was marked by the large amount of litigation over the prices of slaves.[742] The society was in a state of flux. To a superficial observer, it appeared to be in a state of development. The immigration of rich planters leaving exhausted eastern soil is made strikingly clear by the prices sometimes paid for slaves, which were far higher than those in any other state. The peak went over $2000 for a single man.[743] Prices between $1000 and $2000 for men or women were not infrequent.[744] There was every variety of price from $1000 down.[745] Hire was likewise high, usually $100, or between $100 and $200 a year.[746] As in other states, there was also a miscellany of contests between slaveowners, both over torts, and possession or ownership. [748]

Unlike other slave states at this time, Mississippi did not yet seem to have the problem of what to do with lunatic slaves. Taxes went for other things. Between 1844 and 1850 they were first raised to[748a] seventy-five cents[749] and then reduced to thirty cents per slave.[750] Mississippi was being settled and was apparently on the way to becoming a stable society. In 1846, the state finally granted compensation to slaveowners for half the value of slaves executed under process of law.[751] One need but note that this was only fifteen years before the outbreak of the Civil War to see that the state was then still finding herself, and to understand her sorry history after 1865. Nonresidents were soon excluded from the benefits of this act,[752] as were owners who tried to secrete or eloign their slaves to escape the operation of the law.[753]

Mississippi's difficulties and essential weakness stood out in the law. As late as 1850, it denied compensation for executed slaves, or to owners who tried to hide or carry them off "to screen the same from trial." [754] It showed the violent, self-help disposition of many Mississippi settlers, which continued alongside the more civilized paternalistic conduct of the large slaveholders who had finally reached the state. It occurred often enough to require legislative attention, that a master would "carry off, conceal or otherwise dispose of such slave with a view to prevent the trial and conviction of such slave."

This kind of self-help was merely an extension of what had brought these people to Mississippi in the first place—self-help to dodge their creditors. It was then within eleven years of the Civil War, and Mississippi did not have time to become fully civilized before the that war swept away the slave society.

Given the primitiveness of the Mississippi frontier, the struggle between the wilderness and the civilizing elements was more exacerbated than in other parts of the country. In the contest between slaveowners aiming to preserve their property, and nonslaveowners demanding "punishment" (or vengeance), lynch mobs appeared twice in the reported cases between 1830 and 1850. The first time, the life of the accused slave was protected by a relative of the homicide victim.[755] The other reported incident came a few years later.[756] If anything in American history casts doubt on the validity of democracy, it is the respective behavior of the patricians and the "common man" in Mississippi. Apart from these two cases, the majority of death sentences, which reached the appellate courts were reversed,[757] showing that the upper stratum of society[758] had gained control in the state during the 1830's and 1840's.

Nothing changed directly in the stern but narrow law of 1824, penalizing masters for allowing their slaves to trade for themselves.[759] Nor did any reported litigation arise, but an extension of the policy can be seen in the new law forbidding even masters to employ slaves beyond city limits for selling any goods whatever.[760]

Mississippi, like most other slave states, found a continuous problem in sales of liquor to and by slaves. Like her sister states, she enacted a law against it[761] but almost immediately repealed it.[762] Yet the original prohibition was enforced,[763] with the usual leniency toward devices of entrapment.[764] Mississippi also followed the practice of other frontier states in drafting citizens for roadbuilding. She followed other slave states in making this draft include slaves.[765] There are some private statutes granting compensation for services to the state, either by slaveowners or in connection with slaves.[766] In addition, we find some specific statutes, mostly private, on various details of the relation of the slaveowner and the state.[767]

Mississippi had extensive legislation on free Negroes. At first it was hostile,[768] but later showed piecemeal gentleness.[769] But there was almost no litigation. Free Negroes were a sufficiently depressed group that they did not get into court to enforce their rights, and of course, nobody bothered to sue them.[770]

The decades from 1830 to 1850 did not see any attempts to revive the foreign slave trade. Moreover, Mississippi had joined the Union in 1817, when the legal slave trade had already been ended. But for the same reason, the state almost from the first found herself in the gale of abolition.[771] The uncompromising character of her resolutions against abolition foreshadowed the Brooks Adams summary:

> Only a generation ago, the aristocracy of the South deliberately chose a civil war rather than admit the principle that at some future time they might have to accept compensation for their slaves.[772]

Alabama, like Mississippi, was part of the wild South, but did not go to the same extremes. The state was not the same haven for absconding debtors, nor did the cases record lynch mobs, as in Mississippi. Slaves were brought into Alabama from the older eastern slave states. And, perhaps being further east than Mississippi, Alabama was even more exposed to the Abolitionist activities which gathered steam soon after her admission to the Union. Relatively few statutory changes were made, but litigation abounded. In 1849, the legislature improved the provisions for notice which had to be given to the owners of absconding slaves.[773]

Judicial cases showing the movement west and south are legion. As indicated, Alabama was both a transshipment point[774] and a way station.[775] There are also a few instances where slaves were moved west from Alabama.[776] Coming into the Union in 1819 just before the Missouri Compromise, and a fast-growing slave state, Alabama, was subjected to the pull in both directions. There was the insatiable demand of northern industry for "freed" slaves as cheap wage labor, and there was an almost equal demand for more and more slaves within the state. Consequently, the records contain cases of slave stealing evidently designed to bring the slaves north,[777] as well as repeated cases of slave stealing for profit.[778]

As a new Gulf Coast state, Alabama had no problems with the illegal foreign slave trade during the 1830's and 1840's. Exhaustion of the soil in the older eastern slave states led to a stream of slaves coming into Alabama. There was no need to take risks by bootlegging them from Africa.[778a]

It goes without saying that Alabama continued the practice of corporal punishment.[779] With slaves so much in demand as to invite slave stealing for profit, there was ample reason for modes of discipline which did not separate the slave from his work.[779a] But, as in the past, corporal punishment had to be reasonable. Killing a slave by excessive whipping was a criminal offense particularly against an overseer, and excessive whipping by an overseer without fatal results gave rise to civil damages.[780]

During the 1830-1850 period, Alabama had surprisingly little on patrols. To be sure, the statutes recognized them, but even so, only piecemeal and by counties.[781] Alabama went back to the 18th century system of having slaveowners themselves ride patrol,[782] rather than leaving it to hirelings, as in 19th century South Carolina.[783] Although there was quite a bit of litigation during the two decades, not a single case involving patrols reached the appellate courts. It is possible only to draw inferences from cases on other subjects. As will be seen, Alabama was very careful to treat her slaves well, and the personal attachment between master and slave recurred continually. In general, master-slave relations seem to have been peaceful and good. It would follow that though the state instituted patrols, they did not have much occasion to exercise their authority.

One is likewise struck by the wide difference between Alabama and Mississippi, neighboring states admitted to the Union within two years of each other. The key would seem to be the greater fertility of Mississippi. This attracted all sorts of riff-raff who had failed in the eastern slave states. While it also attracted large slaveowners who paid fantastic prices for slaves, the latter were not enough of a leavener. On the other hand, Alabama, not being quite so fertile, drew only those who expected to live systematically in their new environment as they had in their old. Alabama was less of the wild South.

Accordingly, Alabama consistently respected the obligations of masters to care for their slaves and treat them with humanity,[784] to furnish housing,[785] food, clothing[786] and medical attention,[787] and to refrain from excessive punishment.[788] To a large extent these requirements were self-operating. A large number of cases show that masters volunteered good treatment to their slaves.[789] Perhaps because of the continuous influx of new slaves, there were as yet no statutes or cases making separate provisions for care during old age.

Alabama followed the general pattern of the other slave states. Sexual relations between blacks and whites were accepted as a fact of life.[790] But the state went a little further than most in permitting them legally. The law against rape by a Mulatto was inapplicable to rape by a Quadroon.[791] Marriages, on the other hand, were impossible.[792] They would have upset the caste structure. The paucity of cases measures the bare ripple which interracial sexual connections caused in Alabama.

Alabama allowed no exceptions to her statutory requirements for emancipation. Testamentary emancipations were uniformly held to be void.[793]

Though an individual buyer might pay over $2100 for a slave blacksmith,[794] prices were generally lower than in Mississippi. The ordinary maximum was $1200.[795] The cost of hiring slaves on the other hand, was as high, if not higher than in Mississippi, and possibly the highest in the Union.[796] This shows an influx not only of slaveowners, but of persons without slaves who had a moderate amount of money. Probably because of the frontier condition of the state,[796a] and with little control over her slaves, no civil damages could be collected for injuries done by slaves, unless by the master's direct authority.[797]

This contrasts sharply with the law of Louisiana, applying respondent superior,[798] and South Carolina which made a distinction between large plantations where control would be lacking, and ships where the owner was held responsible.[799] Aside from disputes over prices, the Alabama cases contain the usual subjects of litigation. There was breach of warranty of soundness,[800] conversion of slaves,[801] injury to or causing death of slaves,[802] and controversies over levy of execution.[802a] Alabama showed two almost contradictory tendencies. On the one hand, she had huge plantations.[803] On the other, she employed slaves in non-agricultural pursuits.[804] By 1849, holding public auctions for hiring slaves had evidently grown too burdensome, and a general law was passed permitting guardians to hire slaves privately.[806] As a rising slave state attracting planters who had exhausted their soils at home, Alabama soon felt the inconvenience of absentee owners.

In the 1840's, the basic tax on slaves was sixty cents a head;[807] but slaves of non-residents were taxed at two dollars a head.[808] In 1849, taxes were put on a sliding scale[809] and the Legislature continued a special fund to pay compensation for executed slaves.[810] Slave traders were assessed ten dollars a head on each slave offered for sale.[811] The courts however, were not anxious to enforce the criminal penalties of this act, and found loopholes which dispensed with enforcement.[812] Compulsory roadwork was a form of taxation in kind. Where the master neither worked himself nor sent a slave substitute, he was subject to civil penalties.[813] There were as yet no reports of lunatic slaves. Alabama was too new.

The tax acts to set up a fund for compensating owners of executed slaves had already been instituted.[814] Non-residents were excluded from compensation if their slaves had escaped to Alabama.[814a] There were not many cases. Besides an oblique reference,[815] two decisions indicate both a growing importance attached to compensation, and a growing reluctance to execute slaves.[816] The state went as far as any in her unwillingness to destroy slave property by punishing slaves. And unlike Virginia,[817] the slaveowners were in firm control of the situation. Among the capital cases which reached the State Supreme Court, most convictions were reversed or pardoned.[818]

Though less violent than Mississippi, Alabama was still on the frontier. In the 1830's and 1840's citizens tried self help against the state, giving rise to occasional prosecutions for hiding or eloigning slaves charged with crimes.[819] Trading with slaves was a frequently recurring problem. Here, too, the frontier was dominant. The frontiersmen had been dissatisfied with the social structure of the society from which they came. When it suited them, they disregarded the social structure of the society to which they went.[820] Sales of liquor to slaves or purchases from them loomed large in Alabama law.[821] Here, too, the influence of the frontier was evident. Everybody was drinking hard liquor, and slaves were no exception.

Unique in Alabama was the number of Indian slaveholders.[823] Cherokees,[824] Choctaws[825] and Creeks[826] all held slaves. That they did so was accepted as a normal facet of the existing society.

The 1830's and 1840's saw Alabama move in two directions at once with respect to free Negroes. Internally, the laws became steadily milder. Externally, the fear of Abolitionist agitation brought increased restrictions. Slaves were competent witnesses against colored defendants.[827] Free Negroes were treated like slaves in the matter of punishment[828] and the courts hesitated to give judgments of freedom.[829] But during the same years, free Negroes became qualified as witnesses when white men sued them for small amounts.[830] But several years later, the courts were stretching points to decide in favor of freedom rather than slavery.[831] During this latter period there were only two more holdings in support of slavery.[832]

From 1830 to 1850, Alabama, though a coast state, was not plagued by the bootleg foreign slave trade. Nevertheless, she felt the weight of the abolition movement. But Alabama was peculiar in several respects. The overall picture, is that of a hybrid. Second only to Mississippi among the new cotton states, she also had the wherewithal for industry. The fact that she was second, rather than first in cotton attracted a different type of settler. At the same time Alabama had the frontiersman's disregard of law, and his reliance on self help. At a time when American society as a whole had progressed beyond the point, there was a re-emergence of the practice of hiding slaves to frustrate prosecutions for capital offenses.

Missouri was a western state into which it was hoped that

slaveowners would flow, and to a certain extent they did. That slaves were not tied to the soil was the foundation stone of slavery in the state. Several cases record the movement with slaves from the East.[835] At the same time, as Missouri proved not to be good territory for slave labor, slaves were sold south.[836] There were however, fugitive slave cases.[837] Abolition agitation was an integral part of the Missouri Compromise fight, and the date of Missouri's admission into the Union presaged headaches from slaves seeking "freedom" in the North. There was one private act allowing slaves to be brought into Missouri,[838] and one injunction was refused to prevent removal of slaves out of the state.[839]

Missouri being an inland state, was not affected by the ending of the foreign slave trade. Hence there was relatively little evasion of the prohibition during the 1830's and 1840's. In part, Missouri followed the classical slave states in adopting corporal punishment,[840] but she also betrayed her unsuitability for slavery by imposing imprisonment or banishment as well.[841] The state could affort to dispense with slave labor.[842] There were no cases of excessive punishment by owners but one such by an overseer.[843] The statues did however, go out of their way to punish "mischief and dishonesty among slaves."[843a] The burden of administering discipline was a public one for which everyone was liable.

Imitating the slave states, Missouri instituted a patrol law[844] but did not use it. As no cases arose in this field before 1830, so none arose after that year. Missouri had no maximum hour law for slaves for she did not need it. There was not enough demand for slave labor to tempt anyone to excessive hours. After 1830, requirements for due care of slaves were usually carried out as a matter of course. The laws showed themselves not in the violations, but either in voluntary performance or in civil enforcement between private parties.[845] In one case, inhuman treatment by the hirer caused the slave's death. Even here the remedy was a civil suit for damages.[846] Casualness about mistreatment appears in CARPENTER v. STATE,[846a] which was satisfied with forfeited bail where a master had killed his own slave.

In Missouri, as in the other slave states, sex between the races was taken for granted. The terms "persons of color" and "Mulattoes"[847] were constantly used in the statutes. The courts similarly took cross-breeding in their stride.[848]

Mark Twain gave a full-length portrait of Missouri miscegenation in Pudd'nhead Wilson:

> To all intents and purposes Roxy was as white as anybody,
> but the one sixteenth of her which was black outvoted the
> other fifteen parts and made her a Negro. She was a

slave, and salable as such. Her child was thirty-one parts white, and he, too, was a slave, and by a fiction of law and custom, a Negro.[849]

As Missouri was an artificially constituted slave state which was set up for other reason, than its suitability to slave agriculture, it was quick to find emancipation. There were two statutes[850] and numerous cases of emancipation.[851] The state also had a series of laws directed to particular phases of the relations between slaveowners.[852] Prices were moderate only going twice into four figures.[853] But with hires it was different.[854] People without slaves hoped to embark on slave-worked agriculture. Other instances of disputes over property are given in the footnotes.[855]

Missouri did not include individual taxing acts in her later statute books. [856] Nor did the late and sparse institution of slavery in the state bring forth any insane slaves. Missouri did not deal with the problem of compensation for executed slaves. There were neither statues nor cases. On the one hand, slave society was too sparse and too little interested in driving slaves to raise many such cases. On the other, the desire to protect slave property rather than punish the slave was very pronounced, and avoided executions.

The state's methods of trying slaves revealed the artificial nature of its slave system. Trial by judges was preserved, but a jury was optional on the master's request.[857] The community had completely lost sight of the caste structure and failed to recognize that a trial of slaves by judges was generally more favorable to the defense than a jury trial. When it came to practical situations, the preservation of slave property far outweighed the demands for punishment. On appeal, nearly all sentences of death or mutilation were reversed.[858] In one instance, a slave condemned to death was pardoned, but the pardon was held unconstitutional.[858a] In only a single instance was it recorded that a death sentence was carried out.[859]

Unlike Alabama[860] and Mississippi, Missouri had no problems with slave owners spiriting away a slave to dodge the course of the law. Here, too, its artificial character as a slave state was undoubtedly controlling. Slavery existed sparsely and limply. Situations arose infrequently or not at all, where a slaveowner resorted to self help to rescue his slave from the importunities of the law.

The artificial character of Missouri slavery also came to the fore in the lackadaisical attitude toward slaves trading for themselves. Cities were given the power to forbid it,[862] but the only case refused to sustain a conviction for allowing slaves to so trade.[863] Likewise, relations between the slaveowner and the state gave rise to a number of isolated, unusual problems.   The familiar one, sales of liquor, hardly appeared at all.   There was only one case of selling liquor to a slave, and in that one, the conviction was set aside.[864]   But civil damages were granted even for remote consequences. [864a]

Besides one private act authorizing payment of the costs of a prosecution,[865] and a statute forbidding poisonous drugs to be sold to slaves,[865a]it was held that cities could not prohibit slaves from driving drays.[866]   The right to the statutory award for capturing a fugitive slave was lost if the slave escaped a second time.[867]

Missouri began as a state with relative laxity toward free Negroes. Then after 1830, the rules hardened, as Missouri tried to line herself up with the older slave states.   The statute against "mischief" by slaves and free Negroes made its appearance in 1831.[870]   Until 1835, marriages between whites and Mulattoes were legal.   In that year they were made illegal.[871]   It was not until 1843 however, that the state followed the other slave states in excluding free Negroes,[872] but part of this law was promptly made inapplicable to those already in residence.[873]   Individual exceptions also sprang up almost immediately.[874]

By 1846 though, Missouri was engulfed by the abolition panic and forbade teaching Negroes or Mulattoes to read or write.[875]   The exclusion of free Negroes was made more drastic,[876] and persons under twenty-one who would not be entitled to a license to marry if of age, could not be bound out as apprentices.[877]

A measure of its static prosperity, rather than its goodheartedness, appeared in the rule granting free Negroes compensation for time unlawfully held in slavery.[878]   Children of statu liberae were slaves, at least for payment of debts.[879]   This was logical but more severe than the laws of Virginia.[880]   Anticipating DRED SCOTT v. SANFORD,[881] the Supreme Court of Missouri held that free Negroes were not citizens.[882]

Missouri was not concerned with the foreign slave trade, but Abolitionist activities hit her between the eyes.   The state's geographical position accounted for that.   Resolution after resolution or statute was passed by the Legislature inveighing against the campaign of the Abolitionists, or supporting the federal authorities against abolition.[886] There were however, no cases.   Missouri, as an artificial slave community exposed to abolition activities was excited, but in a rather abstract way.

Arkansas was the first state admitted after the Missouri Compromise fight.[887]   She was in every aspect a frontier state, the product of westward migration.   The pioneers brought their slaves, but otherwise they were supposedly exchanging the society they had known for a democracy.

The laws were initially those of Missouri. Equality was thought to be a good thing, so when the settlers wanted to protect slaves, they guaranteed them jury trials. The requirement that slaves be tried by slaveholders had been forgotten. But since Arkansas was better soil for slave labor than Missouri, there was also some of the same mob violence as when the pioneers came to Mississippi.

The state constitution enacted in 1837, indirectly approved the introduction of slaves. The legislature was given power to exclude only those who had committed high crimes.[890] A substantial number of cases reflected the migration to Arkansas from states further east.[891] There was also the practice of moving slaves to avoid execution for debt.[891a]

Arkansas came into the Union so late, that "fugitive slaves" were almost a foregone conclusion. Having just adopted the laws of Missouri, the legislature soon found that Arkansas needed laws of her own for runaway or stolen slaves.[892] Heavier laws were enacted against slave stealing.[892a] As Arkansas had no seacoast, it was not concerned with the past, present or future of the bootleg foreign slave trade. In its statutes, prohibitions against importing slaves illegally from foreign countries were coupled with prohibitions against importing certain slaves from other states.

As a frontier state, Arkansas lost sight of the purpose of corporal punishment for slaves. Lashes or stripes were substituted for fines,[892a] but not for jail offenses. The pioneers apparently forgot the design to not separate the slaves from their work. One can infer only that there was no great labor shortage in Arkansas.[892b] Masters legally had the option of punishing their slaves themselves for any offense less than a felony, and settling with the injured party. A trial was held only if the master refused to compound and pay the damages.[892c] In other instances, corporal punishment was imposed by statute.[892d]

Arkansas adopted the patrol system.[893] This came about partially in imitation of the older slave states, and because Arkansas was at least partially suited to slave agriculture. The system stood half-way between the Eighteenth and Nineteenth century institutions of the eastern states. Slaveholders had to serve as patrollers,[894] but could send substitutes.[895] The captain and his assistant were paid,[896] but could opt to serve without pay,[897] in which case no tax was levied to pay them.[898]

In 1848, a separate patrol act was adopted[899] and the maximum number of men in a patrol was increased from four to ten,[900] which was probably a reaction to Abolitionist activities. The previous five-dollar fine for refusing patrol duty was now made the minimum, with the maximum at $20.[901] This was combined with exemptions,[902] showing that the state was not getting the patrol service it wanted. But there were no cases. Arkansas was still to sparsely populated and too much on the frontier[903] for such matters to reach the courts.

Arkansas was settled much too late to develop restrictions on the slaves' hours of labor. Even the earliest territorial statutes were almost contemporaneous with the Missouri Compromise.[904] The new slave states had to compete with the new industrialism, and made no rules contrary to the latter's limitless working of employees.

The Arkansas Constitution of 1836 provided broadly that "the General Assembly had the power to oblige the owner of any slave or slaves to treat them humanely," but no statute was passed to execute this provision. The cases present a curious pattern. Up to 1850 there were few, undoubtedly due to the sparsity of the population. But those few show the character of the Arkansas settlement. Within the master-slave relation, slaves were either treated well, or ill treatment was condemned.[906] But we also find the strange phenomenon of mob violence against slaves by the slaveowners themselves.[907] One can only infer that the pioneers in Arkansas were not used to owning slaves nor used to command, but the device of instigated mob violence was adopted even by slaveowners from patrician South Carolina.[908] They had evidently caught the spirit of the frontier.

Like the other slave states, Arkansas accepted Mulattoes without comment.[909] But as in other slave societies, marriages were forbidden, although not until 1848.[910] The caste system had to be preserved, but it took time for a frontier society to understand the requirements of a caste system. Rape, and attempted rape were punished by death.[910a] Later rape cases suggest a swinging from a frontier society to a settled caste society, with the usual reluctance of slaveowners to destroy their own property for whatever reason.[911]

In 1850, there was an interesting retrospect upon "that barbarous treatment and excessive cruelty practiced upon them in the earlier period of our colonial history."[912] Of course, this was partly due to the general cruelty of the 17th century[913] and partly due to the fact that the 19th century did not clearly distinguish the early continental colonial practices from those of the West Indies.[914]

Arkansas' adoption of Missouri laws[915] included liberal provision for emancipation.[916] These sections were re-adopted in the last Territorial Code of 1835.[917] Immediately after Arkansas' admission as a state, its own constitution gave the legislature power to pass laws authorizing owners to emancipate their slaves, saving the rights of creditors.[918]

The legislature forthwith put the power into effect,[919] substantially retaining the laws borrowed from Missouri. This code was continued without essential changes until 1850.[920]

Here we see the bright side of the frontier. There was no shifting opposition to emancipation as developed in the older slave states.[921] The implication was that if freed slaves could make a living on the frontier, the frontier was open for them to do so. But the rules had to be strictly followed. An attempted liberation by the probate court was void, because it was not the court which had jurisdiction over manumission.[922] This however, worked both ways. The courts did not hesitate to uphold a decree of emancipation where the objector had let his time to appeal go by.[923] Otherwise, there were no court cases on emancipation. Arkansas was not yet populated either sufficiently or during a long enough period for the subject to come up with any frequency.

Arkansas adopted the ways of a civilized society by enacting various laws to govern the gifts and conveyancing of slaves.[924] The period of adverse possession was five years.[924a] Most of the litigation between slaveowners concerned prices. In general, these were medium.[925] Only three times did the price of a single slave go into four figures.[926] The overall situation was similar to that in Missouri.

Arkansas was moderately suited to slave agriculture. There was no wild demand for slaves as in Mississippi. Hires were likewise in middle figures.[927] Otherwise, both statutes[928] and litigation[929] mirror the frontier disputes among property owners. One case however, suggests the instigation of action by owners against their own slaves, indicating that they either were not used to command, or had forgotten how. In ROSE v. ROSE,[930] a wife asked for a divorce on the ground that the husband encouraged the slaves to disobey her.

Arkansas belonged to the large class of states which enacted periodic tax acts.[931] There were neither statutes nor cases on lunatic slaves. The state was much too new and sparsely settled for this trouble to demand attention. And until 1850, Arkansas had no statute granting compensation to owners of executed slaves. For one thing, the population was still too sparse. For another, the frontier customarily brought violent and unexpected deaths. There would seem to be no reason to compensate those from one particular source.

We have already noted that both the state constitution and its statutes guaranteed slaves the right to a trial by jury.[932] This was the democracy of the frontier triumphant over the sociology of caste—even in a society based on caste. The same spirit of equal opportunity caused Arkansas to require counsel to be assigned for the defense of slaves accused of crimes.[933] Defense of the slave was no longer an obligation of the master as a quasi-feudal lord, but a spirit of fairness demanded that a defense should be furnished in some way. Similarly, felony trials for slaves had to be tried in the same way as felony prosecutions of white persons (except that slaves could not be witnesses).[934] This was evidently considered a benefit to the defendant.

In view of the frontier mentality of the Arkansas slaveowners themselves, the estimate was probably right. A jury of slaveholders would not have recognized their own peculiar property interests. A reading of the statutes did not give the impression that the legislators felt such a process would benefit either the slave or his owner. There were no cases that decided which type of tribunal should try a slave. This was probably due to the fact that no one had objections to the tribunals which were then functioning.

Unlike Mississippi and Alabama, Arkansas had no jurisprudence arising out of attempts to put slaves beyond the reach of the law. This is due, at least partly, to the Arkansas statute allowing masters to compound civilly, slaves' crimes less than a felony.[935] No other state made a similar express provision. Besides, Arkansas had more than any of the other slave states, what may be called a working frontier. The frontiersman's democracy was achieved with a relatively small part of the lawlessness and violence accompanying other frontier communities. There was no further territory to take the slave to.

While the relatively stable freedom of Arkansas' frontier eliminated many problems which plagued the other new slave states, it brought one to the fore; slaves trading for themselves, both with and without the master's consent. The frequency of statutory prohibitions shows how general the practice must have been.[936] On the other hand, there were no cases. Just as Arkansas' relatively free pioneering society, in spite of itself, encouraged slaves to trade for themselves and masters to allow them, so it evidently did not take violations very seriously. No case was ever serious enough to reach the appellate courts.

Arkansas made the usual efforts to prevent sales of liquor to or by slaves,[937] and to prevent whites from gambling with them.[938] A society like Arkansas' would find such rules hard to enforce and was unlikely to take violations very seriously. Slaves were personal estate.[939] Arkansas was organized so late that the problem of whether slaves should be real or personal property had long since been settled. There were some procedural problems however, as between state and slaveowner when slaves were arrested for travelling without a pass.[940] Comparatively peaceful and newly settled though, frontier Arkansas had few contests between slaveowners and the state.

The territory authorized suits to establish freedom to be brought <u>in</u>

forma pauperis. [941] That this was done so soon, again illustrates the attitude of the Arkansas frontier. It was quite willing to accept Negroes. The same is true of the 1835 law permitting free Negroes to have their own gun powder and shot. [941a] But to a large extent free Negroes were classed with slaves, [942] and by 1844 the Legislature resolved that they were not citizens and should be excluded from the state as a response to abolition agitation. Since 1837, statutes had hobbled their immigration [943] to Arkansas.

The internal policies of the state were ambivalent. The right to sue for freedom in forma pauperis was retained, [944] but education was withheld from black or Mulatto apprentices. Money and goods were furnished them instead. [945] Attempted marriages between whites and blacks were void, [945a] confirming the caste system. The Supreme Court of Arkansas held the exclusion of free Negroes to be constitutional, as they were not citizens. [946] This however, was the only case. On the Arkansas frontier, there was apparently not much tension between whites and free Negroes.

As Arkansas had no seacoast, no problems arose from the interdicted foreign slave trade. The state did however, take steps to regulate interstate trade, prohibiting the introduction of slaves for purposes of speculation, and banning those who had committed a high crime. [947] There were no cases. As a practical matter, Arkansas did not seem to have been bothered by illegal importations of slaves. [948] Nevertheless, Arkansas' western and northern position, bordering on streams of frontiersmen who had no use for slavery, made her sensitive to Abolitionist agitation. The resulting resolutions against Abolitionist activity were already considered in connection with Nat Turner's rebellion. [949]

Florida, south of the cotton belt, had a great many statutes on slaves but very little litigation. In fact, there was none at all during her quarter century as a territory from 1819 to 1845. Both before and after admission as a state, she enacted all the usual laws of the slave states. They included statutes on corporal punishment, trading with slaves, slave-stealing, patrols, the exclusion of free Negroes, compensation for executed slaves and prohibition of miscegenation.

Florida was distinctive only in that patrolling was made a duty of the militia and the Indian agent, that patrols were apparently conducted on foot, and that in contrast to South Carolina, free colored sailors were allowed to go ashore while their ship was docked. Unlike Mississippi, slaves could be introduced as merchandise.

While Florida inherited slavery from Spain, [950] it tried to make a profit out of the importation of additional slaves from American states and territories. Not only did it permit slaves to be brought in as merchandise,[951] but also laid a special tax on them.[952]   At the same time, it joined the chorus of Southern states in opposing the Wilmot Proviso,[952a] at least theoretically looking forward to the expansion of slavery into new territory.

Almost immediately after Florida's acquisition, Congress made the Fugitive Slave Law of 1793 applicable to the territory.[953]   Since all American (i.e., non-Spanish) legislation was post Missouri Compromise, it manifested a distinct nervousness about slave stealing.[954] Abolitionist activity extended as far south as Florida.

In this newly settled community however, slaveowners also stole from one another. In 1842, a resolution was adopted against the spiriting away of mortgaged slaves.[955]   The lush Florida landscape encouraged "outlying slaves"[955a] and disappearance among the Seminoles.[955b]   Accordingly, the Indian agent was paid for apprehension of runaways among the Indians.[955c]

Florida being a coast state with a background of slave trade by the Spaniards, was sufficiently conscious of the American prohibition, that she included special laws on the subject.[956]   But the problem does not seem to have presented itself practically, and there were no cases.

Florida inflicted corporal punishment, and more harshly than most slave states. While sixty lashes were originally the maximum,[957] later statutes repeatedly authorized one hundred.[958]   The pillory was used but the defendant did not quite lose his ears.[959]   Plantations with any slaves had to have a white person,[959a] and a white person had to accompany any group of slaves exceeding seven, who were traveling.[959b]

Florida joined the less confident slave states in imposing lashes for "abusive and provoking language" by a "Negro or Mulatto, bond or free" to anyone "not being a Negro or Mulatto."[960]   Firearms were forbidden, except by the owner's permission, showing that the law was designed to uphold the master's control, rather than to guard against revolts.[960a]

Though outside the cotton belt, Florida, flat and fertile, adopted the patrol system.[961]   Patrols had the usual duties of searching slave houses and keeping slaves in subordination. But unlike those of other states, Florida's patrols went on foot.[962]   Florida adopted the same scheme as Arkansas.[963]   Patrols were composed both of slaveowners and hired employees.[964]   But there was a reverberation of 18th century South Carolina in a special injunction "to avoid intoxication."[965]   There were no cases. While Florida adopted the trappings of the established slave states, many of these trappings remained academic.

Florida passed general laws requiring masters to treat slaves with humanity. Assuring the slaves free Sundays is the closest approximation to maximum hour laws that were adopted.[966]   In disputes between hirer and owner, the owner was required to pay medical bills. [967] The state went out of her way to protect the slave in expressly providing that the order of the master should be a defense to the commission of any crime not capital.[968] And cruel and unusual punishment of slaves was a criminal offense.[969] One case indicates a spontaneous desire to treat slaves with humanity, which unfortunately was disregarded.[969] On the whole however, there was less detailed legislation in Florida than in many other states, and no cases.

Mulattoes were taken for granted in Florida as everywhere else. [970] The details of the social attitudes toward sexual relations between the races were mutually contradictory. This was undoubtedly due to a different attitude while the territory was Spanish, and a gradual superimposition of the social structure of the English colonies. Interracial marriages were not forbidden until 1832.[971] Then at one stroke, living in concubinage was also made illegal. This latter prohibition was enforced not only by fine but by the loss of superior civil rights; i.e., holding office, serving as jurors, competence as witnesses,[972] indicating the caste basis of the rule. But while the statutes were savage against rape, or attempted rape of a white woman by a colored man,[973] the courts were reluctant to enforce them. [974]

With Florida being a relatively new acquisition of the United States, few problems of emancipation arose by 1850. But the rules were gradually restricted. In 1822, emancipation was authorized subject only to the ability of the slave to support himself and the rights of persons having claims against the slave. [974a] In 1829, manumission was by statute, conditioned on the freedman's leaving the state.[975] One case arose out of a testamentary provision that the decedent's slaves should be freed six months after his death. [976]

Most Florida litigation to 1850 were contests between slaveowners, usually about prices. In an isolated case, the price reached $1205 for a slave in 1850, [977] but generally the prices or values were in three figures on either side of $500. [978] Hire fluctuated from $30 to over $100 per year.[979] There were a few other statutes, and all deal with the property relations between slaveowners. [980]

There are numerous Florida tax acts on record. None, however, touched upon lunatic slaves. Florida was too recently settled. Slaves were subject to a gradually rising poll tax,[981] and by 1850 the state also collected a license fee for imported slaves.[982] Florida at first granted masters compensation for executed slaves [983] and then repealed the entire law in 1839. [984] From then until 1850, no general compensation was paid for executed slaves. The question evidently did not arise often in practice, since there were no cases.

Florida took the same position as Arkansas, and gave slaves the doubtful benefit of being tried in the same manner as white persons in capital cases. [985] In 1825, the Florida Legislature committed the trial of slaves to juries not of slaveholders, but of householders.[986] There were however, no cases which deal with the composition of the jury trying a slave. A broad policy for the protection of slave property shows itself in the provision for court-appointed counsel where the owner himself had not furnished counsel.[988] In other words, hypothetically, the interests of society surpasses those of the individual slaveowner. However, nailing the ears to posts in case of "perjury"[989] as well as the charge to the prospective witness, [990] here as elsewhere, were designed to make the slave say what was wanted, rather than "nothing but the truth." Florida at least, did not inflict such punishment "without further trial."[991]

Nothing suggests that Florida had the problem of masters hiding or abducting their own slaves to withdraw them from possible criminal prosecution. Having been settled by the Spaniards for several centuries, Florida was no longer a frontier. Habits formed under the Spanish regime tended to make society more stable than those formed by persons running to an unsettled country in order to escape creditors or laws.

However Florida had plenty of trouble with slaves trading for themselves, as well as with masters who authorized their slaves to do so.[992] No case though, reached the appellate courts. It is an interesting exception peculiar to Florida, that slaves were allowed to trade for themselves in "brooms, baskets, mats or things commonly manufactured by slaves,"[993] and that in 1850, the prohibition was lifted against trading in cotton, sugar, syrup or molasses, rice, fodder or meat.[994] Here customs followed the Florida climate, and suggest remnants of the Spanish regime. A heavier penalty was imposed for trading with slaves on Sunday.[995] Sunday laws served a social purpose,[996] and were found convenient to deal with all sorts of problems. There were no cases. It may be inferred that any violations were considered minor.

Florida made the same efforts as other slave states to prevent sales of liquor to and by slaves.[997] But here again, the matter never reached the appellate courts. Florida was still sparsely populated,[998] and such cases were probably not taken too seriously. Florida statutes also forbade a slave to possess domestic animals "in his own right."[999] This provision, which seems tautological under Anglo-American laws of slavery, was probably meant to change the pre-existing Spanish law. Under Roman law slaves had peculium (private property). Under Anglo-American law this was denied. Slaves illegally manumitted were not free, but became the property of the school fund.[1000]

By 1850, Florida had a great many statutes on free Negroes and almost no cases. One of the latter probably holds the key. Where status was questioned, Negroes and Mulattoes were presumed to be free.[1001] Sparsity of population also produced sparsity of litigation. The plethora of statutes shows that Florida intended to go ahead as a full fledged slave state. The territory adopted the usual policy against immigration of free Negroes.[1002] This policy was even enforced internally. Negroes or Mulattoes resident in Indian Territory had to stay there.[1003] But unlike South Carolina[1004] and Georgia,[1005] Florida did not quarantine the colored crews of vessels calling at her ports until 1842.[1005a]

As elsewhere, free Negroes in Florida were singled out for oppressive taxation. Where white men or slaves were assessed at a fraction of a dollar a head, the poll tax on a free Negro was several dollars.[1008] Otherwise, "free" Negroes were often bracketed with slaves.[1009] In addition, they were expressly forbidden to have firearms,[1010] and special statutes dealt with collection of judgments against them.[1011] They were also obligated to work on roads.[1012]

No liquor could be sold to free Negroes,[1013] and in 1847 they were put under compulsory guardians.[1014] But special laws protected them from being made to work on Sundays,[1015] and selling a freeman as a slave was prohibited, though with relatively light punishment for whites. But in 1850, this could lead to a death sentence for Negroes or Mulattoes.[1016]

While Florida was a territory, the federal government especially forbade the importation of slaves.[1017] After her admission as a state, the law of 1808[1018] applied. Otherwise, the abolition of the slave trade left no marks on Florida up until 1850.

Texas had few statutes but a substantial amount of litigation. As the westernmost slave area, Texas was on the receiving end of slave mobility.[1019] Under the Texas Republic, a statute allowed the introduction of slaves from the U.S.[1020] The right to bring in slaves from other states was made an express clause of the Texas constitution.[1021] The Texas Republic passed an act against slave stealing almost as soon as it came into existence.[1022] The next year another law followed,[1023] and in 1840 came an act regulating the sale of runaways.[1023a] Texas was fully conscious of abolition agitation but too far removed from New England for such agitation to have practical consequences.

The Texas Republic, being outside the United States for nine years (1836–45) was a target for foreign slave trade. There was a marked reluctance to enforce the anti-slave trade laws either of Cuba or Texas, or for that matter, of the United States. Illegally imported slaves who had not sued for their freedom could be held as slaves by the purchaser.

The year 1850 saw the first Texas patrol law.[1025] Until then, there were harsh but limited provisions. Slaves had been forbidden to carry guns,[1026] and "insulting or abusive language" to a white person was punished by up to 100 stripes.[1027] Texas had few statutes on slavery up to 1850, but those few establish the basic principles of good treatment.[1028] Mulattoes were taken for granted, but only two cases touch the point collaterally. There were no cases which directly involved sexual relations between blacks and whites. Rape, or attempted rape of a free white woman was punished by the death penalty.[1028b]

Texas allowed emancipation provided the owners sent the emancipated slaves out of the country. The state constitution guaranteed to slaveowners the right to emancipate their slaves, provided that those freed then did not become public charges.[1029] Litigation over prices occupied by far the largest part of relations between slaveowners. Prices were not remarkable, the highest reaching $1,000.[1030] But hires bought the fantastic figure of $200 for two months.[1031]

Texas enacted special tax statutes.[1034] No compensation was paid for executed slaves, but it was generously held that a master did not have to pay the costs of execution in addition to losing his slave.[1035]

Like Arkansas, Texas held slaves but had completely forgotten the psychology of slavery—that the slaveholders as a superior caste, were desirous of preserving their property, an interest which the lower non-slaveholding castes did not share. So a slave defendant in a criminal prosecution was "guaranteed" a trial by jury.[1036] One judicial decision however, showed an inclination to avoid the death penalty.[1037] There were no statutes or cases on hiding or spiriting away slaves to avoid prosecution. Texas was too new a society, too directly concerned with the abolition movement of the 1830s and 1840s, and too sparsely populated for such activities to pose a problem.

Like other slave states, Texas forbade trading with slaves, but unlike others she laid special emphasis on particular articles.[1038] A unique feature was that an owner was allowed to hire his slave to another slave.[1039] Texas followed the other slave states by prohibiting sales of liquor by and to slaves.[1040] In the sparse legislation up to 1850, there were no other statutes on the relation of slaveowners to the state.

Under the Constitution of the Texas Republic, free persons of African descent could reside in Texas only with "the consent of Congress."[1041] In the same year, Congress extended this consent to all who were residents at the time of the Declaration of Independence.[1042] But after that the general laws were implacable, although there were a few private acts granting free Negroes and Mulattoes the right to reside.[1043] On the other hand, poll taxes were the same for whites and free Negroes. [1044] There was some of the same egalitarian spirit of the frontier as in Arkansas.

Case law was uneven. Free Negroes could not be witnesses,[1045] even to take a pauper's oath. [1046] In this respect, Texas was more severe than some other states which allowed a free Negro to make an affidavit, or give other limited testimony. [1047] Both the Texas Republic and the state however, were careful to protect civil rights.[1048] In one case a civil judgment was taken against a free Negro, suggesting that the defendant owned enough property so it was thought worthwhile to sue him. [1049]

The Texas Republic followed the United States in prohibiting the foreign slave trade.[1050]   This was significant, because Texas slaveholders were almost entirely immigrants from the United States. The period of the Texas Republic was 1836-1845. Adopting the anti-slave trade law of the U.S. meant that during these years there was no movement to reopen the legal slave trade. There were no further statutes after Texas' admission as a state. The state was sensitive to abolition activities, although it did not have to deal with them concretely. Consequently, there was a long resolution against the Wilmot Proviso, [1051] and against abolition in the District of Columbia, but nothing else.

In the decades from 1830 to 1850, the slave states were faced with an irresistible tide of industralization and abolition, but had no idea that it was irresistible. The new slave states tried to compete by adding the harshness of a newly industrialized society to the harshness of slavery. Beyond that they offered a document, the United States Constitution, as if the Constitution was the cause, not the product of historical events.

All states which abolished slavery before the Civil War, had abolished it by 1830 (except as specifically mentioned hereafter). Consequently the non-slave states only dealt with limited aspects of the subject, such as questions of slavery antedating abolition, the return of fugitive slaves, emancipation of slaves brought into free territory, free Negroes and prohibition of the foreign slave trade.

Due to the law's delays after the abolition of slavery in New York, the court of last resort still had to decide a few cases under the law of slavery. These were either disputes between slaveowners, [1052] or concerned the care and support of slaves by means of trust legacies.[1053]

The return of fugitive slaves by the non-slave states was the sensitive point in the controversy between the slave society and the wage society. To return fugitive slaves to their southern masters was obviously the last thing the non-slave states wanted to do. At the time, the need for wage labor was so great that rising industrialism could absorb the entire flood of immigration that was coming from Europe. Fugitive slaves not only swelled this volume of badly needed labor, but having been kept unskilled by their owners, could be employed at the lowest possible wages. And all that could be glorified under the name of "freedom". So resistance to the return of fugitive slaves followed as a corrollary from the economic situation of the country. The reasons were economic, but the pretext was noble and high-minded. As J. P. Morgan, Sr. said:

> A man has two reasons for everything he does—a good reason and his real reason.[1053a]

Two statutes were designed to hobble the recovery of fugitive slaves under the then existing Act of 1793.[1054] They made it more burdensome for the party claiming the slave.[1055] Fugitive slave cases were submitted to juries and the alleged fugitive had to be represented either by the district attorney or by assigned counsel.[1056] There were two cases of slaves claimed in New York as fugitives.[1057] In addition to laws directly on fugitives, the legislature repealed the right to take slaves in transit through New York.[1058]

No cases arose on the emancipation of slaves brought into New York. There was only the withdrawal of the privilege of transit, and laws broadening the powers of the New York society for promoting the manumission of slaves,[1059] and extending the society's life to 1854.[1060] There was also one case favorable to the society.[1060a]

New York, in the forefront of the new industrial economy, was beating the drums for abolition. First came a brave resolution on abolition, damning with faint praise the right of each state to determine the internal relation of master and slave, and expressing a misguided anxiety to see "the bright side of things."[1061] It was followed ominously, by another resolution four years later, condemning the House of Representatives for having refused to receive petitions against slavery.[1062] This in turn was followed by three resolutions that slavery should be excluded from newly acquired territory.[1063] These were all resolutions. There were no statutes and no cases.

New York made an exodus, but a slow one, from the thinking of a slave society. The metamorphosis into an industrial society was manifested by the statute to prevent free Negroes from being kidnapped.[1064] They were granted a stunted franchise. They had to meet a property qualification before being admitted to vote, which whites did not.[1065] The New York courts were glad to absolve out-of-state vessels charged with bringing escaped slaves to New York, on technical grounds if convenient.[1066]

But the slaveowner's psychology appears in EXECUTOR v. GILLESPIE,[1067] a testamentary provision for the support of an aged colored servant, and in VANDENBURGH v. TRUAX,[1068] where the same legal consequences were drawn from chasing a colored servant as would have been drawn from chasing a slave. When it came to paying wages, the rules of both systems were used to avoid payment:

> Negro was denied wages because he supposedly could not understand the meaning of an oath.[1069] The crew of another vessel was granted only partial wages because 'the conduct of the libellants was at times perverse and offensive to the officers, and they were deficient in ready subordination and alacrity in the performance of their duties.'[1070]

Colored seamen ran the risk of being imprisoned if their ship docked in a slave state. They sometimes carried over the traditions of slavery by escaping from their vessel.[1071] There were also two other cases.[1072] In both of these, women had children of a different color and tried to pick a man who could be made responsible.[1073] One of the most striking features about New York was the number of cases arising out of the illegal slave trade.[1074]

New Jersey is classed among the non-slave states. Technically however, the state had slavery until 1850. The statute of 1804 provided that persons born after that time should be "free". But slavery was not abolished. There were still 222 slaves in the state by the census of 1850.[1075] Consequently, New Jersey presents not merely cases which carry over from a slave era, but slavery itself.

While slavery was not abolished, it was dying out as expected. After 1830, there was only one new statute, confirming certain manumissions.[1076] But in 1848, the Court of Errors held that the Constitution of 1844 had not abolished slavery.[1077] Both before and after that date, there were several cases arising from the institution modified only by the law for gradual abolition.[1078] But now intertwined with slavery was the callousness of the wage system which turned employees out to starve.[1079]

Free persons of color were qualified as witnesses.[1080] Aside from that, there were three instances of efforts by towns to escape the obligation of supporting a colored pauper.[1081] A single case promoted true emancipation with all its corollaries. A trust was set up for the

tuition of poor children, with an express provision that it should be applied regardless of color.[1082] A few statutes granted private relief to free Negroes [1083] and to colored schools.[1084] One provided that only whites could accept legal notices,[1085] thus marking free colored people as an inferior caste. At the same time, claims for fugitive slaves from other states had to be tried before a jury.[1086]

Since New Jersey had no major port, no statutes or cases touched the slave trade. But New Jersey aligned herself with the non-slave states in opposing the extension of slavery into the territories.[1087]

The legislation of Massachusetts from 1830 to 1850 was devoted to fighting the Fugitive Slave Act of 1793. First, cases under the act were submitted to juries.[1088] Then jurisdiction over cases under the federal act was withdrawn entirely from the Massachusetts state courts.[1089] The obvious question was "Why should all this come now?" The answer lay in the Governor's address of 1846, observing that the state had switched from commerce to manufacturing.[1090] Factories could use all the menial labor they could get. There were the usual pauper statutes, attesting to "freedom" of "free" Negroes.[1091] The demand for labor naturally engendered a statute against kidnapping free Negroes.[1092]

At the same time, the inferior status of "free" Negroes was underlined by a law against miscegenation,[1093] and segregation of colored children in separate schools.[1094] Such laws completed the picture. "Freedom" brought Negroes within the wage economy, making them a depressed caste hired at the lowest possible wages.

Aside from this, the legislature busied itself with resolutions; on slavery in the District of Columbia;[1095] on its extension into the territories or into new states;[1096] on the foreign and interstate slave trade;[1097] the denial by the House of Representatives of the right of petition,[1098] and a protest against the arrest by South Carolina of colored seamen.[1099] Yet no matter how much economic consideration might lie beneath the surface, some people inevitably took the professions of liberty and the "moral evil" of slavery seriously and literally.

There was one Massachusetts case in which a man conveyed away Maryland slaves which he had acquired by marriage.[1100] Until 1850, Massachusetts stretched her policy of "emancipation" to the utmost,[1101] while still recognizing the constitutional provision for return of fugitive slaves.[1102] On at least one occasion, a slave in Massachusetts declined the proferred "freedom."[1103] Beyond this, the cases evince the same attitude as ROBERTS v. CITY OF BOSTON, that free Negroes were considered an inferior caste.[1104] Boston and Salem, like New York, showed their importance as ports by the number of slave trade cases which arose from them.[1105]

Connecticut, from 1830 to 1850, had relatively little concerning Negroes. Some residual slavery survived until 1848,[1106] but the state was neither hunting for "free" wage labor, like industralized Massachusetts, nor for slave labor, like the active slave states. As in Massachusetts, state cooperation with the federal Fugitive Slave Law was withdrawn.[1107] There was enough impetus behind the abolition movement that in 1846 it was proposed to enfranchise free Negroes.[1108]

Schools were segregated, but Connecticut was not inclined to enforce her own restrictions against educating colored children from other states.[1109] The state joined the chorus of resolutions against expansion of slavery into the territories,[1110] freed those slaves brought within her boundaries,[1111] and took the standard precautions against the kidnapping of freemen.[1112] Two cases arose out of the illegal foreign slave trade,[1113] and a few other scattered expressions complete the roster.[1114]

Very little on slavery came from Rhode Island. The Constitution of 1842 said there shall be no slavery,[1115] and gave the vote to all males of 21 or over, subject to a property qualification.[1116] A contemporaneous statute forbade intermarriage between whites and blacks, thus placing blacks in an inferior caste.[1117] Towns were to support their poor, and masters had to support their former slaves.[1118] One to ten years in prison was the punishment for taking a person out of the state against his will.[1119]

In 1850 we find resolutions on slavery and the preservation of the Union,[1120] and on the admission of California and the Fugitive Slave Law.[1121] The only cases concern care of colored paupers and former slaves.[1122]

New Hampshire like other non-slave states, forbade its state officers from aiding the enforcement of the federal Fugitive Slave Act.[1123] Otherwise, legislative activities were confined to resolutions. First came a plan for moderation.[1124] New Hampshire supported the annexation of Texas, on the theory that it would bring in more free than slave states.[1125] The state followed the usual pattern of opposing the extension of slavery into the territories, and calling for abolition in the District of Columbia.[1126] There was only one case, arising in 1837.[1127] It inveighed against selling free persons as slaves, but did not enforce the prohibition.

Pennsylvania was once known as the Quaker state, but the Quaker influence was invisible from 1830 to 1850. First, the state retained slavery until well after 1830. [1128]   Secondly, its citizens were as turbulent as any in the country.   Mob violence operated in both directions; against blacks [1129] and against enforcement of the Fugitive Slave Law. [1130]   And from this northern Quaker state we have a summary of the position of free Negroes in American society:

> A caste in which ignorance, submission and oppression was the badge of this tribe[1131] . . . The blacks were introduced as a race of slaves; whence an unconquerable prejudice of caste. Insomuch, that a suspicion of taint still has the unjust effect of sinking the subject of it below the common level. [1132]

The lone statute of these two decades was aimed against the kidnapping of free Negroes. [1133]   Pennsylvania, as a border state, was justly concerned with this activity. The same statute withdrew jurisdiction over fugitive slave cases from the state courts and repealed old slave laws. Resolutions were likewise few. One opposed the extension of slavery into the territories, [1134] and one, with a generosity not usual among the non-slave states, commemorated the death of John C. Calhoun. [1135]

Specific court decisions cut both ways, as in other "free" states. There was opposition to the Fugitive Slave Act, [1136] but also degradation of "free" Negroes. [1137]   A few cases affirmed the rights of freemen. [1138] It is interesting to note how much of the illegal slave trade was conducted through northern ports, and Pennsylvania contributed her share to slave trade litigation. [1139]   Economic motives, rather than humanitarianism was evidently behind the abolition movement, and did not bear equally against the slave trade. One case recorded the separation of the Black Methodist Episcopal Church from the white. [1140]

Vermont, never having had slavery, had few laws on the subject after 1830. Jury trials were now applied to fugitive slave cases, [1141] a procedural way of accomplishing a substantive result. Soon afterwards, auxiliary enforcement of the federal Fugitive Slave Act was put beyond the jurisdiction of state officials, [1142] and fugitive slaves were granted the remedy of <u>habeas corpus.</u> [1142a] Otherwise, legislative activity consisted of the usual resolutions against the extension of slavery into the territories, against the annexation of Texas, in favor of the right to petition Congress and in favor of abolition in the District of Columbia.[1143]

There are only two Vermont cases touching Negroes in the years 1830 to 1850. One granted regular intestate succession to the illegitimate children of a New Hampshire slave. [1144]   The other states the collateral fact that the plaintiff said he would hire a Negro to whip the defendant.[1145]   This was evidently considered the height of insult and shows how, in "free" Vermont, Negroes were treated as a degraded caste.

Ohio first granted[1146] and then withdrew,[1147] state cooperation in enforcing the federal Fugitive Slave Act.   Otherwise there was only a procedural act on the management of the New Orphans Asylum of colored children.[1148]   There was the usual spate of resolutions during this period,[1149] and several statutes directing a state census of white males only.[1150]

It goes without saying that Ohio sought ways to negate the Fugitive Slave Law.[1151]   The state vacillated on the civil rights of free Negroes. They were, and were not held to be competent witnesses,[1152] but if they were more than 50% white, they were officially accorded political rights, which however, were not always enforced.[1153]   Schools were segregated.[1154]   Civil rights in litigation were sometimes granted and sometimes denied,[1155] and two cases actually enforced the federal Fugitive Slave Act.[1156]

Indiana, like Ohio at this time, had inconsistent laws on the status of free Negroes.   Apprentices were handled without reference to color,[1157] but colored immigrants were barred unless they could furnish a bond.[1158]   And one anti-miscegenation statute followed another.[1159]

State laws aided enforcement of the federal Fugitive Slave Act.[1160]   Like Ohio, Indiana took a census of her white males only.[1161]   Otherwise, the Indiana legislature bubbled with resolutions, the usual ones during these years.[1162]   There were only four cases. Three deal with slaves escaping into Indiana,[1163] and the fourth upheld segregated schools but did not enforce the statute.[1164]

As events moved to their climax, Illinois, Lincoln's home state, was unfriendly to blacks in legislation but favorable in judicial decisions. Blacks and Mulattoes could not give evidence[1165] and were excluded from the militia.[1166]   They could not vote,[1167] nor even reside within the state without producing a certificate of freedom and posting a one thousand dollar bond so as not to become a public charge.[1168]

These inequalities existed side-by-side with a law punishing the kidnapping of free Negroes,[1169] and the resounding declarations that all men were born free and equal, and no slavery should exist in the state.[1170]   The legislative resolutions of this time were in accord with those of other non-slave states.[1171]

On the other hand, judicial decisions on civil rights were nearly all in favor of the free Negro.   Civil judgments were given for battery,[1172] and for services rendered.[1173]   Suits for freedom and related contests were usually decided in favor of freedom,[1174] and the Fugitive Slave Act was frequently not enforced.[1175]   It was not slander to say that a white woman had a child by a Negro,[1176] and assault on a black person with intent to commit murder was punished as such.[1177]

Maine has understandably little on the subject of slavery from 1830 to 1850, but that little included a case on the slave trade.[1178]   It is interesting to see how much of the illegal slave trade was concentrated in New England, which all the while was beating the drums for "freedom" and emancipation.   The Maine statutes show the same ambivalence toward blacks manifested by all the northern states during this period, an ambivalence which has remained until the present day.   There were only two statutes, but one penalized kidnapping a free person or selling him as a slave,[1179] while the other proscribes intermarriage between whites and blacks.[1180]

The legislature twice resolved to keep hands off slavery so far as other states were concerned,[1181] and resolved once, that slavery should not be extended into the territories.[1182]   One other case arose during the two decades.   It upheld a Negro's civil rights.   A slave from Guadeloupe was allowed to sue in his own name for an assault and battery received on board of ship.[1183]

Michigan was French before becoming English, and had slavery under French law.[1184]   After the territory was acquired by the United States, the English laws were repealed in 1821.[1185]   Like other free governments, the territory and later the state, was schizophrenic about free Negroes.   But legislation leaned a little more toward real equality than it did in some other areas.   Voting was limited to whites,[1186] as was the militia,[1187] and free Negroes were excluded from the territory except under severe restrictions.[1188]   Corporal punishment was reserved for Negroes, Mulattoes and Indians.[1189]   Schools were segregated,[1190] but there was no bar against miscegenation.[1191]

However, Michigan did have a state fugitive slave law.[1192]   The first case under the federal Act of 1793 arose in 1848.   After one disagreement, a jury gave damages for the value of slaves who had been enabled to escape to Canada.[1193]   Most noteworthy about this case is that the whites encouraged the blacks to forcibly take escaped slaves out of the possession of Kentuckians who were trying to reclaim them.[1194]   The picture which one gets is that when the whites opposed enforcement of the Fugitive Slave Law, they encouraged the Negroes to obstruct it in a gesture of supposed racial solidarity.   Michigan produced the usual crop of resolutions during the 1830's and 40's, against extension of slavery to new territories, [1195] against s avery in the District of Columbia, [1196] and for the Union.[1197]

Iowa, which was not covered by the Ordinance of 1787, had very little on Negroes and slavery. But she was in tune with the times as slavery was forbidden, [1198] but free Negroes were ineligible to vote. [1199] A resolution calling for establishment of a land office[1200] echoed the defeat of Foot's Resolution in 1830.[1201] Other legislative resolutions related only remotely to the subject of slavery,[1202] and the few judicial decisions were schizophrenic.

There were no judicial cases on slavery in Wisconsin up to 1850. In her statutes we find virtually the same split personality as in other northern states. Kidnapping free persons was forbidden,[1205] but voting[1206] and the militia[1207] were confined to whites. The state did go as far as submitting to the electorate the question of whether Negroes should have the right to vote.[1208] But the electorate evidently turned down the idea, since later statutes still limit voting to whites.[1209] There was, however, no law against miscegenation,[1210] and schools were open to all.[1211] The usual resolutions against slavery were duly passed. [1212]

The admission of California was a subject of the Great Debate in 1850. In the last year of this period (1849-50), California joined the "free" states, prohibiting slavery, and punishing the kidnapping of free Negroes into slavery, [1213] but at the same time it made free Negroes a depressed caste.[1214]

When California adopted her constitution of 1849, she organized herself as a state and applied for admission. Her southern boundary was the Mexican border—latitude 32⁰ and 33/—far south of the Missouri Compromise line. The constitution of 1849 prohibited slavery or involuntary servitude except as punishment for crime.[1216] Admission on this basis would do two things. In the first place, it would admit an odd non-slave state, and thus upset the balance of slave and non-slave states in the Senate. Until then, slave and non-slave states had always been admitted in pairs, and in 1849 there were fifteen of each.

In the second place, admission of a non-slave state with California's boundaries would be in open disregard of any "gentlemen's agreement" which had made the Missouri Compromise work both ways. The terms of the Compromise had in fact prohibited slavery north of the line and left the subject open south of latitude 36⁰ 30/. But until 1849, though slavery had never been confirmed south of the line, in practice the Missouri Compromise was treated as working equally in both directions.

California's application for statehood would at once strike down both parts of this arrangement; the equal balance of slave and non-slave states, and the toleration of slavery south of 36° 30/. Furthermore, the non-slave states were pressing the Wilmot Proviso which stated that slavery should not be permitted in any of the territories newly acquired from Mexico. And at this time, there was a greater and greater flow of fugitive slaves away from the slave states.

On January 29, 1850, Henry Clay presented to the Senate a combined plan to settle the problems posed by the admission of California, by fugitive slaves, and over the question of whether slavery should henceforth be permitted in newly organized territories.[1217] We can say of Clay, much of what Tolstoy said of Kutuzov:

> Kutuzov's merit lay not in what is called 'a stroke of genius,' in making a strategical manoeuvre, but simply in the fact that he was the only one who understood the meaning of what was taking place about him.[1218]

What ensued is known as "The Great Debate". Most of the talking in this "debate" was done by the Senators and Representatives of the slave states. The greatest heat developed from the respective ends of the spectrum of slave and non-slave states in the Senate:

> The recommendation of the president, as I have already said, proposes the simple introduction of California as a State into the Union—a measure which, standing by itself, has excited the strongest symptoms of dissatisfaction in the Southern portions of the confederacy.[1219]

> In that case, California will become the test question. [1220]

There was disagreement between the slave and non-slave states as to who was contending for something concrete, and who was only upholding an abstraction. The southerners argued that their whole "way of life" was at stake, but they also said that they were fighting for a "principle."

> The southern States in convention at Nashville, will devise means for vindicating their rights. They may be able to carry slaves into all of southern California, as the property of sovereign states, and there to hold them, as we have a right to do; and, if molested, defend them, as is both our right and our duty.[1222]

> Sir, it is because we believe that disunion is better than emancipation, that any result is preferable to the attempt to give equality to the two races by legislation, a

belief openly expressed and found fixed in every Southern mind, which has induced those who pursue a policy directed to the production of those results, to call us disunionists.[1223]

Is it then, not certain that if something decisive is not now done to arrest it, the South will be forced to choose between abolition and secession? [1224]

But the Southern Senators and Representatives also claimed that they were fighting for a "principle" and were willing to die for it.

We are contending for principle, and a great principle, a principle lying at the very foundation of our constitutional rights involving, as has been remarked, our property. In a word, involving our safety, our honor, and all that is dear to us as American freemen. Well sir, for that principle we will be compelled to contend to the utmost, and to resist aggression at every hazard and at every sacrifice.[1225]

Unscrupulous men are apt to forget that there is any such restraint as principle, any such monitor in the human bosom as conscience.[1226]

I am certain there is not one of our citizens who would be willing for a moment to weigh it dissolution of the Union in the balance against the dishonor of submission.[1227]

I am free to confess, Mr. President, that I did not expect to hear an argument in the Senate of the United States, emanating from a gentleman so distinguished for his talents and ability in its counsels as the Senator from Kentucky, to prove that it was right to do wrong.[1228]

The South asks for justice, simple justice, and less she ought not to take. [1229]

The slave senators accused the north of contending for nothing other than an abstraction. [1230] But minds outside the Senate understood what was concretely at stake for the non-slave states. In 1848, Governor Briggs of Massachusetts saw that admitting slaves into any territory would tend to keep out emigrants from non-slave states.[1231] The legislature of New Hampshire astutely pointed out the greater prosperity and development of non-slave Ohio as against slave-owning Kentucky directly across the river, and asked: "Do we want to bring this penury into the territories?"[1232]

And interestingly, Jefferson Davis, who had a partial grasp of what was going on around him, gave several concrete reasons for stopping the extension of slavery while he thought he was arguing for its extension.

> What has been the progress of emancipation throughout the whole of our country? It has been the pressure of free labor upon the less profitable slave labor. Slave labor is a wasteful labor, and it therefore requires a still more extended territory than would the same pursuits if they could be prosecuted by the more economical labor of white men.[1233]

Yet at the same time Davis said,

> Mr. President, in all the controversy which has arisen about the validity and extent of the Mexican law, no species of property has been denied the right to enter the territory we have acquired, except slaves. Why is this?[1234]

Clay, aware of the tension, tried to frame his compromises so as not to violate the principles of either side:

> Another principal object which attracted my attention, was to endeavor to frame such a scheme of accommodation as that neither of the two classes of states into which our country is unhappily divided, should make a sacrifice of any great principle. I believe sir, that the series of resolutions which I have had the honor of prescribing to the Senate accomplishes that object,[1235]

Clay then added:

> Now, sir, when I brought forward this proposition of mine, which is embraced in these resolutions, I intended, so help me God, to propose a plan of doing equal and impartial justice to the South and to the North, so far as I can comprehend it, and I think it does yet.[1236]

But the slave states were exercised over the impending loss of the equilibrium in the Senate. They insisted they had just as much right to go into new territories with their slaves as non-slaveholders had with their property. There were also some complaints over the property losses from fugitive slaves. As Clay remarked later in the debate,[1237] the potential loss of equal votes in the Senate caused the greatest concern. It was expressed by one slaveholding delegate after another:

> We should transfer the sceptre of political power at once and forever into the hands of the enemies of our institutions, and the slaveholding states would enter upon a fixed, dreary and hopeless minority in the face of a growing aggression which threatens our very existence. Today we hold a balance in the Senate of the United States, but the entrance of another non-slaveholding state into the Union would turn that balance against us. We shall never be any stronger than we are today. So far as we can read the future, we must expect the disproportion against us to grow.[1239]

> That is to be found in the fact that the equilibrium between the two sections in the Government as it stood when the constitution was ratified and the Government put in action, has been destroyed.

> This will effectually and irretrievably destroy the equilibrium which existed when the government commenced.[1240]

The counter proposal was either to extend the Missouri Compromise line to the Pacific, or to organize the State of California only north of 36° 30/ (or 35° 30/). Extension of the Missouri Compromise line to the west coast had already been broached and rejected in 1847 and again in 1848.[1241] Nevertheless, in 1850 Jefferson Davis brought forward the same proposal, this time as an ultimatum.[1242]

He was right that the admission of California as organized in 1849, would go contrary to the Missouri Compromise as it had been applied since its adoption. He now wanted slavery south of 36° 30/:

> Then, all the territory involved, that of Misouri, was slave territory. The compromise precluded slavery in a part of the territory. Now, according to the position of the Senator, slavery is excluded from the whole territory of California and New Mexico.

> What then would the application of the spirit of the Missouri Compromise require? Clearly that in renewing

the line, the question should be put at rest by declaring that below said line slavery should be permitted.[1243]

Some of the other southern Senators wanted to admit only the northern part of California as a non-slave state.

If all other questions connected with the subject of slavery can be satisfactorily adjusted, I see no objection to admitting all California above the line of 36 degrees and 30 minutes into the Union, provided another slave state can be laid off within the present limits of Texas so as to keep the present equiponderance between the slave and free states of the Union.[1244]

Rep. Brown of Mississippi wanted to secure the right to carry slaves into southern California.[1245]

If the honorable Senator understood me as saying that I am opposed to the admission of California, he is mistaken. On the contrary, I am in favor of the admission of all that part of California lying above the line of $36° 30/$ as a state.[1246]

Clay grasped realities and saw that splitting California would bring in an additional non-slave state, not another slave state. He likewise understood that extending the Missouri Compromise line to the Pacific would mean nothing, since the compromise did not guarantee slavery south of $36° 30/$. And no such guarantee could ever be obtained.

Now with regard to the limits of California. Mr. President, upon that subject an effort was made in the committee to extend a line through California at $36° 30/$ of north latitude, and one member, not satisfied with that line proposed $35° 30/$. A majority of the committee, I believe, were in favor of that amendment; but, on the question being taken for the line of $35° 30/$, a majority were found to be against it. Sir, is it not a little remarkable that this opposition to the line, this attempt to cut California in two by the line $36° 30/$ or $35° 30/$, or by any other line, is a line not coming from the north at all, from whence we might suppose it to be proposed.

For, with respect to the north, there can be no earthly doubt that if there were half a dozen states made out of California, they would all be what are called free states. Moreover, I have understood that all the delegation in the Convention, of course all of them must, because the Convention was unanimous, the whole Convention, all south of the line 35° 30/, as well as north of it, voted against the introduction of slavery.

It cannot, therefore be, and I presume it is not, under any hope, if California should be curtailed in the manner proposed, that there will ever be slavery within her limits, or upon the Pacific at all. The fact, therefore, of the establishment of a new state or new states out of the present limits of California, is merely to add to the objection which has been made by the South of the preponderance and influence of the North, and apprehensions which they entertain from that preponderance and influence of northern power.[1247]

What was done, sir, by the Missouri line? Slavery was positively interdicted north of that line. The question of the admission or exclusion of slavery south ot that line was not settled. There was no provision that slavery should be admitted south of that line.[1248]

But, whether it be great or small, it appears to me that it is the interest and duty, and it should be the inclination of the South, to look at the facts and nature as they exist, and to reconcile themselves to that which is inevitable and impossible. To reconcile themselves to the fact that it is impossible, however desirable it may be in the opinion of any of them, to carry slaves to the countries which I have described.[1248a]

The Southerners also insisted on their right to bring slaves into all newly organized territories,[1249] and complained about the loss of slave property through fugitive slaves.[1250] On this last point, it was Jefferson Davis who saw that any fugitive slave law would be a dead letter in the non-slave states:

So entirely is this the case, that whatever law may be passed at this session, I perceive a disposition of all sides to pass one for the recovery of fugitive slaves, I feel that that law will be a dead letter in any state where the popular opinion is opposed to such rendition.[1251]

The Senators and Representatives of the future Confederacy had lost the capacity for rational thought. In stating their grievances, they tried to govern with their blood pressure rather than with their brains. They often proposed remedies which were no remedies at all. Through the grievances runs a refrain of injured feelings:

> Long years of outrage upon our feelings and disregard of our rights have awakened in every southern heart a feeling of stern resistance.

> Ask yourselves whether it is right to exasperate eight millions of people for an abstraction.[1252]

> Our wrongs are insupportable and can be tolerated no longer. [1253]

> A separation of the Union would involve the immediate connection of the whole South with Mexico and the West Indies, and with England. And under the exasperation which would inevitably attend such an event, the north, its ships, goods, produce and traffic, would at once be excluded.[1254]

> And when to the potency of those elements of power in an attempt (as it may be so) to overturn the Government, you superadded a deep sense of wrong and injury, diffused among a numerous class, embracing extensive sections, and populous and powerful states, can you still say that it is no part of wisdom to give any serious or grave consideration to these combined influences?[1255]

> Am I to understand him, that no degree of oppression, no outrage, no broken faith, can produce the destruction of the Union? Why, sir, if that becomes a fixed fact, it will itself become the great instrument of producing oppression, outrage and broken faith.[1256]

The measures proposed had an almost stupefying air of unreality. The southern delegates started from the premise that they were hopelessly outnumbered, and proceeded to the conclusion that either they should secede without regard to the consequences, or that, though weaker, they could win a test of force. Two entertained the daydream of peaceful secession, and two did some wishful thinking and gave reasons why the slave states would be stronger after secession.

But the basic lines of conflict were clear and simple. The

slaveowners wanted to secede and go to war if necessary, because their economy had been overtaken by the industrial north. First, there was the unanimous chorus of southerners that they were "now" the weaker party, with nostalgic remembrance of times when the balance of forces was the other way.

> You are numerically more powerful than the slave states. You are, in point of numbers, however, greater.[1257]

> In this body, the popular branch of the Government, the North has an overwhelming majority.[1258]

> The North, the populous, teeming, powerful North, confident in its strength, forgetting the early struggle through which it passed in common with the South, forgetting the spirit which animated those who formed the Constitution, a spirit which existed when the South was the stronger and the North the weaker party;

> The slaveholding states would enter upon a fixed, dreary and hopeless minority in the face of growing aggression which threatens our very existence.[1259]

> The South, now the weaker, the minority in the Government, feels oppressively this power, and here the prostration of the great conservative principle in the bond of union.[1260]

> This, combined with the great primary cause, amply explains why the North has acquired a preponderance over every department of the Government by its disproportionate increase of population and status.

> A single section, governed by the will of the numerical majority, has now, in fact, the control of the Government and the entire powers of the system.

> But can this be done? Yes, easily, not by the weaker party, for it can of itself do nothing, not even protect itself, but by the stronger.[1261]

The South perceived itself as "the weaker party," yet it proposed to resort to force "without regard to consequences," and insisted on this position even when the possible consequences were brought home. At times, this resolution took the self-contradictory form of "redress" regardless of consequences, forgetting that "redress" is redress only if the consequences are favorable.

The wishful suggestion of peaceful secession was put forth, thus boggling a little before possible consequences. It was also illogically argued that in a test of force, the South could win despite being in an irretrievable minority. Only Jefferson Davis and Louisiana's Senator Downs tried to give reasons.

Resort to force without regard to consequences was the favorite proposal:

> Well sir, for that principle we will be forced to contend to the utmost, and to resist aggression at every hazard and at every sacrifice.[1262]

> . . . have awakened in every southern heart a feeling of stern resistance. Think what you will, say what you will, perpetrate again and again if you will, these acts of lawless tyranny. The day and the hour is at hand when every southern son will rise in rebellion, when every tongue will say, give us justice, or give us death.

> And if you deny us this right, we will resist your authority to the last extremity.[1263]

> You will find men of all parties, and of every description of politics in the South, standing shoulder to shoulder to defend those rights; which we mean to defend, which we can defend, and which we will defend at all hazards.[1264]

> A spirit equally determined prevails in the South. Throughout that entire region there exists a single purpose in regard to this threatened aggression, and that is, to resist to the last.[1265]

> If California is dragged into the Union in the mode now proposed, the southern states of the Confederacy will feel, that all hope of fraternal compromise has become extinct, and that such intolerable oppression has already been imposed upon them as to justify, nay demand, secession from the Union in order to save themselves from evils still worse than disunion itself.[1266]

> I refer to a determination to redress our wrongs, whatever may be the consequences.[1267]

The Congressman forgot that unless there are favorable

consequences, there can be no "redress". The same was true for Senator Bell of Tennessee:

> I have watched the whole movement for years, and I think I have seen a considerable accession of strength to those who favor extreme measures of resistance and redress among leading men in many of the states of the South, not to say all who are not active participants in the party strife of the day.[1268]

Clay could visualize the possible consequences, which is why he brought forward his compromises:

> I heard a sentiment uttered today which I have again and again heard uttered, and which I have never heard uttered but with a shuddering and apprehension. We are told that upon certain contingencies, upon the occurrence of certain events, the South must take a particular specified course, regardless of consequences.
>
> Regardless of consequences, sir. It is precisely because I do regard consequences, and I apprehend them, not to this or that side of the Union alone, but to all parts, to the entire country, that I am led to the conclusion of making an extreme, of making every effort, the power to make which is yet reserved to me, to avert the greatest of human calamities, not only that could befall this country, but that could befall the whole race of civilized men.[1269]

The reply which was made to this warning would be unbelievable if it were not enshrined in print:

> I am free to confess, Mr. President, that I did not expect to hear an argument in the Senate of the United States, emanating from a gentleman so distinguished for his talents and abilty in its counsels as is the Senator from Kentucky, to prove that it was right to do wrong. Sir, I did not expect to hear him undertake to prove that is was moral and religious and patriotic to refuse to do right, because something important and perhaps disastrous should result from such a course of action.[1270]

This sentiment was matched by the extravagance of Senator Butler, the junior Senator from South Carolina:

> Compromise!   Its name is frailty, its consequences

treachery, giving the stronger party the power to use it as an instrument, and to throw it away at pleasure. The compromises that have been offered fall far short of the occasion. They neither satisfy the present, nor offer security for the future. The stronger power doesn't want them, and the weaker power, in honor, cannot accept them.[1271]

Politics, said Bismarck, is the art of the possible, but the southern legislators had left its gravitational field. There were moments when they said that no violent consequences lay in store for them or for the Union. They even stated that they could secede in peace.

As to there being any conflict of arms growing out of dissolution, I have not thought it at all probable.[1272]

What I mean to assert is, that both of those Senators (Clay, Cass) endeavored to impress upon the country the belief that war must follow on the heels of disunion. Both of them no doubt believe that such is the case, but in my deliberate judgment all that is merely fancy. I cannot see why war should follow on a separation.[1273]

If you who represent the stronger portion cannot agree to settle them on the broad principle of justice and duty, say so. And let the States we both represent agree to separate, and part in peace.[1274]

Clay foresaw the concrete consequences. In the first place secession would not solve any problems for the South.

Well now, let us suppose that the Union has been dissolved. What remedy does it furnish for the grievances complained of in its united condition? Will you be able to push slavery into the ceded territories? How are you to do it, supposing the North, and all the states north of the Potomac which are opposed to it, and in possession of the Navy and Army of the United States?

Can you expect, if there is a dissolution of the Union, that you can carry slavery into California and then Mexico? You cannot dream of such a purpose. If it were abolished in the District of Columbia, and the Union was dissolved, would the dissolution of the Union restore slavery in the District of Columbia? Are you safer in the recovery of your fugitive slaves in a state of dissolution or of severance of the Union than you are in the Union itself?

What would you have if the Union were dissevered? Why, sir, the severed parts would be independent of each other—foreign countries! Slaves taken from one into the other would be there like slaves now escaping from the United States into Canada . . . Well, finally, will you, in a state of dissolution of the Union, be safer with your slaves within the bosom of the States than you are now? [1275]

Clay likewise understood that the dreams of peaceful secession were pipedreams. Secession would mean war. Clay saw not only this, but also the kind of war it would be.

But, I must take occasion to say that, in my opinion, there is no right on the part of one or more of the states to secede from the Union. War and the dissolution of the Union are one and inseparable.[1276]   There can be no dissolution of the Union except by consent or by war. No one can expect in the existing state of things that the consent would be given, and war is the only alternative by which a dissolution could be accomplished.

Such a war too, as that would be, following the dissolution of the Union! Sir, we may search the pages of history, and none so furious, so bloody, so implacable, so exterminating, none of them raged with such violence, or was ever conducted with such bloodshed and enormities, as will that war which shall follow that disastrous event— if that event ever happens—of dissolution.[1277]

Some of the southern senators and congressmen seemed to believe that in some undefined way they could win a passage-at-arms though being the "weaker party".[1278]   Some resorted to historical analogy without stopping to ask whether the cases were analogous.[1279]   Only Jefferson Davis and Sen. Downs of Louisiana tried to reason from contemporary facts why such an outcome might be thinkable.[1280]

Epilogue

POST-CIVIL WAR ECONOMY IN THE FORMER SLAVE STATES

Up until the Civil War, the slave states had been agricultural and the non-slave states industrial and commercial. When the Great Plains were settled, they were devoted to agriculture not suitable for slavery.[1] The Civil War opened the former slave areas to industry and commerce. Slavery was not suited to these, so slavery was abolished.

After the Civil War, commercial and industrial corporations were organized all over the South; at first by special acts and later administratively. As long as special acts were in use, the statute books showed a steady rise in the number of corporations from the end of the Civil War to the 1890's. The transitions from special acts to administrative incorporations was itself a milestone in the expansion of "business." Appendix "A", shows the number and type of businesses incorporated in each of the former slave states, for as long as incorporations were made by special act.

A few states furnish striking examples. The statute books of Tennessee list new incorporations through 1963. In the last years before the Civil War, there had been no incorporations at all. After the Civil War incorporations went into four figures for several straight years.

Even more pointedly, the statutes of South Carolina and Mississippi show the penetration of northern and foreign capital. Among the 210 foreign corpoations authorized to do business in South Carolina in 1914, were Union Typewriter Co., International Harvester, the Postal Telegraph and Cable Co., S. & I. Kress, Cudahy Packing, Singer Sewing Machine, Pullman, Underwood Typewriter, Western Union, National Cash Register, Proctor & Gamble, New England Mortgage Security, Remington Typewriter, Great Atlantic and Pacific Tea Co., Sperry & Hutchinson, Standard Oil, I. E. DuPont de Nemours, American Telephone and Telegraph, F. W. Woolworth, Baldwin Piano, Swift & Co., Hilton Dodge Lumber, United Cigar Stores, and the Prudential Insurance Company.

Among the Mississippi statutes of 1882, was "an act to ratify and confirm the incorporation of the Memphis, Selma and Brunswick Railroad Company,"[2] which lists the railroads from Memphis. There

343

were five from New York, one from Alabama and only five out of the 21 were from Mississippi. From 1906 to 1957 the governors of Alabama sent messages to the Legislature stressing the importance of industrial development.

The message of Gov. B. B. Conner to the Legislature of 1906-7[3] notes that the state has progressed "from a strictly agricultural people, marketing only cotton. Now we have added coal, iron, steel, cement and lumber, and cotton, wood, iron and steel manufacturers and largely advanced mercantile interests." The message of Gov. Chas. Henderson, 1915[4] says "Our state is rapidly becoming an industrial country." While Gov. James Folsom, in 1957[5] talked about industrial development, the Oil and Gas Board, insurance and banking and loan companies, the Securities Commission and the Department of Industrial Relations.

In 1875, the Florida Legislature passed a resolution,[6] declaring "the development and prosperity of the South are primarily dependent upon the construction of railroads and other channels of communication."

Before the Civil War, the South was agricultural. Industry and commerce were centered in New England and New York. Slavery was suited to the kind of agriculture which existed in the southern states. But industry and commerce were not going to remain confined in the northeast. Neither they, nor the agriculture of the newly developed Great Plains had any use for slavery. When industry and commerce were ready to expand into the old slave areas, the Civil War ensued and slavery was abolished. After the war, industrialization proceeded apace.

POSITION OF THE NEGRO AFTER THE CIVIL WAR

Slaves were, by definition, a subordinate caste. They were required to show the deferential attitude of inferiors, except perhaps where subordination was otherwise clear.[7] What should be done with former slaves after emancipation? What should be done with their descendants?

Appendix "B" shows the ups and downs of laws affecting Negroes in the former slave states after abolition. Three periods stand out. First, directly after the Civil War, legislation was designed to improve the position of freedmen and previously free Negroes, assuring them the same right as whites. Second, these laws were junked after 1877. Repressive laws against the Negro population became stricter. But this process did not gather its full force until the 20 years running approximately from 1890-1910. During that time most of the white supremacy legislation was passed.

Most striking were the "separate coach laws," segregating white and black passengers in railroad trains, streetcars, steamboats, depot waiting rooms, lunch rooms, and circus tents. The accommodations were supposed to be "separate but equal," but the statutes were inapplicable to nurses travelling with their employers, and to officers in charge of prisoners. In other words, "separate but equal" was hypocrisy. Segregation was the badge of subordination. When subordination was clear without segregation, segregation was dropped.[8]

Third, these things stood with few exceptions until the end of World War II in 1945. One consequence of World War II was the emergence of independent black republics in Africa. If the blacks in Africa had achieved even nominally equal status with the white nations, could the blacks in America be permanently kept down? The years which followed World War II have step by step discarded anti-Negro legislation. Some of the work was done by the United State Supreme Court,[9] some by Congress, some even by state legislatures.

The ruling by the United States Supreme Court prohibiting racially segregated schools[10] brought a flood of legislation from the ex-slave states designed to circumvent the decision. This reached a paroxysm in Louisiana, which 100 years before had given the greatest latitude to her free Negroes.[11]

In 1967, the United States Supreme Court held laws against miscegenation unconstitutional.[12] This time, the decision encountered no noticeable opposition. In the late 1960's the former slave states proceeded to repeal their anti-integration laws.[13] Separate coach laws began to fade out at the same time.[14] In 1964, the XXIXth Amendment to the United State Constitution forbade the requirement of a poll tax for voting in Federal elections. On October 30, 1974 for the first time in history, a world's heavyweight boxing championship match was held in Africa at Kinshasa, Zaire, instead of in America or Europe, between two sons of Africa—Muhammad Ali and George Foreman—two American Negroes, descendants of slaves. From a minus, two "sons of Africa" had become a plus.